The Secret in Medieval Literature

STUDIES IN MEDIEVAL LITERATURE

Series Editor: Albrecht Classen, University of Arizona

Advisory Board

Werner Schaefke, University of Copenhagen.
Christopher R. Clason, Oakland University.
Andrew Breeze, University of Navarre.
Connie Scarborough, Texas Tech University.
Gloria Allaire, University of Kentucky.
Fabian Alfie, University of Arizona.
Raymond Cormier, Longwood University.
Janina Traxler, Manchester University.
Marianne Ailes, University. of Bristol

Studies in Medieval Literature invites scholars to publish their most powerful, exciting, and forward-looking studies, which will thus become an excellent platform for Medieval Studies at large.

Recent Titles

The Secret in Medieval Literature: Alternative Worlds in the Middle Ages, by Albrecht Classen
Becoming the Pearl-Poet: Perceptions, Connections, Receptions, edited by Jane Beal
Incarceration and Slavery in the Middle Ages and the Early Modern Age: A Cultural-Historical Investigation of the Dark Side in the Pre-Modern World, edited by Albrecht Classen
Dante Satiro: Satire in Dante Alighieri's Comedy and Other Works, by Fabian Alfie and Nicolino Applauso
Dante's Comedy and the Ethics of Invective in Medieval Italy: Humor and Evil, by Nicolino Applauso
Prostitution in Medieval and Early Modern Literature: The Dark Side of Sex and Love in the Pre-Modern Era, by Albrecht Classen
Chaucer's Neoplatonism: Varieties of Love, Friendship, and Community, by John M. Hill

The Secret in Medieval Literature

Alternative Worlds in the Middle Ages

Albrecht Classen

LEXINGTON BOOKS
Lanham • Boulder • New York • London

Published by Lexington Books
An imprint of The Rowman & Littlefield Publishing Group, Inc.
4501 Forbes Boulevard, Suite 200, Lanham, Maryland 20706
www.rowman.com

86-90 Paul Street, London EC2A 4NE

Copyright © 2023 by The Rowman & Littlefield Publishing Group, Inc.

All rights reserved. No part of this book may be reproduced in any form or by any electronic or mechanical means, including information storage and retrieval systems, without written permission from the publisher, except by a reviewer who may quote passages in a review.

British Library Cataloguing in Publication Information Available

Library of Congress Cataloging-in-Publication Data

Names: Classen, Albrecht, author.
Title: The secret in medieval literature : alternative worlds in the Middle Ages / Albrecht Classen.
Description: Lanham : Lexington Books, [2022] | Series: Studies in medieval literature | Includes bibliographical references and index.
Identifiers: LCCN 2022036973 (print) | LCCN 2022036974 (ebook) | ISBN 9781666917864 (cloth) | ISBN 9781666917871 (epub) | ISBN 9781666917888 (paperback)
Subjects: LCSH: Literature, Medieval—History and criticism. | Secrecy in literature. | Mystery in literature. | Other (Philosophy) in literature. | LCGFT: Literary criticism.
Classification: LCC PN682.S316 C53 2022 (print) | LCC PN682.S316 (ebook) | DDC 809/.02—dc23/eng/20220914
LC record available at https://lccn.loc.gov/2022036973
LC ebook record available at https://lccn.loc.gov/2022036974

Contents

Introduction—The Secret in the Literary Discourse: The Challenges of Medieval Literature for Post-Modern Readers — 1

Chapter One: Marie de France: The Lais—The Mysterious Black Ship and Other Secrets in the World of Love — 55

Chapter Two: Nordic Sagas and the *Mabinogi*: Secrets in Medieval Icelandic and Welsh Literature or the Appearance of the Otherworld in the Human Context — 85

Chapter Three: Wolfram von Eschenbach: Parzival—The Secret of the Grail at Munsalvæsche and the Secret Inscription on the Dog Leash in Titurel — 113

Chapter Four: Heldris de Cornuälle's *Roman de Silence*: The Secret of Gender Identity and the Secret of the Self—Nature versus Nurture, a Debate Raging Already in the Thirteenth Century — 135

Chapter Five: Secrets and Mysteries in the World of Heinrich von dem Türlin's *Crône*: The Transformation of the Arthurian and the Grail Romance — 163

Chapter Six: Secrets and the Secret World in *Huon de Bordeaux* Foreign and Yet Not Alien: The Good King Auberon — 187

Chapter Seven: Secrets of the Mystical World: Mysticism and the Absolute Other in Divine Terms — 209

Epilogue: Have We Now Found the Secret? Or Are There No Secrets? — 235

Bibliography — 239

Index 283

About the Author 287

Introduction—The Secret in the Literary Discourse
The Challenges of Medieval Literature for Post-Modern Readers

"Only what is invisible can move us."

—Théodore Jouffroy[1]

THE MYSTERIES OF CONTEMPORARY LIFE

We live today in a very science-driven and data-determined world, and yet, there are many things that cannot be easily explained, if at all, at least rationally. These include the origin of life, the limits of our universe, the meaning of death, whether we have free will or not, and the purpose of our existence.[2] If we believe that we understand a certain percentage of this world, we can count ourselves among the lucky; but in most likelihood, there are more secrets around us than clearly understandable and verifiable facts.

Since the early Middle Ages, people have gone on pilgrimages, often in the desperate hope that some kind of spiritual force might help them in their physical or spiritual needs, especially in medical cases.[3] They visit sacred sites in order to touch relics and thus to draw from the saint's power for their own lives, and they go on pilgrimages, such as to Santiago de Compostela, in the hope of finding meaning for themselves, even if it consists only of having reached that distant goal. As much as we can explain this entire phenomenon through religious analysis,[4] the belief system remains a secret, especially when the individual seeking help from divine forces achieves the desired recovery of health, retrieves lost items, or regains freedom for loved ones.[5] Considering that pre-Christian and non-European cultures were also well attuned to the value of relics, holy sites, and the charisma of a religious leader, a mystic, a saint, for instance, we can thus identify this as a universal and timeless phenomenon (see, e.g., Stonehenge, or Machu Picchu, pilgrimage sites).

Undoubtedly, there is a mysterious aura within objects, whether altars, the Holy Grail, special rings, scepters, crowns, vestments, vessels, or relics of all kinds (skulls, blood, fingers, toes, bones, etc.), and it remains inexplicable to us how that aura actually works or what it is. For the believers, there are no doubts about those secrets, for the non-believers, those are just objects, nothing else. Recent explorations of the so-called "Ding Theorie" (thing theory) have experimented with those secrets and recognized how much they deeply matter, both in the past and the present, but full explanations continue to escape us.[6]

Simultaneously, throughout time individual rulers, religious leaders, artists, and others have exuded a form of holiness, that is, charisma, and chroniclers have regularly worked with this concept of the holy king, or emperor, hence have operated with a secret in which the head of a government or of a Church has been enshrouded. It would be difficult to differentiate neatly between a natural charisma or sanctity which later writers have assigned to a leader, whether we think of Emperor Charlemagne (747–814) or King Oswald of Northumbria (604–641/42), or the biblical King David (r. ca. 1010–970 B.C.E.).[7] Secrets surround us, or they are cast upon us to achieve certain political ends. This observation allows us to move from the political to the religious secret.

Religion, irrespective of how we might define it, serves the critical function of providing esoteric and also evanescent answers to the question regarding the secret of death and the meaning of life, as countless scholars of theology have confirmed and which we do not need to document any further here. The faithful ones often believe that they comprehend what the divine means, according to their Scriptures, but death remains, after all, one of the ultimate secrets.[8] In this sense, religion carries great importance because it helps people to come to terms with final questions regarding their lives and the meaning of their existence, whether in real terms or as the result of illusions and imagination. In that regard, religion is constituted by the existence of secrets, or it is the manifestation of the very secrets behind all being. Theologians, anthropologists, psychologists, sociologists, historians, and philosophers have debated those issues all over the world and this already for centuries, if we think, to name just some of the most famous thinkers, E. B. Tylor and James Frazer, Sigmund Freud, Emile Durkheim, Karl Marx, Mircea Eliade, Stewart Elliot Guthrie, E. E., Evans-Pritchard, Clifford Geertz, and others.[9]

Despite, or particularly because of the high level of technology determining all of our modern lives, there is a huge interest among the public in science fiction movies, novels, video games, and the like, and in mystery at large. The German TV series "Dark" proves this point most dramatically and epitomizes powerfully the global intrigue with and interest in the secret world of time travel, the human quest for identity and culture, the relevance of history, and the fear of an imminent apocalypse. "It ran for three seasons from 2017 to 2020. In the aftermath of a child's disappearance, *Dark* follows characters from the fictional German town of Winden as they pursue the truth. They follow connections between four estranged families to unravel a sinister time travel conspiracy that spans several generations. The series explores the existential implications of time and its effect on human nature."[10]

The other great success story predicated on the concept of the secret, now in narrative terms, was J. R. R. Tolkien's *The Lord of the Rings*, which started in 1937 with his *The Hobbits* and then developed over the years to the full into a much larger, almost epic work, completed in 1949. It continues to be the probably best-selling book ever, with more than 150 million copies sold, obviously because it so intriguingly explored a world of secrets and dark powers.[11] We also can refer to the modern bestseller novelist J. K. Rowling with her amazingly successful *Harry Potter* novels (1997–2007), perhaps a series of more advanced types of fairy tales on a higher, more complex level that demonstrate that the interest in and fascination with the world of fantasy, magic, sorcery, and hence secrets continue to be cornerstones of human culture even today.[12] In all of these cases, certain information is either not accessible or deliberately withheld. Society is divided into those who know and those who do not know, with the former being the privileged ones because they hold the key to power and insights.

However, we also know of secrecy which is employed in order to protect a person, such as in the case of religious confession, or in legal cases. The priest's promise to keep the confession a secret implies that the individual is granted direct communication with the divine and can hope to be forgiven after repentance and atonement. Similar conditions rule in the legal courts, but then we also can refer to secret societies, religious cults, or political groups. Secrets always imply communication or the lack thereof, and a strategy of exerting or controlling power.[13] Writing, the arts, music, but then also medicine and philosophy are often predicated on the secret; they are accessible, but the outsider or novice first needs to learn the keys to open the doors to the world behind. So, in a way, we might associate all knowledge with secrets, at least globally speaking.

Fantasy provides entertainment because it takes the individual outside of his/her normal existence and provides creative images, characters, and actions.[14] This makes it possible for us to analyze, in reverse order, what kind of imaginations dominated the storyteller or their audiences.

When we consider that both *Harry Potter* and *The Lord of the Rings* are directly embedded within a somewhat medieval context, we can easily grasp how much the modern reader, movie goer, or video game player continues to be obsessed with the mysterious elements and desires to dream or fantasize about other worlds, other modes of time, and other types of lives and living in the past (and future). There are many reasons why those sequels have enjoyed, and continue to do so, such enormous popularity. Without going into any details here, we can be certain that the appearance of secrets that mystify much of the background of the respective stories, played a major role in that regard.

Moreover, we can be certain that our post-modern lives are generally filled with countless secrets, except that we are often not quite aware of them or do not sense that all our "facts" are more assumptions or claims than being truly factual. Modern technology, for instance, represents a huge challenge for most of us. We happily use the internet, social media, TV, and countless electronic gadgets, but who could fully claim to understand all aspects of the mechanisms or structures that make them even possible. Our existence seems to be determined by rationality and transparency, but in reality, to be honest, we know less and less while we think that we know more and more. This is not to imply, of course, that we should return to the Middle Ages and believe in miracles again, using, for example, the hundreds of miracle tales composed by the Cistercian Caesarius of Heisterbach, as guiding narratives for our own lives. There is no point at all to turn to preaching against modernity; we exist in the here and now. However, to explore people's concepts about secrets in earlier times allows us to gain more cultural-historical sensitivity regarding different epistemes and alternatives to the dominant scientific and medical discourse of our time.[15]

To resort to a bit of polemics, in order to feel satisfied with our existence, we accept and embrace secrets or mysterious gadgets as ever more dominant features of our existence, whether we think of robots or laptops, of remote control of our houses or TV. It is more convenient not to question things as they surround us and thus to live comfortably with countless secrets than to investigate and examine them thoroughly. Of course, there are many experts who know their own area thoroughly, but no one can claim to have solved all mysteries and secrets in life, not even the notorious "Renaissance person." Almost paradoxically, the more technology assumes central importance today, the more secrets surround us and make us, in the twenty-first century, subject to a constantly growing degree of ignorance.

Things regularly happen that escape our critical analysis, and yet they seem to be most real. But we do not have much control over them, if any. Life is a curious phenomenon, and it would be rather preposterous to claim that we fully understand what is going on within our own existence and beyond either by way of relying on a rational hermeneutics or religious concepts. Even within the sciences, there are constantly new discoveries, large and small.

New creatures, for instance, commonly appear deep down in the sea at levels to which no human being can penetrate; those operate very differently than any other living creatures we have known so far. Similarly, the outer space is filled with phenomena that seem to be miraculous, and even the best astronomers or physicists have difficulties coming to terms with many of them. Astrology, for many people in the twenty-first century an entirely debunked approach to divination or the determination of one's future destiny, continues to hold sway in many quarters, maybe, particularly because of its secretive nature and irrational approach, or because it provides irrational relief from stress, threat, and fear, and supports narcissistic tendencies, as most recent research has confirmed many times.[16]

And, as the Covid-19 pandemic has taught us once again, our world is shockingly controlled by viruses, in the tera-billions and more, constantly changing, adapting, mutating, thereby threatening our existence, but also offering countless opportunities. After all, life mostly consists of viruses, but we know very little about them.[17] I venture to say that scientists would ultimately agree with the insight that the basic origin of life continues to remain a secret. We have made huge progress today in describing and explaining the phenomena we call existence, but we cannot create life and do not have real power to prevent it from dying—quite apart from the question of why we would want to live longer than the normal human life span.[18] Nevertheless, the overarching significance remains that all life is framed by secrets, or mysteries, as much as poets, philosophers, and scientists have tried to come to terms with them in a critical or imaginary fashion.

Indeed, we do not have to go so far as to the bottom of the sea or to the outer limits of our space in the universe to realize that there are forces around us that cannot be grasped factually and yet that make their working felt, even in a very everyday-life context. The relationships between two people, friends, or a married couple, operate in a way that is often just marvelous, but they are not easily explainable. I call them secrets. Similarly, we are surrounded by objects which seem to take on an identity on their own and operate as if they were objects, such as armor, swords, chess pieces, dice, keys, jewelry, nets, rings, and tools.[19] Any of them could turn into a carrier of private or intimate meaning and hence secrets. What happens to them, through them, with them, and beyond them when we operate with their help remains a secret, and we can perceive their agency, if that is the right word, only as a hunch.[20]

In many cases, the immediate explanation turns to religion, or to magic, as an alternative form of religion, but we would not have to go that far because the interaction between human beings and objects might operate in a secretive manner without any particular divine intervention because they operate on their own or pursue their own agency. Moreover, individuals tend to interact with others (in a negative concept) by way of secrets, keeping information hidden from them and using the unexplained phenomenon to their own advantage. The unique word, the key to a lock, just as in the world of modern computers (passwords), commands considerable power and proves to be relevant, exerting influence and control. In fact, the more knowledge we acquire, the more sensitive it becomes to protect it from hackers, manipulators, liars, and fakers. Of course, there is a universal thirst for knowledge, for facts, but the desire to mystify the world, to control certain information and to keep it away from others, appears to be just as strong, as ominous and opaque all that might be.

Here I am trying to differentiate more carefully between magic, sorcery, and necromancy on the one hand, and secrets on the other. The latter constitutes some powers that exist and make themselves visible or noticeable to humans, but the latter do not gain a full understanding of the phenomenon itself and can only try to learn to engage with those secrets that can be natural forces, mysterious otherworlds, objects with their own agency, or ominous beings such as fairies, berserks, giants, dwarfs, etc.[21] Even modern scientists, such as famous Albert Einstein (1879–1955), recognized that despite all the best scientific investigations of our universe, a secret always lies behind it all, perhaps waiting for us, or, more probably, not caring much about us as a human race.[22] According to Katrin Horn, secrets define the divine itself, that is, God, or they are the very links to the other dimension[23]; hence, they are associated with supernatural forces in life, which both medieval literature at large and modern fairy tales mirror directly (886). Those phenomena she calls "Lebensgeheimnisse" (886; secrets of life). Moreover, as she underscores, the secret is the synthesis of archaic knowledge and rational thought (889).[24]

To do justice to this highly complex phenomenon, we should also admit that secrets are often also a simple part of ordinary human life, not associated with religion, magic, sciences, and the like, although I will not engage with this further in the following chapters. People have always kept secrets from each other out of fear, embarrassment, shame, or pride. This can be nicely illustrated by one popular case in late medieval or early modern literature in which a man tests his wife's loyalty and willingness to keep a secret about her husband. Like in many other rather misogynist tales, often serving specifically didactic purposes, he shares a fake secret with her, but then hits her also in her face, which enrages her so much that she immediately betrays him and thus recklessly endangers his life.

A very late version of this motif can be found, for instance, in the collection of entertaining and erotic tales by the Italian poet Giovanni Francesco Straparola, his *The Pleasant Nights* (*Le piacevoli notti*), first printed in 1550, and many times thereafter. This collection exerted a tremendous influence on early modern and even modern literature, especially because of the inclusion of many examples of the genre of fairy tales, predicated on the imaginary and fanciful, at times even exploring bestiality leading to a happy outcome for two lovers.[25]

In the very first story, a young man, Salardo, inherits, after his father's death, the entire estate, but he deliberately disregards the old man's three strong recommendations: a) not to reveal a secret to his wife, irrespective of how much he would love her; b) not to adopt a child that would not be of his own blood; and c) not to enter the service of a lord and so to preserve his freedom and independence. The son, however, disregards his father's advice completely, adopts a child and enters the service of a lord, which all seems to work out well, making him believe that his father must have been an utter fool. Hence, he then checks on his wife's seemingly impeccable loyalty since she has always demonstrated complete love for her.

Salardo steals the marquis' favorite falcon and entrusts it to a friend, Fransoe, for safekeeping. Then he kills one of his own falcons and pretends to his wife that this was the one he had taken away from his lord so that the latter would stop going hunting all the time, which exhausts his supporters, friends, and servants alike. His wife, however, is enraged and severely criticizes him, and when he then slaps her face badly because she refuses to eat from the cooked falcon, she goes to the marquis immediately the next morning and betrays her husband to him. The marquis is so angry about this vile deed that he orders Salardo's execution without delay. His property would then be divided into three parts, one going to the wife, the second to the son, and the third to the executioner. When the son learns of this, he volunteers to be the hangman for his own father, which would allow him to keep also that portion of his father's wealth for himself. The narrator implies that the deceased father, the young man's grandfather, had been right in that regard, and also with respect to the danger of entering the service of a lord.

In the last minute, just shortly before the execution, Salardo's friend comes forward, pleads with the marquis to spare the other man's life due to his complete innocence, and then produces the lost falcon as proof of the accused friend's innocence. Salardo then reveals the entire story to the marquis, who deeply apologizes to him and restores all of his honors and property. Salardo, in turn, sends his son off into misery, never to be seen again, whereas his wife flees into a convent where she dies soon thereafter.

The outcome of this story proves to be highly misogynistic, but we can refer to it after all as an example of a different dimension of secrets, that is, secrets of a mundane kind, not to be shared with an untrustworthy husband, or wife, as in this case. The motif of this story and related accounts can be traced back to many earlier sources, such as the anonymous *Buch der Sieben weisen Meister* (ca. 1450), which by itself was a German translation of a Latin text (*Septem sapientes*), which in turn had been based on a Jewish version, etc., all of which is taking us as far back as to second- or third-century India and its

Pañatantra. The French translation, *Sept Sages de Rome*, foundational for the later European reception, had appeared already in ca. 1160, the first German translation, *Diokletians Leben* by Hans von Bühel, in 1412.[26]

The various poets' hatefulness against women is obvious, but what matters here is the extent to which all of them operated with the notion of the secret. But this secret is really only a ploy to test the wife who immediately falls for it and reacts with utter disloyalty, especially after she has been physically abused by him. Moreover, what love story in world literature would not be predicated in one way or the other on the secret, since love is the veritable secret by itself, as the fifth story told on the first day *The Pleasant Nights* powerfully illustrates. Similar situations determine both ancient and medieval, both Renaissance and Baroque literature, but this kind of secret will not be discussed here further.

Instead, the focus will rest on secrets associated with spiritual, religious, and other matters from out of this world. We might say, more esoteric secrets addressing more existential concerns. Nevertheless, the late example provided by Straparola underscores nicely the complexity of the issue itself, which could be relevant both in ordinary, mundane conditions—such as sharing or keeping important information from others—and also in cases of highest importance both for a courtly or heroic protagonist and for society at large.

SECRETS IN LITERATURE

I deliberately blend here the concept of "the secret" as an epistemological phenomenon with "the miracle" and "the wonder" as a religious experience. The latter topic has already found intensive attention by Caroline Walker Bynum, who identifies it as a "response to something novel and bizarre that seemed both to exceed explanation and to indicate that there might be reason . . . behind it."[27] Moreover, she also stressed that for people in the Middle Ages the engagement with wonder was a step toward new, spiritual knowledge, as it was expressed especially by such intellectual giants as St. Augustine, Aelfric, Bernard of Clairvaux, Bonaventure, or Jacques de Vitry. In the modern world, by contrast, wonder appears to be an expression of how little we know, as I myself have indicated several times above, especially because even the sciences and medicine cannot answer all of our questions.[28]

For this study, hence, many different features of the unknown, the mysterious, the inexplicable, and the incomprehensible will come into play since they prove to be much more influential in medieval and early modern imagination and fantasy than we might have assumed.[29] While Church-based literature (miracle stories, hagiographical texts, visionary accounts, etc.)

consistently refers to the power of Christ, God, the Virgin Mary, the saints, or the Holy Ghost, or secret powers, so to speak, secular, courtly literature above all teems with themes and motifs of the "secret," that is, with an ineffable force of great significance, quasi-religious, but often indeterminate and yet highly influential, whether we think of the magician Merlin, of Morgan le Fée, the mysterious Grail, fairies and nixies, and magical objects, such as rings, swords, armor, nets, crowns, mirrors, and the like.[30] As much as we would regularly catalog those as products of imagination, as much we would also have to acknowledge that throughout time and across the globe people have projected secret powers that exert their influence on human life and remain somehow inexplicable. We could go so far as to claim that there is no existence without secrets, maybe because existence itself constitutes a miracle or a secret.

ONE THOUSAND AND ONE NIGHTS

The best example of this phenomenon might be the Arabic story of "Ali Baba and the Forty Thieves," which the French translator Antoine Galland (1746–1715) added to his collection *Les mille et une nuits* (1704–1715) as no. 270, claiming that he had learned about it from a Syrian Maronite storyteller, called Hanna Diyab, from Aleppo, Syria, who told him the story while in Paris. As in the case of all fairy tales the world over, the original date or poet cannot be confirmed, but we know that this account has exerted global popularity up to the immediate present, both in literature and film, in visual artworks and musical compositions.[31] Ali Baba learns the secret of the magical charm, "Open Sesame" (French: Sésame, ouvre-toi; Arabic: افتح يا سمسم), and can thus open the door to the treasury kept by the forty thieves. It does not seem to be truly magic that is at play here, more a secret, that is, word magic with which the poor woodcutter Ali Baba learns how to gain access to the cave with all the valuable objects.[32]

There are many examples in medieval literature, both East and West, but then also in literature from other parts of the world, where something miraculous happens and yet which does not find its explanation in a religious or magical manner. That means, we cannot always refer to a Christian, Muslim, Hindu, or a necromantic reason for certain phenomena which appear and impact the protagonists' lives. Things at times operate, move, arrive, help, or harm all by themselves without any divine intervention, as if driven by their own energy and propulsion. They demonstrate a surprising agency and a certain degree of character as if they were independent to some extent.

MEDIEVAL PERSPECTIVES

Recent discussion of *The Thing* (*Dingtheorie*) has begun to explore those confusing and yet intriguing phenomena.[33] As Anna Mühlherr formulates in the introduction to a new volume dedicated to this topic:

> Gegen das modern-'aufgeklärte' Verständnis von Dingen als 'stummen' Objekten menschlichen Handelns werden hier Mensch-Ding-Hybride, Macht oder Eigensinn der Dinger, Dinge als Aktanten oder Akteure gesetzt.

[Here we place hybrids of humans and objects, the power or the idiosyncrasy of things, things as actors or respondents against the modern-'enlightened' concept of things as 'quiet' objects of human actions].[34]

Those are not necessarily secrets in the common sense of the word, but certainly puzzling and often inexplicable phenomena tantamount to secrets. After all, the protagonists in various literary texts are often not in charge, do not employ magic or charms in the usual sense of the word, and yet they are able to transform a situation with the help of independently operating animals or objects. We are thus dealing with active powers of a non-religious kind that interact with the human figures. Those are not involved in magic either, do not employ charms, have not studied necromancy, and do not appeal to demons, the devil, or other dark forces.[35]

Similarly, they do not pray to God, to a saint, or to a martyr; instead, they encounter a new dimension or new forces which suddenly appear in human life and interact with people, either in support or causing damage. Or, as is often the case as well, those forces operate on their own and are not really concerned about humans as negligible factors. Poets, however, often respond to those secrets, allowing them to come to the forefront and to display themselves in the literary context. Scholars, however, have normally ignored them because they do not seem to fit into any of the traditional hermeneutic categories, and they appear like the results of pure imagination. Little wonder that those secrets tend to emerge in texts which we have traditionally identified as fairy tales.[36]

Those are secrets that have a huge impact on human life because the hero is suddenly able to carry out his/her task, to achieve the impossible, or to enter into new spheres and dimensions—not hell, not heaven, but maybe the underworld, caves, or mountain-tops. They represent a different dimension that is certainly at play, but which is not a mystical vision or revelation. Neither God nor the devil emerges in such circumstances; instead, something secretive makes its presence felt and assists or threatens the individual.

Thus, to make it absolutely clear, the present study is not going to be a book about magic or religion, or mysticism, but about the sense of the secret itself, a quasi-religious experience that is reflected in countless literary examples, such as the early medieval religious charms, the appearance of werewolves, the role of dwarfs and dragons, true riddles, magical swords (Excalibur, Colada, etc.), mysterious processions of exotic and wondrous beings, etc. The world human beings live in is not limited by heaven and hell, however defined, and it is obviously much bigger than even the best scientists today can figure out completely. There always remain some mysteries; we confront ever new forces and phenomena that challenge us, spiritually and materially, in our existence and rationality, and hence we keep growing and living. The number of questions concerning the why and the what is probably never going to decrease; they are simply part and parcel of all life itself, the biggest riddle we human beings face all the time.

Medieval philosophers and scientists talked about the macrocosm and microcosm; we moderns are aware of the nanosphere and the extraterrestrial space at the outer edge of the universe, which is expanding at a rapid pace, not slowing down, as the big bang theory had suggested. We know that people interact with each other in a curious way, loving or hating each other. Some people are close friends, others ignore everyone else. So, what bonds individuals, what connects them and makes them to cohesive, social beings? A reference to God in that regard would be a too simplistic way out, whereas the admission that this is all a secret might be too elusive. And yet, as this book will demonstrate, there are many forces in life that we all can observe, experience, feel, and interact with, and yet do not know really what they are all about.

WHAT IS A "SECRET"?

The term "secret" has already been identified as a useful epistemological category for a discussion of things medieval, but then mostly in the context of explorations, magic, and mysteries, commonly of a religious kind.[37] Keeping secrets, using secrets, and detecting secrets within the early medieval discourse has been the topic of Benjamin A. Saltzman's recent monograph.[38] The secrets of nature, often implying monstrosity, the supernatural, and the divine, viewed at times through a scientific lens (Roger Bacon), is the theme pursued by Robert Bartlett.[39] For many mystics, their visions and revelations constituted a form of secrets since the experience of the Godhead in their awake condition proved to be beyond all rational and physical explanations, making it impossible to translate those ineffable experiences into comprehensible human terms.[40]

The term "secret" carries considerable hermeneutic difficulties with it, having been used by so many different poets, writers, artists, and philosophers throughout time. Here, however, I want to stay away from the medical concept behind the word (referring to gynecology), from mysticism (with one exception, see the respective chapter below), magic, and theology. Otherwise, I would be forced to explore the vast field of medieval religious thought, from St. Augustine to Martin Luther, for instance, insofar as the transcendence of the material limitations in human life immediately leads over to a secret dimension, which ordinary rationality cannot grasp. The secret would then be tantamount to God Himself, or the divine sphere, and entering a secret would then have to be understood as the ultimate encounter with God, the merging of the soul with the divine, that is, the ultimate non-material experience possible.[41] Francesco Petrarch (1304–1374) used the term "secret" in his eponymous dialogue narrative, *De secreto conflictu curarum mearum* (*My Secret Book*, ca. 1347–1353), for the exploration of his inner self in exchange with St. Augustine who teaches him to keep one's mortality in mind and to search for happiness not in the material dimension of things but in the world of spirituality.[42] In Augustine's words,

> the first step in avoiding the distresses of this mortal life and raising the soul to higher things is to practice meditation on death and on man's misery; and that the second is to have a vehement desire and purpose to rise. (14)

Of course, Petrarch is not really concerned with secrets in this context and instead uses the term "secret" as a concept of human ignorance of the true goals in life. As he teaches his disciple, "The desire of all good cannot exist without thrusting out every lower wish. . . . All these [objects] you must first learn to count as nothing before you can rise to the desire for the chief good" (25). In the more secular context, we hear only about secret associations or federations and secret scripts, but not about secrets in epistemological, narrative, and philosophical terms.[43]

Undoubtedly, intellectuals in the Middle Ages were rather familiar with the work of the *Secreta secretorum*, a twelfth-century translation of the pseudo-Aristotelian *Kitab sirr al-asrar* from the tenth century, which contained many different suggestions and much advice about healthcare, bathing, herbs, anatomy, magic, alchemy, astrology, and popular wisdom. It was highly popular far into the late Middle Ages, greatly appreciated as a major source of ancient wisdom.[44] Similarly, the thirteenth-century treatise of *Secretum mulierum*, commonly attributed to Albertus Magnus or to one of his students and drawing on Hippocratic, Galenic, and Aristotelian theories, operated profoundly with the notion of the secret in a biomedical context. The human body constitutes, until today, a mystery, or a secret, often operating all by itself without our doing or our control.[45]

In other words, already in the Middle Ages, if not especially then, the term *secretus* exerted a considerable appeal and opened new dimensions readily available for all kinds of imagination and fantasy,[46] while the authors of the relevant texts certainly endeavored as best as they could to explore the world of medicine. The birth of a child has always been a miracle, a secret, and it was discussed at great detail already in the Middle Ages (Hildegard of Bingen) and the sixteenth century, such as in the case of the famous medical doctor Eucharius Rösslin (ca. 1470–1526), who gained much popularity with his first major treatise on midwifery, his *Der Rosengarten* (The Rose Garden) in 1513, which was soon translated even into English as *The Birth of Mankind* in 1540, and also into other languages such as Czech.[47] I will return to this topic below in a slightly different context. But here we need to keep in mind that all knowledge can be identified as a secret that only the initiated and experts can really understand, something which medical experts know only too well, and this until today.

The goal of this study, however, will be much more humble, yet also eye-opening, and innovative, addressing a variety of medieval narratives where strange, inexplicable phenomena appear, which challenge the protagonists and drive the account forward in a significant way. Full explanations are normally not given, probably because they would have been impossible or would have destroyed the poetic and aesthetic value of the secret itself.

GOTTFRIED VON STRASSBURG

One small example of what medieval secrets mean would be the famous dog Petitcreiu in Gottfried von Strassburg's *Tristan* (ca. 1210) whose iridescent fur makes it impossible for the protagonist to figure out what color might be hidden here. Whereas before Tristan had been in complete control of his world, the appearance of the dog with its magical fur reveals that the master of the world of the courts does not comprehend the alternative dimension. Nevertheless, Tristan attempts to gain this dog for his beloved because it guarantees, as he is told, its owner to enjoy happiness resulting from the music produced by the bell hanging around its neck. But that happiness is fake, it is the outcome of sensuous deception, and Isolde realizes that quickly. While listening to that music, she observes a false sense of happiness, so she realizes that this personal comfort really threatens her notion of true love. In order to preserve that love, she pulls off the bell and thus destroys the music, or the false sense of happiness. Her happiness rests, as she insists for herself, inside, so the music that she destroys represents a dangerous illusion.

Whereas up to that point, Tristan had been completely in charge of his own life, had been a master strategist and commander of all forces affecting his individuality as a member of the court, the encounter with the secret represented by these confusing colors indicates that he is losing this control; instead, the secret is taking over his existence.[48] There is no possible explanation of the secret associated with Petitcreiu, except that it alerts the reader to the fact that true love cannot be purchased, manipulated, instrumentalized, or materialized. At the same time, Petitcreieu signals that the nature of love will remain a secret for human beings.

In concrete terms, the dog carries a bell hanging from a necklace, and whoever listens to that music immediately feels a deep sense of happiness, losing any previous worries, fears, depressions, or frustrations. This music works almost like a wonder drug and removes also all feelings of love, sorrow, longing, and despair in Isolde's heart. As soon as she realizes this sudden change of her heart, that is, the lifting of all of her sadness and desire for her lover, she recognizes the danger of this secret music and destroys it by tearing off the bell. Thus, the wonder brought about by the sound of the bell is destroyed, and there is no longer any secret about this amazing dog, a secret and wonder in the world of the courts which threatens, however, the very essence of love, another form of secret, which counteracts the efforts by official society to control lovers and to discipline those who do not act in conformity with public expectations.[49]

Early on, Tristan had appeared as the wonder child in terms of music, able to play all known instruments with ease, and being competent, particularly in others with which no one at the Cornish court is even familiar, and whereas throughout the romance he had demonstrated his mastery of music whenever he needed it for his political strategies, or for personal purposes, the confrontation with Petitcreiu throws the protagonist into doubts, confusion, and lack of understanding. The secret of the sounds created by the bell remains hidden to him; or, he misunderstands its properties and hence misappropriates it.[50] While music has always tended to be a medium of entertainment and pleasure, Gottfried clearly signals that its misunderstanding or misappropriation, or its mysterious nature, could lead to an existential danger for society at large because it addresses an epistemological dimension most people do not have access to.

There are hardly any explanations by the narrator as to the secret behind the dog and its bell, but it is a clear example of that phenomenon of love. If not even Tristan can figure out the "true" color of the fur and the meaning of the sound of the music, then Petitcreiu escapes human understanding; the dog remains a secret, here disregarding a few discreet comments by the narrator. As he informs us, the dog was delivered to Duke Gilân from Avalon, the Arthurian utopia, or the world of the fairies. A goddess had sent it out of love and friendship for Gilân, who is single and apparently happy enough with his more or less intimate relationship with that goddess (15797–817).

The narrator gives highest praise for this amazing dog, which shines forth through its color and inner charm, so it seems, and the fictional characters Gilân, Tristan, and Isolde react the same way, being stunned by this animal phenomenon having originated from another world (Avalon). However, no poet would ever be able to describe either its appearance or its properties, as the narrator emphasizes, which also applies to Tristan, the smartest person in the entire romance, as we may assume (15820–21). The more the narrative gaze focuses on the animal's appearance and delights in its iridescence, the less the reader/listener succeeds in imagining what this stunning dog really looks like; its dazzling appearance makes it impossible to describe in detail the charm of this canine secret.

For Gilân, Petitcreiu constitutes his entire happiness: "sînes herzen spil von Avaliu" (15799; his heart's delight from Avalon), so it represents a messenger from a utopian world. Tristan realizes this as well, especially when he listens to the music created by the bell which eliminates all of his sorrow and infuses him with complete happiness (15850–55). He is not even filled with thoughts of Isolde any longer, so he stares at this miracle of a dog, without being capable of fully comprehending what has happened to him in the presence of Petitcreiu. The operative term for this moment proves to be "wunder" (15869), which Krohn translates simply as "Wunder" (miracle), and Whobrey follows him in the exact same way.[51]

Gottfried did not resort to any religious explanation of this phenomenon, and did not refer to any necromantic forces, to infernal powers, or to anything spiritual behind this dog. We only know that it originated from the world of fairies, spites all human spectators, and has a magical impact on them when they listen to the music of the bell. It is a secret *par excellence*. There are no indications of any kind of magic involved, and the dog's charm is not owed to any religious and diabolic forces, although we hear that it had been sent to Gilân by a goddess in the world of utopian Avalon, "der feinen lant" (15808; the land of the fairies), as a sign of her love and friendship (15810). Its beauty and intrigue prove to be of such a quality that no human words can be used to express them, and not even the master linguist and artist Tristan commands any capacity to comprehend this secret. However, to reiterate the crucial characteristic of this dog, it is not the product of magic, and there are no religious explanations for its miraculous properties.

Petitcreiu is simply a secret, and not even Tristan is able to decipher or to decode it.[52] He looks at the fur and realizes that he cannot distinguish among the colors of the fur, meaning that he as the master epistemologist is no longer capable of handling his own world. Interestingly, by contrast, when Isolde receives the dog and listens to the music, she quickly realizes the extent to which it works like a drug, making her happy, removing all of her feelings of sorrow and pain; hence, her longing for Tristan. Consequently, she pulls off the bell and thus destroys the music; in other words, she deconstructs the secret that is supposed to make her feel happy and resorts to her own feelings of true but sorrowful love, determined at that point by deep pain. Does Isolde perhaps therefore understand more of the other secret, her love of Tristan than the male protagonist? She explicitly turns away from this wonder dog with its dangerous music: "nune welle got der guote, / daz ich in mînem muote / iemer vröude âne in gehabe!" (16385–87; now, may God the Good One prevent it that I will ever feel happiness in my mind without him). Once having removed the bell, there is no more music, and this fake form of happiness thus has disappeared, which allows Isolde to stay true to her deep feelings, irrespective of all the pain which comes along with them.

OTHER EXAMPLES

We observe another set of secrets in the anonymous Old French *Huon de Bourdeaux* from the second half of the thirteenth century where the young protagonist encounters the King of Fairies, Auberon, who was later to become the source for Shakespeare's *A Midnight Summer's Dream* from ca. 1595 or 1596.[53] Auberon himself represents a secret, a mysterious being of enormous powers which appear to be magical but belong to a different category, for which we should use the term "secret" as the heuristically most fitting word. Huon strikes a close friendship with him and receives two major gifts from the king, first a goblet from which people can drink only if they have never told a lie and are stellar representatives of complete virtuousness. Secondly, he gives him a horn—similar to the horn Oliphant in the *Chanson de Roland*—with which Huon would be able to call for Auberon's immediate help in case of an emergency. Neither object is associated with magic, demons, or infernal powers, and they are not viewed in any religious terms. Hence, they are simply secrets that no one can understand; they plainly exist and serve the protagonist in many subsequent scenes.

There are other wonders and mysterious phenomena in *Huon de Bordeaux*, which I will discuss in a separate chapter. It is fitting that Auberon is the lord of the kingdom of fairies, a domain separated from the world of King Arthur and from the real existence, hence a territory characterized by a secret that never finds a full explanation. Auberon himself reveals a little about himself when he states: "I know all the secrets of paradise / And can hear the angels singing up there. / I will never grow old / And never die, unless it is my choice" (3557–61). Similar miraculous phenomena emerge in other contemporary works, such as in Der Stricker's *Daniel von dem Blühenden Tal*, some of which appear to be robotics, magical objects, and mysterious instruments; and all of them ultimately help the protagonist to achieve his goals and to triumph over all dangers and opponents at the end.

We also need to take into consideration the large corpus of medieval charms, which are best known today from early medieval manuscripts (e.g., "Merseburger Zaubersprüche"). There are many approaches possible to identify them, associating them with medicine, religion, political, and military power.[54] Those charms continued to be popular throughout the ages, in fact, well into the fifteenth and sixteenth centuries, though they have survived mostly in little-known manuscripts. The effort to use magical words to achieve medical healing, to overcome military opponents, to find lost objects, etc., can be explained using a variety of hermeneutic approaches, including anthropology and religion.[55] But in their concrete context and function, charms represent most interesting secrets known only to insiders and experts, which opens a wide window toward medieval epistemology, medicine, spirituality, and power. Again, the term "secret" proves to be highly useful in this context because the charms were not associated with demons, though in the course of time they assumed specifically Christian features and utilized religious formulas such as the "Pater noster" or "amen" to reach out for divine help.

To return to our initial reflections, whether charms or magical spells, whether prayers or incantations, the phenomenon itself proves to be widespread and pertaining to the dimension of healing, power, riches, spirituality, and even military successes. Courtly love such as expressed by Tristan and Isolde in Gottfried von Strassburg's version could be identified as a secret as well, and remains one until today, though most people would not think of specifying it as a secret in a magical sense. The term itself refers to an amorphous dimension of profound influence and power, but it does not associate the one who uses the secret or who deciphers it with a specific divine entity. Nevertheless, there is always a certain sense of a secret when medieval poets reflect on the topic of love—it is, after all, a phenomenon that tends to escape all rational and critical examinations.

Particularly this more flexible perspective regarding secrets makes it possible to incorporate many different texts from the entire European literature where we find numerous examples of inexplicable, mysterious, ominous, or fascinating objects, events, locations, and texts which cannot be easily deciphered or decoded, if at all. Secrets are mostly beyond the rational grasp and yet require a uniquely critical analysis outside of the traditional logical framework. They certainly matter essentially especially in pre-modern fictional (but also scientific and medical) texts.

Addressing secrets requires a highly interdisciplinary approach to medieval literature because they appear throughout the ages in many different languages and cultures, and also in a variety of genres. In the modern world, we still talk about secrets, and there is, for example, within the US government, the important branch of the Secret Service—perhaps a far-fetched analogy to medieval secrets, although courtly politics and diplomacy then were also often shrouded in secrecy.[56] A literary confirmation for this phenomenon can be found in the anonymous Middle High German *Herzog Ernst* (*Duke Ernst*; ms. A., ca. 1170; ms. B., ca. 1220), where Emperor Otto has retired to his private chamber together with his nephew, the Count Henry of the Palatinate, to discuss with him their secret plans to promote their military campaign against Duke Ernst of Bavaria: "heimlîch an eime rate" (1277; in a secret meeting). They are not aware that just at that moment the latter has arrived late at night, unrecognized by the guards, and has already entered the military camp. Just when the secret meeting has begun, Ernst and his advisor Wetzel enter the chamber, and Ernst can slay Henry, who had maligned him and was really responsible for the terrible war, while the emperor manages to escape at the last minute with his life.[57]

The literary projection was, of course, only a fictional projection of what probably happened all the time in courtly life. But this kind of secrecy, a practical, political maneuver or strategy, is not the topic the subsequent chapters are engaged with. Nevertheless, even this small episode in *Herzog Ernst* signals how much secrets, secret negotiations and discussions, and efforts to keep certain information private, for instance, mattered already at that time.

Of course, children throughout time have greatly enjoyed secrets and played with that notion quite extensively within their fantasy. By contrast, many medieval poets carefully operated with the notion of the secret to open up new dimensions of epistemology, beyond religion as such, and they indicate, whenever those secrets are mentioned, that there are active agents behind the scene whom the poets themselves could not address, whether we think of the Grail in Wolfram von Eschenbach's *Parzival* (ca. 1205) or the hawk man in the *lai* "Yonec" by Marie de France (ca. 1170).

The contributors to the recent volume on *Geheimnis und Verborgenes im Mittelalter* study the appearance, functions, and impact of secrets and their demarcation from the public domain are examined in essays from the fields of history, philosophy, theology, and literary and cultural studies.[58] The editors have combined investigations on the ordeal, church-imposed atonement, mysticism, alchemy, the concept of paradise, the notion of the mythical Atlantis, sacred objects and reliquaries, voyeurism, spirituality, and other topics directly or indirectly correlated with the obscure. All this, however, amounts to a rather disjointed collection where anything which sounds even faintly mysterious is grouped under the category of the secret.

My intention, by contrast, is to collect a variety of literary-historical and religious cases of secrets that certainly impact the texts' developments and the protagonists' characters, without us ever fully comprehending the meaning or causality, such as in the Old Welsh *Mabinogion*. The interest here is focused on the functions of the secret as a narrative motive of great relevance from the early to the late Middle Ages, always addressing uncanny epistemological ends, but certainly of great influence, whether the nixies in the anonymous *Nibelungenlied* (ca. 1200) or the werewolf in Marie de France's "Bisclavret."

We also need to discriminate between "magic," "miracle," and "the secret," since I do not want to blend religious and pseudo-religious aspects with the epistemological aspect when fictional individuals just do not know what to make out of phenomena that they encounter and are then in need of outside explanations. This is wonderfully illustrated by Priest Lamprecht's early Middle High German *Alexander* (ca. 1170), one of the many versions of Alexander the Great's accomplishments discussed both in European and Arabic, then also in Persian and Indian sources. Here I leave aside all the miracles he has encountered on his exploration and conquest of the Orient, and focuses only on a secret object that he receives from an old man who protects the wall to Paradise which Alexander would never be able to penetrate with military force. In fact, the guardsman simply sends him away and gives him a curious rock as a reminder of his blasphemous attitude believing that he could even fight against and win over God by conquering Paradise.[59] After a long consultation with his advisors, Alexander indeed agrees to abandon the conquest and to return home, carrying the mysterious stone with him. However, back in Greece, none of his wise men is able to identify the true properties of the rock although many of them have studied gems and jewels for a long time and claim to be experts in the lapidary sciences. (7035–40).

Only when he has finally called in a wise old man, a Jew who is admired by everyone,[60] do they learn the secret hidden in the rock. He immediately understands the full property of this object and identifies it as the most precious stone in the world (7102–04). To demonstrate this, he has the rock placed on one of the dishes of a scale, and the other one filled with many gold coins, but the rock is always heavier than those although it is not larger than the size of a human eye. The narrator explicitly describes the spectators' amazement: "daz was ein michil wunder" (7030; that was a great marvel). The solution to the secret is that the rock represents God's message to people to stay away from greed since none of the money or gold would ever outweigh the little stone. No material goods would ever be good enough for one's salvation, an idea that only a divine message can convey to people. Hence, it is a kind of miracle, but more a divine message to teach a lesson, hence it is a secret which the old Jew alone is able to solve or to explain by means of the practical demonstration, an intellectual challenge, we might say, which only those can address who command deep knowledge and learning.

Thereupon, he demonstrates the other, almost dialectical message contained in the rock. This time, the other dish is filled with some earth and a feather (7138–43), and it forces the other one with the stone to rise up, which indicates, as he explains, that people are nothing but soil or feathers, hence heavy and earthbound and easily pass away at the end of their life—we are all subject to death. The Jew appeals to Alexander and his men to abstain from sinful behavior, especially greed and arrogance, to observe humility, and to live a God-fearing life because all people are nothing but mortal and will die for sure. Once the riddle has been solved, the king pays his respects to the Jew and sends him home with all honors. The poet has thus crowned his literary achievement with the inclusion of this phenomenon, which I identify as a secret that only the wisest of them all can solve since he knows about the temporality of all human existence and admonishes Alexander to keep the afterlife in mind.[61] This is, generally speaking, a miracle, but it falls into a unique category that is better characterized as a secret because of the hidden message within the rock.

As much as medieval poets addressed many different aspects of human existence trying to offer rational explanations, as much they were also deeply concerned with addressing the ineffable, if not even the apophatic, particularly in religious terms. However, we often also face profane contexts where the secret functions as an agent all by itself, such as in Heinrich von dem Türlin's *Diu Crône* (ca. 1280), which I will analyze at length below. To do full justice to that particular perspective, I will also include a chapter on mysticism, but that is a topic already covered so extensively by other scholars that their research would not help us much further in the present context. My interest will here not focus on mysticism as such in religio-historical terms. Instead, I suggest that we recognize the visions reported about as alternative forms of secrets, that is, the sudden intervention of the "Other" in ordinary human life in a secretive medium, the revelation

Secrets in *Sir Gawain and the Green Knight*

Much discussed already, the Middle English alliterative romance *Sir Gawain and the Green Knight* from the late fourteenth century also offers many insights into medieval concepts of secrets.[62] The entire set-up with the Green Knight who appears at King Arthur's court during Christmas time and demands that someone accepts his offer to dare the challenge of mutual decapitation seems to be a rather playful operation. But it really proves to be a matter of life and death, at least for Gawain. Of course, he succeeds in cutting off the stranger's head using the ominous axe, but when it is his term a year later to submit to the other knight, he knows that he has virtually no chance to survive. Of course, the Green Knight is only testing his bravery and courage, and would not want to see him dead, but he delights in probing his possible fear and hence his knightly honor. At the end of the scene at the Green Chapel, after the game has been completed and Gawain has survived despite all odds, he himself admits that he had previously received from Morgan le Fay a magical means to reattach his head to his own body, a kind of cheating in this deadly matter.

Gawain himself trusted, in a way, some magical trapping, the green belt which the lady of the caste Hautdesert had given him as a gift. According to her claims, it would have guaranteed his life, which thus should have assured Gawain that his opponent would not kill him. However, her husband, Bercilak, who is really the Green Knight, and Gawain had made an agreement to exchange with each other whatever they would have caught and gained during the day. Bercilak goes hunting and returns with the prey, each one of them representing one of Gawain's own physical characters. Gawain, by contrast, stays behind and is surprised for three days, or early mornings, by the lady who tries to seduce him. Observing his own honor and respect for his host, Gawain resists all of her attempts and accepts nothing but her kisses, which he can calmly exchange with the host in the evening. But Gawain then keeps the belt as a secret object, does not divulge its existence, although Bercilak certainly learns about his "failure" from his own wife. Consequently, Bercilak then punishes him for this failure during the capitation scene at the Green Chapel by wounding his opponent at his neck and then mocks him softly for his "loss" of honor, although he does not really mean it.

For Gawain, this realization represents a deep embarrassment, and he bursts out with a highly misogynist and traditional lambasting of women as men's arch-temptresses (2416–28). Then he departs and returns to King Arthur's court, where he openly admits his failure to uphold his honor in the face of the threatened execution by the Green Knight. Of course, the latter basically brushes this aside: "However, you lacked a little, sir, and your loyalty was wanting, / But that was not for wild wickedness, nor wooing either, / But because you loved your life; thus the less I blame you" (2366–68). Morgan le Fay had really wanted to challenge her brother, King Arthur, and then his wife, Guenevere; this also reveals that she is really Gawein's aunt. As Bercilak indicates, the entire set-up served as a strategy to test Arthur's and Gawain's inner strength, and this in a playful manner. However, Bercilak's ability to transform into a Green Man who could not be killed still represents a profound secret that finds no full explanation and is also not supposed to be revealed. This also applies to the countless images of the "green man" in tile works, paintings, frescoes, and sculptures particularly in contemporary England.

Neither here nor in any other medieval narrative is the secret of Morgan le Fay fully exposed, and she serves ominously as a constant reminder of the vast difference between the material existence of the Arthurian court and the other dimension.[63] We do not learn where she derives her power from, and it also remains unclear why she is so hateful of King Arthur and his court. A big secret really veils the background of the entire romance, and many others insofar as this mysterious woman operates on her own and defies all male efforts to identify her and maybe to wrest power from her. She might be identified as a witch, as a goddess, as a fairy, or as a sorceress, and she certainly operates in the twilight between knightly society and the world of magic and the secret, between the religious and the secular, between the male and the female. Her ultimate secret consists in her resistance to be categorized, to be identified as female, for instance, and to human efforts to determine individuals in narrow, specific terms.[64]

Secrets in Heinrich Kaufringer's Late Medieval Verse Narratives: An Exemplary Exploration

To round off these preliminary observations, we can also reflect on the simple situation in human life when an individual deliberately dissimulates to deceive other people, keeping his own identity a secret. Not every secret is associated with spiritual forces, with magical powers, or mystical visions, and yet those secrets then also indicate what determines an individual within a larger social context, at times within a religious dimension. For instance, in Heinrich Kaufringer's verse narrative, "The Mayor and the Prince" (ca. 1400), a young student in Erfurt is suspected of being involved in a string of burglaries because he spends his money profligately and without any care. No one knows anything about him, so the city council sends the mayor to inquire about his background, but the young man refuses to oblige the mayor. Resorting to a subterfuge, however, he pretends to make his money as a gigolo, receiving plenty of money from each housewife and each maid. This revelation deeply shocks the mayor and the council members, who feel confirmed in their sense of sexual inferiority and know not at all how to defend themselves against this threat to their honor, dignity, and social status. Hence, they implicitly decide to ignore it all and let things pass to avoid being exposed in their personal failures, at least as they now perceive it.[65]

The mayor, however, one day observes the young student crossing the marketplace, and he involuntarily smiles thinking about what he believes the young man down there is up to—maybe he even derides the other husbands who are, as he believes, in the process of being cuckolded—and is then forced by his wife to reveal the cause for this. For a second time, hence, a secret is revealed, and this one is also only the result of deception. But whereas the mayor was the victim of the student's rhetorical strategy, here, in this situation, he becomes a victim of his erotic imagination.

As one might expect, once the wife is aware of the alleged sexual services provided by the student for a hefty fee, she voices moral disgust, but in secret (!) she feels rejected by the student and senses some degree of envy and jealousy. Hence, she begins to woo the student and actually manages to invite him in when she believes her husband to be away on a business trip. This is their secret, "haimlich gieng er da zehant / zuo dem lieben puolen sein" (250–51; secretly he went right away to his beloved mistress); that is, they rely on the secret set-up, and yet this quickly collapses and becomes exposed.

In reality, the husband had deceived her and now catches the couple *in flagrante* when they are taking a bath. The mayor removes their clothes to hold them captive, and then returns with food and wine, asking his wife to serve the guest properly because now, with him in their presence, it has become a "public" visit that requires respectful treatment. They both are then allowed to get dressed and must act in official roles which restores the husband's honor, as the young man also affirms. When the husband then tries to pay the "debt" on his wife's behalf, this embarrasses the student, who then finally reveals his real secret, that he is the son of the king of France and had only pretended to be a male prostitute to make fun of the mayor and the councilmen. At that point, he also tries to make amends and promises the mayor that he as a merchant would never have to pay any taxes on the goods that he would buy or sell in France and that he would be under the king's protection wherever he would go (25). The secrets have all been resolved, and the dangerous consequences have been avoided.[66] The audience is invited to laugh about these confusions and misunderstandings, but it remains important that the poet here endeavors to resort to the concept of the secret as a major vehicle in human communication or as a significant factor of miscommunication, an issue that current research has not yet taken fully into consideration.[67]

In "The Search for the Happily Married Couple" (no. 8), a man is deeply frustrated with his wife because she is too frugal for him, whereas he enjoys throwing parties and inviting friends. Although the entire city community is filled with praise of her virtues, he can't stand living with her, so he goes on a long journey, not to entertain himself, but with the purpose of searching for at least one married couple who would display complete happiness. Of course, the foolish protagonist is not able to achieve his goal, although twice he believes to have found such an ideal couple. In the first case, he suddenly learns that behind the façade of the couple's happiness there rests a deep secret. Once she had had an affair with the local priest, whom the husband then slew. He then extracted the skull and prepared it as a cup from which she has to drink wine once every evening as a perpetual reminder of her transgression. No one knows about the priest's death, since the body is well hidden in a secret grave. But in private, the wife has to carry out that awful ritual every night as her punishment (47).

The second couple who also seems to lead a truly happy life proves to be just as much a deception because they only pretend to be happy. In reality, she had been a nymphomaniac whose uncontrollable sexual desires made her commit endless adultery. The husband, in his desperation, finally went to a distant land, kidnapped a strong young peasant, and made him his wife's sex slave, a topic we would not find again in any other medieval text. Unknown to everyone in town, the man is kept in a cave deep in the wine cellar, where the wife enjoys copulating with him regularly. She conceived a number of times, but all of their subsequent children are fathered by the slave, which the husband admits with chagrin to the protagonist: "But my honor is deeply hurt, in secret and silently. The same wine and food that I enjoy every day I personally bring to the peasant for his dinner. I take better care of him, by my honor, than of myself in order that he may sleep with my wife so that she will be sexually satisfied and does not look for the pleasure of sex elsewhere, as she used to do" (49).

Once the protagonist has learned the truth of this case and has realized the secret behind the façade of fake happiness, he returns home and enjoys his own marriage despite his wife's frugality which proves to be far less important compared to the major transgressions her husband had observed in other cases. Life is filled with secrets, and Kaufringer illustrates this universal truth both here and in other of his verse narratives. However, in this case, the secrets pertain to the tension between private and public life; they represent the hidden existence that the individuals do not want to reveal to society, out of shame and embarrassment. It is quite indicative that both husbands whose wives had transgressed their marriage vow to resort to private spaces to deal with their personal conflicts, that is, either the private chamber or the cellar. Throughout time, and so already in the Middle Ages, people have had to cope with such problems, and Kaufringer deserves particular credit for thematizing this tension so dramatically.

On top of these secrets, however, he also elaborated on secrets in religious and epistemological terms, which illustrates powerfully that the term "secret" carries numerous meanings and reveals a number of different hermeneutic levels. In the very first tale, "The Hermit and the Angel," a hermit desires to explore the world after a long life in his isolated cell but not necessarily out of a vain worldly curiosity, but, as the narrator states explicitly, in order to observe God's countless miracles, as mentioned in the Psalms 67:36: "mirabilis deus in sanctis suis." However, as the narrator also alerts us from the start, no human mind would ultimately be powerful and skilled enough to comprehend God's working: "The human mind cannot grasp the wonders that God works, and no one can ever grasp it all" (1). This concept goes back to the biblical text and was rephrased many times throughout the Middle Ages, such as in the work by the ninth-century Fulda abbot Rabanus Maurus.[68] Of course, there is a clear difference between the secret in the private lives of the various burgher protagonists, commonly reserved for their marital conditions, and the secrets in divine terms. Nevertheless, the shared denominator proves to be the inability of the outsider to look beyond the factual screen and to peer into a secret world. Miracles would thus be the physical manifestation of God's secrets, though the spectator would not have any chance of comprehending the actual nature and properties of these phenomena.

This proves to be the case in Kaufringer's tale as well where the hermit explicitly emphasizes to the stranger pilgrim, who is really an angel, "All my intentions are directed toward the goal of how I could learn about God's miracles, which happen everywhere; there are many that are unaccountable for. I want to understand what they are; that is my desire" (1). He is too old and too pious to search for worldly adventures or erotic experiences, but he still does not have any clue as to what he might be in for once he would have witnessed the ways in which the world is operating. The angel, however, is happy that this provides him with an opportunity to accompany him, and the hermit welcomes him as a fellow in the assumption that he would be a good person and companion on this pilgrimage.

The situation at first looks good for both since they are welcomed and treated in a very generous fashion by an innkeeper. However, the angel quickly turns out to be a monstrous person, murdering the host's little child, and snuffing it to death with a pillow. On the second day, they stay with another innkeeper, and the angel steals his most precious chalice. To the poor hermit's chagrin, when they are then badly mistreated and abused by an innkeeper the third night, the stranger hands over the chalice as payment for their miserable night. Finally, the hermit is already about to despair over all these horrible acts, the stranger murders a young man by way of throwing him into a river where he drowns. The old man is completely distraught over all those horrible acts and calls out: "Help, why is God asleep that he does not take revenge on you for the evil deeds, of which you commit so many? Indeed, I no longer want to walk with you, neither here nor there" (5).

To his great surprise, however, at that moment the angel reveals his true identity and teaches him some of God's secrets, or secret workings, miracles, but in a rather different sense of the word. All the horrible actions were part of the larger divine plans and could not be judged by human moral, ethical, legal, or religious criteria. There are very good reasons why those people had to die or why the chalice was stolen and handed over to that evil person. The angel offers perspectives regarding God's intentions which the hermit, hence we as the audience, can barely comprehend because divine justice proves to be far removed from human justice. Consequently, the angel concludes his remarks with the following statement: "Therefore, my dear brother, return to your cell, because all the wonders that God does happen only for good purposes. No longer question anything and follow my teachings, which will give you protection for ever" (6).

The hermit accepts those recommendations and acknowledges that the miracles performed by God, or divine secrets, are beyond his comprehension, so all he can do is to embrace them as such and live his own life undisturbed by the torturous quest for knowledge about those secrets out in the world which no human mind can satisfactorily analyze and understand.[69] As recent scholarship has observed, this approach to human epistemology was rather characteristic of the genre of late medieval verse narratives where the poets felt free to experiment with challenging issues and problematic cases in human life.[70] However, we can also trace those perspectives backward to late antique and early medieval theology (St. Augustine), while they found maybe their most impressive manifestations in the arguments by William Ockham. According to him, God often orders certain things or brings about conditions that are irrational or contradictory within the human context and thus appear to be secrets (my word). Even the great authority, Thomas Aquinas (1225–1274), had already confirmed this understanding of God who could do wonders that people would not be able to understand.[71]

Kaufringer's *mæren* stand out within the wide genre of related texts because the poet experimented on a regular basis with the notion of the secret. While this term pertains to the power and workings of God here in this world as illustrated in the first narrative, in many others we discover the inclusion of secrets or secretive operations as tools in the lives of the various protagonists, often when their love affairs are involved, such as in "The Canon and the Cobbler" (no. 9). The critical issue always proves to be the separation of the interior and the exterior, of the material and the sacred, of the human and the divine. While Kaufringer's protagonists tend to play with secrets to cover their private issues, he was obviously also deeply aware of the larger secrets, normally appearing as miracles, but in "The Hermit and the Angel" as God's secret strategies which human beings cannot grasp at all. We face, in other words, a phenomenon that is simply called "the secret," but which proves to be an issue of great epistemological concerns for a wide range of medieval poets.

OUTLOOK

On that basis, both theoretically and established, we can now turn to our actual investigation, drawing from a wide range of sources, taking us from early medieval magical charms, secrets in themselves, to the late medieval mystical discourse, and the appearance of mysterious goddesses and objects; the focus here will rest on what we can learn about secrets in the pre-modern world, that is, on a hidden world where things happen that are supposed to be removed from public awareness, from the knowledge by the uninitiated, or protected from abuses by the masses.

I have already alluded to many possible analogies between medieval and modern secrets, and we really ought to dismiss the Weberian concept as a fallacy to a certain extent. Especially when we incorporate the world of Romanticism from around 1800, deeply steeped in its re-discovery of the Middle Ages, we can easily recognize the continuous workings of secrets in human imagination, if not lives. Secretive spaces, objects, people, and visions appear even in the so-called Realist literature from the late nineteenth century. And who would be willing to declare the twenty-first century free from secrets?

Not every secret is something positive; violence (sexual or otherwise) happens in secret spaces, especially rape, thieves and murderers operate in secret to stay obscured from the public view, and so forth.[72] Some of the best examples for that phenomenon would be, apart from Rowling's most popular series of novels, *Harry Potter*, the masterpiece of Latin-American literature, Gabriel García Márquez's *Cien Años de Soledad* (1967),[73] Michael Ende's novel for young readers, *Momo* (1973),[74] and Patrick Sueskind's *Parfüm* (1985).[75] Since the secret continues to be of such great relevance for contemporary readers, we discover here a remarkable epistemological bridge to pre-modern literature, whether we think of the various novels dealing with *Melusine* (Jean d'Arras, 1393; Coudrette, ca. 1400; Thüring von Ringoltingen, 1456), or the anonymous *Fortunatus* (1509), where a mysterious fairy appears and offers the protagonist magical powers (eternal wealth or eternal wisdom, etc.). The secret has always been powerfully at play, though often removed from the public gaze, and so it has also escaped, to some extent, the critical examination, certainly a desideratum this book wants to cover.

SOCIOLOGICAL PERSPECTIVES OF SECRETS

The standard reference works on the Middle Ages do not include any entry/lemma on the "secret" (such as the *Lexikon des Mittelalters*), and major lexica or encyclopedia dedicated to the humanities appear to have ignored this topic as well.[76] Of course, most learned individuals in the Middle Ages were familiar with the highly popular *Secretum Secretorum*, a pseudo-Aristotelian text originally composed perhaps in Greek, later translated into Arabic, and from there into Latin (Europe) and probably also into many other languages in Asia. The earliest version might date from the ninth or tenth century, and it purports to be a letter by Aristotle to his student Alexander the Great, containing a wide range of instructions about many different topics, including basic ethics for a king, the alchemical properties of plants, gems, other natural objects, or numbers. The unknown author explicitly predicated his work on the notion of the secret nature of deep knowledge, which obviously appealed deeply to medieval audiences.[77] Secrets have always been with us and are part of human epistemology, if not of all human actions which take place in private, in the dark, away from society for many different reasons.[78]

We might face here an archetypal phenomenon, the intrigue exerted by that which is kept hidden, as a secret. But this does not only apply to science and medicine, to alchemy and astrology, but it also pertains to the religious component, the witnessing of the Godhead as a privilege for the prophet, mystic, or visionary. Aleida and Jan Assmann go so far as to identify the secret as the foundational myth of culture.[79] We could thus define the secret as the deliberate product of a process intended at creating an interior dimension for an exterior materiality or activity, which thereby becomes the foundation for spirituality, aesthetics, sciences, ethics, and morality. This does not amount to a full theory or definition of the secret, but it can serve as the starting point for our subsequent reflections on the secret in medieval and early modern literature.[80] We can add, however, that all scientific investigation of nature, spirituality, aesthetics, ethics, and morality imply the creation of interiority, that is, an understanding of the hidden structures, concepts, and ideas behind the physical phenomena.[81] Thinking, feeling, faith, spirituality, imagination, and other human faculties are predicated on the secret, that is, on that what is hidden from plain view and constitutes the essence of all being, all culture, and all ideas.[82]

This would also come close to our critical awareness of the ultimate secrets in nature today. Although contemporary scientists have been able to penetrate ever more deeply into even the nano-dimension of the physical world, or into the furthest spaces of the universe, the ultimate realization has regularly implied that the more we know the less we really know.

THE THEORY OF THE SECRET BY GEORG SIMMEL

In epistemological terms, Georg Simmel had already formulated some of the key components underlying the very nature of the secret observing that it defines the very relationship between people since many know much about the other individuals, but no one knows everything about everyone else.[83] We are, after all, secretive beings and unique in our identity which is rarely completely divulged to others. We might even be unaware of many dimensions in our own selves and grow throughout our lives by way of discovering ever new secrets about ourselves and our social environment. Moreover, all religion is the result of the realization of secrets in this world and the beyond which some individuals were privy or graced to discover and which they then share with the rest of their group either completely or in excerpts. Thus, discussing secrets amounts to an exploration of religion, science, and psychology at the same time.[84]

In fact, as Simmel emphasizes in his *Soziologie: Untersuchungen über die Formen der Vergesellschaftung* (1908; Sociology: Investigations of the Forms of Socialization), "the hiding of realities by negative or positive means, is one of man's greatest achievements."[85] The secret is the pathway and locked gate to another world, with the manifest world deeply influenced by the former. Applied to historical analysis, Simmel notes, "[t]he historical development of society is in many respects characterized by the fact that what at an earlier time was manifest, enters the protection of secrecy; and that, conversely, what once was secret, no longer needs such protection but reveals itself" (330–31). He perceived a form of evolution of secrecy insofar as "what originally was done consciously, sinks to the level of consciously mechanical *routine*, and, on the other hand, what at an earlier stage was unconscious and instinctive, rises to the clarity of consciousness" (331). Both positive and negative features are associated with the secret, either when a person is hiding his/her best values out of humility, or when a person is hiding immoral and evil thinking.

Secrecy serves, above all, to give particular power to something extremely valuable, accessible only to one individual or to a small group of initiated: "The secret gives one a position of exception; it operates as a purely socially determined attraction" (332). This also implies the establishment of charisma, superior political power, and public esteem because the leader (political or religious) stands apart from the crowd and surrounds him/herself with secrecy, hiding the "actual" nature of this power from public view (333). However, the very projection of a secret dimension can also be conditioned by the desire to deceive ordinary people as to the true source of political or religious authority, which might be nothing but dissimulation (333). All this, however, always comes along with the (perhaps deliberate?) possibility of betrayal, revelation, and discovery because the secret "creates the tempting challenge to break through it, by gossip or confession—and this challenge accompanies its psychology" (334). More generally put, "the secret is a form which constantly receives and releases contents: what originally was manifest becomes secret, and what once was hidden later sheds its concealment" (335). Leaders and rulers in the pre-modern era were hence shrouded in secrecy, while the individual was in its inner core manifestly public and transparent (hence: confession and repentance in the Church) (336). In modern times, so Simmel, the reverse has taken place, with the government having increasingly lost all of its secrecy, whereas the individual, qua its individuality, has become much more secret and inscrutable (336). In short, to paraphrase

Simmel further, politics have turned mostly public, and individuality has turned mostly private, or secret (337).

Simmel also points out that the secret serves a social group to maintain its public standing, whether it is the cast of clerics or aristocrats, members of the military (knighthood) or medical experts. Both the Holy Grail in medieval romances (Wolfram von Eschenbach's *Parzival*, ca. 1205) and the Masonic Order in Wolfgang Amadeus Mozart's *Magic Flute* (K. 620; premiered in 1791) easily come to mind, but there are countless other examples, such as the secret Himalayan valley of Shangri-La in James Hilton's *Lost Horizon* (1933).[86] As we can observe, "[t]he sociological significance of the secret is external, namely, the relationship between the one who has the secret and another who does not. But as soon as a whole group uses secrecy as its form of existence, the significance becomes internal: the secret determines the reciprocal relations among those who it has in common" (345). However, almost no secret remains as such as soon as it is known by more than one person. Virtually all secrets reveal themselves, in part or in total (346), at least in the political arena: "The flight into secrecy is a ready device for social endeavors and forces that are about to be replaced by new ones. In these cases, secrecy constitutes a sort of transitional stage between being and not-being" (347), and we could go so far as to claim that the secret needs its self-revelation in order to maintain its very own property, even though that revelation tends to be only partial, as in the case of the secret world of the Mountains where the secret order of the Assassins resides—for a medieval example, see The Stricker's *Daniel von dem Blühenden Tal* (ca. 1220).[87]

Seen through Simmel's lens, then, the secret enjoys particularly political, religious, and psychological significance, apart from its role in law, science, medicine, finance, and business.[88] I will leave aside his lengthy discussion of secret societies as a historical phenomenon, and only refer to his last thought that the "secret society is so much considered an enemy of the central power that, even conversely, every group that is politically rejected, is called a secret society" (576). Secrecy discriminates between insiders and outsiders and projects a hidden world of power and influence, which was certainly a major aspect of pre-modern culture.

THE SECRET AS THE SPICE OF LIFE

Similarly, the treatment of love, either in poetry or paintings, in music or sculptures, in treatises or romances, always amounts to the discovery of most intimate secrets associated with the individual's most inner core. We might also formulate that love is the secret par excellence and defines the very properties of human existence. If that holds true, then we are on firm ground to embrace medieval courtly love poetry, for instance, as most formidable research material to explore the meaning of love, as it also pertains to us.[89]

As Aleida and Jan Assmann formulate, no human society has ever released all secrets to its members, so we have always to assume that "das Gesagte stets vor einen Hintergrund des Ungesagten zu veranschlagen ist" (that what is spoken has consistently to be understood as something beyond that which is not spoken about).[90] Even though we live today in the western world in a society strongly determined by publicity and transparency, it appears as rather questionable whether secrets have thus disappeared from our existence. The more we command knowledge of ever more aspects in material terms, the more we seem to be facing ever new secrets beyond the limits that we just moved forward. The arcane has not been removed from our existence; it has simply taken on different shapes and properties, that is, we know both more and actually less, especially because we increasingly rely on the computer to store our knowledge. To study this phenomenon of the secret thus invites also medievalist approaches, if not primarily pre-modern ones, and this book will attempt to bring to the larger conversation the multiplicity of medieval voices addressing, describing, examining, and presenting secrets in many different contexts.[91]

Of course, secrets matter centrally also in fairy tales, but this would not be a contradiction to the previous claim since this genre was so deeply steeped in medieval culture and history and predicated on the workings of unknown forces, both evil and good.[92] As Hans Rudolf Picard has already observed, taking into consideration the inability of the human mind to grasp fully the world we live in:

Der im Märchenerzählen sich vollziehende, also ästhetische Umgang mit der Situation von dem Unbekannten, wie er im Märchen gegeben ist, kann als ein narratives Analogon jener menschlichen Beschränkung angesehen werden. Es ist eine ins Erzählerische abgemilderte Form von Beschwörung, in der Intention analog jenen magischen Handlungen, die die anthropologische-existentielle Grundsituation vor dem Undurchschaubaren zu bewältigen versuchen.[93]

[The aesthetic engagement with the situation of the unknown, as it takes place in the telling of fairy tales, as a basic fact of this genre, can be regarded as a narrative analogy to that human limitation. It is a mitigated form of incantation given in the narration, which is, in its intention, analogous to the magical actions through which people have tried to come to terms with the anthropological-existential foundations in face of the impenetrable.]

DEFINITIONS

We should not close this introduction without at least an attempt at defining secrets, a term which seems to be rather self-evident as to its common usage both today and in the past. We could easily comment that when a person withholds information from another, then this becomes a secret. Secrets can be a set of data or visions, objects or texts kept in private, away from the public, for religious, political, or economic reasons. Certain medicines, or poisons, are secrets, and new scientific discoveries might at first be treated as secrets. But we could also include the notion of the secret as being an epistemological phenomenon that challenges the outsider and protects the insider from divulging his/her knowledge about something. The concept of the "secret" finds application in many different aspects of human life, whether in religion (confession), business, in the military, in politics, economics (taxes), and literature.[94]

To deal with secrets constitutes a drive to gain new political influence, to acquire power withheld up to that moment, to gain riches, to learn about the mysteries of God, to comprehend scientific processes, or rather, to circumvent those in order to pursue a parallel goal with mysterious means, etc. The German writer Günter Kunert commented on secrets once by observing,

[das Geheimnis ist] das Wesen der Sache, die besagt: nur Fiktionen seien Antriebe menschlicher Sehnsucht. Alles Verborgene oder als verborgen Angenommene, das sich den Anschein letztgültiger Wahrheit selber verleiht, erweist sich stärker denn jede Autorität, deren Befehle es bricht, selbst wenn, was als Rätsel stellvertretend für Wahrheit stand, nur Enttäuschung bringt: jedes neue Rätsel erneuert die forschende Unruhe; Suche und Weg wiederholen sich unstillbar.[95]

[the secret is the essence of the thing, which means: only fictions are the drives for human desire. Everything that is hidden or assumed to be hidden, which takes on the pretense of ultimate truth, proves to be stronger than any authority since it breaks its orders, even if that what constituted, at least representatively, the truth through the riddle, then leads to complete disappointment. Every new riddle demands once again the searching unrest. Search and the path repeat themselves unquenchably.]

The *Oxford English Dictionary* offers a range of definitions, all based on textual examples going as far back as to the fourteenth century: "Kept from public knowledge, or from the knowledge of persons specified; not allowed to be known, or only by selected persons," "Removed from the resort of men; retired, remote, lonely, secluded, solitary; hence, affording privacy or seclusion," "Secluded from observation," "Of actions, negotiations, agreements, etc.: Done or entered into with the intention of being concealed; clandestine,"

"Of doctrines, ceremonies, language, signs, methods of procedure, remedies, and the like: Kept from the knowledge of the uninitiated," "Of feelings, passions, thoughts: Not openly avowed or expressed; concealed, disguised; also, in stronger sense, known only to the subject, inward, inmost. Hence said of the heart, soul, etc.," "Abstruse, recondite; beyond ordinary apprehension or beyond unaided human intelligence. Of a person or thing: Pertaining to or dealing with mystical or occult matters," "Hidden from sight; not discernible or visible; unseen (chiefly poetic)," "Of a door, chamber drawer, passage, or mechanical contrivance: Designed to escape observation or detection," "Of an agent: That works in secret. Of a person: That is secretly (what is expressed by the noun)," or "secret life n. a private life of a nature concealed from the common observer; spec. one consisting of covert sexual dealings."[96]

The famous *Deutsches Wörterbuch* by Jacob and Wilhelm Grimm offers the valuable linguistic observation that the modern German word "Geheimnis" (secret) did not emerge until the sixteenth century; in earlier time, the common term for "secret" was "heimlîche" or "heimlichkeit."[97] They observe that the origin of the term and concept appears to have rested in the religious dimension ("mysterium"), as we will observe in the case of the Old High German magical charms. We hear of secrets in the context of science, politics, then of secrets as means to create magical or artistic illusions for entertainment and the arts, in law, and the marking of personal properties.

Secrets are, in short, the opposite of knowledge, and they defy the human interest in and concern with self-control. But they are not completely elusive to our comprehension and pertain more to a non-linear, non-analogous dimension of phenomena than the the rational, material dimension. Dealing with secrets in a wide variety of literary (The Grail) and non-literary contexts (charms) will open many valuable perspectives regarding human epistemology in the pre-modern world, which can then shed light also on our contemporary perception of reality, or rather, lack thereof. This "ontologie du secret," as Pierre Boutang has called it,[98] pertains to all epistemology, but this book will refrain from philosophical, religious, or scientific investigations of the secret.

We could easily and meaningfully draw, for instance, intensively from late antique (St. Augustine) and early medieval theology (Notker Balbulus), and then combine those comments with remarks by high and late medieval theologians who more or less consistently confirmed the inability of the human intellect to comprehend the nature of God (Meister Eckhart), but this would lead us too far into the domains of religion and philosophy.[99] Instead, I will mostly examine how medieval poets engaged with the unknowable, the uncanny, the powerful behind the material dimension, and thus how the medieval discourse already laid the foundation for the ultimate epistemology which continues to challenge us until today. Relying on medieval voices in that regard facilitates the analysis of the other world, however defined, through a convex mirror that ultimately allows us to recognize ourselves today once again in face of the "other" dimension.

In Thomas of Cantimpré's famous book of bees (*Bonum universal de apibus*; ca. 1263–1270), we learn of a highly insightful anecdote about St. Augustine, Bishop of Hippo, which nicely situates the notion of the secret in a religious context. The bishop is said to be walking along the beach outside of Hippo, when he comes across a boy who has dug a little hole in the sand and who is pouring some water from the sea into it with a spoon. Asked about his project, he relates that his intention is to transfer all the water in the sea into his little hole. When the bishop objects that this would never be possible, the boy retorts that it would be rather possible for him to achieve that goal than it would be realistic to assume that Augustine would be able to fathom the meaning of the Holy Trinity in his new book:

> Cogitatu, ait, voluis et estuas volumine brevi concludere, quid sit illud individue trinitatis inexplicabile sacramentum. Et hoc quidem antequam possis, isti fosse parvule potius totius maris undas infundam.[100]

> [In your thoughts, he said, you consider how to conclude in a brief volume what the inexplicable sacrament of the indivisible trinity might be. Before you will succeed in that, I will rather manage to pour the waves of the entire sea into this small hole.]

Thereupon the little boy disappears from Augustine's view, and the theologian realizes the truth of his words since the secret of God's divinity is not open to human intelligence. However, the availability of the Holy Scriptures offers, so Thomas of Cantimpré, a chance to approximate that secret after all through a thorough and intensive study and reflection. Yet, he did not mean that the secret could be truly solved, as he then concludes: "Non transgrediaris ergo terminus constitutos et pium semper modum habeas in scripturis" (830; Do not transgress hence the given limits and have always a pious goal in mind when studying the Scriptures).

When I will discuss the treatment of secrets in a wider range of European medieval texts, I will not rely on one definition of this phenomenon only. Instead, the "secret" stands in as a metaphor for a range of strategies to hide information, to let deep and unexplainable forces enter human existence, and to allow objects or people to interact with the protagonist in a rather independent manner. There are political secrets, scientific and medical secrets, personal secrets, emotional secrets, erotic secrets, spiritual secrets, and secrets that exist all by themselves and do whatever they want on their own as independent agents. Medieval literature is profoundly determined by the existence of secrets.[101]

It does not need further discussion that medieval rulers and their princes, advisors, and others regularly resorted, just as their modern contemporaries do, of course, to secret negotiations and consultations, such as we know about Emperor Otto in the anonymous *Herzog Ernst* (who retires to his private chambers during a war campaign to consult with his counselor, Count Henry of the Palatinate about the next steps in their efforts to defeat the protagonist, the Bavarian Duke Ernst, as I have discussed already above. We can be certain that secret meetings of such a kind were common in medieval and early modern courts, just as they are today, but this does not need to be expounded further here.

If secrets are of such importance within the political, scientific, medical, and military context, separating those who are in the "in" from those who are on the "out," then it comes as no surprise that literary and religious poets felt strongly encouraged to operate with the secret as an epistemological phenomenon in their works as well. Quite often, I think, we can observe in the individual cases a deeper sense of the secret, maybe bordering on the sacred, or paralleling it in secular terms. It might be worth considering the related experience of grace and the gesture of giving gifts as leading to the realization of something secret, or larger, in human existence. As Alice Brittan now observes,

> In the twenty-first century, we might imagine grace as a striking and refined quality that is pleasurable to encounter but certainly not fundamental to anyone's existence or to the beliefs and practices that hold us together or drive us apart. For millennia, though, it has been recognized as essential to the vitality of inner life, as well as to the large-scale shifts in perspective and legislation that improve the way we live as a society. Grace is also astonishing-always-as the enormously insightful readings in *The Art of Astonishment* show. Brittan reveals the concept's breadth as sacred and secular, ancient and recent, lived and literary. And in so doing, she shows us how the act of reading is like grace-social but personal, pleasurable, and essential.[102]

Grace is not quite the same as the confrontation or engagement with secrets, but there is always the sense of an alternative power beyond our own consciousness which bestows itself upon us in a surprising and inexplicable fashion. Medieval poets were, perhaps naively, but perhaps deeply insightfully, often very close to that phenomenon and included references to it into their texts to alert their readers/listeners to the possibility of an otherworld, so we might be able to profit from a careful analysis of a wide range of relevant texts determined by secret objects, events, or people even for modern epistemology.[103]

My first task hence consists of identifying and analyzing examples of secrets as hermeneutic challenges in a variety of medieval European texts. Next, I will try to contextualize the phenomenon itself and explore its existential meaning. As we will observe most centrally, here we will discover an entire discourse on the "secret" in a wide range of textual contexts. To restate it one more time, the issue here does not consist of the discourse on magic, or on religion, but on an epistemologically different discourse of considerable significance both in the Middle Ages and also in subsequent centuries.

As much as I will refrain from discussing religious texts from that time period, with the exception of mystical visions that I will deal with in the last chapter, as much it is also important to keep in mind that there are significant parallels and overlaps. While religious texts such as the famous *Imitatio Christi* by Thomas à Kempis, composed between 1416 and 1427, addressed essential aspects of Christian spirituality deeply influenced by the *Devotio moderna* as practiced in Deventer, above all,[104] secular poets throughout the Middle Ages addressed spiritual or magical forces and phenomena. The focus of the subsequent chapters will rest primarily on the latter, but it seems appropriate to conclude here with at least one lengthy quote from Thomas's work to illustrate the proximity of both dimensions to each other. Investigating secrets as such hence represents a fascinating balancing act. Since the *Imitatio Christi* is now available in an excellent new German translation, I begin with that and then render it into English:

> Hochgelehrte Worte machen weder heilig noch gerecht; allein ein tugendhaftes Leben erwirkt uns Gottes Huld. Was mich betrifft, so will ich lieber Reue empfinden als ihre Definition kennen. Wüsstest du die ganze Bibel auswendig und dazu die Aussprüche aller Philosophen, was nützte dir das alles ohne Liebe zu Gott und ohne seine Gnade? (I, 3)

> [Deeply learned words make you neither holy nor just; only a virtuous life helps us to gain God's grace. As far as I am concerned, I want to feel rather repentance than to know its definition. Even if you knew the entire bible by heart and the statements by all philosophers, what good would it do to you without love for God and without His grace?]

Granted, Thomas aimed for God's secrets, and he admonished his audience to search for them in their own hearts, but it is still a beautiful comment that undergirds the entire quest for secrets and reveals a profound understanding of their true meaning in human life, as it was then also formulated by many secular medieval poets. The very realization that there are secrets in all existence, that we cannot know everything, and that there are forces beyond our

Introduction—The Secret in the Literary Discourse 37

control, signals the presence of different dimensions. The literary and mystical examples that I will examine below confirm this observation deeply. But since I am not going to engage with Dante in particular, who obviously had much to say about the secret of physical and spiritual life, I would like to conclude with a lengthy quote from his *Divina Commedia*, which reveals much about the essential understanding of metaphysical epistemology:

> Oh quanto è corto il dire e come fioco
> al mio concetto! e questo, a quel ch'i' vidi,
> è tanto, che non basta a dicer 'poco.'
>
> O luce etterna che sola in te sidi,
> sola t'intendi, e da te intelletta
> e intendente te ami e arridi!
>
> Quella circulazion che sì concetta
> pareva in te come lume reflesso,
> da li occhi miei alquanto circunspetta,
>
> dentro da sé, del suo colore stesso,
> mi parve pinta de la nostra effige:
> per che 'l mio viso in lei tutto era messo.
>
> Qual è 'l geomètra che tutto s'affige
> per misurar lo cerchio, e non ritrova,
> pensando, quel principio ond' elli indige,
>
> tal era io a quella vista nova:
> veder voleva come si convenne
> l'imago al cerchio e come vi s'indova;
>
> ma non eran da ciò le proprie penne:
> se non che la mia mente fu percossa
> da un fulgore in che sua voglia venne.
> A l'alta fantasia qui mancò possa;
> ma già volgeva il mio disio e 'l velle,
> sì come rota ch'igualmente è mossa,
>
> l'amor che move il sole e l'altre stelle. (*Paradiso* 33.121–45)[105]

[How incomplete is speech, how weak, when set
against my thought! And this, to what I saw.
is such—to call it little is too much.

Eternal Light, You only dwell within
Yourself, and only You know You; Self-knowing,
Self-known, You love and smile upon Yourself!

That circle—which, begotten so, appeared

in You as light reflected—when my eyes
had watched it with attention for some time,

within itself and colored like itself,
to me seemed painted with our effigy,
so that my sight was set on it completely.

As the geometer intently seeks
to square the circle, but he cannot reach,
through thought on thought, the principle he needs,

so I searched that strange sight: I wished to see
the way in which our human effigy
suited the circle and found place in it—

and my own wings were far too weak for that.
But then my mind was struck by light that flashed
and, with this light, received what it had asked.

Here force failed my high fantasy; but my
desire and will were moved already—like
a wheel revolving uniformly—by

the Love that moves the sun and the other stars.]

NOTES

1. Théodore Jouffroy [1796–1842], *Cours d'esthetique: suivi de la thèse du mème auteur sur le semtiment du beau et de deux fragments inédits* (Paris: Hachette, 1843); for an online version of the English translation, see https://archive.org/details/introductiontoet00jouf (vol. 1).

2. See now, for instance, Nils Ch. Rauhut, *Ultimate Questions: Thinking about Philosophy*. 4th edition. Penguin Academies (New York, Munich, et al.: Pearson Longman, 2021); Patrick Masterson, *In Reasonable Hope: Philosophical Reflections on Ultimate Meaning* (Washington, DC: The Catholic University of America Press, 2021).

3. Cf., for instance, *Encyclopedia of Medieval Pilgrimage*, ed. Larissa J. Taylor, Leigh Ann Craig, et al. (Leiden and Boston: Brill, 2010).

4. This topic has been discussed already for a very long time, but see, most recently, Vincent Bierce, *Le sentiment religieux dans La Comédie humaine: foi, ironie et ironisation* (Paris: Classiques Garnier, 2019).

5. *Pilgrimage in the Middle Ages: A Reader*, ed. Brett Edward Whalen. Readings in Medieval Civilizations and Cultures, XVI (Toronto: University of Toronto Press, 2011); Denys Pringle, ed., *Pilgrimage to Jerusalem and the Holy Land, 1187–1291*. Crusade Texts in Translation (Farnham, Surrey, and Burlington, VT: Ashgate, 2012);

as to miracles, see Benedicta Ward, *Miracles and the Medieval Mind: Theory, Record and Event 1000–1215* (London: Scolar Press, 1982); Michael E. Goodich, *Miracles and Wonders: The Development of the Concept of Miracle, 1150–1350*. Church, Faith and Culture in the Medieval West (Aldershot: Ashgate, 2007); cf. also the contributions to *Mirakel im Mittelalter: Konzeptionen, Erscheinungsformen, Deutungen*, ed. Martin Heinzelmann, Klaus Herbers und Dieter R. Bauer. Beiträge zur Hagiographie, 3 (Stuttgart: Steiner, 2002); and to *The Cambridge Companion to Miracles*, ed. Graham H. Twelftree. Cambridge Companions to Religion (Cambridge: Cambridge University Press, 2011). The literature on this topic is legion.

6. *"Die Tücke des Objekts": vom Umgang mit Dingen*, ed. Katharina Ferus and Dietmar Rübel.

Schriftenreihe der Isa-Lohmann-Siems-Stiftung, 2 (Berlin: Reimer, 2009); Pia Selmayr, *Der Lauf der Dinge: Wechselverhältnisse zwischen Raum, Ding und Figur bei der narrativen Konstitution von Anderwelten im "Wigalois" und im "Lanzelet."* Mikrokosmos, 82 (Frankfurt a. M., Bern, et al.: Peter Lang, 2017). Anglophone and other research have not yet fully responded to these theoretical concepts developed in recent years. Noteworthy exceptions are the study by Bettina Bildhauer, *Medieval Things: Agency, Materiality, and Narratives of Objects in Medieval German Literature and Beyond*. Interventions: New Studies in Medieval Culture (Columbus, OH: The Ohio State University Press, 2020), and Jane Bennett, *Vibrant Matter: A Political Ecology of Things* (Durham, NC: Duke University Press, 2010); see also the contributions to *Object Fantasies: Experience and Creation*, ed. Philippe Cordez, Romana Kaske, Julia Saviello, and Susanne Thürigen. Object Studies in Art History, 1 (Berlin and Boston: Walter de Gruyter, 2018).

7. Jerzy Strzelczyk, *Święci Władcy Europy*. Biblioteka Długosza, 3 (Częstochowa: Wydawnictwo Naukowe Uniwersytetu Humanistyczno-Przyrodniczego, 2020). I thank the author for pointing out his study to me. See now the contributions to *The Legend of Charlemagne: Envisioning Empire in the Middle Ages*, ed. Jace Stuckey. Explorations in Medieval Culture, 15 (Leiden and Boston: Brill, 2022); cf. also my literary-historical investigation of more or less the same topic, *Charlemagne in Medieval German and Dutch Literature*. Bristol Studies in Medieval Culture (Cambridge: D. S. Brewer, 2021).

8. There is a legion of scholarly and not so scholarly literature on this topic; see, for instance, Roland Göck, *Die letzten Rätsel dieser Welt: unerklärliche Phänomene, letzte Geheimnisse, Jenseits des Begreifens, Mythen und Mysterien, Grenzen des Wissens* (Augsburg: Weltbild Verlag, 1994); Werner Huemer, *Warum wir durch den Tod nicht sterben: die großen Geheimnisse am Ende des Lebens* (Leipzig and Frankfurt a. M.: Deutsche Nationalbibliothek, 2021). As to the phenomenon of death, see the excellent historical study by Romedio Schmitz-Esser, *Der Leichnam im Mittelalter: Einbalsamierung, Verbrennung und die kulturelle Konstruktion des toten Körpers*, translated by Albrecht Classen and Carolin Radtke as *The Corpse in the Middle Ages: Embalming, Cremation, and the Cultural Construction of the Dead Body* (orig. 2014) (Turnhout: Harvey Miller Publishers, Brepols, 2020).

9. For a simple but convenient introduction, see, for instance, Austin Cline, "Why Does Religion Exist?," *Learn Religions*, Sep. 4, 2021, learnreligions.com/

why-does-religion-exist-250557. For more details in practical and theoretical terms, see William Hasker, *God, Time, and Knowledge* (Ithaca, NY: Cornell University Press, 1998); Edward R. Wierenga, *The Nature of God: An Inquiry into Divine Attributes* (Ithaca, NY: Cornell University Press, 2003); Beate Pongratz-Leisten and Karen Sonik, *The Materiality of Divine Agency*. Studies in Ancient Near Eastern Records (SANER), 8 (Berlin and Boston: Walter de Gruyter, 2015). In my understanding, the anthropological approach by Clifford Geertz appears to be one of the most rational and convincing concepts, "Religion as a Cultural System," Clifford Geertz, *The Interpretation of Cultures: Selected Essays* (London: Fontana Press, 1993), 87–125. But see also Andrey Korotayev, *World Religions and Social Evolution of the Old World Oikumene Civilizations: A Cross-cultural Perspective* (Lewiston, NY: Edwin Mellen Press, 2004); Daniel L. Pals, *Eight Theories of Religion* (Oxford: Oxford University Press, 2006).

10. For an excellent overview of the various episodes and the individual characters, see https://en.wikipedia.org/wiki/Dark_(TV_series) (last accessed on Nov. 21, 2021). There is no scholarly examination out in print yet, as far as I can tell. So there is no good alternative to this site.

11. Wayne G. Hammond and Christina Scull, *The Lord of the Rings: A Reader's Companion* (London: HarperCollins, 2014); Anna Dawson, *Studying the Lord of the Rings*. Studying Films Ser. (Oxford: Auteur Publishing, 2021).

12. Claudia Fenske, *Muggles, Monsters and Magicians: A Literary Analysis of the Harry Potter Series*. Kulturelle Identitäten, 2 (Frankfurt A. M. et al.: Peter Lang, 2008); for the latest update on sales, translations, and developments, see the well-documented website online at: https://en.wikipedia.org/wiki/Harry_Potter (last accessed on July 8, 2019). There is no comparable scholarly study regarding the latest media data regarding the current reception process.

13. Alois Hahn, "Geheimnis," *Vom Menschen: Handbuch Historische* Anthropologie, ed. Christoph Wulf (Weinheim and Basel: Beltz Verlag, 1997), 1105–18. He adds that secrets can serve to establish confidence, mutual trust, and shared values and ideals. All secrets, secret operations, or communications are reliant on the presence of silence, that is, the deliberate observation of no-communication to keep the majority of people out of the insider group. The establishment of secrets proves to be tantamount to setting up taboos. Only those who are inducted into a special group or organization are trusted with the knowledge of secrets. Hahn also refers to the privilege, first formulated by the *Magna Carta* ca. 1215, that "Nemo tenetur seipsum accusare" (1111), which we know today in the US Constitution as the privilege of taking the Fifth, meaning that an individual has the right to invoke his or her right against self-incrimination under the Fifth Amendment of the United States Constitution. It emerged in England as part of the *Common Law* and became well established in the seventeenth century.

14. See the seminal study by Tzvetan Todorov, *The Fantastic* (1970: Ithaca, NY: Cornell University Press, 1975); see also now *Exploring the Fantastic: Genre, Ideology, and Popular Culture*, ed. Ina Batzke, Eric C. Erbacher, and Linda Hess (Bielefeld: transcript, 2018). Cf. also the contributions to *The Cambridge Companion to Fantasy Literature*, ed. Edward James and Farah Mendlesohn (Cambridge: Cambridge

University Press, 2012). For the relationship between literature and fantasy, see András Horn, *Das Schöpferische in der Literatur: Theorien der dichterischen Phantasie* (Würzburg: Königshausen & Neumann, 2000); for global perspectives, pursuing the entire history of European literature from Greek antiquity to the modern world, seen under the umbrella of emotions/fantasy versus rationality, see Silvio Vietta, *Literatur und Rationalität: Funktionen der Literatur in der europäischen Kulturgeschichte* (Munich: Wilhelm Fink, 2014). See now Albrecht Classen, "Imagination, Fantasy, Otherness, and Monstrosity in the Middle Ages and the Early Modern Age," *Imagination and Fantasy in the Middle Ages and Early Modern Times: Projections, Dreams, Monsters, and Illusions*, ed. Albrecht Classen. Fundamentals of Medieval and Early Modern Culture, 24 (Berlin and Boston: Walter de Gruyter, 2020), 1–229.

15. See now the contributions to *Darstellung und Geheimnis in Mittelalter und Früher Neuzeit*, ed. Jutta Eming and Volkhard Wels. Episteme in Bewegung, 21 (Wiesbaden: Harrassowitz, 2021), online available free of charge at: https://www.harrassowitz-verlag.de/pdfjs/web/viewer.html?file=/ddo/artikel/81693/978-3-447-11548-3_Kostenloser%20Open%20Access-Download.pdf#pagemode=thumbs (last accessed on May 30, 2022). The editors compiled this volume in order to investigate, as they identify it in the title for the book series, epistemes in motion.

16. Sophie Page, *Astrology in Medieval Manuscripts* (Toronto and Buffalo: University of Toronto Press, 2002); *De Frédéric II à Rodolphe II: Astrologie, divination et magie dans les cours (XIIIe–XVIIe siècle)*, ed. Jean-Patrice Boudet, Martine Ostorero, and Agostino Paravicini Bagliani. Micrologus Library, 85 (Florence: SISMEL—Edizioni del Galluzzo, 2017); *The Astrological Autobiography of a Medieval Philosopher: Henry Bate's Nativitas (1280–81)*, ed. and intro. by Carlos Steel, Steven Vanden Broecke, and David Juste and Shlomo Sela. Ancient and Medieval Philosophy, XVII (Leuven: Leuven University Press, 2018). For the latest scientific analysis of this phenomenon, astrology, which underscores the very presence of the belief in secrets in the twenty-first century, see Ida Andersson, Julia Persson, and Petri Kajonius, "Even the Stars Think that I am Superior: Personality, Intelligence and Belief in Astrology," *Personality and Individual Differences* Nov. 2011, online at: https://www.sciencedirect.com/science/article/pii/S0191886921007686 (last accessed on May 16, 2022). They observe: "Though embracing astrology might seem innocent, it is nonetheless possible that it facilitates uncritical thinking and favours biases. Further, belief in astrology correlates with belief in multiple other pseudosciences as well as with belief in conspiracy theories . . . which indicates that it might not be all that harmless." And they conclude, which is quite relevant for our investigation, "since astrological predictions and horoscopes tend to be positively framed, this reinforces grandiose feelings and thus might appeal even more to narcissists. Note that narcissistic traits correlated with the belief that astrology is supported by science . . . which leads to a speculation that narcissists may generally be more fact resistant. Other interesting findings was that the higher the level of intelligence, the lower the belief in astrology . . . as well as that agreeable people tend to report believing in astrology more. Seeing how most personality predictors were small in magnitude, this leaves room for many other variables influencing belief in astrology. Speculatively, additional predictors could be cohort-effects, educational levels, occupations, and others."

17. This is not my research area, but see Santiago F. Elena and Ricard Solé, *Viruses as Complex Adaptive Systems* (Princeton, NJ: Princeton University Press, 2019); Raj Chari and Isabel Rozas, *Viruses, Vaccines, and Antivirals: Why Politics Matters* (Berlin and Boston: Walter de Gruyter, 2022). See also the contributions to the journal *Viruses*, published by MDPI, online at: https://www.mdpi.com/journal/viruses (last accessed on May 16, 2022).

18. Erwin Schrödinger, *What is Life?: The Physical Aspect of the Living Cell: with Mind and Matter: & Autobiographical Sketches* (Cambridge: Cambridge University Press, 1992); Andreas Losch, *What is Life?: On Earth and Beyond* (Cambridge: Cambridge University Press, 2017); Jeremy J. Baumberg, *The Secret Life of Science: How It Really Works and Why It Matters* (Princeton, NJ: Princeton University Press, 2018); the literature on this topic, both scientific and esoteric, serious and ridiculous, is legion. Undoubtedly, however, the more modern sciences progress, the more people tend to grapple with ultimate questions about themselves, which are really religious in nature.

19. Bettina Bildhauer, *Medieval Things: Agency, Materiality, and Narratives of Objects in Medieval German Literature and Beyond*. Interventions: New Studies in Medieval Culture (Columbus, OH: The Ohio State University Press, 2020); Albrecht Classen, "Symbolic Significance of the Sword in the Hero's Hand: *Beowulf*, The *Nibelungenlied*, *El Poema de Mio Cid*, the *Volsunga Saga*, and the *Njál's Saga*. Thing Theory from a Medieval Perspective," *Amsterdamer Beiträge zur älteren Germanistik* 80 (2020): 346–70; see also Philippe Cordez, *Treasure, Memory, Nature: Church Objects in the Middle Ages* (2015, in German; 2016, in French; London and Turnhout: Harvey Miller Publishers, 2020). See also the contributions to *Dingkulturen* (2018). Oddly, however, hardly any efforts have been made to move beyond the materiality of those objects and to examine their agency, hence the secret behind the physical appearance. For one valuable exception, see John Carey, *Magic, Metallurgy and Imagination in Medieval Ireland: Three Studies*. Celtic Studies Publications, XXI (Aberystwyth: CSP-Cymru Cyf/Casemate Academic, 2019).

20. Warren Tormey, "Magical (and Maligned) Metalworkers: Understanding Representations of Early and High Medieval Blacksmiths," *Magic and Magicians in the Middle Ages and the Early Modern Time: The Occult in Pre-Modern Sciences, Medicine, Literature, Religion, and Astrology*, ed. Albrecht Classen. Fundamentals of Medieval and Early Modern Culture, 20 (Berlin and Boston: Walter de Gruyter, 2017), 109–48; see now id., "Wholeness, Holiness, and Wondrous Healing: Wellness and Formulaic Performativity in The Anglo-Saxon Herbal Healing Guides," *Mediaevistik* 35 (forthcoming).

21. See now the contributions to *Magie und Literatur: Erzählkulturelle Funktionalisierung magischer Praktiken in Mittelalter und Früher Neuzeit*, ed. Andreas Hammer, Wilhelm Heizmann, and Norbert Kössinger. Philologische Studien und Quellen, 280 (Berlin: Erich Schmidt Verlag, 2022). The contributors engage with many different features of the magical, with runes, fairies, and magicians, but there is no specific theoretical framework to capture all of them. I propose to rely more simply on the term "secret" because it does not limit our hermeneutic approaches.

22. John Bowker, *Knowing the Unknowable: Science and Religions on God and the Universe*. Library of Modern Religion, 2 (London: I. B. Tauris, 2009). The abstract online describes the critical point as follows: "Albert Einstein once remarked that behind all observable things lay something quite unknowable. And the motivation for his own work in physics stemmed from something as apparently innocuous as his father first showing him a compass when he was a boy. Yet, the wonder and inspiration of that moment, which he never forgot, led ultimately to his own stupendous scientific breakthroughs. This book explores that special territory perceived by Einstein: where the unknown takes over from everything that is understandable, familiar, explicable." See also Jean Petrucelli, *Knowing, Not-Knowing, and Sort-of-Knowing: Psychoanalysis and the Experience of Uncertainty* (London: Karnac Books, 2010). The number of publications on this topic, both scholarly/scientific and mythologizing, is legion.

23. Katrin Horn, "Geheimnis," *Enzyklopädie des Märchens*, ed. Rolf Wilhelm Brednich. Vol. 5 (Berlin and New York: Walter de Gruyter, 1987), 882–92; here 886.

24. Hedwig von Bei, *Das Märchen: Sein Ort in der geistigen Entwicklung* (Bern and Munich: Francke, 1965).

25. Giovan (sic) Francesco Straparola, *The Pleasant Nights*, ed. and trans. by Suzanne Magnamini. The Other Voice in Early Modern Europe. The Toronto Series, 40 (Toronto: Centre for Reformation and Renaissance Studies, 2015).

26. *Die Historia von den sieben weisen Meistern: Nach der Gießener Handschrift 104 mit einer Einleitung und Erläuterungen*, ed. Ralf-Henning Steinmetz. Altdeutsche Textbibliothek, 116 (Tübingen: Max Niemeyer, 2001); Udo Gerdes, "Die sieben weisen Meister: Zyklische Rahmenerzählung orientalischer Herkunft, " *Die deutsche Literatur des Mittelalters. Verfasserlexikon*, ed. Burghart Wachinger et al. 2nd completely rev. ed. Vol. 8 (Berlin and New York: Walter de Gruyter, 1992), 1174–89. For a digitized version of the Universitätsbibliothek Heidelberg, manuscript Cod. Pal. germ. 149 from ca. 1450, see https://digi.ub.uni-heidelberg.de/diglit/cpg149block /; for a contemporary manuscript, also Universitätsbibliothek Heidelberg, Cod. Pal. germ. 106, see https://digi.ub.uni-heidelberg.de/diglit/cpg106/; for the Frankfurt a. M. Universitätsbibliothek manuscript ms. qu. germ 12 from 1471, see https:// sammlungen.ub.uni-frankfurt.de/msma/id/3654381, for the Strasbourg print version in German by Johann Prüss, 1478/1497, see https://daten.digitale-sammlungen.de /0002/bsb00027804/images/index.html?id=00027804&groesser=&fip=eayayztswea yaewqfsdreayaxseayasdasw&no=5&seite=7. The print version by Heinrich Knoblochtzer, also in Strasbourg, 1483, is available at https://daten.digitale-sammlungen .de/~db/0002/bsb00027806/images/ (all last accessed on May 20, 2022). The history of this motif with the loyal dog is outlined in great detail by Jean-Claude Schmitt, "Hundes Unschuld," *Enzyklopädie des* Märchens, ed. Rolf Wilhelm Brednich. Vol. 6 (Berlin and New York: Walter de Gruyter, 1990), 1362–68.

27. Caroline Walker Bynum, "Wonder," *American Historical Review* 102.1 (1997): 1–26; here 24.

28. Bynum, "Wonder" (1991), 11. She exemplifies this phenomenon particularly with regard to hagiographical literature, such as the narratives about Christina the

Astonishing by Jacques de Vitry, but then also the accounts by Bonaventure and Caesarius of Heisterbach (miracles).

29. *Imagination and Fantasy in the Middle Ages and Early Modern Times: Projections, Dreams, Monsters, and Illusions*, ed. Albrecht Classen. Fundamentals of Medieval and Early Modern Culture, 24 (Berlin and Boston: Walter de Gruyter, 2020).

30. Bettina Bildhauer, *Medieval Things: Agency, Materiality, and Narratives* (2020); Albrecht Classen, "Symbolic Significance of the Sword in the Hero's Hand: *Beowulf*, The *Nibelungenlied*, *El Poema de Mio Cid*, the *Volsunga Saga*, and the *Njál's Saga*. Thing Theory from a Medieval Perspective," *Amsterdamer Beiträge zur älteren Germanistik* 80 (2020): 346–70.

31. Paulo Lemos Horta, *Marvellous Thieves: Secret Authors of the Arabian Nights* (Cambridge, MA, and London: Harvard University Press, 2017). There is a vast amount of information about this story and its reception available online.

32. Michelle Karnes, *Medieval Marvels and Fictions in the Latin West and Islamic World* (Chicago and London: University of Chicago Press, 2022), addresses the same issue, placing examples of the Latin West next to those of the Arabic world. I did not yet have a chance to put my hands on it and could only draw from the abstract posted online.

33. See, for instance, Bettina Bildhauer, *Medieval Things: Agency, Materiality, and Narratives* (2020); Albrecht Classen, "Symbolic Significance of the Sword in the Hero's Hand: *Beowulf*, the *Nibelungenlied*, *El Poema de Mio Cid*, the *Volsunga Saga*, and the *Njál's Saga*. Thing Theory from a Medieval Perspective," *Amsterdamer Beiträge zur älteren Germanistik* 80 (2020): 346–70. For a useful research overview, though slightly dated by now, see Kellie Robertson, "Medieval Things: Materiality, Historicism, and the Premodern Object," *Literature Compass* 5 (2008): 1060–80; 10.1111/j.1741–4113.2008.00588.x

34. *Dingkulturen: Objekte in Literatur, Kunst und Gesellschaft der Vormoderne*, ed. Anna Mühlherr, Heike Sahm, Monika Schausten, and Bruno Quast, together with Ulrich Hoffmann. Literatur | Theorie | Geschichte, 9 (Berlin and Boston: Walter de Gruyter, 2018), 3.

35. There is much new research on magic; see the contributions to *The Cambridge History of Magic and Witchcraft in the West: From Antiquity to the Present*, ed. David J. Collins (Cambridge: Cambridge University Press, 2015); *Magic and Magicians in the Middle Ages and the Early Modern Time: The Occult in Pre-Modern Sciences, Medicine, Literature, Religion, and Astrology*, ed. Albrecht Classen. Fundamentals of Medieval and Early Modern Culture, 20 (Berlin and Boston: Walter de Gruyter, 2017); John Carey, *Magic, Metallurgy and Imagination in Medieval Ireland* (2019); *The Routledge History of Medieval Magic*, ed. Sophie Page and Catherine Rider. The Routledge Histories (London and New York: Routledge, 2019).

36. Albert Wesselski, *Märchen des Mittelalters* (Berlin: H. Stubenrauch, 1925).

37. *Secrets and Discovery in the Middle Ages: Proceedings of the 5th European Congress of the Fédération Internationale des Instituts d'Études Médiévales (Porto, 25th to 29th June 2013)*, ed. José Meirinhos, Celia López Alcalde, and João Rebalde. Textes et études du Moyen Âge, 90 (Barcelona and Rome, 2017). The emphasis here rests on prophecy, the mysterious nature of God, the secrets of relics, divination,

women's medical conditions (their secrets), secrets hidden in legal documents (falsifications), and just a little on love secrets in medieval literature.

38. Benjamin A. Saltzman, *Bonds of Secrecy: Law, Spirituality, and the Literature of Concealment in Early Medieval England*. The Middle Ages Series (Philadelphia, PA: University of Pennsylvania Press, 2019). He focuses on the ill-conceived notion by individuals that they could keep a secret from God, and this within the legal context. In his abstract, online, the author states: "Whereas today the bearers of secrets might be judged for the consequences of their reticence or disclosure, Saltzman observes, in the early Middle Ages a person attempting to conceal a secret was judged for believing he or she could conceal it from God. In other words, to attempt to hide from God was to become ensnared in a serious sin, but to hide from the world while deliberately and humbly submitting to God's constant observation was often a hallmark of spiritual virtue. Looking to law codes and religious architecture, hagiographies and riddles, Bonds of Secrecy shows how legal and monastic institutions harnessed the pervasive and complex belief in God's omniscience to produce an intense culture of scrutiny and a radical ethics of secrecy founded on the individual's belief that nothing could be hidden from God." (http://kvk.bibliothek .kit.edu/view-title/index.php?katalog=BVB&url=https%3A%2F%2Fwww.gateway -bayern.de%2FBV046646213&signature=jvEkSVcNH9_pWETsEw0OjcpdHd-EZ -Z2YzWV9yz3ccQ&showCoverImg=1; last accessed on May 16, 2022).

39. Robert Bartlett, *The Natural and the Supernatural in the Middle Ages* (Cambridge: Cambridge University Press, 2008).

40. Hildegard Elisabeth Keller, *My Secret is Mine: Studies on Religion and Eros in the German Middle Ages*. Studies in Spirituality, 4 (Leuven: Peeters, 2000); Joanna Godlewics-Adamiec and PawełPiszczatowsky, "Mystisches Geheimnis zwischen Sprachschöpfung und bildhafter Aussage, " *Geheimnis und Verborgenes im Mittelalter: Funktion, Wirkung und Spannungsfelder von okkultem Wissen, verborgenen Räumen und magischen Gegenständen*, ed. Stephan Conermann, Harald Wolter-von dem Knesebeck, and Miriam Quiering. Das Mittelalter: Perspektiven mediävistischer Forschung. Beihefte, 15 (Berlin and Boston: Walter de Gruyter, 2021), 89–106.

41. K. Rahner, "Geheimnis," *Lexikon für Theologie und Kirche*. 2nd completely rev. ed. by Josef Höfer and Karl Rahner. Vol. 4 (Freiburg i. Br.: Herder, 1960), 593–97.

42. Francesco Petrarch, *The Secret, with Related Documents*, ed. with an intro. by Carol E. Quillen. The Bedford Series in History and Culture (Boston: Bedford/St. Martin's, 2003); for an English translation, see Petrarch: *Petrarch's Secret: or The Soul's Conflict with Passion. Three Dialogues Between Himself and S. Augustine*, trans. from the Latin by William H. Draper (Westport, CT: Hyperion Press, 1911). See also the contributions to *Petrarch and Boccaccio: The Unity of Knowledge in the Pre-Modern World*, ed. Igor Candido. Mimesis, 61 (Berlin and Boston: Walter de Gruyter, 2018).

43. There is no lemma for "Geheimnis" (secret) in *Das Lexikon des Mittelalters*, ed. Robert-Henri Bautier. Vol. IV (Munich and Zürich: Artemis, 1989), 1172–73, there are only lemmata for "Geheimbünde" (B. Hergemöller; secret associations) and "Geheimschriften" (P. Ladner; secret texts) in Das *Lexikon des Mittelalters*, ed. Bruno Mariacher. Vol. IV (Munich and Zürich: Artemis, 1989), 1172–73.

44. See, for instance, Steven J. Williams, *The Secret of Secrets: The Scholarly Career of a Pseudo-Aristotelian Text in the Latin Middle Ages* (Ann Arbor, MI: University of Michigan Press, 2003); William Eamon, *Science and the Secrets of Nature: Books of Secrets in Medieval and Early Modern Culture* (1994; Princeton, NJ: Princeton University Press, 2021), who addresses, at least preliminarily, the literature of secrets, knowledge and power, revealed arcana, natural magic, and the secrets of nature. Cf. also Regula Forster, *Das Geheimnis der Geheimnisse: die arabischen und deutschen Fassungen des pseudo-aristotelischen "Sirr al-asrār"—"Secretum secretorum."* Wissensliteratur im Mittelalter, 43 (Wiesbaden: Reichert, 2006); *Trajectoires européennes du "Secretum secretorum" du Pseudo-Aristote (XIIIe–XVIe siècle)*, ed. Catherine Gaullier-Bougassas, Margaret Bridges, and Jean-Yves Tilliette. Alexander Redivivus, 6 (Turnhout: Brepols, 2015).

45. Helen Rodnite Lemay, *Women's Secrets: A Translation of Pseudo-Albertus Magnus's* De secretis mulierum *with Commentaries*. SUNY Series in Medieval Studies (Albany, NY: SUNY Press, 1992). See also Britta-Juliane Kruse, *Verborgene Heilkünste: Geschichte der Frauenmedizin im Spätmittelalter*. Quellen und Forschungen zur Literatur- und Kulturgeschichte, 239 (Berlin and New York: Walter de Gruyter, 1996). For a good edition of the original Latin text and a Spanish translation, see José Pablo Barragán Nieto, *El "De Secretis Mulierum" atribuido a Alberto Magno: estudio, edición crítica y traducción*. Textes et études du Moyen-Age, 63 (Porto: Fédération Internationale des Instituts d'Études Médiévales; Turnhout: Brepols, 2012). See now *Science and the Secrets of Nature: Books of Secrets in Medieval and Early Modern Culture*, ed. William Eamon (Princeton, NJ: Princeton University Press, 1994);

46. *Imagination and Fantasy in the Middle Ages and Early Modern Times: Projections, Dreams, Monsters, and Illusions*, ed. Albrecht Classen.

47. Eucharius Rößlin, *Der swangern Frauwen vnd Hebammen Rosegarten* (1513; Wutöschingen: Antiqua-Verlag, 1994); Eucharius Rösslin, *When Midwifery Became the Male Physician's Province: The Sixteenth Century Handbook "The rose garden for pregnant women and midwives newly Englished."* Trans. from the German and with an intro. by Wendy Arons (Jefferson, NC, and London: Macfarland, 1994); https://fn.bmj.com/content/79/1/F77.full (last accessed on May 27, 2022).

48. Gottfried von Strassburg, *Tristan*, newly edited on the basis of the edition by Friedrich Ranke, trans. into New High German, with a commentary and an epilogue by Rüdiger Krohn (Stuttgart: Philipp Reclam jun., 1980); Albrecht Classen, "Hunde als Freunde und Begleiter in der deutschen Literatur vom Mittelalter bis zur Gegenwart: Reaktion auf den 'Animal Turn' aus motivgeschichtlicher Sicht," *Etudes Germaniques* 73.4 (2018): 441–66.

49. Albrecht Classen, "Soundscapes in Medieval German Literature," to appear in *A Companion to Sound Studies in German-Speaking Cultures*, ed. Rolf Goebel (Rochester, NY: Camden House, forthcoming); for a modern perspective, see now Rolf J. Goebel, "Auditory Resonance: A Transdisciplinary Concept?," *Humanities* 11.6 (2022): 6; https://doi.org/10.3390/h11010006 (last accessed on May 27, 2022).

50. Anna Sziráky, *Éros Lógos Musiké: Gottfrieds 'Tristan' oder eine utopische renovatio der Dichtersprache und der Welt aus dem Geiste der Minne und Musik?*.

Wiener Arbeiten zur germanischen Altertumskunde und Philologie, 38 (Bern, Berlin, et al.: Peter Lang, 2003). She does not, surprisingly, take into consideration this particular scene and examines instead the philosophical, spiritual, and musicological aspects of music.

51. Gottfried von Strassburg, *Tristan and Isolde, with Ulrich von Türheim's Continuation*, ed. and trans., with an intro. by William T. Whobrey (Indianapolis, IN, and Cambridge: Hackert, 2020), 196. Cf. now Albrecht Classen, "Music as a Universal Bond and Bridge Between the Physical and the Divine: Transcultural and Medieval Perspectives," *Rupkatha Journal on Interdisciplinary Studies in Humanities* 13.3 (2021): 1–30; online at: https://rupkatha.com/V13/n3/v13n301.pdf; or: DOI: 10.21659/rupkatha.v13n3.01.

52. Anna Sziráky, *Éros Lógos Musiké*.

53. *Huon of Bordeaux: First Modern English Translation* by Catherine M. Jones and William W. Kibler. Medieval & Renaissance Text Series (New York and Bristol: Italica Press, 2021); see my review in *Mediaevistik* vol. 34 (forthcoming). I will dedicate a separate chapter to this text to explore the various secrets more in detail.

54. Verena Holzmann, *"Ich beswer dich wurm vnd wyrmin . . ." Formen und Typen altdeutscher Zaubersprüche und Segen*. Wiener Arbeiten zur germanischen Altertumskunde und Philologie, 36 (Bern, Berlin, et al: Peter Lang, 2001); Christa M. Haeseli, *Magische Performativität. Althochdeutsche Zaubersprüche in ihrem Überlieferungskontext*. Philologie der Kultur, 4 (Würzburg: Königshausen & Neumann. 2011); Ernst Wolf, *Beschwörungen und Segen. Angewandte Psychotherapie im Mittelalter* (Cologne, Weimar and Vienna: Böhlau, 2011); Chiara Benati, "*À la guerre comme à la guerre* but with caution: Protection Charms and Blessings in the Germanic Tradition," *Revista Brathair* 17.1 (2017): 155–91.

55. For a global anthropological examination of secrets, see Alois Hahn, "Geheimnis" (1997), 1105–18.

56. Gerd Althoff, *Spielregeln der Politik im Mittelalter: Kommunikation in Frieden und Fehde* (Darmstadt: Wissenschaftliche Buchgesellschaft, 1997). He differentiates, for instance, between "colloquium familare," "colloquium secretum," and "colloquium publicum" (157–84).

57. *Herzog Ernst: Mittelhochdeutsch/Neuhochdeutsch, in der Fassung B mit den Fragmenten der Fassungen A, B und Kl nach der Leithandschrift*, ed, trans., and commentary by Mathias Herweg (Stuttgart: Philipp Reclam jun., 2019). For the common tension between the public and the private already in the pre-modern world, see the contributions to *Das Öffentliche und Private in der Vormoderne*, ed. Gert Melville and Peter von Moos. Norm und Struktur, 10 (Cologne, Weimar, and Vienna: Böhlau, 1998).

58. *Geheimnis und Verborgenes im Mittelalter* (2021); that volume is based on the contributions to the symposium *17. Symposiums des Mediävistenverbandes* (March 19–22, 2017, Bonn). I had been quite ignorant of that event when I conceived of the idea to write this book. There is some overlap, and there are some shared ideas, but the entire concept and content of this study deviates extensively from that volume and pursues its own approach.

59. *Das Alexanderlied des Pfaffen Lamprecht (Strassburger Alexander)*. Text, Nacherzählung, Worterklärungen by Irene Ruttmann (Darmstadt: Wissenschaftliche Buchgesellschaft, 1974), 6932–46; see also Lamprecht, *Alexanderroman. Mittelho chdeutsch/*Neuhochdeutsch, ed. Elisabeth Lienert (Stuttgart: Philipp Reclam jun., 2007), where the edition differentiates between the two manuscript versions; for critical comments on the text and its treatment of "the foreign," cf. Albrecht Classen, "The Amazing East and the Curious Reader: Twelfth-Century World Exploration through a Writer's Mind: Lamprecht's *Alexander*," *Orbis Litterarum* 55.5 (2000): 317–39; id., "Globalism before Globalism: The Alexander Legend in Medieval Literature (Priest Lambrecht's Account as a Pathway to Early Global Perspectives)," *Esboços: histories in global contexts Florianópolis* 28/49 (Aug./Sept. 2021): 813–33, set./ dez. 2021.ISSN 2175-7976 DOI https://doi.org/10.5007/2175-7976.2021.e79311). See also the contributions to *Herrschaft, Ideologie und Geschichtskonzeption in Alexanderdichtungen des Mittelalters*, ed. Ulrich Mölk. Veröffentlichungen aus dem Göttinger Sonderforschungsbereich 529 "Internationalität nationaler Literaturen," 2 (Göttingen: Wallstein Verlag, 2002). The literature on this mythical account of Alexander in East and West is legion.

60. Here we encounter an amazing example of great respect for a Jew by a Christian author from the late twelfth century; Albrecht Classen, "Jewish-Christian Relations in Medieval Literature," Peter Meister, ed., *German Literature Between Faiths: Jew and Christian at Odds and in Harmony*. Studies in German Jewish History, 6 (Oxford, Bern, Berlin, et al.: Peter Lang, 2004), 53–65; id., "Complex Relations Between Jews and Christians in Late Medieval German and Other Literature," *Jews in Medieval Christendom: "Slay them Not,"* ed. Kristine T. Utterback and Merrall Llewelyn Price. Études sur le judaïsme médiéval, 60 (Leiden and Boston: Brill, 2013), 313–38.

61. Cf. now Falk Quenstedt, *Mirabiles Wissen: Deutschsprachige Reiseerzählungen um 1200 im transkulturellen Kontext arabischer Literatur:* Straßburger Alexander, Herzog Ernst, Reise-*Fassung des* Brandan. Episteme in Bewegung, 22 (Wiesbaden: Harrassowitz Verlag, 2021), 128–266, esp. 256–63. He limits himself, however, to the notions of miracle and marvel.

62. *Sir Gawain and the Green Knight: A Dual-Language Version*, ed. and trans. by William Vantuono. Garland Reference Library of the Humanities, 1265 (New York and London: Garland, 1993); for critical reflections, see, for instance, *A Companion to the Gawain-Poet*, ed. Derek Brewer and Jonathan Gibson. Arthurian Studies, 38 (Woodbridge, Suffolk; Rochester, NY: D. S. Brewer, 1997).

63. Carolyne Larrington, *King Arthur's Enchantresses: Morgan and Her Sisters in Arthurian Tradition* (London: I. B. Tauris, 2006); Jill M. Hebert, *Morgan le Fay, Shapeshifter*. Arthurian and Courtly Cultures (New York: Palgrave Macmillan, 2013).

64. Leila K. Norako, "Morgan le Fay," *The Camelot Project*, online at https://d.lib.rochester.edu/camelot/theme/morgan (last accessed on April 21, 2022).

65. Heinrich Kaufringer, *Werke*, ed. Paul Sappler (Tübingen: Max Niemeyer, 1972); see my English translation, Albrecht Classen. *Love, Life, and Lust in Heinrich Kaufringer's Verse Narratives*. 2nd rev. ed. Medieval and Renaissance Texts and Studies, 467. MRTS Texts for Teaching, 9 (2014; Tempe, AZ: Arizona Center for Medieval and Renaissance Studies, 2019). I will quote from my own translation.

66. Marga Stede, *Schreiben in der Krise: Die Texte des Heinrich Kaufringer. Literatur—Imagination—Realität* (Trier: Wissenschaftlicher Verlag, 1993), 41–48. For a global study of the pan-European verse narrative, including the texts by Kaufringer, see Klaus Grubmüller, *Die Ordnung, der Witz und das Chaos: Eine Geschichte der europäischen Novellistik im Mittelalter: Fabliau—Märe—Novelle* (Tübingen: Max Niemeyer, 2006).

67. Michaela Willers, *Heinrich Kaufringer als Märenautor: das Oeuvre des cgm 270* (Berlin: Logos-Verlag, 2002); Coralie Rippl, *Erzählen als Argumentationsspiel: Heinrich Kaufringers Fallkonstruktionen zwischen Rhetorik, Recht und literarischer Stofftradition*. Bibliotheca Germanica, 61 (Tübingen: Francke, 2014).

68. Vulgate, Psalms 35:7, "Justitia tua sicut montes Dei; judicia tua abyssus multa. Homines et jumenta salvabis, Domine," which then translated into Raban's "Sed nemo omnia judicia Dei penetrare potest, quoniam scriptum est: 'Judicia Dei abyssus multa.'" The full Latin name is: Hrabanus Maurus. Rabanus Maurus, *Poenitentium Liber ad Otgarium*, in *Patrologia Latinae*, ed. J. P. Migne (Paris: Migne, 1852), 112:1398–424; I am indebted here to the study by Christopher P. Flynn, "Fontenoy and the Justification of Battle-Seeking Strategy in the Ninth Century," to appear in *Mediaevistik* 35.

69. Albrecht Classen, "Rabbi Nissim and His Influence on Medieval German Literature: Rudolf von Ems's Der guote Gêrhart and Heinrich Kaufringer's 'Der Einsiedler und der Engel': Jewish Wisdom Teachings in the Middle High and Early Modern German Context," *Aschkenas* 108.4 (2017): 349– 69. doi:10.1515/ asch- 2017- 0015. Most likely, both Kaufringer and the author of the *Gesta* had access to Rabbi Nissim's version, either in Yiddish or a Latin translation unknown to us. I have recently also discovered a French play from 1341 where the same motif is used to convey a religious message about the workings of God in this world: Albrecht Classen, "Das Paradox der widersprüchlichen Urteil[s]sprechung und Weltwahrnehmung: göttliches vs. menschliches Recht in Heinrich Kaufringers 'Die unschuldige Mörderin'—mit paneuropäischen Ausblicken und einer neuen Quellenspur ('La femme du roi de Portugal')," *Neuphilologische Mitteilungen* CXX.II (2019): 7– 28.

70. See the contributions to *Mären als Grenzphänomen*, ed. Silvan Wagner. Bayreuther Beiträge zur Literaturwissenschaft, 37 (Berlin: Peter Lang, 2018).

71. Thomas Aquinas, *Summa theologiae*, IIa IIae, q 154, a.2, ad 2; here quoted from Bee Yun, *Wege zu Machiavelli* (2021), 143. Yun identifies this phenomenon, people's epistemological limitation, as "Weltkontingenz" (146; world contingency).

72. Lena Behmenburg, "Die Semantisierung des Raumes: Öffentlichkeit und Geheimnis," eadem, *Philomela: Metamorphosen Eines Mythos in der deutschen und französischen Literatur des Mittelalters* (Berlin and Berlin: Walter de Gruyter, 2009), 244–58. She focuses on the violent treatment of Philomena in Ovid, Chrétien de Troyes, and Georg Wickram's works, where each time the secret space matters centrally to keep the crime a secret.

73. *The Palgrave Handbook of Magical Realism in the Twenty-First Century*, ed. Richard Perez and Victoria A. Chevalier (Cham, Switzerland: Palgrave MacMillan, 2020); *Magical Realism and Literature*, ed. Christopher Warnes and Kim Anderson Sasser (Cambridge: Cambridge University Press, 2020).

74. Alexander Oberleitner, *Michael Endes Philosophie im Spiegel von "Momo" und "Die unendliche Geschichte"* (Hamburg: Meiner, 2020).

75. Alexander Kissle and Carsten S. Leimbach, *Alles über Patrick Süskinds "Das Parfüm"* (Munich: Heyne, 2006).

76. See, for instance, *Lexikon der Geisteswissenschaften: Sachbegriffe—Disziplinen—Personen*, ed. Helmut Reinaler and Peter J. Brenner (Vienna, Cologne, and Weimar: Böhlau Verlag, 2011).

77. Mahmoud Manzalaoui, "The Pseudo-Aristotelian Kitab Sirr al-asrar: Facts and Problems," *Oriens* 23–24 (1974): 146–257; Steven J. Williams, "The Early Circulation of the Pseudo-Aristotelian 'Secret of Secrets' in the West," *Micrologus* 2 (1994): 127–44; Regula Forster, *Das Geheimnis der Geheimnisse: die arabischen und deutschen Fassungen des pseudo-aristotelischen Sirr al-asrar / Secretum Secretorum*. Wissensliteratur im Mittelalter, 43 (Wiesbaden: Reichert, 2006); for some online versions, see: https://archive.org/details/threeproseversio01steeuoft; https://www.colourcountry.net/secretum/, and, most importantly because it is a digitized manuscript, https://openn.library.upenn.edu/Data/0023/html/lewis_e_016.html (all three last accessed on May 16, 2022).

78. Rüdiger Brandt, *Enklaven—Exklaven. Zur literarischen Darstellung von Öffentlichkeit und Nichtöffentlichkeit im Mittelalter. Interpretationen, Motiv- und Terminologiestudien*. Forschungen zur Geschichte der älteren deutschen Literatur, 15 (Munich: Wilhelm Fink, 1993); id., "his stupris incumbere non pertimescit publice. Heimlichkeit zum Schutz sozialer Konformität im Mittelalter," *Schleier und Schwelle: Archäologie der literarischen Kommunikation V*. Vol. 1: *Geheimnis und Öffentlichkeit*, ed. Aleida und Jan Assman (Munich: Wilhelm Fink, 1997), 71–88; Lena Behmenburg, *Philomela: Metamorphosen eines Mythos in der deutschen und französischen Literatur des Mittelalters*. Trends in Medieval Pilology, 15 (Berlin and New York: Walter de Gruyter, 2009), 244–58.

79. Aleida Assmann and Jan Assmann, "Das Geheimnis und die Archäologie der literarischen Kommunikation: Einführende Bemerkungen," *Geheimnis und Öffentlichkeit* (1997), 7–16.

80. Conermann, Wolter-von dem Knesebeck, and Quiering, ed., *Geheimnis und Verborgenes im Mittelalter* (2021), do not enter into any significant ruminations on the meaning of the secret and only summarize the various approaches by the individual contributors.

81. See the excellent anthology, *The Marvels of the World: An Anthology of Nature Writing Before 1700*, Rebecca Bushnell. Penn Studies in Landscape Architecture (Philadelphia, PA: University of Pennsylvania Press, 2021); see also the contributions to *Reading the Natural World in the Middle Ages and Renaissance: Perceptions of the Environment and Ecology*, ed. Thomas Willard. Arizona Studies in the Middle Ages and Renaissance, 46 (Turnhout: Brepols, 2020).

82. See the contributions to *Secrecy and Concealment: Studies in the History of Mediterranean and Near Eastern Religions*, ed. Hans G. Kippenberg and Guy G. Stroumsa. Numen. Studies in the History of Religions, 65 (Leiden and New York: E. J. Brill, 1995).

83. *Simmel-Handbuch: Begriffe, Hauptwerke, Aktualität*, ed. Hans-Peter Müller and Tilman Reitz (Berlin: Suhrkamp, 2018); *Simmel-Handbuch: Leben—Werk—Wirkung*, ed. Jörn Bohr, Gerald Hartung, Heike Koenig, and Tim-Florian Steinbach (Stuttgart: J. B. Metzler, 2021). See also Stephan Moebius, *Simmel lesen: moderne, dekonstruktive und postmoderne Lektüren der Soziologie von Georg Simmel* (Stuttgart: Ibidem-Verlag, 2002).

84. Georg Simmel, *Soziologie: Untersuchungen über die Formen der Vergesellschaftung*. Gesamtausgabe, vol. II. Suhrkamp-Taschenbuch Wissenschaft, 811 (1908; Berlin: Suhrkamp, 1992), 383–455; Burkard Sievers, *Geheimnis und Geheimhaltung in sozialen Systemen*. Studien zur Sozialwissenschaft, 23 (Opladen: Westdeutscher Verlag, 1974). See also Georg Simmel, *Essays on Art and Aesthetics*, ed. and with an intro. by Austin Harrington (Chicago and London: The University of Chicago Press, 2020).

85. *The Sociology of Georg* Simmel, trans., ed., and with an intro. by Kurt H. Wolff (Glencoe, IL: The Free Press, 1950), 330.

86. Albrecht Classen, "Hermann Hesses *Glasperlenspiel* (1943) und James Hiltons *Lost Horizon* (1933). Die Intertextualität zweier utopischer Entwürfe," *Studia Neophilologica* 72 (2000): 190–202.

87. Albrecht Classen, "Assassins, the Crusades, and the Old Man from the Mountains in Medieval Literature: With an Emphasis on The Stricker's *Daniel von dem Blühenden Tal*," *Marginal Figures in the Global Middle Ages and the Renaissance*, ed. Meg Lota Brown. Arizona Studies in the Middle Ages and the Renaissance, 47 (Turnhout: Brepols, 2021), 123–40.

88. Burkard Sievers, *Geheimnis und Geheimhaltung in sozialen Systemen*. Studien zur Sozialwissenschaft, 23 (Wiesbaden: VS Verlag für Sozialwissenschaften, 1974), criticizes that modern sociology has not sufficiently picked up the critical discourse on the secret as developed by the founders of this academic field, such as Georg Simmel and Wilhelm Stok. Cf. also Joachim Westerbarkey, *Das Geheimnis: Zur funktionalen Ambivalenz von Kommunikationsstrukturen* (Wiesbaden: VS Verlag für Sozialwissenschaften, 1991).

89. Horst Wenzel, "'Öffentlichkeit und Heimlichkeit in Gottfrieds, Tristan,'" *Zeitschrift für deutsche Philologie* 107 (1988): 335–61; id., "Das höfische Geheimnis: Herrschaft, Liebe, Texte," *Schleier und Schwelle*, vol. I (see note 41), 53–69.

90. Aleida and Jan Assmann, "Das Geheimnis und die Archäologie" (1997), 11.

91. See the many contributions to *On the Margin of the Visible: Sociology, the Esoteric, and the Occult*, ed. Edward A Tiryakian (New York: Wiley, 1974). We could, and this for good reasons, re-write all of cultural history as an evolution of secrets and secrecy.

92. Albrecht Classen, "The Fairy Tales by the Brothers Grimm and Their Medieval Background," *German Quarterly* 94.2 (2021): 165–75.

93. Hans Rudolf Picard, "Ei wie gut, daß niemand weiß, daß ich Rumpelstilzchen heiß'!: Das Geheimnis und seine Entdeckung im Märchen," *Schleier und Schwelle* (see note 41), vol. 3: *Geheimnis und Neugierde* (1999), 253–59; here 253.

94. Thomas Marxhausen, "Geheimnis," *Historisch-kritisches Wörterbuch des Marxismus*, vol. 5 (Hamburg: Argument-Verlag, 2001), cols. 48–53. Surprisingly,

even the WWW does not provide good entries on this topic; see, however, https://de.wikipedia.org/wiki/Geheimnis (last accessed on Nov. 18, 2021).

95. Günter Kunert, "Der verschlossene Raum," id., *Die geheime Bibliothek* (Berlin and Weimar: Aufbau Verlag, 1973), 9–10. He formulated these valuable thoughts as a kind of introduction to a selection of fictional texts which are all characterized by an inquisitiveness of the secret behind their own fictionality. In his text (not a story, not an autobiographical account, not a meditation) "Die geheime Bibliothek" (The Secret Library), he imagines a hidden library in the cellar area of a real library where all those novels, poems, or verses are kept which have never been written down. "Die unfertigen, von weichen Wellen der Wachträume weggespülten Werke würden mehr über den sagen, der sie denkt, als seine Bücher, die im Laden stehen, zerfleddert beim Antiquar, weil die unaufgeschriebenen, die fötalen, dem Dichter direkter zugehörig sind, ihn schamloser offenbaren als die immer wieder abgeschliffenen, geänderten, von der Form deformierten" (71; The unfinished works, washed away by the soft waves of daydreams, would say more about the one who is thinking them than his books which are standing on the bookshelf in the bookstore, in tattered shape in the used book store. Those books that were not written, the fetal ones, belong more directly to the poet and expose him more shamelessly than those that are deformed through the constant grinding and revisions). In the end, the narrator emphasizes that he has to be most careful from now on, protecting himself against an unknown intruder. The first thing for him to do would be to remove his twelve-volume autobiography, "damit kein auch noch so imaginärer Fremder Dinge über mich erfährt und möglicherweise verbreitet, die mir selber gänzlich unbekannt sind, weil sie sich niemals ereignet haben" (72; so that a stranger, even if he is entirely imagined, learns things about me and perhaps shares those which are entirely unknown to myself because they have never happened). Kunert operates in all of these narratives with a concept of the secret which could be explained as a mask or screen between our world and another one, imaginary or simply hidden.

96. *Oxford English Dictionary*, last modified in Sept. 2021; online at: https://www-oed-com.ezproxy2.library.arizona.edu/view/Entry/174537?rskey=8TUVib&result=1#eid (last accessed on Nov. 19, 2021).

97. *Deutsches Wörterbuch von Jacob und Wilhelm Grimm*, online at: https://woerterbuchnetz.de/?sigle=DWB&lemid=G04862#1 (last accessed on May 16, 2022).

98. Pierre Boutang, *Ontologie du secret* (Paris: Presses Universitaires de France, 1973). Ultimately, Boutang examines the secret behind all being, questions the relationship between matter and form, and probes the meaning of consciousness, which was also one of the cornerstones of medieval philosophy, such as by Thomas Aquinas (386).

99. Bee Yun, *Wege zu Machiavelli: Die Rückkehr des Politischen im Spätmittelalter.* Beihefte zum Archiv für Kulturgeschichte, 91 (Vienna, Cologne, and Weimar: Böhlau, 2021), 80–81. Summarizing Augustine's teachings in that regard, he emphasizes the following, which is really worth quoting at length: "Den Menschen sind die Möglichkeiten versperrt, die Welt und ihren Ablauf rational zu begreifen, und seine Handlung und die Handlung der gesamten Bürgerschaft im Hinblick auf

ihren Nutzen zweckmäßig zu gestalten.... Er behauptet, dass die vernünftige Erkenntnis des Menschen prinzipiell von der Sünde getrübt ist und daher dem Akt des Glaubens unterworfen werden muss" (People lack the possibility to grasp the world and its development in rational terms and thus to model their actions and the actions of the entire citizenship regarding their practical utility.... He claims that human epistemology is principally undermined by sinfulness and hence must be submitted to the act of faith). Later, Yun notes that in the later Middle Ages "[d]er Abstand zwischen der menschlichen Welt und der üblichen Ordnung des Universums . . . immer stärker betont und schließlich sogar als unüberbrückbar begriffen [wurde]" (110; scholars emphasized ever more the distance between the human world and the rest of the universal cosmos and finally considered it as unbridgeable). Yun cites, for instance, the teachings by William Ockham (ca. 1287–1347) according to whom God is omnipotent and not subject to any necessity (140), which can be easily traced back to Augustine and theologians/philosophers from the early Middle Ages. Yun's arguments, directly aimed against the claims by famous Hans Blumenberg, who insisted that Ockham and others constituted a new beginning, the rise of modernity, seem to be convincing especially because he presents solid textual evidence for the long tradition of such perspectives (see also 143–47).

100. Julia Burkhardt, *Von Bienen lernen. Das* Bonum universale de apibus *des Thomas von Cantimpré als Gemeinschaftsentwurf: Analyse, Edition, Übersetzung, Kommentar*. 2 vols. Klöster als Innovationslabore, 7 (Regensburg: Schnell & Steiner, 2020), vol. 2, 821.

101. Just as I completed the manuscript of this volume, I learned about parallel efforts by the contributors to the collection of articles, *Darstellung und Geheimnis in Mittelalter und Früher Neuzeit*, ed. Jutta Eming and Volkhard Wels (2021). There are some comparable approaches, particularly regarding Wolfram von Eschenbach's *Parzival* (Matthias Benz) and Heinrich von dem Türlin's *Diu Crône* (Jutta Eming), but overall, the notion of the secret is often conceived more in metaphorical or abstract terms, which does not help much in grasping the epistemological dimensions of the secret in high and late medieval literature. While my interests are focused on developing pan-European perspectives, uncovering shared concepts and ideas across the premodern languages and cultures, this volume is primarily dedicated to medieval and early modern German literature and thus tends to reiterate much of what previous research has already stated, discussed, or investigated.

102. Alice Brittan, *The Art of Astonishment: Reflections on Gifts and Grace* (London: Bloomsbury Publishing, 2022). I have copied this summary from the webpage advertising her book.

103. I would like to express my gratitude to my dear colleagues Marilyn L. Sandidge, Westfield State University, MA, and Christopher R. Clason, Oakland University, Rochester, MI, for their critical reading of parts of the manuscript and for their helpful suggestions and corrections. Fidel Fajardo-Acosta, Creighton University, Omaha, NE, was so kind as to serve as a reader for the publisher and made valuable suggestions. All remaining mistakes are, of course, my own. I am particularly pleased with the topic that I am pursuing here because it represents a new and heretofore little considered topic relevant for medieval literature, not focused on religion or magic, but on

the workings of the otherworld, the invisible and yet powerful, as the motto above nicely indicates. It is my hope that the insights we can glean from medieval literature regarding the role and functions of secrets can be applied, in one way or the other, to our own existence where we are also confronted by many situations that leave us baffled and confused, helpless or inspired, although we cannot really tell what it was that touched us. As to magic, see the contributions to *Magic and Magicians in the Middle Ages and the Early Modern Time* (2017); and to *The Book and the Magic of Reading in the Middle Ages*, ed. Albrecht Classen. Garland Reference Library of the Humanities, 2118 (New York and London: Garland Publishing, 1999).

104. *The Imitation of Christ: Being the Autograph Manuscript of Thomas à Kempis, De Imitatione Christi*, ed. Charles Ruelens (London: Elliot Stock, 1885). This is the facsimile of the Brussels manuscript. See now the excellent new German translation, Thomas von Kempen, *Von der Nachfolge Christi: Die Weisheit des mittelalterlichen Klosters*. Übersetzt und herausgegeben von Bernhard Lang (Stuttgart: Philipp Reclam jun., 2022), 7–8; cf. my review in *Mediaevistik* 35 (forthcoming). For a biographical sketch and the cultural-historical context, see Albrecht Classen, "Thomas a Kempis," in *Literary Encyclopedia* (2005), http://www.litencyc.com/php/speople.php?rec=true&UID=2 (last accessed on June 1, 2022); John Welch, *An Interior Life: Rummaging Through the Christian Tradition* (Mahwah, NJ: Paulist Press, 2022).

105. Dante Alighieri, *Paradiso*. The Italian text with an English verse translation, intro., and commentary by Allen Mandelbaum (Berkeley, CA: University of California Press, 1982).

Chapter One

Marie de France
The Lais—The Mysterious Black Ship and Other Secrets in the World of Love

It is quite understandable that many modern readers of the *lais* by the Anglo-Norman poet Marie de France (ca. 1190) feel strongly reminded of fairy tales because she includes numerous fabulous creatures, magical objects, and mysterious events affecting the various protagonists that clearly escape any rational explanation. Of course, there is nothing wrong with adding such narrative elements since they help the poet to develop her verse narratives more effectively and to formulate, ultimately, her key messages about essential concerns in human life. How to explain them, however, represents a considerable challenge for us as modern scholars/readers and what to make out of these secretive forces and figures.

Those cases have been studied already for a long time by many Marie de France scholars; apart from the fact that we have available excellent text editions and translations, we can also count on numerous in-depth examinations, so there might be the danger here of carrying the proverbial owls to Athens when I try to examine some of her *lais* once again in the current context, the secret.[1] Nevertheless, in this chapter I propose a particular interpretive angle in accordance with the overall focus of the present study, that is, investigating how Marie engaged with secrets in her texts and how she has the protagonists operate with them successfully without us, as the audience, ultimately being allowed to understand them fully.[2] To be sure, there are many secrets, and they constitute an epistemological challenge that the verse narratives themselves do not overcome or dismiss, quite deliberately; there are many riddles to be solved, and this until today, both in life and in the poetic works, such as Marie's verse narratives.

There is universal agreement that Marie's *lais* belong to some of the best medieval literary texts from her time (late twelfth century), providing entertainment, excitement, social comments, and reflections on values and emotions. There is, in particular, little wonder that the magical elements have fascinated scholars much, though I would question whether we have yet found really convincing answers as to their meaning.[3] It is one thing to deal with miraculous ponds or fairies, with giants or dwarfs, and it is a very different thing to have shape-shifting hawk men ("Yonec") or a mysterious ship that transports the protagonists all on its own ("Guigemar") to his predestined goal.

Throughout medieval literature, we hear of many mechanical trappings that amount to be robots or automata, whether in Béroul's or Thomas of Brittanny's *Roman de Tristan*—see the *salle aux images*—or in any of the many versions of *Floire and Blancheflor* (the tomb for Blancheflor), especially in Konrad Fleck's Middle High German romance, whether in The Stricker's *Daniel von dem Blühenden Tal* or the *Lancelot en prose*.[4] But those are constructions, machines, gadgets, if not robots, and we know in essence who created them with what purpose. Those are not secrets and do not add to our investigation of that magical world of which Marie de France, apparently was fond.

In essence, virtually all of her *lais* are determined by the miraculous phenomenon of love; but it cannot always become a reality because social and political constraints prevent it from happening. In many ways, the poet did not intend to elucidate all aspects in her narratives to the fullest and obviously enjoyed playing with a variety of secrets that cannot be revealed easily, if at all. Love, of course, proves to be the greatest mystery of them all, but it is buttressed consistently by the workings of secret objects or creatures that help the individuals to overcome nearly insurmountable barriers and smoothen challenges.[5]

Deus Amanz

There are medical or pharmaceutical aids to make love possible, such as in "Deus Amanz," where the learned aunt of the princess concocts a powerful potion to give the squire the necessary strength to carry his beloved up to the top of the mountain. But there is no particular secret about it since this aunt is apparently a learned person studying and working in Salerno as a medical expert who knows much about herbs and roots (100) and has the necessary skills to provide him with the right drug (steroid?) which would enable him to carry her up to the mountain. We are not told any specifics about it and only know that it is a liquid with enormous power ("beivre," 134).[6] Once consumed, it would refortify or invigorate the young man and give him so much strength that he then could carry her up all the way to the top of the mountain.

This aunt is not creating magic; instead, she carefully studies the man's physical constitution (132), which makes it possible for her to proceed and create this amazing potion strong enough to return power to his entire body, veins, and bones (138). The potion is contained in a little vial which the maid then carries for him while he tries to accomplish the near-impossible achievement. All would then have worked well if he had accepted her advice to drink from that vial, but he suddenly changes his mind and becomes stubborn, believing that he could achieve his goal without medical help. The princess grows increasingly worried, knowing all too well that he is near exhaustion, but she cannot push him to accept the potion. Miraculously, however, he reaches the top, contrary to all expectations, but there he collapses and dies from a broken heart. As tragic as it certainly proves to be, as miraculous the subsequent events turn out because the princess sinks to the ground with him and then tosses the vial on the ground where it spills since it was useless for them both. Once the liquid has flown out, however, a true miracle happens, a secret that the aunt might not even have foreseen. As soon as the potion has spilled all over the ground, many flowers and herbs begin to grow and transform the mountain top to a colorful garden, as we are invited to imagine. The liquid had been concocted from roots and herbs, and those now, released, plant themselves in the barren ground, producing the very fertility which the young woman had wanted to possess herself (218–19).

The emphasis on the roots hidden in the potion confirms that the aunt had simply worked with natural products, which would have certainly worked their effects if the squire had accepted the liquid to strengthen himself. His refusal to take it indicates his toxic selfishness and exclusive focus on the masculine competition with the princess's father. Tragically, however, he succumbs to his physical exhaustion and hence death. The narrator does not hide anything about the potion, even though the specifics are not mentioned. For the audience within the narrative, however, the sudden development of a flower bed, or a garden with herbs, high up there, represents a miraculous development since they do not know about the potion and its origin.

We, as the audience, by contrast, learn in very specific terms from the narrator who had created the potion, how it was created, and what its impact on nature proves to be. This is not a secret. The narrator traces the entire process of the potion's concoction to its end-use, though the young man never profits from it because he always wants to achieve his own goals all by himself, so without any external help.[7]

The aunt working in Salerno finds a direct parallel in the Irish Queen Isolde in Gottfried von Straßburg's *Tristan and Isolde* (ca. 1210) who has not only produced a poison for the tip of her brother Morold's sword, which causes enormous problems for the wounded Tristan, but she is also an expert in combating the infection when Tristan comes to Ireland under the pseudonym

Tantris to find healing there. Isolde does not create a secret at all; she works long and hard to treat her patient and can eventually restore his health, which confirms her outstanding medical expertise, along with her pharmaceutical knowledge.[8] We could also point out the historical reality of Salerno where, as we know, female physicians operated successfully, such as Trotula, who might have been the model for Marie's concept here.[9] Hence, we have to be careful in determining what was considered a secret in medieval literature and what was learning, knowledge, and science.

Guigemar

The situation in "Guigemar" constitutes a very different case that deserves more extensive examination because here we come across a true secret, the black ship, which is never resolved and remains hidden within the narrative. Guigemar, as a young man, is not interested in the other sex and lives a life of self-contentment, not wooing any lady. Although a young adult, he seems to be stuck in a stage of pre-puberty, at least in biological terms. At the same time, as the narrator emphasizes, he proves to be a worthy knight, gaining much esteem for his major accomplishments on a variety of battlefields. Yet, women do not interest him at all, a shortcoming of nature, as the narrator comments (58). This continues until one day he becomes badly injured during a hunt during which he had tried to kill a hind with a fawn. There are no comments about the cruelty of this action, but strangely, the arrow with which he had shot at the hind's forehead bounces back and badly injures Guigemar, perhaps meaningfully in his thigh as a sexual allusion.[10] Miraculously, before the hind dies, it (she) informs the protagonist that he would never receive any healing, that no medicine would ever help him until a woman would intervene, that is, a woman he would be madly in love with and she with him. Only when both would experience great suffering for each other would he have a chance of recovery. Once the hind has pronounced this destiny for Guigemar, it requests to be left alone to die in peace.[11]

Is this a curse, as June Hall McCash has argued, or is this a promise, an outline of what future will hold for the protagonist? I lean toward the latter because the experience of love is the most wonderful transformation Guigemar could ever expect in his life, and the wound is only a catalyst for him to find his future beloved.[12]

The protagonist does just that and wanders off by himself, not waiting for his hunting companions. The secret of the hind is not explained, there are no answers for why the arrow bounced back and then even could hurt Guigemar so badly. But the narrative aims at developing a symbolic love story which requires that the young man departs from there and disappears from his family and friends. The hind might have known what is happening next, but as mysterious as this speaking animal proves to be, as startling is the next strange phenomenon. Guigemar encounters a black ship in a harbor, but there is no crew on board. We are alerted to the fact that the entire ship is completely black: "There was no peg or spike / that was not made completely of ebony" (156–57, "ebenus"). If not strange enough, once Guigemar has placed himself on a bed and fallen asleep, the ship immediately takes off, as if driven by an automatic engine, directed by an unknown mind. The bed itself can only be identified as a piece of highly symbolic furniture, as the narrator's description indicates.[13] As was popular in the Middle Ages, Marie endeavored to employ some ekphrastic elements in the presentation of the bed, elaborating, for instance, the cover, the pillow, the cloth, and the calendabra, and Guigemar expresses his great astonishment about this marvel of craftsmanship. However, the bed had also tempted him to lie down, while the ship was already moving out of the harbor, making it impossible for the protagonist to get back to land. In other words, Guigemar is kidnapped, but we do not know by whom and with what purpose, at least not at the beginning.

In a certain way, both the hind and the ship are part of the same plan, as if they communicated with each other behind the scene and beyond the animal's death. By contrast, Guigemar is stunned, does not know what to do, "ne seit ke faire" (196), and feels helpless and confused in face of his desperate situation. But the narrator seems to know more of what is going on within the schema of the unfolding events, outlining what his future will hold for him, whereas Guigemar lies down on the bed, praying to God for his safeguard, but he does not think of the hind's words, although those should be present in his mind particularly now as the black ship moves completely on its own, yet another automaton, operating better than any ship even today could do, not relying on a crew, a captain or a pilot.

Obviously, such a magical ship operates on behalf of a higher power, of which neither the protagonist nor we as the audience know anything. But there are specific clues as to the purpose of this arrangement because Guigemar needs to meet his future beloved. The wound in his thigh is already a sign that his old self-protected identity is broken and that he ready for the first experience of love. The ship itself never communicates with him; it's only an object, but it seems to be driven by something or someone, which remains a secret throughout the tale.

To understand this situation better, that is, to gain a better grasp of the symbolic meaning of the ship, we can also look at Konrad von Würzburg's *Partonopier und Meliur* (ca. 1280), which was based on the Old French *Partonopeus de Blois* (ca. 1170, hence, predating most of Chrétien de Troyes's, at least according to one school of thought).[14] The young protagonist, the nephew of King Clogier, ruler over "Kärlingen" (235; France), one day gets lost in the course of a hunt and is left behind all by himself in the

Ardennes forest. After having climbed a mountain to gain an overview, he discovers the ocean in the distance and turns in that direction, reaching the shore already at night. There he discovers an extraordinarily decorated ship, similarly embellished as the ship in Marie's "Guigemar," and similarly empty, with no soul to be seen. Assuming that it would be safer to spend the night on the ship than on the beach, where wild animals could attack him and the horse, he embarks it and soon falls asleep on a bed, which is not described at all (644–59).

Without him knowing what is going on, the ship starts moving by itself, which the narrator emphasizes deliberately (669–71). When Partonopier wakes up and realizes where is, he bursts out in tears and laments his destiny, but he does not experience a shipwreck, and instead is mysteriously guided to a city across the sea, which is later identified as Constantinople. That location is also completely empty, as he believes, and then his adventure continues because he is royally treated there by a host of invisible servants, then retires in a bedroom, where he is visited at night by an invisible woman, who soon becomes his mistress. She had actually arranged all that, the ship, the invisibility, and the bedroom. Whether she also had been involved in Partonpier getting lost in the forest, we cannot tell, but it would be a logical consequence. Meliur is the young queen of that city and needs him to wait for three and a half years during which he would not be allowed to see her physically. Obviously, she considers him to be too young to marry her, and she also wants to test his inner strength to observe the taboo. Only then she would cancel the magic, introduce him to her court, and marry him officially.

All this pleases Partonopier, and he spends a wonderful time there, finding entertainment during the day and sexual pleasures at night with Meliur. But the romance then continues with news reaching him that his father and uncle have died and that his mother desperately needs him to defend the country. Again the ship arrives and transports him back, which takes fifteen days which he spends sleeping, all pre-arranged by Meliur, who commands major magical powers over long distances. The story continues from there which we do not need to pursue further without losing the connection with Marie's *lai*. Suffices only to point out that Partonopier later transgresses the taboo and makes Meliur visible with the help of a magical lamp, and this upon the urging of his mother and the archbishop of Paris who are afraid that this princess might be the devil but completely misjudge this young woman who has simply learned great magical powers, as she explains to him in great detail (8029–292).

Meliur badly laments Partonopier's failure to observe her order, expels him from her court, and thus forces him to return home where he has to struggle hard for many years to recover his former self, to reach maturity, and finally to return in order to win a major tournament for Meliur's hand, which leads to a happy end for both.

The magical ship no longer appears after Partonopier has been expelled, and instead he is placed on an ordinary ship with a normal crew, who is instructed by Meliur's sister Irekel to take good care of him and to transport him back to France, to the city of Blois (9158–70). And much later, once Partonopier is allowed to return to Constantinople, magic no longer surfaces since the secret has been exposed and destroyed due to Partonopier's ignorant mother and the archbishop.[15]

In Marie's narrative, by contrast, the ship remains a mystery; it always knows, so to speak, when it must be ready to transport the two protagonists across the sea. It takes, by its own volition, so to speak, Guigemar directly to a young lady who is imprisoned by her old husband so that he might be able to force her to love him—clearly an absurd notion, despite all of his efforts even by means of wall frescoes allegedly teaching a lesson about love which ought to apply to her. The ship finds the harbor below the tower where the lady is 'incarcerated,' which allows her and her maid to retrieve the badly wounded knight and to take him up to their tower. At first, however, in clear contrast to the situation in *Partonopier und Meliur*, the lady is afraid of the ship and wants to flee when it steers by itself into the harbor (270–71), but her maid encourages her to be bold and to enter the ship, where they discover the sleeping knight.

Subsequently, the lady treats the knight with great medical care and helps him to heal his wound, but both are then wounded by the arrow of love, and spend a year and a half together, just as the hind had told him. We are not informed about the true nature of that animal, and why the ship 'knew' exactly where to take Guigemar, but this love relationship evolves rapidly, and the two enjoy each other unperturbed until they are discovered. As a sidenote, she never conceives, but Marie never engages much with the practical consequences of love relationships within family life.[16]

The old husband, egregiously jealous, is ready to kill Guigemar, but he is also afraid of him since he is immediately ready to defend himself, and therefore he first inquires with him where he had come from and how he had reached this almost inaccessible coast. This requires the protagonist to retell his entire story once again, which appears, however, very unbelievable to the husband, as it would most audiences. Yet, he demands proof from him, so they all go down to the harbor where, as to be expected, the ship has just arrived, obviously completely in the know about what is going on in Guigemar's life and bent on participating and helping to move the love story along. He is put on the ship, which then, again all by itself, immediately takes off and returns him to his home country. The ship is a material agent, an object operating in close conjunction with the protagonist, but it is also somehow connected with the hind.

Both anthropologists and folklorists have already identified numerous other references to such magical ships, all of which appear as secrets that refuse easy, if any, full explanation. In many ancient fairy tales and in religious narratives we hear of mysterious ships made out of all kinds of materials that transport the protagonist, saints, martyrs, female victims, brave knights, etc., across a body of water and appear to serve a specific purpose. Saints such as Jacob, Vitus, Maurilius, and so on, receive extraordinary ships or manage to traverse the ocean with God's help. In Scandinavian legendary tales, there are numerous references to magical ships that travel at enormous speed and quickly take the protagonist to his/her goal. Ancient Egyptian and Old Norse mythology associate the gods or heroes with ships that transport them to the other world, such as the ship "Skiðblaðnir" owned by the God Freyr. Some fairy tales know of ships that can be folded together and put away, whereas others operate, as in Marie's *lai*, all by themselves, such as in the *Flóamanna saga* (ch. 26). The same motif can be traced as far back as to Homer's *Odyssey* (ch. 8) where the ship can read people's minds and steer itself without a rudder.[17]

The poor lady has to stay behind and suffers badly, being treated like a prisoner, and locked into a tower (655–66).[18] However, eventually, after two years she happens to discover that the door to her prison is suddenly open, so she can leave, and her steps take her directly to the harbor to drown herself out of desperation. But the ship, like a trusted friend, is already waiting for her, and hardly has she entered it when it takes off and transports her off to Brittany, where she later meets her lover who can liberate her from her captivity by another lord, master of the harbor where she had arrived. Scholars have mostly focused on the secret codes which both of them had implemented in his shirt (by her) and her belt (by him). What matters here is the intriguing treatment of the ship which operates all by itself and yet does not seem to be completely free either, maybe being subject to the ultimate force of love so that it can bring the two lovers together.

We face here a wonderful example for the latest theoretical approach to literature, "Thing Theory," since the ship is an agent and as such intervenes directly in the protagonists' lives, realizing their true needs and promoting their desires to achieve happiness in love. Recent scholars have investigated objects such as dishes, gifts, armor, precious jewels, the Grail, arrows, tablets, reliquaries, rings, and all kinds of shining objects, but not a ship.[19] We are told about its completely black appearance only once; otherwise, we only learn that there is a bed on which the protagonist can rest during the voyage. But there is no crew, at least no visible one; and the ship knows exactly what to do, when to arrive, where to land, whom to take, and where to deliver that person. There are no explanations for this phenomenon in "Guigemar," although we are not the only one who are puzzled since the old husband questions Guigemar's explanation of how he reached that land and is then stunned to learn that that specific ship has arrived in the harbor at exactly that moment when Guigemar needs to prove the veracity of his account. The husband believes that a ship without a crew would certainly represent a risk to the other man's life (615–17), and he would not mind it if he drowned at sea. Since the ship is there, indeed, they take Guigemar on it, but he does not suffer from a shipwreck at all. He and the ship are, so to speak, of the same mind since he needs to be transported back home: "Od lui s'en vet en sun pais" (620).

Similarly, once the lady has found the door to her prison cell open and no one on guard, the ship, again as an independent agent, is ready for her and moves her close to her lover, which then soon reaches the culmination point, with Guigemar amassing a small army, defeating and killing the lord holding his beloved, which then concludes this *lai*. The closer we examine it, the more secrets we encounter, and none of them finds a satisfactory explanation. Both objects (ship) and animals (hind), but then also prison gates, and to some extent also the knots in the shirt and the belt defy rational answers and yet contribute crucially to the development of this love story. Guigemar would not have found his beloved without being propelled out of his world through magic; his lady would not have been able to welcome him without the help provided by the ship. Guigemar's life is spared because the ship is in the harbor at the nick of time after the lovers have been caught *in flagrante*, and the prison door cooperates as well after more than two years wait time for the lady to find a way out of her predicament, and then the ship takes her on and brings her to Brittany and hence close to her lover. The narrator grants us some glimpses into the world of secrets, but she does not reveal the truth and prefers to keep it all a secret, which altogether might be considered a series of metaphors of love itself, the greatest secret of them all.[20]

I would not associate any of those elements (the hind, the ship, the knots, etc.) with religion,[21] but simply call them secrets, epistemological challenges hovering intriguingly between the spiritual and the material, connecting the individual with another world that shows itself kind enough to help these two lovers, but does not reveal its actual essence or identity.[22] Hence, the term 'secret' in its open-ended character seems to be most fitting for all of these phenomena. They defy all critical efforts to explain and define them; they are associated with forces we might feel, might even see or hear, but those are forces that remain ineffable, unfathomable, inexplicable, and mysterious. As we clearly sense in Marie's "Guigemar," the protagonists are determined by secrets, by some powers that support them, which the poet does not associate with God, or any divine force. Things happen in the background which control and guide the events in the foreground, but none of the characters in this *lai* have the faintest idea about the true causes behind their own actions. But the poet does not want to reveal the secrets, and prefers, quite obviously, to leave it that way to increase both the charm of her tale and to challenge her audience to probe the issues more in depth and creatively.

Bisclavret

In her famous story of the werewolf, "Bisclavret," Marie goes even one step further and has the male protagonist appear as a living secret, although he himself does not seem to understand what is happening in his life. He is forced to leave society for three days per week during which he transforms into a werewolf. This might be a horrible situation, for himself and his wife— there are no children ever mentioned—and she actually reacts with terror when she finally learns the truth about her husband's regular disappearance. The critical issue here, however, is not the fact that Bisclavret transforms into a werewolf, but that this is a secret he cannot divulge to anyone, not even to his wife. She forces him, however, to reveal what he is doing during those three days, and even to relate to her what he is doing with his clothing, which is crucial for his return to human shape.

The narrator emphasizes explicitly that both Bisclavret's lord and his neighbors greatly appreciate him as a worthy knight who "noblement se cunteneit" (18; "conducted himself nobly"). There would be nothing wrong with him except for his regular disappearance during the week with no one knowing his whereabouts, not even his wife. She is rightly worried and understandably fears that he might have an affair with another woman, which is certainly not the case. However, Bisclavret knows only too well that his entire existence depends on preserving his transformation into a werewolf as an absolute secret: "Trouble will come to me if I tell you, / for I will divide you from my love / and destroy myself in doing so" (54–56).

Unfortunately for him, she ultimately exerts so much pressure that he must reveal to her the secret, and even tell her the location where he hides his clothing. For the poor woman, this is all too much, and being completely overwhelmed by this horrible news, she decides to use another knight who had wooed her already for a long time to eliminate Bisclavret from her life. Indeed, once that knight has removed the clothing from the hiding place, the protagonist is forced to stay in his shape of a werewolf, not being able to shift back into human form. Curiously, however, during his life in the wilderness, and also afterward at King Arthur's court, there are no negative aspects reported about him. People wonder about his disappearance, they worry and search for him, but with no luck. But, although he is roaming the forest as a wild beast, the narrator does not tell us anything about him hunting prey or attacking people. We are, in other words, confronted with a mystery that no one can tackle and solve in any way.

A year later—Marie likes to take big steps in chronological terms to accelerate her narrative account—the king goes hunting, and the company comes across the werewolf, which they immediately want to kill, being deadly scared of it. When the beast is already surrounded and about to be torn to pieces, it espies the king and throws itself at his feet, begging him for mercy in the way how people would do in times of great need. To the king's credit, he recognizes these gestures as signs of "sen de hume" (154; "human understanding"), calls off the hunt and takes the werewolf with him to his court where it is treated like a member of nobility because, as he says, it has "entente e sen" (157; "intelligence and understanding"). The king is delighted about this wonder and then orders that the werewolf be treated with respect as an equal among the knights: "Every day it went to bed / among the knights and close to the king" (176–77).

Surprisingly, the werewolf displays a most noble and kind character and receives full recognition by the entire court company. Bisclavret, to return to his actual name, never leaves the king's side and constantly demonstrates his love for him (184), so no one questions this most unusual arrangement. But the beast remains a secret until the king's vassal, who had stolen Bislavret's clothing and then married his wife, happens to attend court festivities. The werewolf immediately recognizes and attacks him, which puzzles everyone since otherwise it had never displayed any aggression to anyone. Afterwards, the court happens to visit the castle where Bisclavret's wife resides, and the werewolf rushes up to her and bites off her nose, which then motivates people to question the lady and force her to reveal the truth about her first husband. Upon the king's advice, they place Bisclavret in a room with clothing for him, leave him alone, and this then achieves his transformation back into human shape.

The wife is then banished and sent into exile, accompanied by her husband. Many of the female descendants in the future are then born without a nose, as a sign of the shame brought upon them by Bisclavret's wife. No doubt, one mystery is piled upon another, and none of them finds a satisfactory explanation. We do not know why this worthy knight is so much shamed or humbled by being forcefully transforming into a werewolf. The narrator does not inform us about his activities during his 'exile' in the forest, and we are also left in the dark as to Bisclavret's future insofar as there are no words about his destiny. Does he ever assume the shape of a werewolf, or is he then free of this destiny?

What we can say for sure is that Bisclavret's wife is scared to death when she learns the truth about her husband disappearing in the forest as a ferocious beast. We are also told that the werewolf performs quite peacefully once the king has adopted him, as he demonstrates aggression only when he encounters his wife and her new husband. By contrast, we know nothing about the reason for his transformation, why it lasts particularly for three days per week, and we cannot tell whether the curse, if that's the right word, continues to hold for him after he has bitten off his wife's nose and subsequently, with the help of his clothes, has recovered his human shape.

Of course, we could simply argue that here we face literary liberty, Marie's imagination which was not bound by realistic limitations, although she drew from oral sources and might also have been familiar with a motif developed already by the troubadour Peire Vidal (fl. ca. 1183–1204), included in his song "De chantar m'era laissatz" (ca. 1194) (PC 364.16) and elaborated in a narrative *razo* explaining the song. There we are told that he was in love with a woman nicknamed Na Loba de Pennautier and disguised himself as a wolf and ran through the forest making shepherds believe he was a real wolf so they would chase and catch him and bring him to his beloved Na Loba.[23] But in her introduction, Marie makes clear how much she drew from collective memory among the Bretons who knew from ancient times that it was a rather common phenomenon that special individuals turned into werewolves. She defines this creature as follows: "The werewolf is a wild beast: / when it is in that frenzy, / it devours people and does great harm. / It lives in and roams the great forests" (9–12).[24]

However, in her own *lai*, Marie conceives of the werewolf in very different terms, clearly abstaining from any negative comments on the beast, except that the hunters are terrified when they witness the werewolf and are prepared to kill it on the spot. But Bisclavret's wife reacts similarly and cannot tolerate the idea of being married to and living with a man who turns into such a beast for three days of the week. For the king, by contrast, the horrible shape of that creature does not matter at all because it has demonstrated to him its human character, its inner nobility.

Similarly, the entire royal court accepts Bisclavret upon the king's order, and indeed, nothing evil happens at all, until the one vassal arrives who had committed the crime against Bisclavret. As Marie finally insists: "The adventure you have heard / was true have no doubt" (315–16), meaning that for her the secret of this werewolf carries great relevance, though she refrains from revealing the critical cues to unravel this riddle. Instead, we as the audience are required to examine the symbolism and to figure out what the appearance of a werewolf within a narrative framework determined by the topic of love would tell us about the essence of human life, about inner nobility, trust, loyalty, and honor.

Of course, we can easily understand Bisclavret's wife and her reaction; to imagine that her husband transforms into such a beast is just terrifying her. But this only means that a) she does not understand the situation at all; b) that the couple has completely lacked in communicating with each other; c) that Bisclavret knows of a horrible secret in his life thath he cannot divulge to his wife because otherwise, he would lose her and himself at the same time, as it then actually happens; and d) that there is a secret behind human existence that cannot be understood by us. Certain forces have imposed something on this worthy knight to transform into such a dangerous beast, but we do not know why and for what reason. But we can tell that Bisclavret knows very well that this transformation, once revealed to his wife, would destroy their marriage.

There is something horrifying, particularly for this woman, whose husband does not trust her to be strong enough to sustain the truth about him. But the king's huntsmen react the same way and would have killed him if he had not demonstrated humbling gestures toward the king recognizing him as his lord. The narrator herself comments directly that werewolves devour people when they are "en cele rage" (10; "in that frenzy"). Nevertheless, all that is later forgotten or ignored when Bisclavret as a werewolf lives at the royal court. And Bisclavret himself is consistently identified as a highly noble and worthy knight whom the king loves dearly, as is shown at the very end when the king finds him sleeping on the bed in his original human shape: "The king ran to embrace him; / more than a hundred times he hugs and kisses him" (300–01). What is going to happen with the werewolf in the future? Is Bisclavret now free from the curse, or will that simply continue, without his former wife bothering him? We do not know, and Marie appears unwilling to clarify any of those questions, obviously content with leaving us with numerous questions, if not rather secrets, just as the werewolf is a secret by itself.

Of course, there are numerous references to this creature in other literary works, such as in the late twelfth-century Old French *Guillaume de Palerne* (ca. 1194–1197; preserved in only one manuscript, thirteenth-century Paris, Arsenal FR, 6565), where the prince of Sicily is kidnapped by a werewolf who subsequently turns out to be his most trustworthy and almost miraculous helper in many different adventures. Then there is the anonymous French verse narrative *Melion* and the Latin *Arthur and Gorlagon*. In *Guillaume de Palerne*, the werewolf even carries a name, Alphonse, and he is also a human being, the son of the king of Spain, who had to take on the shape of the werewolf because of the evil treatment by his stepmother, Brande. His father had remarried after his first wife's death, the daughter of the king of Portugal. But she was jealous of Alphonse and wanted to secure the throne for her own son, Brandin. Having covered Alphonse's body with a magical potion Brande had concocted herself, having been extensively trained in the necromantic arts, she had brought about the young man's transformation from a human shape into that of a werewolf. Poor Alphonse tried to avenge himself, attacking Brande, but her people protected her and chased the beast away, which escapes to Apulia in southern Italy.

During the next two years, the werewolf grows into a strong and fierce creature, but we are not told anything about its 'evil-doing' there. Instead, Alphonse learns about the treason to be committed against Guillaume and comes to his rescue, whereupon the real adventure story sets in.[25] At the end of the romance, once when the protagonist's problems have been solved, the werewolf enters the king's prison—Guillaume holds him, his son, and his men as captives in Palermo at that moment after having defeated them in a battle—and displays the same humility toward the king as the werewolf in "Bisclavret," which moves the king to grant the beast complete protection everywhere. Thereupon he relates the entire story of his second wife's nefarious actions against his own son, Alphonse, but still regards it as somewhat doubtful because she had always told him not to believe those evil rumors directed against her. But Guillaume confirms that the werewolf is a most noble and highly intelligent creature who had helped him out of many perils, saving his life, indeed, numerous times. The king then forces his wife to come to his rescue, and she completely admits her guilt, begs for mercy, and helps Alphonse to restore his original human shape and form (7748–51), which soon after completes that romance, with the werewolf having disappeared since Alphonse has returned to human society with the help of counter magic applied by the originally evil stepmother.[26]

Marie de France certainly tapped into a major European, if not an archetypal myth and operated with it successfully to develop one of her *lais* with the intention to reflect on marital problems resulting from lack of communication, mutual distrust, lack of compassion, and understanding. Recent scholarship has raised critical perspectives with regard both to the wife in this story and to Bisclavret, but we can content ourselves here with the final observation that the protagonist's hidden life represents a secret somehow associated with clothing as cultural markers. The wife has those removed, and without them, the werewolf cannot shed its monstrous appearance until the end of the story when those clothes are restored. The conflict between husband and wife are quite obvious, both determined, so it seems, by considerable character weakness and perhaps also lack of love. The outcome is rather tragic for her, though she remains married to the other knight and has children with him. For Bisclavret, the situation seems to look positive since he regains his human appearance and is reintegrated into the king's court, and this with great joy. But Marie does not comment on Bisclavret's future and does not leave any clue as to why this man is forced to transform into a werewolf for three days of the week.[27]

Eliduc

One of the most mysterious secrets in Marie's *Lais*, however, proves to be the weasel, much-discussed and rarely fully understood. This little mammal from the Mustela family (as a genus), as modern biologists have confirmed it, has attracted from very early on symbolic readings, such as in folkloric magic and religions, but then also in the late-antique *Physiologus* (ca. 2nd century C.E.), which was extremely popular throughout the Middle Ages and used as a textbook in many different contexts, served particularly Christian writers as an important symbolic animal, maybe representing the human soul or God's love for people.[28] The individual narratives can easily be traced back to Indian, Hebrew, or Egyptian sources, but this would not concern us here. As Michael J. Curley succinctly summarizes, "Both directly and through numerous intermediaries, *Physiologus* became an established source of Medieval sacred iconography and didactic poetry and was used in the preaching manuals and religious textbooks of the later Middle Ages.[29]

Many different animals are mentioned and allegorized here, although the selection is far removed from what we are wont to expect from the fable tradition (Aesop), which Marie de France was very familiar with herself, since she composed her own collection of fables, ca. 1190.[30] Instead, we confront here both real and mythological creatures, such as the antelope, the swordfish, the pelican, the owl, the eagle, the phoenix, the hedgehog, the fox, the elephant, and then, oddly and completely out of order, so to speak, the siren, Amos the Prophet, an agate stone, oyster stone, or pearl, the fig tree, the panther, the whale, etc.

The *Physiologus* also contains a chapter on the weasel (no. XXXV), which people should never eat since it is forbidden as unclean already in the Old Testament (Lev. 11:29). The narrator then explains the most bizarre method for the female weasel to get pregnant and to conceive. She "receives the seed of the male in her mouth and, having become pregnant, gives birth through her ears" (50). The gender of the new birth is determined by whether it comes out of the right or the left ear. Something wicked is associated with either form of delivery (50). The narrator correlates the weasel with the viper and other earth-bound creatures which do not listen to Christ's teaching. The allegorical explanation pertains to the rich in this world:

> who lay one ear to earthly desires and stop up the other, adding new sins to past ones. Thus, they do not hear the voice of the enchanter (that is, the preachers). Indeed, they blind their eyes with earthly desires and rapine, so that they desire neither to hear nor to serve divine commands with their ears nor to regard heaven with their eyes nor even to consider him who is above the heavens and perform works of goodness and justice. (50)

In some way, the weasel is accused of being an allegory of those who do not want to listen to God's words through the preachers' mouths and would later have to listen to those words during the Day of Judgment.

None of that applies, however, to the way how Marie de France discusses the weasel, which performs a miraculous miracle and remains a secret for which there are no good answers available, especially because it would be rather speculative to identify this animal in the present context as an allegory or as a religious symbol. Various medieval authors such as Bruno Latini (1220–1294; *Libri di Tresoro*, L I, CL XXXI) and Konrad von Würzburg (*Die Goldene Schmiede*, ca. 1275; the Virgin Mary as a weasel which brings to life the ermine, the future killer of the basilisk, a symbol of evil and death) included references to the weasel, which later also became an important iconographic motif in Christian art, such as in Florence, on the door to the baptistry (ca. 1403–1424), where it represented Christ.[31]

The famous German mystic, philosopher, and theologian Meister Eckhart (ca. 1260–ca. 1328), discussing in one of his sermons the superiority of the power of herbs, water, or stones, refers to the very same motif of the weasel. As he relates, once a snake and a weasel fought against each other, and the latter then fetched an herb, wrapped that into something (?) else, and tossed it against the snake, which made the latter burst apart and die. Eckhart praises the weasel's wisdom, but he also adds that both words and stones have great properties through their correspondence with the stars and the heavenly powers. All of this, but particularly the weasel's deep knowledge of the herb's inner strength suggests to him that the soul ought to elevate itself into the highest sphere of all of creation and thus step into the light of the angels, which then would lead it over to the divine light.[32]

In Marie's "Eliduc," the situation for the protagonist proves to be most complicated, and only at the end when his wife voluntarily withdraws from their marriage can he pursue his new goal, marrying a British princess and enjoying complete happiness with her. The situation for Eliduc from the start was a complex one, having enjoyed his king's full confidence and trust until malignment and evil rumors destroyed his reputation. Being forced into exile, Eliduc turns to the Kingdom of Exeter where he liberates a besieged older king from his enemy. In that process, the princess falls in love with him, and he follows suit, although he is happily married back home. Nevertheless, after his political and military stance at the original king's court has been reestablished, Eliduc returns to Exeter and elopes with the princess. However, during their crossing of the Channel a mighty storm threatens to capsize their ship and kill them all. One of the sailors shouts out that this is all the result of Eliduc's adultery with the princess, who should be sacrificed to calm down God's anger as expressed by the storm. The princess, finally learning the truth about Eliduc's true family situation and being deeply distraught, collapses and falls into a coma. Her lover kills the sailor and steers the ship safely to their harbor. But the princess remains unconscious, and Eliduc places her body on an altar in a recently deceived hermit's cell. Only then does he see his wife, but he begins a steady ritual to pray in front of the altar and thus to the comatose princess.

One of the lady's maids discovers this practice and reveals it to her mistress. The worthy woman visits the chapel and so discovers the seemingly dead body of the foreign princess. At that moment, a weasel comes out of its hiding place and one of the lady's male servants slays it. All this would not be particularly sensational if then not another weasel appeared realizing the death of its mate. Soon thereafter, the second weasel reappears with a particular flower in its teeth which it then places into the mouth of the other one. This has a miraculous effect, reanimating the dead weasel, a true miracle, or secret.

The lady observes this phenomenon with astonishment, quickly calls upon the servant to catch or strike that weasel—explicitly not to kill, at least those words are missing here (1056)—and to secure the flower, the true secret. The servant is skillful enough to achieve the desired goal, striking the weasel so that it has to drop the flower, which the lady immediately picks up and uses it on the comatose maid, who is thus brought back to life. From here, both the weasel and the flower disappear from the narrative horizon, and we only hear about the two women conversing with each other, whereupon the wife then withdraws from her marriage to make room for the maid who truly loves Eliduc who returns the same feeling for her.[33]

The allegorical comments in the *Physiologus* do not fully help us to understand what is going on in this scene. Approaching it objectively and factually, we can only observe that there are two weasels, obviously companions, like husband and wife, or two female friends.[34] They exist in the area underneath the altar. The first one had crawled over the body of the seemingly dead maid, for which reason the servant had struck it as a kind of punishment and killed it (1035). The other weasel realizes the tragedy and yet knows of a miraculous herb or flower with which death can be reversed. Marie does not identify it any further and only comments on the red color of the petals. The lady immediately understands the meaning of this scene, because the first dead weasel is revived. But the lady does not call for the servant to kill either one of the two weasels; she only orders him to hold that animal back: "Retien la!" (1055). There is no interest in her mind to get the weasel killed as if it were an ordinary rat or another vermin. All she wants from the weasel is the flower, which she also secures with the servant's help, whereby she can awake the maid from her seeming death (1064). More the narrator does not divulge about the two weasels, though the one struck by the servant to secure the flower might be badly hurt.[35] It is hit, for sure, and thus has to drop the flower, but in contrast to the first weasel, it is not killed.

We can be certain that the weasel represents a mysterious creature that commands knowledge over life and death, that is, this animal is aware of what death means in the case of its companion and has sufficient intelligence and experience to identify a specific herb or flower that has the power to revive a killed being and bring it back to life. There are no explanations for this wonder in the text; the lady herself is greatly surprised and only reacts with great speed to gain access to that flower. But since we do not learn anything about the fate of the weasel or the flower, the narrator simply leaves us in the dark because the secret does not need to be solved. Instead, the *lai* then focuses on the lady's decision to make room for her husband to pursue his new love. She herself withdraws from this life, establishes a monastery, and becomes its abbess. Eliduc and his new wife live happily together, but in their old age, she joins the monastery as well, whereas Eliduc enters a monastic community as well.

All three people entertain a friendly correspondence with each other and closely follow God's commands, so there are no bad feelings about the new marriage on part of the first wife who actually welcomes the young woman as a friend and fellow sister. As is so often the case, Marie only touches upon the secret with the weasel and the magical flower, and then moves on after the young princess has been revived. We as the audience might be puzzled by and even bothered about the secret, but there is no interest by the poet to illuminate us further. We are supposed to be content with the secret and to acknowledge it as such. Little wonder that scholarship has hence not bothered much to investigate it further, although the flower known only to the weasel represents a true miracle that cannot be repeated. But there is a striking parallel to "Deus amanz" because the magical potion spilled out on the top of the mountain, a steroid, as we would say today, quickly produces many herbs and flowers to grow, all representatives of the lost love which the two young people had tried to achieve but lost again because of his masculine self-centeredness.

We could also speculate that the weasel or the red flower represents Christ since death is overcome, and life is restored. As is characteristic of Marie's verse narratives, both here and elsewhere the explanation for the secret hovers between Christianity and ancient pagan religions and cultures. But the poet, an Anglo-Norman speaker, succeeded at any rate to combine various old traditions to such an effect that she could utilize those ancient images and examples as metaphors of true love within her own courtly context.[36]

Yonec

In "Yonec," we are confronted with yet another secret; and obviously, Marie was deeply fond of operating with such miraculous elements to enrich and to deepen her narratives. In this case, an unhappy lady maintains a miserable life, literally her very old husband's prisoner, not allowed to speak with other people freely or to leave her tower where she is kept as a captive. This goes on for more than seven years, without her ever getting pregnant, when the woman is suddenly visited by a strange creature, a goshawk, which turns out to be a knight who is deeply in love with her and wants to enjoy an affair with her. Again, like in "Bisclavret," we face the situation of shape-shifting, but this time it is the opposite way around, the attractive young knight had taken on the shape of the hawk in order to visit his beloved. As the knight confirms to her, and hence to us, this ability to take on the appearance of a goshawk represents a secret: "Si li segrei sunt oscur" (123), but she would not have to be afraid of it.

The knight had loved her already for a long time, and yet he had not been able to visit her without the lady having expressed this wish explicitly (133). In modern terms, only through telepathy, or feelings of strong love, had he been able to visit her finally and present himself both as a goshawk and then as a knight and lover. Since he can assure her of his solid Christian faith, all of her concerns about this stranger are abated, and since she finds him extremely attractive, nothing stands in the way of them enjoying an affair with each other. She even gets the additional proof through a strategy she plays on the old woman guarding her (her husband's sister), pretending to be dangerously sick and being in need of a priest's support to give her the last rites. But in her place, the knight takes the host and drinks from the chalice, which is the ultimate proof of him being fully devoted to Christ. We are not informed how he managed to take on her shape, but neither the priest nor the old maid have any suspicion, so this critical test confirms the knight's faithfulness and hence the fact that he is not a demon, a devil, a ghost, or something like that.

However, neither the lady nor the audience ever learns anything about his background, his origin, his family, or his personal conditions, which is similar to the love affairs in "Guigemar," "Le Fresne," and "Eliduc." We are only told that he is a king and comes to see his beloved in another kingdom. But the experience of love granted to her by this man is all that she needs, which soon transforms her entire appearance, since her whole body begins to radiate once again. This, of course, makes her husband suspicious, and the secret is soon revealed to him. However, there is a double edge to this development because his discovery helps him to learn about his wife's adultery, but the true secret is the hawk-man, whose true identity and powers actually remain a secret both to his beloved and to her husband. The outcome of the *lai* does little to solve the issue, if that would have been the poet's intention in the first place. After all, the story is not titled after the mysterious knight, whom the narrator introduces as Muldumarec, an onomastic reference to ancient Celtic traditions upon which the Breton stories were apparently based and which transpire here in Marie's version in adapted form.

The perhaps earliest version of this shape-shifting knight visiting his beloved lady appears already in *The Compert Mongain* (*Birth of Mongan*) from the early twelfth century, contained in the manuscript *Lebhor eta h-Uidre* (*Book of the Dun Cow*). A very similar story forms part of the prose sections in *Dinnshenchus*, also from the early twelfth century but based on a didactic treatise on Irish topography from the ninth or tenth century. A fifteenth-century variant of this motif can be found in the *Book of Fermoy*, with Manann'an mac Lir assuming the form of Fiachna Lurga, king of the Ulster Dalriada.[37]

At any rate, Marie utilizes this motif to her full advantage, operating with a most mysterious secret which makes it possible for this knight—later we find out that he is a king—to visit his imprisoned lady and to enjoy her love to the fullest. However, tragedy strikes, as is often the case, the jealous husband figures out what is going on behind his back and has spikes attached to the window through which the hawk comes flying in which mortally wounds the knight in his bird shape when he returns to visit his lady.[38] The betrayal happens because the old woman spies on her lady and observes, with great fright, the transformation of the bird into a man (277). We never learn how this miracle is even possible, and who might have granted this power to the knightly lover, but it serves him well, just as in the case of Guigemar, to overcome a nearly impossible barrier to his lady and to spend a long time with her. Strangely, as much as he seems to know the future and can foretell what will happen to his lady after the betrayal and him having received his mortal wounds, he does not demonstrate any awareness of those spikes in the window set up as a trap. He informs her that she is pregnant with their son whom she is to call 'Yonec,' who would then grow up as a worthy and noble character: "he will avenge him and her, / he will kill their enemy" (331–32), which then is actually going to pass.

While the hawk-man then departs, leaving behind a trail of blood, she manages to climb out of a window and to gain her freedom, following the trail which takes her through a mysterious landscape, even through a hill ("boge," 346), then through a city and up to a castle. Having crossed several chambers, she finally reaches her lover's bedroom, where is resting on his bed expecting his death. He alerts her about the imminent danger which she would soon face when the people would learn about their lord's death as a result of his love for this lady: "it will be well known among my people / that they have lost me for your love" (405–06).

Before she departs again, as instructed by him, he turns over a magical ring which would make her husband forget everything that has happened with his wife and her lover. Then he gives her his sword which she is to keep for their son when he is reaching adulthood. The dying prince also foretells her in great detail where and when this moment of passing on the sword would happen—at a tomb in his honor placed in an abbey. Theses mysterious prophecies will later become true, although there are no explanations of how that might have been possible. Perhaps, as we might speculate, the knight knew of the spikes, knew that he would be killed, but he had to go through his destiny, parallel to or in imitation of Christ's passion.

Some indications might support such a reading which might seem rather speculative at first. When, many years later, the family visits that abbey and come across that tomb, the mourners inform them: "He had been king of this land; / there was never anyone so courtly. / He was attacked at Caerwent, / killed for the love of a lady" (515–18). The people had waited ever since for his son to come forward as the worthy successor to his slain father. Having heard those words, the lady calls out to her son and reveals the story of his origin, and also of the 'treason' committed against him by the old husband: "E cum si sires le trahi" (534). Almost in parallel to "Deus amanz," once having revealed the full background, she faints and falls onto the tomb, whereupon her son grabs the sword and cuts off the old man's head, who is now suddenly identified as "parastre" (540). His mother is honorably buried together with her original lover, and Yonec is chosen as the new king of their country, which concludes this *lai*.

Considering the knight's amazing foresight and actually active planning for the future of his son and his people, it seems most puzzling that he does not know in advance of the trap set for him which then kills him: "Dieus! qu'il ne sout la traison" (295; "God! he did not know the treason). But the lady is really responsible for the tragic development because she wishes her lover to come to her, which forces him to arrive, despite the mortal danger waiting for him (307–09). In fact, he had precisely predicted this outcome, as he confirms after having been fatally wounded: "I told you truly what would come of this" (321). Even earlier, he had warned his beloved to observe moderation, otherwise he would lose his life: "we will be betrayed in such a way / that I could never leave here / without dying of it" (208–10).

We would misread this narrative if we identified the hawk-man with Christ, although his death caused by the spikes placed in the window reminds us of the Passion. He dies out of his love for her and as a result of this love, so he is a very different person than the squire in "Deus amanz," who ultimately thought only about himself and tried to prove his masculinity to the king and his court. The hawk-man clearly confesses his faith in the Creator, performs the standard rites of all Christians, and thus is to be regarded as an ordinary member of courtly society, irrespective of his ability to shift his shape into a goshawk.

There are interesting parallels to Marie's "Lanval" where the mysterious figure is the fairy who comes to the protagonist's rescue. But there, Lanval ultimately departs from King Arthur's court, from human society, and disappears with his lady to the utopian world of Avalon, after he had experienced tremendous disappointments with the world of the courts and the vicious and untrustworthy king.[39] The secret figure in "Yonec" comes to the lady indirectly through her wishing his appearance, although she does not yet know him. And he has to leave again, at the end with mortal wounds, because her husband has succeeded in trapping his competitor. In "Lanval," the protagonist has to flee from this world to find happiness, in "Yonec" happiness comes to her, but not without death immediately lurking for her lover.[40]

CONCLUSION

To conclude, Marie de France operates most skillfully with many different kinds of secrets in her various *lais*. She knows fully well that those secrets would demand some explanations, but those never come forward. We are supposed to accept that a ring can make a jealous husband forget everything that happened in his miserable marriage. There are no further questions about the existence of a hawk-man, although both the lady and the old maid express great fright when they witness his appearance. The narrator does not make any effort to explain the existence of this secret, just as in the case of "Bisclavret." Human existence is not, as Marie indicates, all that firm in the traditional appearance of things and people. By the same token, traditional marriage is not necessarily the final ideal; instead, the poet presents many cases of unhappy marriages and projects alternatives which border, however, on the miraculous, and are consistently predicated on a secret. For this poet, the world in which her protagonists operate is filled with inexplicable forces, powers, objects, and creatures. All those receive full respect by the narrator, and as such they are acknowledged in their own agency. Marie does not probe the etiology of everyone and everything appearing on her narrative stage; instead, she fully recognizes, perhaps even appreciates, the great significance of secrets.

Human beings are not always supposed to understand everything, especially since they are driven by inexplicable forces, such as love and hatred. We are hence left behind perhaps more puzzled than illuminated, but there is always a deep sense of satisfaction with which Marie concludes her *lais*. Undoubtedly, this poet embraced secrets as essential components in a world which human epistemology and intelligence cannot fully fathom and penetrate.[41] By contrast, the power of love determines virtually every aspect of human society, which might be the biggest secret of them all. Because of love, death occurs numerous times, sorrow fills the world, but hope remains after all because the future looms nearby. There is a strong sense that those magical objects (ring, sword, ship, etc.) can be relied on to help the lovers to achieve their objectives, to be together with their partner. But the price to be paid is very high as well, death.

NOTES

1. R. Howard Bloch, *The Anonymous Marie de France* (Chicago and London: The University of Chicago Press, 2003); Glyn S. Burgess, *The Lais of Marie de France: Text and* Context (Athens, GA: The University of Georgia Press, 1987); A *Companion to Marie de France*, ed. Logan E. Whalen. Brill's Companions to the Christian Tradition, 27 (Leiden and Boston: Brill, 2011); Sharon Kinoshita and Peggy McCracken, *Marie de France: A Critical Companion.* Gallica, 24 (Cambridge: D. S. Brewer, 2012); Albrecht Classen, *Reading Medieval European Women Writers: Strong Literary Witnesses from the Past* (Frankfurt a. M.: Peter Lang, 2016), 83–118. For a concise summary of what we know about Marie, see Albrecht Classen, "Marie de France," *The Literary Encyclopedia*, ed. Robert Clark, online at: (http://www.litencyc.com/php/speople.php?rec=true&UID=5494; Sept. 2003); id., "Smart Marie de France Knew the Ways of this World—Medieval Advice Literature (Fables) and Social Criticism in Its Relevance for Us Today," *International Journal of History and Cultural Studies* 5.4 (2019), online at: https://www.arcjournals.org/pdfs/ijhcs/v5-i4/4.pdf (last accessed on May 16, 2022). There are numerous excellent websites, including Wikipedia, that provide solid information about Marie de France.

2. The best recent edition and translation into English is *The Lais by Marie de France: Text and Translation*, ed. and trans. Claire M. Waters (Peterborough, ON: broadview editions, 2018).

3. Laetitia Rampau, "Die *aventure* der *escriture*: Zu einem poetologischen Strukturprinzip der *Lais* von Marie de France," *Das Wunderbare in der arthurischen Literatur*, ed. Friedrich Wolfzettel (Tübingen: Max Niemeyer, 2003), 249–80; eadem, "Der Sprung nach Avalon: Ritter, Ross und Raum bei Marie de France und Chrétien de Troyes," *Raumerfahrung—Raumerfindung. Erzählte Welten des Mittelalters zwischen Orient und Okzident*, ed. eadem and Peter Ihring (Berlin: Akademie Verlag, 2005), 119–48.

4. Christian Buhr, "*dar nâch underkusten sich diu bilde mê danne tûsent stunt.* Automaten und Sprechpuppen in der deutschen und französischen Literatur des hohen Mittelalters," *Technik und Science-Fiction in Mittelalter und Früher Neuzeit*, ed. Brigitte Burrichter and Dorothea Klein. Würzburger Ringvorlesungen, 17 (Würzburg: Königshausen & Neumann, 2018), 87–108; see also E. R. Truitt, *Medieval Robots: Mechanism, Magic, Nature, and Art*. The Middle Ages Series (Philadelphia, PA: University of Pennsylvania Press, 2015). Strangely, both have overlooked entirely the important study by Lambertus Okken, *Das goldene Haus und die goldene Laube*:

Wie die Poesi ihren Herren das Paradies einrichtete. Amsterdamer Publikationen zur Sprache und Literatur, 72 (Amsterdam: Rodopi, 1987).

5. Much of Marie de France scholarship is dedicated to the topic of love in her works; see, for example, S. Foster Damon, "Marie de France: Psychologist of Courtly Love," *PMLA* 44 (1929): 96–96; Roger Dubuis, "La notion de *druerie* dans les Lais de Marie de France," *Le Moyen Âge Revue d'Histoire et de Philologie* 98 (1992): 391–413; cf. the contributions to *Amour et merveille: Les Lais de Marie de France*. Collection Unichamp, 46 (Paris: Champion, 1995); Sharon Kinoshita, "Two for the Price of One: Courtly Love and Serial Polygamy in the *Lais* of Marie de France," *Arthuriana* 8.2 (1998): 23–55; Tovi Bibring, "'Quant il le pout partir de sei!' Les départs amoureux dans les Lais de Marie de France," *Atant m'en vois: Figures du départ au Moyen Âge*, ed. Nelly Labère and Luca Pierdominici. Piccola biblioteca di studi medievali e rinascimentali, 4 (Fano: Aras edizioni, 2019), 333–62; Elizabeth Liendo, "The Wound that Bleeds: Violence and Feminization in the *Lais* of Marie de France," *Neophilologus* 104 (2020): 19–32.

6. I have regularly consulted the *Anglo Norman Dictionary* to verify Waters translation: https://www.anglo-norman.net/entry/ (last accessed on Jan. 31, 2022).

7. Sarah Eddings, "Infertility and the Marvel-Less in Marie de France's *Deus Amanz*," *Romance Notes* 57.1 (2017): 157–65; Ju Ok Yoon, "Lettre, Love, and Magic in Marie de France's *Les Deus Amanz*," *The Journal of English Language and Literature* 58.3 (2012): 427–46 (with an English summary); June Hall McCash, "The Mulier Mediatrix in the Deus Amanz of Marie de France," *Courtly Arts and the Art of Courtliness*, ed. Keith Busby and Christopher Kleinhenz (Cambridge: D. S. Brewer, 2006), 455–65; Minnie B. Sangster, trans. Walter A. Blue, "A Study of the Legend and the Location of 'Les Deux Amanz' from the Middle Ages to Modern Times," *Le Cygne: Journal of the International Marie de France Society* 4 (1998): 11–27.

8. Gottfried von Strassburg, *Tristan and Isolde, with Ulrich von Türheim's Continuation*, ed. and trans., with an intro. by William T. Whobrey (Indianapolis, IN, and Cambridge: Hackett Publishing, 2020), ch. 11, 96–106, here 102–03: "Concerning my lady's skill at medicine and her treatment of the patient, I will keep it short. Within twenty days she was able to help him be tolerable to everyone so that no one avoided him because of the wound but was instead willing to stay with him." See also the mostly unjustly ignored study by Peter Meister, *The Healing Female in the German Courtly Romance*. Göppinger Arbeiten zur Germanistik, 523 (Göppingen: Kümmerle, 1990); more broadly, Tomas Tomasek, *Gottfried von Straßburg* (Stuttgart: Philipp Reclam jun., 2007); Christoph Huber, *Gottfried von Straßburg: Tristan*. Klassiker-Lektüren, 3. 3rd, newly rev. and expanded ed. (2000; Berlin: Erich Schmidt Verlag, 2013).

9. *The Trotula: An English Translation of the Medieval Compendium of Women's Medicine*, ed. and trans. by Monica H. Green. The Middle Ages Series (2001; Philadelphia, PA: University of Pennsylvania Press, 2002); see also Green's individual studies on this topic, *Women's Healthcare in the Medieval West: Texts and Contexts*. Collected Studies Series, 680 (Aldershot: Ashgate, 2000); Pietro Greco, *Trotula: la prima donna medico d'Europa*. Profilo di donna, 7 (Rome: L'asino d'oro edizioni, 2020). For women's role in late medieval Europe, see Britta-Juliane Kruse,

Verborgene Heilkünste: Geschichte der Frauenmedizin im Spätmittelalter. Quellen und Forschungen zur Literatur- und Kulturgeschichte, 5 (Berlin and New York: Walter de Gruyter, 1996).

10. For a somewhat daring thesis regarding this wound and its effect upon Guigemar, see Elizabeth Liendo, "The Wound That Bleeds: Violence and Feminization in the *Lais* of Marie de France," *Neophilologus* 104.1 (2020): 19–32. For older accounts with similar themes, such as in Geoffrey of Wales's *Itinerarium Kambriae*, see Leslie Brook, "Guigemar and the White Hind," *Medium Ævum* 56 (1987): 94–101; cf. also Antoinette Knapton, *Mythe et psychologie chez Marie de France*. North Carolina Studies in the Romance Languages and Literatures, 142 (Chapel Hill, NC: University of North Carolina Department of Romance Languages, 1975), 69.

11. Matilda Tomaryn Bruckner, "Speaking Through Animals in Marie de France's *Lais* and *Fables*," *A Companion to Marie de France* (2011), 157–85; see also Ashley Lee, "The Hind Episode in Marie de France's *Guigemar* and Medieval Vernacular Poetics," *Neophilologus* 93.2 (2009): 191–200.

12. June Hall McCash, "The Curse of the White Hind and the Cure of the Weasel: Animal Magic in the *Lais* of Marie de France," *Literary Aspects of Courtly Culture: Selected Papers from the Seventh Triennial Congress of the International Courtly Literature Society; University of Massachusetts, Amherst, USA, 27 July – 1 August 1992*, ed. Donald Maddox, Sara Sturm-Maddox (Cambridge: D. S. Brewer, 1994), 199–209; e.g., 204.

13. Karin Lerchner, *Lectulus Floridus: Zur Bedeutung des Bettes in Literatur und Handschriftenillustrationen des Mittelalters* (Cologne, Weimar, and Vienna: Böhlau Verlag, 1993); Hollie L. S. Morgan, *Beds and Chambers in Late Medieval England* (Woodbridge, Suffolk: Boydell&Brewer, 2017).

14. For the European context, see the contributions to *Partonopeus in Europe: An Old French Romance and Its Adaptations*, ed, and with an intro. by Catherine Hanley, Mario Longtin, and Penny Eley. *Mediaevalia* 25.2, Special Issue (Binghamton, NY: The Center for Medieval and Renaissance Studies, 2004). Konrad von Würzburg, *Partonopier und Meliur*, ed. Karl Bartsch. Deutsche Neudrucke. Reihe: Texte des Mittelalters (Berlin: Walter de Gruyter, 1970); for a review of the relevant research literature, though by now a little dated, see Rüdiger Brandt, *Konrad von Würzburg*. Erträge der Forschung, 249 (Darmstadt: Wissenschaftliche Buchgesellschaft, 1987), 152–73; Anja Kühne, *Vom Affekt zum Gefühl: Konvergenzen von Theorie und Literatur im Mittelalter am Beispiel von Konrads von Würzburg "Partonopier und Meliur."* Göppinger Arbeiten zur Germanistik, 713 (Göppingen: Kümmerle, 2004).

15. Cf. Sebastian I. Sobecki, "A Source for the Magical Ship in the *Partonopeu de Blois* and Marie de France's *Guigemar*," *Notes and Queries* 48.3 (2001): 220–22.

16. Logan Whalen, "A Matter of Life or Death: Fecundity and Sterility in Marie de France's *Guigemar*," *Shaping Courtliness in Medieval France*, ed. Daniel E. O'Sullivan and Laurie Shepard (Woodbridge: D. S. Brewer, 2013), 139–149.

17. Reimund Kvideland, "Schiff," *Enzyklopädie des Märchens*, ed. Rolf Wilhelm Brednich. Vol. 11.3 (Berlin and New York: Walter de Gruyter, 2004), 1416–21. See also Michael McCaughan, "Symbolism of Ships and the Sea: From Ship of the Church to Gospel Trawler," *Folk Life* 40.1 (2001): 54–61.

18. Albrecht Classen, *Freedom, Imprisonment, and Slavery in the Pre-Modern World: Cultural-Historical, Social-Literary, and Theoretical Reflections*. Fundamentals of Medieval and Early Modern Culture, 25 (Berlin and Boston: Walter de Gruyter, 2021), 110–19, with more secondary literature there.

19. James Paz, *Nonhuman Voices in Anglo-Saxon Literature and Material Culture* (Manchester: Manchester University Press, 2017); see now the contributions to *Dingkulturen: Objekte in Literatur, Kunst und Gesellschaft der Vormoderne*, ed. Anna Mühlherr, Heike Sahm, Monika Schausten, and Bruno Quast. Literatur—Theorie—Geschichte, 9 (Berlin and Boston: Walter de Gruyter, 2018); to *Abecedarium: erzählte Dinge im Mittelalter*, ed. Peter Glasner, Sebastian Winkelsträter, and Birgit Zacke (Berlin: Schwabe Verlag, 2019); see also the monograph by Bettina Bildhauer, *Medieval Things: Agency, Materiality, and Narratives of Objects in Medieval German Literature and Beyond*, Interventions: New Studies in Medieval Culture (Columbus, OH: The Ohio State University Press, 2020).

20. Much has been written on "Guigemar," but rather little about the secrets we have identified here. See, for instance, Kinoshita and McCracken, *Marie de France* (2012), 24–26, 51–52, 72–75, et passim.

21. Enrique Galván Alvarez, "Aspectos místicos y religiosos del amor cortés en *Guigemar*, de María de Francia," *Nerter* 11 (Fall 2007): 97–105.

22. Thomas L. Reed Jr., "Marie de France's *Guigemar* as Art of Interpretation (and Ambiguity)," *Speaking Images: Essays in Honor of V. A. Kolve*, ed. Robert F. Yeager and Charlotte C. Morse (Asheville, NC: Pegasus Books, 2001), 1–26.

23. *Biographies des troubadours: textes provençaux des XIIIe et XIVe siècles*, ed. Jean Boutière, Alexander Hermann Schutz, and Irénée Marcel Cluzel. Bibliothèque Méridionale, First Series, 27 (Paris: Didier, 1950), 245–49.

24. For further comments, see Waters, ed. and trans. (2018), 145, n. 2.

25. *Guillaume de Palerne: An English Trans. of the 12th Century French Verse Romance*, trans. and ed. Leslie A. Sconduto (Jefferson, NC, and London: McFarland, 2004), 261–340. Cf. eadem, *Metamorphoses of the Werewolf: A Literary Study from Antiquity Through the Renaissance* (Jefferson, NC, and London: McFarland, 2008); Gaël Milin, *Les chiens de Dieu: la représentation du loup-garou en Occident, XIe–XXe siècles* (Brest: Centre de recherche bretonne et celtique, Université de Bretagne occidentale, 1993); Matthew Beresford, *The White Devil: The Werewolf in European Culture* (London: Reaktion Books, 2013); Manfred Bambeck, *Wiesel und Werwolf: typologische Streifzüge durch das romanische Mittelalter und die Renaissance*. Landeskundliche Vierteljahrsblätter, 36.1 (Stuttgart: Steiner, 1990). The old studies by Wilhelm Hertz and Rudolf Leubuscher, *Der Werwolf/Werwölfe und Tierverwandlungen im Mittelalter: Zwei ungekürzte Quellenwerke in einem Band* (1862; Norderstedt: Books on Demand, 2018), continue to be of great value for us because of their global anthropological and folkloric perspectives. The werewolf motif has been highly popular also in contemporary culture, both in movies and novels; see, for example, Brent A. Stypczynski, *The Modern Literary Werewolf: A Critical Study of the Mutable Motif* (Jefferson, NC, and London: McFarland, 2013). For the ancient sources of the werewolf myth, see Daniel Ogden, *The Werewolf in the Ancient World* (Oxford: Oxford University Press, 2020, online; in print in 2021).

26. There is much more to the myth of the werewolf than I can summarize here. It was present already in classical antiquity; there are similar phenomena in other non-European cultures, and we hear about the werewolf really throughout times in global terms, which is often documented in surprisingly good online encyclopedias and others, such as *Wikipedia*. See, however, Stephen O. Glosecki, "Wolf and Werewolf," *Medieval Folklore: An Encyclopedia of Myths, Legends, Tales, Beliefs, and Customs*, ed. Carl Lindahl, John McNamara, and John Lindow (Santa Barbara, CA, Denver, CO, and Oxford: ABC-CLIO, 2000), vol. 2, 1057–61. See now Eleanor Hodgson, "Rewriting the Werewolf: Transformations of Bisclavret in Guillaume de Palerne," *French Studies Bulletin: A Quarterly Supplement* 37 (138) (2016): 9–13.

27. As is often the case with Marie's *lais*, they invite many different interpretations, often driven by new theoretical approaches, even if those do not necessarily uncover new insights; see, for instance, Emily McLemore, "Queer Bodies, Sexual Possibility, and Violent Misogyny in Bisclavret," *Le Cygne: Journal of the International Marie de France Society* 7.1 (2020): 9–31; Dorothy Gilbert, "The Beast in You: On Teaching Bisclavret," *Le Cygne: Journal of the International Marie de France Society* 7.2 (2020): 53–68; Ahmed Muhammed Faleh Banisalamah, "Gender, Reason, and Androgyny in the Role of Righteousness in Marie de France's 'Bisclavret,'" *Interactions: Ege Journal of British and American Studies/Ege İngiliz ve Amerikan İncelemeleri Dergisi* 26.1–2 (2017): 55–63; Jennifer K. Cox, "Symbiotic Werewolves and Cybernetic Anchoresses: Premodern Posthumans in Medieval Literature," *Quidditas: Online Peer-reviewed Journal of the Rocky Mountain Medieval and Renaissance Association* 36 (2015): 84–105; Victoria Blud, "Wolves' Heads and Wolves' Tales: Women and Exile in *Bisclavret* and *Wulf and Eadwacer*," *Exemplaria: A Journal of Theory in Medieval and Renaissance Studies* 26.4 (2014): 328–46.

28. *Physiologus*, trans. Michael J. Curley (Chicago and London: University of Chicago Press, 1979); cf. now Nikolaus Henkel, Studien zum Physiologus im Mittelalter. Hermaea: Neue Folge, 38 (Tübingen: Max Niemeyer, 1976); see also the contributions to *Bestiari tardoantichi e medievali: i testi fondamentali della zoologia sacra cristiana*, ed. Francesco Zambon with Roberta Capelli, Silvia Cocco, Claudia Cremonini, Manuela Sanson, and Massimo Villa. Classici della letteratura europea (Florence: Bompiani, 2018), and to *Christus in natura: Quellen, Hermeneutik und Rezeption des 'Physiologus,'* ed. Zbyněk Kindschi Garský and Rainer Hirsch-Luipold. Studies of the Bible and Its Reception, 11 (Berlin and Boston: Walter de Gruyter, 2019). For an art-historical approach, see Christian Montésinos, *Les étranges symboles des cathédrales, basiliques et églises de la France médiévale. Les lieux de la tradition* (Paris: Éditions Dervy, 2018). For more symbolist readings of the weasel, see Thomas Shearer Duncan, "The Weasel in Religion, Myth and Superstition," *Washington University Studies* 12 (1924–1925): 33–66; see also this online bibliography dedicated to the weasel: http://bestiary.ca/beasts/beastbiblio150.htm (last accessed on Jan. 31, 2022).

29. *Physiologus*, trans. Curley (1979), 1.

30. Marie de France, *Fables*, ed. and trans. Harriet Spiegel. Medieval Academy Reprints for Teaching (Toronto, Buffalo, and London: University of Toronto Press, 1994).

31. S. Braunfels, "Wiesel," *Lexikon der christlichen Ikonographie*, ed. Engelbert Kirschbaum SJ, Vol. 4: *Allgemeine Ikonographie* (Rome, Freiburg i. Br., Basel, and Vienna: Herder, 1972), 528. For the passage in Konrad's poem of the *Goldene Schmiede*, ed. Edward Schröder. 2nd ed. (Göttingen: Vandenhoeck & Ruprecht, 1969), see vv. 156–65; cf. 157–58. Cf. Sabine Obermaier, "Frauenlob und der 'Geblümte Stil,'" *Handbuch Frauenlob*, ed. Claudia Lauer and Uta Störmer-Caysa, together with Anna Sara Lahr. Beiträge zur älteren Literaturgeschichte (Heidelberg: Universitätsverlag Winter, 2018), 147–79; here 156–60.

32. Meister Eckhart, *Deutsche Predigten und Traktate*, ed. and trans. Josef Quint (Munich: Carl Hanser Verlag, 1955), sermon 18, 235.

33. For a somewhat daring, but I believe successful approach to identifying the essential narrative motif here with the love relationship between the famous French philosopher Peter Abelard (d. 1142) and his mistress and later wife, Heloise, see Albrecht Classen, "Guildeluëc in Marie de France's 'Eliduc' as the Avatar of Heloise? The Destiny of Two Twelfth-Century Women," *Quaestiones Medii Aevii Novae* (Poland) 20 (2015): 395–412.

34. See Waters, ed. and trans. (2018), 351, n. 1

35. Although the appearance of these two animals plays a significant role in the *lai*, if they are not even the fulcrum of the entire sequence of events, transforming death to life, scholars have tended to ignore the weasels altogether; see, for instance, Kinoshita and McCracken, *Marie de France* (2012), 125–30; Bloch, *The Anonymous Marie* (2003), 83–89, et passim. Glyn S. Burgess, "Marie de France and the Anonymous Lays," *A Companion to Marie de France* (2011), 116–56; here 151, mentions the weasels in passing. But see June Hall McCash, "The Curse of the White Hind and the Cure of the Weasel" (1994), for further reflections on the symbolic meaning of those animals.

36. Danielle Gurevitch, "The Weasel, the Rose and Life after Death: Representations of Medieval Physiology in Marie de France's *Eliduc*," *Restoring the Mystery of the Rainbow: Literature's Refraction of Science*, ed. Valeria Tinkler-Villani and C. C. Barfoot (Amsterdam: Brill/Rodopi, 2011), 209–23; Jacques Ribard, "Le Lai d'Yonec est-il une allégorie chrétienne? *The Legend of Arthur in the Middle Ages: Studies Presented to A. H. Diverres by Colleagues, Pupils, and Friends*, ed. P. B. Grouot, R. A. Lodge, C. E. Pickford, and E. K. C. Varty (Cambridge: D. S. Brewer, 1983), 160–69.

37. Tom Peete Cross, "The Celtic Origin of the Lay of Yonec," *Studies in Philology* 11 (1913): 26–60; here 29–33; online at: https://www.jstor.org/stable/pdf/4171667.pdf. Cross offers many other parallels between Marie's "Yonec" and medieval Irish literature. See also Marbury Bladen Ogle, "Some Theories of Irish Literary Influence and the Lay of *Yonec*," *Romanic Review* 10 (1919): 123–48; for more recent studies of this phenomenon of Irish-Celtic sources used by Marie de France, see R. N. Illingworth, "Celtic Tradition and the *Lai of Yonec*," *Études Celtiques* 9 (1961): 501–20; Joanne Findon, "Supernatural Lovers, Liminal Women, and the Female Journey," *Florilegium: The Journal of the Canadian Society of Medievalists/La revue de la Société canadienne des médiévistes* 30 (2013): 27–52; Matthieu Boyd, "The Ring, the Sword, the Fancy Dress, and the Posthumous Child: Background to the Element

of Heroic Biography in Marie de France's *Yonec*," *Romance Quarterly* 55.3 (2008): 205–30.

38. Jean-Marie Kauth, "Barred Windows and Uncaged Birds: The Enclosure of Woman in Chrétien de Troyes and Marie de France," *Medieval Feminist Forum* 46.2 (2010): 34–67.

39. Cassidy Leventhal, "Finding Avalon: The Place and Meaning of the Otherworld in Marie de France's *Lanval*," *Neophilologus* 98.2 (2014): 193–204; Albrecht Classen, "Outsiders, Challengers, and Rebels in Medieval Courtly Literature: The Problem with the Courts in Courtly Romances," *Arthuriana* 26.3 (2016): 67–90; Will Hasty, *The Medieval Risk-Reward Society: Courts, Adventure, and Love in the European Middle Ages* (Columbus, OH: The Ohio State University Press, 2016), 176–87.

40. Emma Campbell, "Political Animals: Human/Animal Life in *Bisclavret* and *Yonec*," *Exemplaria: A Journal of Theory in Medieval and Renaissance Studies* 25.2 (2013): 95–109; Haoyu Irene Xia, "La Symbolique des oiseaux de proie dans trois lais des douzième et treizième siècles," *The French Review: Journal of the American Association of Teachers of French* 89.4 (2016): 93–105; Catherine Nicolas, "'Sun parastre ad le chief tolu': Vengeance, jugement et amour dans le lai d'*Yonec*," *Babel: Littératures Plurielles* 42 (2020): 115–32.

41. For a variety of critical approaches, see, for example, Joanne Findon, "Supernatural Lovers, Liminal Women, and the Female Journey," *Florilegium: The Journal of the Canadian Society of Medievalists/La revue de la Société canadienne des médiévistes* 30 (2013): 27–52; Anna Gęsicka, "Sacrum et profanum dans Yonec de Marie de France (XIIe siècle)," *Quêtes Littéraires* 3 (2013): 9–15; Seeta Chaganti, "The Space of Epistemology in Marie de France's 'Yonec,'" *Romance Studies* 28.2 (2010): 71–83.

Chapter Two

Nordic Sagas and the *Mabinogi*

Secrets in Medieval Icelandic and Welsh Literature or the Appearance of the Otherworld in the Human Context

To do real justice to the issue of the secret in the medieval world, or in medieval literature at large, we would need to cast our net as widely as possible, which thus would mean also to include relevant examples of secrets—or mysteries—as discussed in the literary framework beyond the "narrow" Continental limits. I would have also liked to consider the situation of contemporary Arabic, Hebrew, or Persian literature, but my own competence in that regard is rather underdeveloped, or non-existent. Instead, in the present chapter, going in the very opposite direction, I focus on literary examples from both the Scandinavian north and in Wales, which will underscore the great importance that this topic has had throughout time and across the world as a universal phenomenon of great significance.

As we will observe here once again, secrets function often as expressions of deep forces beyond the human limits which emerge sometimes and then disappear again, which the literary protagonists observe with awe, fear, respect, and also deep puzzlement. If the observations and interpretations offered here gain traction as solid evidence, we could then expand on them and invite other scholars to consider what non-European poets had to say about this phenomenon.

Many times, oral poetry and heroic poetry, which were often very similar to each other or even the same, touched on obscure forces which certainly exist but mostly hide from people's ordinary awareness. Of course, with the arrival of the Christian Church also north of the Alps in late antiquity, much of the ancient knowledge was increasingly repressed or simply went into hiding away from public view. However, poets throughout the centuries engaged with those after all and allowed brief glimpses of those aspects and forces to surface and make their presence known, at least fleetingly.[1]

Some of the most dramatic examples would be the Old English *Beowulf* (ca. 700) where the Swedish protagonist arrives in Denmark and volunteers to fight first against the man-eating monster Grendel and then against his horrendous mother who is hiding deep down in the sea in a cave from ancient times, as documented by the mighty weapons scattered around there. Beowulf succeeds in securing victory over both creatures, but at the end of his life, he has to fight against yet another monster, the dragon, hiding in its lair within a mountain, who then wounds him mortally, although it has to die as well. In short, Beowulf battles against secret forces and ensures that they are excised from human society, even at the cost of his own life.[2] Whereas cannibalistic figures such as Grendel and his mother are rather uncommon in medieval literature,[3] dragons played a huge role, which now can be explained better by way of identifying them as emblematic creatures representing secrets, or the underworld, the other dimension, the depth, or the roots of all existence, without having a really religious connotation.[4] As the Icelandic sagas and the *Mabinogi*, among many other texts, indicate, as much as human society existed all by itself, as much it was also challenged by other forces that remain inexplicable and dark, whether they are threatening or simply making their presence felt. When protagonists such as Beowulf and Siegfried kill their respective dragons they put a lock on the door to the underworld and thus end the communication with the ominous dimension beyond human life. By contrast, Tristan's killing of the dragon in Ireland only serves him to gain the privilege to claim Isolde's hand in marriage for his uncle, King Mark, such as in Gottfried von Straßburg's *Tristan* (1210). There, the dragon is certainly ravaging the country, threatening even the king and his court, but it does not represent a secret, a dark force, or a mystery.

Secrets emerge, of course, many times in Old Icelandic literature, especially in *Saga* texts, such as in the famous *Egil's Saga*,[5] written down in the early thirteenth century but recording events that date back almost three hundred years to the Viking age. It is one of many other sagas, such as the *Njál's Saga* or the *Laxdaela Saga*, all of which contain both much historical information about land settlements in the north, especially Iceland, and about conflicts between individuals and entire families. However, apart from accounts concerning battles, murder, law-making, legal courts, political meetings, and setting up farms or voyaging across the northern Atlantic, the Baltic Sea, or even further south for the purpose of pillaging or raiding—as if that were a very ordinary activity they commonly carried out during the summer months—we also learn much about the people's worldviews, attitudes, mentality, imagination, fears, desires, and concepts about nature and spirits.

Before I engage with the medieval *Mabinogi*, let us first examine some of the Icelandic evidence for the specific use of secrets in epistemological terms.

In *Egil's Saga*, for instance, perhaps composed by Snorri Sturluson in the early thirteenth century, we learn immediately that people believe that Ulf, the son of Bjalfi and Halbera, is a shapeshifter who wanders at night and controls people thereby (3). The narrator refers to a man called Bjorgolf who is identified as a descendent of a mountain giant, "as his strength and size bore witness" (10).[6] Occasionally we hear of berserks, such as those in King Harald's army (14), though there are no further comments about them, not even any qualifying remarks. At least we are told that they could not be injured in battle because "iron could not bite" them (14)—maybe animal warriors, as Vincent Samson has suggested.[7] Then there is a note about the sorceress Thorarna in Skallagrim and some of her men who are identified as shapeshifters (42), the meaning of which remains rather obscure. However, other figures describe them in fearful terms: "they are more like giants than human beings in size and appearance" (42).

Although somewhat unrelated, the narrator then includes an explanation about those shapeshifters who "take on the character of animals, or went berserk, became so strong in this state that no one was a match for them, but also that just after it wore off they were left weaker than usual" (48). They experience an extraordinary frenzy and become frightfully powerful, but only for a very short period, which leaves everyone around them rather baffled because this secret is never solved. We are simply confronted with those figures and cannot penetrate any deeper into their personality and powers. In some cases, we even learn that shapeshifting is actually commonly identified as a unique and important characteristic of important figures, such as Onund, who is introduced as follows, revealing the complexity of this secret feature in mighty persons: "He was well-built and the strongest man in his district. Not everyone agreed that he was not a shape-shifter. Onund had often travelled to other countries" (145).

In *Njál's Saga*, probably contemporary to the *Egil's Saga*, there are some fleeting comments on magic, and shape-shifters, but most noticeable is a remark on a berserk named Otryng whom everybody fears greatly (178).[8] He is said to be untouchable by fire or swords, which Thangbrand, the son of Count Vilbaldus of Saxony, who had been sent to Iceland on behalf of King Olaf Tryggvason to preach the new Christian faith, then uses to challenge the people and to make them accept the new Christian faith. They build three fires, the first blessed by the heathens, the second by the Christian missionary, and the third unblessed (178). Thangbrand then sets the condition: "If the berserk fears the one which I blessed but walks through your fire, then you must accept the faith" (178). The berserk then indeed walks through the first fire without suffering any injuries or harm. But he does not want to walk through the second fire because he claims that he is "burning all over" (179). Afraid of evil consequences for him and his people, he attacks with his sword, though to no avail because of the power of the Christian God: "Thangbrand struck him on the arm with his crucifix and a great miracle happened: the sword fell from the berserk's hand. Then Thanbrand drove his sword into the berserk's chest, and Gudleif hacked at his arm and cut it off" (180). The berserk is then finished off, and Gest and his people accept the Christian faith as promised in their agreement—but certainly under duress.

Neither the origin nor the true character of this berserk is fully explained, but since he was the last bulwark, so to speak, against the spread of Christianity at that location, the narrator does not see any need to expand on this episode further or to engage with the secret of the berserk or the secret of the Christian faith. It all remains a secret, and probably for good reasons because the Christian poet did not want to give more credit to this pagan culture than necessary.

We could also identify Njál's ability to foresee the future as one of the major secrets, especially because this skill is not associated with the Christian faith, is not conditioned by his learning or wisdom, and constitutes an internal power that he possesses. More clearly, as we actually often hear in medieval literature, there are at times references to monsters, such as when Thorkel Bully travels to the Baltic Sea and encounters "a creature half-man, half beast" (202), which he battles for a long time and can finally kill. He also has to fend off a flying dragon south of Estonia, which is only mentioned just in passing without any explanations. All that matters for the narrator is that he can report these astounding feats of this mighty man and then has them depicted in wood carvings in his room back home (203). The secrets related here are not divulged and only serve to increase the protagonists' fame and glory, or their ominous, evil, and uncanny character. However, the narrator clearly indicates that those berserks or shapeshifters belong to an ancient culture and possess extraordinary strength which finds no real explanation. This is, in fact, closely related to the account of the Middle High German *Nibelungenlied* (ca. 1200) where the Netherlandish hero Siegfried is said to have defeated the king of the dwarfs, Alberich, and thus gained not only possession of the infamous invisibility cloak, but also of the rulership of the underworld. Moreover, he killed a dragon and took a bath in its blood, which made his body impenetrable and completely protected, apart from a little spot on his shoulder blade, sort of his Achilles' heel.[9] We could call this fictional imagination, mythical projection, or heroic idealization, but this does not change the fact that neither Siegfried's superhuman strength, his victory over the dwarfs, and his defeat of the dragon remain inexplicable, incomprehensible, and hence a secret. The Icelandic sagas contain many complementary elements and are equally little interested in offering rational answers; instead, we are confronted with mysteries or simply secrets.

This phenomenon finds also a very common expression in some people's ability to prophesy the future, such as in the case of the old woman Saeunn who is belittled by the family members for her allegedly foolish predictions but who truly knows what the future will hold, often with catastrophic consequences (214). The same applies to the man named Ranolf Thorsteinson who has a vision and recognizes in it the future doom of Njál and his family. But as ominous as this vision proves to be, the only reaction is that Hjaltic says: "You have seen a witch-ride; it always occurs before great events" (215). Subsequently, however, other people also recognize signs of the imminent attack and find even evidence to confirm the truth of their observations. Njál himself comments: "I look around the room and imagine that I see both gable-walls gone, and the table food all covered with blood" (217). When Grim and Helgi return home much earlier than anticipated, which was predicted by Bergthora, the imminent doom becomes even clearer, which ultimately leads to the burning of the entire house with the family in it. However, there are no rational explanations for the various individuals' ability to predict the future. As much as the poet is deeply concerned with legal issues and the formation of a rational and transparent legal system, as much he invested in the topics of the supernatural, withholding in that process any specific explanations because, as we may say, the secret is only to be observed, but not to be understood.[10]

Then there are also dreams which help the individual to foresee what will happen soon thereafter, such as in the case of Flosi (232), a feature which finds many parallels in medieval literature, including the *Nibelungenlied* begins with Kriemhild's ominous dream about her falcon which is torn to pieces by two eagles (stanzas 13–14). The falcon represents Siegfried, her future husband, who will be killed by Hagen, King Gunther's court steward, with the king's indirect approval.[11] For the poet, there is no doubt about the validity of this, and several other dreams in this epic poem, and the composer of *Njál's Saga* harbored equally little doubt about that secret phenomenon. Why and how this was possible, however, is never revealed.

There are also references to magic, so when we hear of a man "named Svan who lived in Bjarnarfjord on a farm called Svansho, to the north of Steingrimsfjord. Svan was skilled in magic; he was the brother of Hallgerd's mother, and he was overbearing and vicious to deal with" (20). We do not learn what kind of magic he could practice until somewhat later when he can conjure fog and monsters (24), which hold back the enemies for some time, but there is no doubt about his superior powers and their secret impact on this world.[12] The poet, however, only touches on this mysterious power and quickly moves on, as if the appearance of magic would not need any further comments. As powerful and meaningful *Njál's Saga* certainly is, as reflected also by many scholarly efforts,[13] as puzzling and resisting it proves to be when it comes to secretive forces, dream prophecies, and berserks.

When we briefly consider the contemporary *Laxdaela Saga* (ca. 1245), we also face the topic of life after death and the trouble caused by a deceased vexing the living. Killer-Hrapp was a disturber of peace all of his life, but after he had passed away, things do not improve. On the contrary: "his corpse would not rest in its grave; people say he murdered more of his servants in his hauntings after death and caused grievous harm to most of his neighbors" (78).[14] Although Killer-Hrapp operates only as a ghost, he seems to exert tremendous power in concrete physical terms and is able to cause even death to his former servants. The situation is getting so bad that the "farm at Hrappstead had to be abandoned and Vigdis, Hrapp's widow, went west to her brother Throstein Black the Wise" (78). People then consult with the wise Hoskuld Dalla-Kollsson who visits the grave, has the body dug up, and reburied far away, and achieves thereby at least some results, though he cannot lay to rest the uncanny phenomenon altogether: "After this, Hrapp's hauntings abated a little" (78). Tragically, however, soon thereafter, once his son Sumarlidi has taken over the farm, "He went mad, and died soon afterwards" (78), as if his father's evil spirit had invaded and then destroyed him.[15]

In a later episode, we learn that Killer-Hrapp's spirit had the power to return and threaten the lives of the living, such as one of the farmhands in the service of Olaf Hoskuldsson (Olaf the Peacock). Although Olaf does not want to believe him that the ghost is about to kill him if he enters the barn again, he accompanies hione evening to drive the cattle back in, and he carries his valuable spear with him for potentially great danger. The farmhand enters the barn but comes flying out of it because the apparition has appeared to him: "Killer-Hrapp is standing in the door of the byre and he tried to catch hold of me, but I've had enough of wrestling with him" (103). This forces Olaf to confront the ghost himself, and a bitter fight erupts in which his spear is broken. However, when Olaf then rushes against him, "Hrapp sank into the ground where he had been standing, and that was the end of their encounter" (103). As the narrator insists, however, the conflict was real as the broken spear demonstrated, with Olaf holding the shaft and Hrapp the spearhead. The next day, Olaf and some of his men visit Hrapp's grave, dig out the corpse, burn the undecayed bones, and scatter the ashes in the sea. The narrator does not comment any further about the reality or fantasy of this report, and yet emphasizes that "Olaf found his spear-head there" (103). Subsequently, no further ghostly appearance bothered people, which finishes the story of this unpleasant man, Killer-Hrapp, who defied all norms of human life by exerting his power even long after his death in most concrete forms.[16] Since his body had not decayed, the normal forces of nature did not apply to him, but there are no explanations for this phenomenon.

Little wonder then that the narrator repeatedly refers to the power of dreams witnessed both by Olaf (117) and Gudrun (119–22), which appear to predict the future and thus connect the individual with another dimension of existential powers. Significantly, however, not all those who hear about the content of a dream simply accept it, such as in the case of An the Black, whose dream about a horrible woman who attacked him with a knife and cut him open is met by Kjartan's and the others' laughter (171). It remains uncertain here whether they are correct in making fun of his dream or not, which leaves much of this episode in an uncanny limbo, although this chapter is soon followed by one reporting about Kjartan's death (173–77). And only then do we hear of An the Black again, who had been assumed to be dead and had only been caught by a swoon. In that swoon, however, he had the same dream, except that now the terrible woman in his dream restores his health, which then becomes the case in reality as well (176). The fact of An the Black's sudden recovery, and his dream experience deeply frighten the people around him, a reaction which underscores that we are with this narrative not simply within a fictional realm where everything is possible. On the contrary, which underscores the impact of the dream, of magic, and the appearance of strange creatures and beings on people, those who observe An the Black's return to the living feel just as shocked as those people who witnessed the revenant Killer-Hrapp. In other words, the secret that the people witness proves to be just as much a secret as it is for us as modern readers.

In the chapter on Gudrun's second marriage, for instance, we are first told about a man called Kotkel who had arrived from the Hebrides in Iceland only recently. Without further ado, the narrator simply tells us: "They [Kotkel and his family] were all extremely skilled in witchcraft and were great sorcerers" (125). For quite some time, that power is apparently not applied in any particular way, until later when the neighbors begin to complain about their "thieving and sorcery" (128). In fact, Thord Ingunnarson becomes a major figure to oppose them and summons them to the Althing, which motivates Kotkel to practice his magic against him: "Then Kotkel erected a large ritual-platform and they all climbed onto it; there they chanted potent incantations—these were magic spells. And presently a tempest arose" (129). This tempest is aimed against Thord while he is out on the sea on his ship, and although Thord then tries with all his might to cope with the thread, a major wave then suddenly makes the ship keel, and all men on the ship drown (129). Kotkel and his family subsequently leave and settle elsewhere, but they continue to cause trouble and experience much hostility by the people (131). Eventually, once more spells have been issued and a boy has been killed by it, Kotkel and his people are pursued and executed. While the narrator has nothing to say about the specifics of their sorcery, he is much concerned with providing authentication for his account by way of referring to a cairn of stones where Kotkel and Grima had been stoned to death (135). The chapter then concludes with references to a curse that Hallbjorn Sleekstone-Eye, one of Kotkel's men, issues before he is drowned as punishment for his association with Kotkel. The narrator then bluntly comments: "This curse is considered to have been very effective" (136).[17]

Already the next chapter talks about another evil character, the outlaw Stigandi who exerts occult power over the ewes at Hundadale by means of his evil eye. When he is then captured, the men put a bag on his head and then stone him to death, but not before he can cast an evil spell on the land, looking through a tear in the bag: "Stigandi could glimpse the hillside on the opposite side of the valley. It was a fine stretch of land, rich with grass; but suddenly it was as if a whirlwind came and turned the whole sward upside down, so that no grass has ever grown there since" (137–38). Then the narrator also includes references to trolls (180) and miraculous healing by means of a special kind of stone, as in the case of the badly wounded Grim who is suffering from a heavy loss of blood. But Thorkel, who had caused that wound in their battle, takes a "healing-stone and rubbed it on the wound; then he bound it to the arm, and all the pain and swelling disappeared at once" (192). This proves to be a direct reminder of the magical healing flowers in Marie de France's "Eliduc," though neither here nor there do we receive any explanations or are we supposed to understand this phenomenon rationally.

All this seems a bit surprising considering that we hear in the same context of a Christian priest, Snorri, and the pagan magic is then not even discussed further. But it also remains unclear what kind of healing stone that might have been. Thorkel, to be sure, does not speak any magical formula, does not utter a spell, and he is actually not even identified as a particularly learned magician. The priest himself does not emerge as a particularly different person from them all, demonstrating only interest in serving Thorkel's personal interest, addressing a marriage possibility and the need to carry out an act of revenge for the death of the woman's first husband. Although being a priest, Snorri thinks and acts like all the other major leaders of the Icelandic society: "And as regards the vengeance for Bolli, I think it very likely that something will have been done about that before this year is out" (193).

We can break off at this point, satisfied with this plethora of data confirming the existence of magic, extraordinary powers, trolls, berserks, shapeshifters, and sorcerers as reflected on by these Icelandic poets in their sagas. There is never any question regarding the authenticity of those phenomena; instead, the issue is always only what can and must be done about those secrets, as we can call all those phenomena collectively. Even though the sagas mostly reflect a historical dimension, that is, land settlement, conflicts, wars, legal arrangements, marriages, and the history of the various families (dynasties) and their protagonists, we clearly recognize a strong interest as well in reflecting on secrets in whatever form they might manifest themselves.

Almost consistently, the various poets unmistakably indicate the presence of mysterious powers as they interact with the individual heroes and their families. But both magic and sorcery, berserks and shapeshifters do not occupy the dominant positions and emerge only marginally. However, even there, at the margin, they play a significant role and indicate the extent to which they could be considered as dangerous. At any rate, those secrets exist for the poets who incorporate them subtly into their accounts of the history of these Icelandic heroes. When those secrets emerge from the dark and the hidden, they deeply trouble the ordinary people who try as much as they can to overcome them, to repress them, to remove them, or simply to handle them as efficiently and radically as possible.[18] However, epistemologically speaking, when the secret forces make their presence felt, they shock and unsettle the social environment, and defy any easy explanation, if any might even be possible. We could thus claim that the sagas operate not only with the historical accounts as they can be verified but also with secret forces as they had exerted an uncanny influence on people under many different circumstances.[19]

Next, let us examine one of the most famous medieval Welsh poems, the so-called *Mabinogi*, which is predicated in many different ways on the appearance of the secret by itself. As a brief reminder, however, both here and elsewhere, I use the term "secret" in a broader sense, referring to all phenomena in people's lives that do not find any rational explanation and border on or are part of another dimension. The term "secret" here implies, as we have now observed numerous times, a sense of human helplessness against magical forces or against the appearance of creatures or beings from another world who operate on their own and defy any rational explanation.[20]

We can explore this topic with little difficulty when we turn to the medieval, or Middle Welsh *Mabinogi*, which consists of four branches, some of which will be the topic of the following reflections. They were composed by an anonymous poet in the late eleventh or early twelfth century—but perhaps even earlier, as some scholars have argued, suggesting the period prior to the conquest of England by Duke William the Conqueror in 1066—and have survived in two fourteenth-century manuscripts—the White Book of Rhydderch or Llyfr Gwyn Rhydderch, written circa 1350 (today housed in the National Library of Wales, Aberystwyth), and the Red Book of Hergest or Llyfr Coch Hergest (today housed at Jesus College, Oxford), written about 1382–1410—and a number of thirteenth-century fragments.[21] Scholarship has long established that these *Mabinogi* (plural) represent major pre-Arthurian prose narratives which include, however, early Arthurian elements and figures and are related with the poems *Culhwch and Olwen*, *Owain* or *The*

Lady of the Fountain, then *Peredur*, and finally *Gereint and Enid*.[22] There would be much to say about each branch, and to discuss the various opinions voiced about these Middle Welsh masterpieces. But most major reference works already include detailed plot summaries and outline significant topics and tropes discussed by the poet/s, so it would not be necessary to reiterate much of the fine research of the last decades, and even a century and more.[23] In short terms, these branches contain the following materials, comprising eleven tales altogether that address the lives of superhuman humans with some kind of divine origin, which commonly leaves us rather baffled in face of these secrets. Here is a convenient, well-formulated structural summary of the *Mabinogi*:

> Pwyll Pendefig Dyfed (Pwyll, Prince of Dyfed) informs us about Pryderi's parents and his birth, loss, and also recovery.
> Branwen ferch Llŷr (Branwen, daughter of Llŷr) primarily deals with Branwen's marriage to the King of Ireland. Pryderi appears but does not assume a major part.
> Manawydan fab Llŷr (Manawydan, son of Llŷr) treats Pryderi's return home with Manawydan, brother of Branwen, and describes the misfortunes that befall them there.
> Math fab Mathonwy (Math, son of Mathonwy) principally treats the eponymous Math and Gwydion, who come into conflict with Pryderi.[24]

It is not my intention here to probe particularly the literary-historical framework and connections with older sources, or the overall message conveyed by the poet/s. Instead, the focus will rest primarily on the various comments included in some of these narratives on the experience and encounter with the uncanny, the otherworld, the magical, and hence with the secret dimension in all of human existence, and this in close connection with the many other examples of mysterious phenomena as discussed in contemporary narratives and poems. The *Mabinogi* lends itself particularly well for this purpose because, as we can immediately recognize, the essential intention by the poet/s was to reflect on the interaction between humans and figures or powers from another world, and this in a definitely non-Christian context, creating fear, inviting awe, and a deep sense of the power of magic.[25]

At the risk of isolating individual episodes too much, instead of offering a comprehensive interpretation, the purpose here can only be to highlight specific interactions with and explorations of secrets in the *Mabinogi*. The very first tale of Sage, Prince of Dyfed, actually known as Pwyll, confirms this observation because on his hunt he has a mysterious encounter and faces a huge challenge to his entire existence, similar to Guigemar in Marie de France's eponymous *lai*, although the topic of love, as in Marie's tale, does not concern the Welsh poet directly. Sage runs into a conflict with the King Arawn of the otherworld kingdom over a stag that the latter's dogs have killed. Sage had driven those curious dogs—all completely white with the exception of their totally red ears—away and had allowed his own dogs to take over the prey. Arawn finds this extremely insulting, and he threatens Sage to ruin his reputation as a punishment—if we don't have to assume that he had staged this setting to gain the help by Sage in this secret matter. But Sage submits, begs for forgiveness, and is granted a chance to remedy this terrible situation. Arawn knows that he needs Sage to overcome his own enemy, but this will be possible only if the two shift their shapes and assume the identity of the respective other, living like that for a whole year in each other's place. As part of the plan, Sage needs to fight against the enemy in a duel, but he is not to strike him a second time after he has wounded him. Only under that condition would the enemy surely die.

It is not clear why Arawn needs Sage to carry out that deed in his place, but the representative of the otherworld cannot achieve his own goal, so it seems. We might even suspect that Arawn had arranged the hunt in such a way that he would meet Sage and set him up to make him obliged to Arawn. After all, Sage is completely surprised about the situation with the stag and the curious dogs, does not pay attention to the fact that those dogs belong to someone else, and does not take into consideration their highly unusual skin color (white and red ears), and is hence badly embarrassed when Arawn appears. However, Sage is smart and polite enough to submit to this king and beg for his mercy, promising to do anything in his might to remedy the situation.

The poet had introduced Arawn as "a king of the Otherworld" (16), but his opponent is also a king in that world called Summerbright (Hafgan),[26] so Arawn might be a representative of Winter. Whatever we might want to assume, the crucial component is that Sage immediately accepts the proposition and takes on Arawn's appearance, while the latter changes into Sagan, with no one noticing any difference on either side. The otherworld is projected as fabulous in many respects, with the queen being of extraordinary beauty, but Sagan never touches her in bed and always sleeps with his back to her, as attractive as she might be, obviously because he knows only too well that the curious swapping of places with the king of the otherworld requires from him close observation of all rules and stipulations. We might even speculate that this set-up could have influenced later the similar situation in *Sir Gawain and the Green Knight* where the protagonist faces a major seduction attempt by the host's wife but resists because he is deeply aware of the challenge he is facing to his honor and values as a knight.

Insofar as Sage closely follows Awarn's rule and does not attempt to kill the opponent once he has wounded him badly, although the other king encourages him to finish the job, there is no more any revival, and Sage aka

Awarn can thus successfully take over the entire kingdom of the otherworld with no other person contesting his authority and all the nobles paying homage to him. Shortly thereafter, the two men meet again, Awarn transforms both of them back into their own shape, and they part as good friends. As we subsequently learn, their switching of roles had been of greatest profit for both. Awarn realizes Sage's extraordinary loyalty to him, not having ever touched his wife or having talked to her at night. The couple then breaks out in great praise of the other man, and she confirms: "That's quite a bond you inspired" (21). On the other side, Sage's nobles confirm that 'he' had never ruled better than during the past year, and so he realizes what great nobility inspires Awarn. Sage then continues on his own with the same ideal behavior as a ruler and thus receives the highest accolades from his subjects, while he maintains his friendship with Awarn and hence the close alliance with the otherworld. People learn about the secret shared by those two men, and Sage then receives a new moniker, being called "Sage the Otherworld Ruler" (21).

The most important features of this account might actually be those that receive the least attention. If the poet had not specified that Awarn was king of the otherworld—at first contested, of course, but after Sage's accomplishment the unquestioned ruler there—we would not even suspect anything uncanny about this situation. We do not learn much about that otherworld but can be certain that the curious appearance of the hunting dogs—white with red ears—signals alienation, even if only in traces. Of course, Awarn and Sage meet during an ordinary hunt, but it is clear from the beginning that the king of the otherworld needed to have a mighty proxy fighter to overcome his opponent there. We are not informed why Awarn is not in any position to defeat the other king, but we know for sure that he needs Sage rather desperately.

The positive outcome of the one year during which each man spends his time in the other man's body might be a matter of little concern, and yet we grasp here a unique situation insofar as the transition between both worlds is described as a most ordinary feature. All that it takes here is that Awran and Sage exchange their physical appearances. Otherwise, both operate in very traditional terms and impress their subjects with their generosity, wisdom, support, and honor. Even though Awarn's wife expresses considerable frustration to her husband after the year has passed and the right man has begun again to make love with her and talk to her, complaining bitterly: "you haven't even turned your face to me, let alone more" (20), the couple realizes quickly that Sage had demonstrated most honorable behavior. Awran thinks to himself: "he's a real friend" (20), and she states, "That's quite a bond you inspired. Nothing would make him break it, not even me" (21).

The narrative makes us almost forget that Sage is engaged with the king of the otherworld, which is not specifically defined and appears to operate as a mirror image of the real world in the here and now. The aristocratic protagonists go hunting, engage in knightly conflicts, listen to bards, drink, make friends, and relax, as Sage experiences (19). Despite his initially aggressive terms, Awran apparently seeks Sage's friendship and needs to rely on him to overcome his enemy. In other words, for the Middle Welsh poet, there was only a small barrier between the real world and the otherworld, without telling us clearly what the difference might have been. The only real difference consists of Awran's magical abilities to carry out a shape-shifting process, but otherwise, there are no efforts by the poet to project any mythological dimension.[27] Instead, he emphasizes the most harmonious male bonding between both men (20), and neglects to comment any further on the mythical status of King Awran. Since they both from then on regularly exchange gifts and warm up to each other continuously, we are invited to think that the otherworld is not really far away from the physical, human world, with both epithets almost incorrectly connected with the key terms. We are encouraged to think of the otherworld as being just as concrete and factual as our own world, except that the inhabitant of that other domain commands magical powers, though Awran is not omnipotent and still needs help from Sage by way of switching their positions for the duration of a year. To be sure, the poet presents to us a significant literary secret, and never really cares about resolving it because the otherworld does not function here as a threat or as a superpower. Instead, as the outcome indicates, Sage and Awran establish a close friendship and enjoy their contacts across the two dimensions, as if those kingdoms were simply neighboring countries. It is also worth noting that Sage never demonstrates any fear, amazement, or wonder when he learns that the other man is the king of the otherworld. He is only concerned with gaining Arawn's grace and friendship since he acknowledges him as his superior and accepts that he did wrong to him claiming the dead stag for himself when Arawn's dogs had done the kill.

In the second narrative of the First Branch, the same protagonist climbs to the top of a hill, the Mound of Arberth, where he is told that he would experience a magical spectacle there: "whenever any nobleman sits there, he can't walk away without one of two things happening: either he suffers wounds or blows, or else he sees a wonder" (22). This set-up evokes the typical Arthurian scene in later romances when the king refuses to sit down for dinner at Christmas time before a wonder or miracle has happened. In the romances based on Geoffrey of Monmouth's historical account, especially those by Chrétien de Troyes, this wonder is then closely associated with one of the main knights who then pursue that phenomenon and thus face their critical challenge.

Here, by contrast, Sage does not engage in a knightly adventure; instead, he witnesses the strange appearance of a noble lady who passes by the mound riding at a slow pace with her horse. However, when one of Sage's men tries to follow her, he does not achieve his goal, can never even get close to her, until she has then disappeared. In modern terms, we would characterize this situation as a warp in the relationship of time and space, which makes it impossible for anyone closing the gap with the lady. The narrator describes it simply, but without revealing the secret behind it: "But the faster he hurried, the farther in front of him she ended up. When he realized he couldn't possibly catch up with her, he went back to Sage" (22).

Sage requests his man to fetch the fastest horse they have, but even then, the task proves to be impossible, although the lady continues to ride at the same slow pace. As much as the man tries his hardest, little does he succeed to catch up with her: "Meanwhile, his horse was exhausted, and when it had helplessly slowed to a walk, he went back to where Sage was waiting" (22).[28] If it were not completely anachronistic, it would be worth endeavoring here a comparison of this episode with the concept of time and its relativity as described by the modern German author of novels for young readers, Michael Ende, in his novel *Momo* (1973).[29] I am not aware of any other medieval literary example where the notion of time itself is reflected so exceptionally as here in *Mabinogi*, and the entire effort to come to terms with its relativity constitutes a remarkable secret all by itself. Sage realizes that some magic is involved, but he has a squire try his best once again the next day, though with the same negative results: "And the more his spurs cut up the horse's sides, the farther she was ahead of him, and her pace was no faster than before" (23). Only on the third day—certainly, a highly symbolic number both here and in countless other cases throughout western culture—with his own horse saddled and ready to go for the time when the lady appears, does the situation change. However, Sage at first fails just like the two other men before him, but this time, out of frustration, he calls out to her and begs her to wait for him. Indeed, words uttered by him achieved the desired results, as she then waits for him and is prepared for their conversation in which she reveals that she had passed by in such a mysterious fashion in order to meet him personally and to ask for his love, and then actually for his hand in marriage.

We have learned in recent years that medieval poets projected many more highly active, independent, and self-motivated female characters than we had assumed previously. But this woman, Rhiannon, daughter of Hyffaid the Old,[30] proves to be the most energetic and powerful female figure since she is fighting her father's plans to marry her to an unwanted man and has now used magic—similar to Meliur in Konrad von Würzburg's *Partonopier und Meliur* (ca. 1280), based on the Old French *Partonopeus* (ca. 1170, i.e., prior to Chrétien de Troyes; or ca. 1180, influenced by the latter, which seems rather unlikely)[31]—to reach out to the man with whom she is really in love, Sage. The latter is deeply impressed and does not hesitate immediately to pledge his love for her and to promise to marry her at the time and place she would stipulate (25).[32] In fact, she accepts this right away and then organizes the wedding feast herself, demonstrating an uncanny level of personal independence which is barely matched by other medieval fictional women.

However, already after the main meal of the wedding dinner, the situation becomes highly convoluted and mysterious because a giant man arrives and requests from Sage to have a wish fulfilled. He is Flash, son of Fame, whom Rhiannon's father had wanted to marry her to against her will. Since Sage vaguely promises to fulfill Flash's request, though a close reading of his words would qualify that reading—"if I can get it, it's yours" (26)—he has to hand her over to him, which irritates Rhiannon deeply. However, she knows of a magical trick how to deceive Flash and teaches Sage what to do in this situation to rescue her from Flash. By means of a mysterious little bag Sage uses to receive food at a feast organized by Rhiannon for Flash, without the bag ever getting filled, he can coax the giant to step into the bag and make it finally full, which then traps him. To get out of that ominous bag and to survive, he has to promise to let go of his claim on Rhiannon, who then both can conclude their wedding feast happily. They spend their first night together with full satisfaction, and then depart for his homeland, Dyfed (30).

As unique as the entire situation appears to be at first sight, we can recognize numerous parallels with similar episodes in medieval literature, such as in Gottfried von Straßburg's *Tristan* (ca. 1210) where King Mark of Cornwall, recently married to the Irish princess Isolde, promises the Irish knight Gandin anything he might wish for in return for him playing music on his rote. Of course, Gandin has only Isolde in mind and then demands her as his reward. Although Mark tries to reject this, Gandin reminds him of his royal promise and then offers himself to fight in combat for his right. Since Tristan is not present at that moment, and since no one dares to accept the challenge, Mark proves to be helpless and has to let Isolde go. Of course, later Tristan appears and manages to trick Gandin in the same way and thus to recover Isolde, but there are no real secrets involved.[33]

The situation in the *Mabinogi* is very differently organized, and certainly involves elements from a mysterious other dimension of sorcery, magic, or other sources of powers. Here, Rhiannon instructs the male protagonist on how to overcome the uncanny danger, although we are left with more questions than answers. While Flash seems to operate as a normal knight, maybe comparable to Gandin, he really belongs to the world of monsters, giants, or magical beings. In many respects, however, Rhiannon shares much with him in that regard; otherwise, she would not have known how to deceive him by means of that mysterious bag that cannot be filled "unless a landed nobleman of wealth and property gets up and stand with both feet in the bag and says, 'Enough has been put in here'" (28). But those are precisely the words given to Sage who closely follows his wife's instructions since he would not know otherwise how to cope with the secret of Flash's role in all of that. Ironically, poor Sage has to suffer being badly lambasted by Rhiannon for his foolishness of promising anything that Flash might request, but he and his wife are saved because she is smarter than both men and knows how to counter Flash's rhetorical trickery which had put Sage into this embarrassing bind. Moreover, she becomes an active partner in the strategy to defeat Flash when she pushes him to accept the challenge posed by Sage, ridiculing him in his seemingly lacking manhood (28).

However, once Flash has been caught, then badly beaten while still in the bag, an agreement is reached between them, and Flash voluntarily abandons his claims on Rhiannon and returns home where he needs to take a bath to recuperate from his bad treatment (29). Subsequently, Rhiannon and Sage enjoy each other and live happily in their marriage for three years, but she does not conceive, which makes his people complain badly about her, urging him to marry another woman to have a much-needed heir. Sage requests one more year before he would make a decision and follow their advice, but then she suddenly delivers a male baby (31). Even though this might signal the calm and regular development of their marriage, the secret world does not give them a rest.

Although six women are charged with watching over the baby, they all, along with Rhiannon, fall asleep, and the next morning the baby is gone. The women plot a vicious strategy to protect themselves from being charged for their terrible negligence, kill some puppies, smear the blood on Rhiannon, and scatter bones on top of her to make it look as if she had cannibalized her own child. Despite public demands to have her executed for this horrible crime, her husband refuses, but allows her to be punished; she is condemned to stay at the city gate of Arberth and to tell every traveler who might care to listen to her own story, and then to carry him into the city (32). This mystery then continues because we learn of a similar case, this one involving a horse in the possession of Teirnon Roaring Torrent which always loses its foal as soon as it is borne. Teirnon finally keeps guard during the particular night when the next foal is to be born and discovers to his shock that a monstrous arm reaches through the window to grab the foal. Teirnon cuts it off at the elbow, whereupon there is much screaming and crashing outside. He tries to follow the monster, who is similarly hurt as Grendel in *Beowulf*, but since Teirnon remembers that he had left the door open, he returns and discovers on the doorstep a little baby boy wrapped in brocaded silk (33), who is, of course, Rhiannon's child, which is revealed only years later.

Teirnon and his wife raise the boy who grows tremendously and quickly demonstrates his true origin through his appearance, but when they realize that he is really Sage's son, they turn him over, which leads to universal happiness since Rhiannon is cleared of all charges and the couple gains its rightful heir. However, the narrator entirely neglects to explain anything further about the strange phenomenon of the claw stealing first the boy and then the foals. The creature can get away into the dark of the night, but leaves behind its claw, just as Grendel had to do after Beowulf had ripped its arm out of the socket.[34] We are left wondering what the shared interest might be that leads the monster to steal the newborns. They are not eaten, as Grendel did with his victims at Hrothgar's court, but the disappearance of the baby boy has severe legal consequences for Rhiannon. As much as she had been associated with the otherworld before her marriage, as much she appears to be entirely powerless to defend herself against this strange force and is ultimately liberated from her shameful punishment almost by accident.

To be sure, Teirnon is not a Welsh Beowulf, but he rescues Sage's son from the monster's possession and eventually returns him, after he had raised him for years, to his rightful parents.[35] Like in many fairy tales, the theft of the baby boy and of the foal takes place at night, and no one ever finds out who the thief might be. We are also left wondering why Teirnon does not continue with his pursuit, why he is keeping watch all by himself, and why he naively forgets to lock the door when he rushes out into the dark. Altogether, the narrator of the *Mabinogi* refuses to provide reasonable answers and prefers to leave us with secrets that find no explanation. But the first branch altogether serves to underscore the mythical origin of the new ruler, Sage's son, Carey, or Pryderi, that is, the source of anxiety, or concern, dispute, fear, etc., at least for Rhiannon, who proves to be the greatest victim of them all despite her nearly divine origin.[36] Mark Williams questions, however, the extent to which she has real control over magic since her powers are limited to magical accouterments, whereas the really powerful enchanters are all men.[37] But there is enough mystery involving her to confirm that she is critical in the treatment and development of secrets by the anonymous poet, although we are never fully informed about the true properties or nature.

In the Second Branch, we are not really exposed to comparable secrets, but mysteries still prevail, particularly pertaining to the king of Wales, Benedict Crow, or Bendigeidfran, who is a giant and "was too big to fit inside any house" (40). The poet does not demonstrate any particular interest in the mysterious aspect and instead focuses more on the political aspects and the family history. In particular, the relationship with the Irish King Matholwch is at stake, who marries Benedict's sister, Blanche Crow, or Branwen, who "was one of the three chief matriarchs of this island" (40). After some conflicts, Benedict gives his brother-in-law a unique gift, a cauldron that can restore a man's life once his corpse has been thrown in, although the restored individual would not be able to speak (43).

This cauldron had been a gift from an Irish giant and his wife, who was of a much larger size than even him (43). Those two had then stayed in Wales with Benedict, who was subsequently forced to try to kill them because his subjects feared them and were deeply worried about their presence which had caused much hostility and fear. The assassination did not work, despite all efforts with blacksmiths and bellows to burn them to death, and instead, the couple could break free, and they along with their progeny were then settled around the country. Again, the narrator leaves it at that and does not bother with providing any rational explanations since he is dealing with mythical accounts that cast a shroud of secrecy over the history of the entire land.

After the first year of a happy marriage, people begin to blame Blanche Crow for the insult that the king had suffered back in Wales, which then leads to her expulsion from the court into the kitchen where she has to do the baking and is regularly punched by the butcher. Eventually, she manages to send a secret message to her brother via a tamed bird, and he then arrives with an army crossing the sea. But of course, he is so tall that people mistake him for a forest and a mountain.

Once having arrived, they pursue the fleeing Irish who have withdrawn behind the river Shannon, which cannot be crossed by anyone because of sucking stones. However, Benedict, due to his size, can lie down and make himself into a bridge for his army, saying meaningfully: "A great leader . . . must be a bridge for his people" (48). Many tragic events then follow, but those do not concern us here, apart from Benedict's and his sister's death. The narrator also includes comments about a floating sword" (52), a magic cloak (52),[38] mysterious singing birds (53), and then a most ominous closed door which keeps seven men under the leadership of Manawydan from remembering any of their pain and suffering, until Heilyn son of Gwyn breaks the taboo. The result is devastating for them: "all the loss they'd ever felt, and all the relatives and friends they'd ever lost, and all the harm that ever touched them flooded in as raw as if they were facing it again, right there, all at the same time—and the worst was when it finally became real to them that their lord was dead" (54).

The narrator is not at all concerned with solving the secrets and leaves them as opaque as they are, but the account itself underscores the importance of those secrets and mysteries as foundational for the early history of the kingdom. We would mistake the account if we read it as pure fantasy or imagination; instead, here we confront a deep sense of a different world, a different time when giants still existed, when magical objects were in place, and when ominous events took place. The poet as a historian obviously operated with a deep sense of the presence of secrets and integrated them at liberty (or by default, depending on the responses to the original oral sources) in order to convey at least a hunch of magical forces, objects, and people operating in the past. In light of that observation, we are actually getting closer to unraveling the mystery of those secrets because their very incomprehensibility defines their true nature.

For our purposes, it does not matter whether the Four Branches were composed by a group of poets or by a single author, as J. K. Bollard has suggested.[39] What matters is that here, maybe more explicitly than in many other medieval narratives, the secret, the magic, and the mysterious figure so prominently and claim their own stake without demonstrating any willingness to reveal their true nature. The *Mabinogi* thus represent a true epistemological challenge, probably because it is so deeply steeped in Welsh mythology. As Mark Williams has recently observed,

> All this underscores the point that the author of the Four Branches was conspicuously interested in theorizing magic. In doing so, he—writing somewhere in Wales around the year 1100—managed to anticipate the terms of an anxious debate about metamorphosis which soon engaged some of the finest theological minds in Christendom. This owed much to his characteristic thoughtfulness, and it may be down to him that metamorphosis evidently became a significant intellectual concern among Welsh literary men at the time. Most famously, a pervasive interest in changes of shape is visible in the poems in the voice of the so-called "legendary Taliesin"—himself a shapeshifting transmigrant—many of which may be late twelfth-century and thus almost certainly postdate the Four Branches.[40]

Indeed, magical powers, the role of enchanters, and hence a plethora of secrets dominate these *Four Branches*, as perhaps most dramatically illustrated in the Fourth Branch where two magicians create a fitting female partner for Blondie by means of their sorcery and their connection to the vegetal powers of nature:

> The two magicians took the flowers of the oak, and the flowers of the broom, and the flowers of the meadowsweet, and used them to create the single most beautiful and beguiling woman any man ever saw. They christened her the way they did in those days and named her Fleur. (84)

This woman, Blodeuwedd, later falls in love with another man, Gronwe, and he urges her to find out a way Blondie could be killed, which seems almost impossible unless a whole sequence of actions would have been carried out. She can, however, coax him to reveal all the details, which she secretly informs her lover about, who can then actually attack Blondie, striking him with the specially prepared spear, which wounds him tragically: "Blondie transformed into an eagle and flew off, screaming horribly" (88), and he is not seen again thereafter for a long time because he leaves for the forests.

The account later concludes, however, with Blondie being rescued by the magician Gwydion who knows how to return him into his human shape by means of verses composed by him. Fleur receives her adequate punishment, being transformed into an owl, whereas Gronw tries in vain to escape to his own land. Blondie challenges him and can kill him with a spear in the same location where he himself had been hit. Although Gronw holds up a stone to protect himself, Blondie is too strong to fail in this matter, and so he can kill his opponent. Until the present, as the narrator confirms, "there is a stone slab with a hole through it which is still called Gronw's Stone" (91).[41]

We could go into many more details of the Four Branches and uncover additional secrets. Similar as in the Icelandic Sagas, for the Welsh poet/s the presence of magic was a very common occurrence, though we as the audience are not privileged with any specific understanding of how those charms or spells work. All we are supposed to know is that powerful forces exist behind or beyond human life, some of which individual magicians or sorcerers grasp to instrumentalize for their purposes. But the secrets remain as such both here in the *Mabinogi* and in the Icelandic Sagas, commonly associated with tragedy in human lives.[42] We recognize clearly that the various poets freely played with this phenomenon and recognized it as a powerful force that had to be reckoned with, even though there was hardly ever any explanation. The presence of secrets provided semantic, philosophical, religious, and ultimately epistemological depth to all those poems. The less we are informed about the full nature of those strange phenomena and figures, the more those emerge as meaningful. The key, however, for the answers to the question what or who they really are remains hidden, if not lost, and this from the very beginning in the Middle Ages.

NOTES

1. H. R. Ellis Davidson, "Shape-Changing in the Old Norse Sagas," *Animals in Folklore*, ed. Joshua R. Porter and William M. S. Russell (Cambridge and Totowa, NJ: D. S. Brewer; Rowman & Littlefield for Folklore Soc.; Rowman & Littlefield for Folklore Soc.; Rowman & Littlefield Publishers; 1978), 126–42; Stephen Mitchell, "Magic as Acquired Art and the Ethnographic Value of the Sagas," *Old Norse Myths, Literature and Society*, ed. Margaret Clunies Ross (Odense: University Press of Southern Denmark, 2003), 132–52; Ulla Asmark, "Magikyndige kvinder i islændingesagaerne – terminologi, værdiladning og kausalitet," *Arkiv för Nordisk Filologi/ Archives for Scandinavian Philology* 121 (2006): 113–20.

2. *The* Beowulf *Manuscript: Complete Texts and* The Fight at Finnsburg, ed. and trans. by R. D. Fulk. Dumbarton Oaks Medieval Library, 3 (Cambridge, MA, and London: Harvard University Press, 2010).

3. Andrea Maraschi, "Taboo or Magic Practice? Cannibalism as Identity Marker for Giants and Human Heroes in Medieval Iceland," *Parergon: Journal of the Australian and New Zealand Association for Medieval and Early Modern Studies* 37.1 (2020): 1–25. A very late medieval "heroic" epic, *Der Wunderer* (ca. 1500) is also predicated on the idea of a cannibalistic monster; see Albrecht Classen, "*Der Wunderer*. Hybridität, Erzähllogik und narrative Fragmentierung in der Literatur des deutschen Spätmittelalters," *Wirkendes Wort* 66.3 (2016): 371–84. The narrative of cannibalism gained in traction only after the discovery of the New World by Europeans, many of whom projected the notion of cannibalism on the indigenous population because they had heard of a variety of religious ceremonies among them. See Philip P. Boucher, *Cannibal Encounters. Europeans and Island Caribs, 1492–1763*. Johns Hopkins Studies in Atlantic History and Culture (Baltimore, MD, and London: Johns Hopkins University Press, 1992). Cannibalism has always represented one of the strongest taboos, and so also in the Middle Ages, and yet, there are reported cases. See Geraldine Heng, "Cannibalism, The First Crusade and the Genesis of Medieval Romance," *differences: A Journal of Feminist Cultural Studies* 10.1 (1998): 98–174.

4. Timo Rebschloe, *Der Drache in der mittelalterlichen Literatur Europas*. Beiträge zur älteren Literaturgeschichte (Heidelberg: Universitätsverlag Winter, 2014); Thomas Honegger, *Introducing the Medieval Dragon* (Cardiff: University of Wales Press, 2019). The common tendency is, however, to view the dragon through a Christian lens and to identify it with evil incarnate, for instance, and less with autochthonous forces well beyond any moral or ethical judgments.

5. *Egil's Saga*, trans. Bernard Scudder, ed. with an intro. and notes by Svanhildur Óskarsdóttir (London: Penguin, 1997). For the critical edition of the original, see *Egills saga*, ed. Bjarni Einarsson (London: Viking Society for Northern Research, 2003; available now online at http://www.vsnrweb-publications.org.uk/Egla/Egils_saga.pdf); for another online version, issued in May 1997, see https://www.snerpa.is/net/isl/egils.htm; cf. also *Egills saga: Með formála, viðaukum, skýringum og skrám*, ed. Bergljót Kristjánsdóttir and Svanhildur Óskarsdóttir. Sígildar sögur, 2 (Reykjavík: Mál og menning, 1994). For critical comments, see the excellent volume, *A Companion to Old Norse-Icelandic Literature and Culture*, ed. Rory McTurk. Blackwell Companions to Literature and Culture, 31 (Malden, MA, Oxford, and Carlton, Victoria, Australia: Blackwell, 2007); and *Egil, the Viking Poet: New Approaches to 'Egil's Saga,'* ed. Laurence de Looze, Jón Karl Helgason, Russell Poole, and Torfi H. Tulinius. Toronto Old Norse and Icelandic Series, 9 (Toronto, Buffalo, and London: University of Toronto Press, 2015).

6. See now Timothy Bourns, "Becoming-Animal in the Icelandic Sagas," *Neophilologus* 105.4 (2021): 633–53.

7. Vincent Samson, *Die Berserker: Die Tierkrieger des Nordens von der Vendel- bis zur Wikingerzeit*. Ergänzungsbände zum Reallexikon der Germanischen Altertumskunde, 121 (Berlin and Boston: Walter de Gruyter, 2020), 128–32, 169–95; see also M. Frog, "Rituelle Autoritäten und narrativer Diskurs: Vormoderne finno-karelische Sagenüberlieferungen als analoges Modell für die Annäherung an mittelalterliche Quellen," *Magie und Literatur: erzählkulturelle Funktionalisierung magischer Praktiken in Mittelalter und Früher Neuzeit*, ed. Andreas Hammer, Wilhelm Heizmann,

and Norbert Kössinger. Philologische Studien und Quellen, 280 (Berlin: Erich Schmidt Verlag, 2022), 153–207; here 192–96.

8. *Njal's Saga*, trans. with intro. and notes by Robert Cook. World of the Sagas (London: Penguin, 1997); see also the older, yet still valuable translation, *Njál's Saga*, trans. from the Old Icelandic with intro. and notes by Carl F. Bayerschmidt and Lee M. Hollander (New York: New York University Press, 1955). For a digital version in English, see https://sagadb.org/brennu-njals_saga.en (last accessed on April 28, 2022). Cf. the contributions to *New Studies in the Manuscript Tradition of Njál's Saga: The historia mutila of Njála*, ed. Svanhildur Óskarsdóttir and Emily Lethbridge. The Northern Medieval World: On the Margins of Europe (Basel, Berlin, and Boston: Walter de Gruyter, 2018). For many other editions, translations, and studies, see the official webpage, http://www.njala.is/en/burnt-njal/burnt-njal-in-icelandic/ (last acccessed on April 28, 2022). For discussions of the various manuscripts containing the text, see Jan Alexander van Nahl, "Digital Norse," *The Routledge Research Companion to the Medieval Icelandic Sagas*, ed. Ármann Jakobsson and Sverrir Jakobsson (London: Routledge, 2017), 344–53.

9. *The Nibelungenlied with The Klage*, ed. and trans., with an intro. by William Whobrey (Indianapolis, IN, and Cambridge: Hackett Publishing, 2018), 9–10, stanzas 86–101, and 75–78, stanzas 896–905.

10. Jan Wehrle, *Das Übernatürliche erzählen: die erzählerische Darstellung übernatürlicher Phänomene in sechs Isländersagas* (Munich: utzverlag, 2021).

11. Dreams in the Middle Ages have been discussed already from many different perspectives; see, for instance, Jan Wehrle, "Dreams and Dream Theory," *Handbook of Medieval Culture: Fundamental Aspects and Conditions of the European Middle Ages*, ed. Albrecht Classen (Berlin and Boston: Walter de Gruyter, 2015), vol. 1, 329–46; cf. also Steven F. Kruger, *Dreaming in the Middle Ages* (Cambridge: Cambridge University Press, 1992); Albrecht Classen, "Transpositions of Dreams to Reality in Middle High German Narratives," *Shifts and Transpositions in Medieval Narratives. A Festschrift for Dr. Elspeth Kennedy*, ed. Karen Pratt (Woodbridge, Suffolk: D. S. Brewer, 1994), 109–120; Guntram Haag, *Traum und Traumdeutung in mittelhochdeutscher Literatur: theoretische Grundlagen und Fallstudien* (Stuttgart: S. Hirzel, 2003). For a brief summary, with further reflections on the correlations between medieval and modern dreams, though written not for an academic audience, see Albrecht Classen, "Dreams and Visions, in a Historical Perspective," *The Living Pulpit* Oct. 17, 2020; http://www.pulpit.org/2020/10/dreams-and-visions-a-historical-perspective/ (last accessed on April 22, 2022).

12. See the contributions to *Magic and Magicians in the Middle Ages and the Early Modern Time: The Occult in Pre-Modern Sciences, Medicine, Literature, Religion, and Astrology*, ed. Albrecht Classen. Fundamentals of Medieval and Early Modern Culture, 20 (Berlin and Boston: Walter de Gruyter, 2017).

13. Richard F. Allen, *Fire and Iron: Critical Approaches to Njáls saga* ([Pittsburgh, PA]: University of Pittsburgh Press, 1971); Lars Lönnroth, *Njáls saga: A Critical Introduction* (Berkeley, CA: University of California Press, 1976); Theodore Ziolkowski, *The Mirror of Justice: Literary Reflections of Legal Crises* (Princeton, NJ: Princeton University Press, 1997).

14. *Laxdœla Saga*, trans. with an intro. by Magnus Magnusson and Hermann Pålsson (London: Penguin, 1969); for references to the critical edition and other translations, see 43–44. As to corpses and their afterlife, see Romedio Schmitz-Esser, *Der Leichnam im Mittelalter: Einbalsamierung, Verbrennung und die kulturelle Konstruktion des toten Körpers*. Mittelalter-Forschungen, 48. 2nd unchanged ed. (2014; Ostfildern: Jan Thorbecke Verlag, 2016), 431–44, 467–71; see also the English translation by Albrecht Classen and Carolin Radtke (Turnhout: Brepols, 2020).

15. I can only touch here on the phenomenon of madness, which has always represented a profound challenge to all rationality. It would go too far to identify madness with a secret in the traditional sense of the word, but it certainly represents a different perception of reality and has always been regarded both with horror and awe, with incomprehension and contempt. See Andrew Scull, *Madness in Civilization: A Cultural History of Insanity from the Bible to Freud, from the Madhouse to Modern Medicine* (Princeton, NJ, and Oxford: Princeton University Press, 2015); see also the contributions to *Hermeneutics of Textual Madness: Re-Readings*, ed. M. J. Muratore. 2 vols. Biblioteca della Ricerca: Mentalità e scrittura, 38 (Fasano, Italy: Schena Editore, 2016). In my own study included here, "Madness in the Middle Ages—An Epistemological Catalyst? Literary, Religious, and Theological Perspectives in Caesarius of Heisterbach's *Dialogus Miraculorum*," vol. I, 339–68, I examine madness through a religious-narrative lens. For a philosophical-historical study of madness, see Andreas Brenner, "Mystiker und Wahnsinnige, eine Beängstigung der Philosophie: Die Ausgrenzung a-rationaler Erkenntnisformen als Methode," *Religion und Gesundheit: Der heilkundliche Diskurs im 16. Jahrhundert*, ed. Albrecht Classen. Theophrastus Paracelsus Studies, 3 (Berlin and Boston: Walter de Gruyter, 2011), 381–96. He refers, interestingly, especially to Arthur Schopenhauer, Immanuel Kant (both as strong opponents), and, as the most fascinating voice confirming the validity of the secret beyond all human rationality, the Italian poet, Alda Merini (1931–2009) and the German poet Friedrich Hölderlin (1770–1843).

16. Aline G. Hornaday, "Visitors from Another Space: The Medieval Revenant as Foreigner," *Meeting the Foreign in the Middle Ages*, ed. Albrecht Classen (New York and London: Routledge, 2002), 71–95; she summarizes much of the older research on this topic. See also the useful anthology *The Ghost Story from the Middle Ages to the Twentieth Century*, ed. Helen Conrad-O'Briain and Julie Anne Stevens (Dublin: Four Courts Press, 2010). The standard study, however, continues to be Jean-Claude Schmitt, *Ghosts in the Middle Ages: The Living and the Dead in Medieval Society*, trans. Teresa Lavender Fagan (1994; Chicago: University of Chicago Press, 1998).

17. H. R. Ellis Davidson, "Hostile Magic in the Icelandic Sagas," *The Witch Figure: Folklore Essays by a Group of Scholars in England Honouring the 75th Birthday of Katharine M. Briggs*, ed. Venetia Newall (London: Routledge & K. Paul; 1973), 20–41.

18. Rebecca Merkelbach, *Monsters in Society: Alterity, Transgression, and the Use of the Past in Medieval Iceland*. The Northern Medieval World (Berlin and Boston: Walter de Gruyter, 2019).

19. See now the contributions to *Myth, Magic, and Memory in Early Scandinavian Narrative Culture: Studies in Honour of Stephen A. Mitchell*, ed. Jörg Glauser,

Pernille Hermann, Stefan Brink, Joseph Harris, and Sarah Künzler. Acta Scandinavica, 11 (Turnhout: Brepols, 2021). Cf. also the influential study by Stephen A. Mitchell, *Magic, Ritual and Witchcraft in the Nordic Middle Ages*. The Middle Ages Series (Philadelphia, PA: University of Pennsylvania Press, 2011). For some critical responses to this seminal investigation, see now Thomas A. DuBois, "Magic and Witchcraft Historicized, Localized, and Ethnicized: A Response to Stephen Mitchell's *Witchcraft and Magic in the Nordic Middle Ages*," *Magic, Ritual, and Witchcraft* 8.1 (2013): 82–89; and Ronald Hutton, "Stephen Mitchell's *Witchcraft and Magic in the Nordic Middle Ages*: An Assessment and Appreciation," *Magic, Ritual, and Witchcraft* 8.1 (2013): 75–81.

20. For broader perspectives, including anthropological and religious aspects, see Peter Orton, "Pagan Myth and Religion," *A Companion to Old Norse-Icelandic Literature* (2007), 302–19. As much as scholars have worked already on the many elements of myth and religion in the sagas, as little have they examined those secrets as epistemological functions in a variety of narrative contexts.

21. For a convenient modern English translation, see *The Four Branches of the Mabinogi*, ed. and trans. by Matthieu Boyd (Peterborough, ON: Broadview Press, 2017). The purpose of this translation, however, was to make the text primarily available and accessible for North American undergraduate students. See also *The Mabinogi and Other Medieval Welsh Tales*, ed. and trans. Patrick K. Ford (Berkeley, CA: University of California Press, 2019); and *The Mabinogion*, trans. Sioned Davie. Oxford World's Classics (Oxford: Oxford University Press, 2007). For the critical edition, see *The Mabinogi*, ed. Proinsias Mac Cana. 2nd ed. (1977; Cardiff: University of Wales Press, 1992). See also Proinsias Mac Cana, *The Mabinogi*. Writers of Wales (Cardiff: University of Wales, 1992). For important source studies, see Andrew Breeze, *The Origins of the Four Branches of the Mabinogi* (Leominster, Herefordshire: Gracewing, 2009); Nikolai Tolstoy, *The Oldest British Prose Literature: The Compilation of the Four Branches of the Mabinogi* (Lewiston, NY, Lampeter, Wales, Queenston, Victoria: Edwin Mellen Press, 2009). See also E. A. Rees, *The Mabinogi Decoded* (Birmingham: University of Birmingham, 2012). Cf. Albrecht Classen, "Multilingualism and Multiculturalism in the Pre-Modern Age: Medieval Welsh and Icelandic Literature in a Literature Survey Course. Interdisciplinary Approaches on a Pan-European Level," *Leuvense Bijdragen* 102 (2018–2020): 357–82. Ludwig Mühlhausen, ed., *Die vier Zweige des Mabinogi (Pedeir Ceinc y Mabinogi)*. 2nd rev. and expanded ed. Buchreihe der Zeitschrift für celtische Philologie, 7 (1925; Tübingen: Max Niemeyer, 1988), XII, claimed that the archetype manuscript was probably created in the Cistercian abbey of Strata Florida in western Wales around 1200. But this cannot be well documented.

22. Thomas Parry, *A History of Welsh Literature* (Oxford: Clarendon Press, 1955); Ifor Williams, *The Beginnings of Welsh Poetry* (Cardiff: University of Wales Press, 1990); *The Celtic Heroic Age: Literary Sources for Ancient Celtic Europe and Early Ireland and Wales*, ed. John T. Koch and John Carey (New York: David Brown, 2003); see now also the contributions to *The Cambridge History of Welsh Literature*, ed. Geraint Evans and Helen Fulton (Cambridge: Cambridge University Press, 2019).

23. See, for instance, Diane Korngiebel, "Mabinogion, The," *Encyclopedia of Medieval Literature*, ed. Jay Ruud (New York: Facts on File, 2006), 416–17. The entry by Roy S. Rosenstein, "*Mabinogion*," *The Oxford Dictionary of the Middle Ages*, ed. Robert E. Bjork, vol. 3 (Oxford: Oxford University Press, 2010), 1062, is so minimal that it is almost not even worth mentioning. Herbert Pilch, "Mabinogion," *Lexikon des Mittelalters*, vol. VI (Munich and Zürich: Artemis & Winkler Verlag, 1993), 54, is barely better. By strong contrast, the more recent online encyclopedias, including *Wikipedia*, offer much more detailed information, background data, references (see below).

24. The respective article in Wikipedia is quite respectable, see https://en.wikipedia.org/wiki/Mabinogion (last accessed on April 26, 2022). This entry also offers extensive information about the influence of the *Mabinogi* on modern literature, scholarly references, an excellent bibliography, a list of translations, and, most importantly, digital links to previous editions and translations. While *Wikipedia* is often not quite trustworthy, this article represents a notable exception.

25. Albrecht Classen, "Imagination, Fantasy, Otherness, and Monstrosity in the Middle Ages and the Early Modern Age," *Imagination and Fantasy in the Middle Ages and Early Modern Times: Projections, Dreams, Monsters, and Illusions*, ed. Albrecht Classen. Fundamentals of Medieval and Early Modern Culture, 24 (Berlin and Boston: Walter de Gruyter, 2020), 1–229; here 155–57; see also Mark Williams, "Magic and Marvels," *The Cambridge History of Welsh Literature* (2019), 52–72.

26. The translation could also be: Summersong since "haf" is "summer" and "cân" is "song." See Boyd, trans. (2017), 17, note 1.

27. Proinsias Mac Cana, *Celtic Mythology* (London: Hamlyn, 1970); see also E. A. Rees, *The Mabinogi Decoded* (2012), 154–73, who oddly tries to correlate the major figures in the Middle Welsh texts with the various gods in classical Greek Mythology. This seems to be more speculation than an argument based on solid evidence.

28. Indirectly, the poet raises here significant time-space issues and reflects on relativity which would have certainly intrigued a physics researcher such as Albert Einstein. For the phenomenon of time in the Middle Ages, see Ken Mondschein and Denis Casey, "Time and Timekeeping," *Handbook of Medieval Culture: Fundamental Aspects and Conditions of the European Middle Ages*, ed. Albrecht Classen (Berlin and Boston: Walter de Gruyter, 2015), vol. 3, 1657–79. Although they cover a wide range of time-related themes, they did not include this highly unusual episode in the *Mabinogi*. Ken Mondschein, *On Time: A History of Western Timekeeping* (Baltimore, MD: Johns Hopkins University Press, 2020), 147–77, offers further reflections, including on the relativity of time, but then no longer pertaining to the Middle Ages. For the concept of medieval time taking, see Gerhard Dohrn-van Rossum, *History of the Hour: Clocks and Modern Temporal Orders*, trans. Thomas Dunlap (1992; Chicago and London: The University of Chicago Press, 1996).

29. Alexander Oberleitner, *Michael Endes Philosophie im Spiegel von "Momo" und "Die unendliche Geschichte"* (Hamburg: Meiner, 2020); Gernot Böhme, "Zeitphilosophie in Michael Endes '"Momo,'" *Philosophie im Spiegel der Literatur*, ed. Gerhard Gamm. Zeitschrift für Ästhetik und allgemeine Kunstwissenschaft. Sonderheft, 9 (Hamburg: Meiner, 2007), 79–89; Jana Mikota, "Zeitdiebe in

unterschiedlichen Jahrzehnten: narratologische Untersuchungen zu Zeit—Raum—Figur in ausgewählten Beispielen," *Kinder- und Jugendliteratur und Narratologie*, ed. Carsten Gansel and Hermann Korte. Deutschsprachige Gegenwartsliteratur und Medien, 2 (Göttingen: V & R Unipress, 2009), 67–79; Albrecht Classen, "Reflections on Key Issues in Human Life: Gottfried von Strassburg's Tristan, Dante's Divina Commedia, Boccaccio's Decameron, Michael Ende's Momo, and Fatih Akın's Soul Kitchen Manifesto in Support of the Humanities—What Truly Matters in the End?," *Humanities Open Access* Nov. 16, 2020, online at: https://www.mdpi.com/2076-0787/9/4/121 (last accessed on May 16, 2022).

30. Jessica Hemming, "Reflections on Rhiannon and the Horse Episodes in *Pwyll*," *Western Folklore* 57.1 (1998): 19–40; Christopher G. Nugent, "Reading Riannon: The Problematics of Motherhood in *Pwyll Pendeuic Dyuet*," *Domestic Violence in Medieval Texts*, ed. Eve Salisbury, Georgiana Donavin, and Merrall Llewelyn (Gainesville, Tallahassee, et al., FL: University Press of Florida; 2002), 180–202.

31. *Partonopeus in Europe: An Old French Romance and Its Adaptations*, ed. and with an intro. by Catherine Hanley, Mario Longtin, and Penny Eley. *Medievalia* 25.2 (2004).

32. As to women's agency in medieval literature, see Albrecht Classen, "Female Agency and Power in Gottfried von Strassburg's *Tristan*: The Irish Queen Isolde: New Perspectives," *Tristania* XXIII (2005): 39–60; id., "The Agency of Wives in High Medieval German Courtly Romances and Late Medieval Verse Narratives: From Hartmann von Aue to Heinrich Kaufringer," *Quidditas* 39 (2018): 25–53 (online at: https://rmmra.byu.edu/files/2018/12/39.pdf); id., "The Agency of Female Characters in Late Medieval German Verse Narratives: "Aristotle and Phyllis," Dietrich von der Gletze's "Der Borte," "Beringer," and Ruprecht von Würzburg's "Die zwei Kaufleute," *Totius mundi philohistor: Studia Georgio Strzelczyk octuagenario oblata*, ed. Małgorzata Delimata-Proch, Adam Krawiec, Jakub Kujawiński (Poznań: UAM/Adami Mickiewicz University Press, 2021), 227–42.

33. Gottfried von Strassburg, Tristan and Isolde *with Ulrich von Türnheim's* Continuation, ed. and trans., with an intro., by William T. Whobrey (Indianapolis, IN, and Cambridge: Hackett, 2020), ch. 19, vv. 13097–450.

34. Daniel F. Pigg, "Who is Grendel in *Beowulf*? Ambiguity, Allegory, and Meaning," *Imagination and Fantasy in the Middle Ages and Early Modern Times: Projections, Dreams, Monsters, and Illusions*, ed. Albrecht Classen. Fundamentals of Medieval and Early Modern Culture, 24 (Berlin and Boston: Walter de Gruyter, 2020), 303–19.

35. E. A. Rees, *The Mabinogi Decoded* (2012), 47–54, again offers a rather speculative interpretation associating this branch of the narrative with classical mythology.

36. Mathieu Boyd, ed., and trans., *The Four Branches of the Mabinogi* (2017), 36, note 1. See also Caitlín Matthews, *Mabon and the Mysteries of Britain: An Exploration of the Mabinogion* (London and New York: Arkana, 1987), 29–30.

37. Mark Williams, "Magic and Marvel," *The Cambridge History of Welsh Literature*, ed. Geraint Evans and Helen Fulton (2019), 52–72. He outlines the long history of research on magic in medieval Welsh literature, going as far back as to Matthew Arnold, who coined the phrase Celtic "natural magic" in his 1867 monograph, *On the*

Study of Celtic Literature. My interest here has nothing to do with any evaluations of Welsh versus British or Continental literature with respect to magic and imagination. As we have observed already many times, secrets appear all over the face of medieval and also early modern literature, and they constitute, also in Middle Welsh texts, a fundamentally important phenomenon in epistemological terms.

38. This is the same motif as in the Middle High German *Nibelungenlied*, with Siegfried winning the cloak of invisibility from the king of dwarfs, Alberich. *The Nibelungenlied with* The Klage, ed. and trans., with an intro. by William Whobrey (2018), stanzas 94–98.

39. J. K. Bollard, trans., *The Mabinogi: Legend and Landscape of Wales* (Llandysul: Gomer, 2006); for a contrastive view, see Mac Cana, *The Mabinogi* (1992), 35 et passim.

40. Mark Williams, "Magic and Marvel" (2019), 64–65.

41. There are striking parallels of this entire account with the *lai* "Equitan" by Marie de France—attempted murder of the seneschal by his wife and her lover, the King Equitan—and the *Nibelungenlied* where Hagen learns from Kriemhild where Siegfried has the one vulnerable spot on his body, and through which he then can throw the spear to kill his nemesis.

42. Mark Williams, "Magic and Marvel" (2019), 68–69. He also observes the other characteristic feature of Welsh magic: "Again, in contrast to other European literary traditions, Welsh magic makes strikingly little use of elaborate 'technology'—it is short on magic rings, girdles, books, and the like. Such examples as there are seem to possess an uncanny, archaic quality, with a particular prominence given to cauldrons and hanging bowls, the 'cauldron of rebirth' in the Second Branch, Branwen uerch Lyr ('Branwen daughter of Llŷr')—a kind of resurrection machine—being the most signal example" (68).

Chapter Three

Wolfram von Eschenbach
Parzival—The Secret of the Grail at Munsalvæsche and the Secret Inscription on the Dog Leash in *Titurel*

A young aristocratic couple enjoys, after a lengthy process of deliberation, testing, and probing, the privilege granted by their elders to spend time together in a forest setting, a clearing, with tents set up, numerous maids, and servants pursuing their business serving those two. The noble maid, Sigune, is situated in her quarter, while her lover, Schionatulander, is standing in a creek nearby trying to catch fish. Everything looks like a rather innocent, idyllic outing with all the ordinary pomp of aristocratic society, but now in a sylvan framework.[1] Suddenly, the forest resounds with the barking of a single hunting dog, apparently directly on the trail of its prey, though it is not followed by any hunters and appears to act all on its own, driven by its blood thirst and killer instinct. As much as hunting was part and parcel of all courtly culture, the arrival of this mysterious dog proves to be highly ominous and immediately indicates that the love between these two young people might be doomed.

The young man immediately drops his fishing rod and runs, although he is barefoot, through the forest and toward the dog, catching it and bringing it back to his mistress, while the deer disappears in the sylvan thickets. The dog had run away from its master because it had been overly excited to catch the game, but Schionatulander is fast enough to track down the dog and to hold it back, turning it over to Sigune as a gift, while the hind disappears for a while, yet leaving behind a trail of blood. As much as the dog had been the hunter, now the young man turns into a hunter, but he catches much more than just an animal, that is, the leash, hence a narrative, and ultimately a secret which will determine his future life, that is, his almost imminent death.

The dog at first does not matter so much in this story told by the Middle High German poet Wolfram von Eschenbach in his fragmentary tale of *Titurel* (ca. 1220), probably his last poetic attempt after he had composed his dawn songs, the grail romance *Parzival*, and the chanson de geste, *Willehalm*.[2] Instead, the leash assumes central importance because there is some writing on it, created by gemstones applied to an "Arabian braid, very tightly woven by the loom" (364, stanza 137).[3] Sigune, the happy recipient of this duplicit or ambivalent gift, a secret by itself, eagerly begins to read the words and soon realizes that they constitute a whole narrative account about unhappy, and actually tragic lovers, with death on their trail, just as the dog, intent on killing the hind, has basically brought death to these two young people.

The situation with *Titurel* proves to be most curious, and there might not be an actual parallel to it in medieval literature and beyond because Wolfram had simply picked up some narrative strands left over in his own *Parzival* (ca. 1205) and here developed them further, though he still left them as fragments, maybe as symbols of the close intertwining of life and death, happiness, and sorrow. The same observation could be made with regard to Wolfram's previous works, including his famous dawn songs, where he deliberately deviated from the literary tradition and created his individual approach to this genre.[4] However, we will then observe that the text on the dog leash escapes from Sigune's grip because the animal runs away from her being so overly anxious to follow the bloody trail of its prey and having no patience for her reading interests.

Wolfram deliberately plays here with the rich connotations of "wilderness" and the "wild," and associates it with the reading process and the experience of love, all forces that prove to be the results of secrets and remain mysterious even at the very end of the poet's texts.[5] As soon as the knot in the leash has been released, that is, as soon as one of the textual knots have been loosened, meaning the unraveling of the entire account, the dog can run away, taking the text with it, hence the secret of the correlation between love and death. The external fragment is thus replicated within the poem, where the text literally runs away and leaves the reader wondering about the outcome.[6]

Sigune then demands from Schionatulander to follow the dog and to bring it back to her because if she cannot complete the narrative on the leash, the young man would never enjoy her love. In *Parzival*, however, we are already aware about Schionatulander's efforts to regain the dog. Young Parzival encounters, once he has left his mother's sylvan retreat Soltane, the lady Jeschute resting in her camp. Although he has no sexual interests in her, he grabs food, forces her to relent a valuable ring and a brooch, and to kiss him because his mother Herzeloyde had provided him with some foolish advice about how to perform in the world of the courts. Satisfied with his 'conquest,' Parzival then left and continued his voyage to King Arthur's court, but he leaves behind many tracks of his presence at the camp. When Jeschute's husband Orilus arrives, he notices immediately the changes and disruptions in the camp, and he charges his wife of having committed adultery, although that is not true at all. Ultimately, much later Parzival, having matured considerably, can whitewash Jeschute of that charge and explain to Orilus the situation itself, which closes that history. But we also learn at first that Orilus had returned from a joust with a young knight over a dog, which the latter had wanted to conquer from him. This young knight was Schionatulander, and he died in that encounter (58, book 135). In the course of further events, we hear of Parzival meeting his niece, Sigune, several times who holds the corpse of her lover in her lap, like a new *pietà*. She griefs so much about Schionatulander's death that she eventually dies.

In *Titurel*, Wolfram backtracks the origin of this story and elaborates further on it so as to explain in depth the root cause of the tragedy, although both the dog (Gardeviaz—Guard Thy Way) and the leash with its mysterious text remain secrets and are never fully explained. Wolfram obviously enjoyed elaborating the relationship between the physical dimension and the meaning of secrets as they pop up often in his works. Sigune has the end of the leash tied to a tent pole, but she cannot read the whole text unless she loosens the knot. The dog immediately realizes its opportunity, jerks, and is set free, so it can run away and continue with its blood-thirsty pursuit. This leaves Sigune behind, deeply grieved and wounded—the gemstones had scratched her palm when she tried to hold the leash, but also very much determined to demand from her lover to demonstrate his worthiness as a knight by following the dog and retrieving it, that is, of course, the leash and hence the text written on it with those gemstones.

As the narrator explains about Gardeviaz: "It had run away from Ehkunat in the same way that day. She called out to the damsels. They had found food for the bercelet. They scampered quickly back into the pavilion, but the hound had slipped out through the tent-wall. Soon he could be heard in the forest" (366, stanza 157). For Sigune, all this means that she cannot learn the outcome of the mysterious, but certainly tragic story embossed on the leash, and she cannot live any longer without knowing what happened with the lovers talked about in that mysterious story. As she emphasizes to Schionatulander:

> There was adventure written on the rope. If I am not to read that to its end, then I care nothing for my land of Katelangen. All the wealth anyone might offer me—even if I were worthy of accepting it—I would rather possess that writing. (367, stanza 165)

This then forces Schionatulander to pursue the dog, and the rest is history, as I have outlined already above. Love and death thus intertwine in Wolfram's

Titurel, and as much as we would like to understand this conundrum, we are left with nothing but a fragment and have to figure out for ourselves what the poet might have implied. However, we are not alone in that regard as already the medieval audience does not seem to have enjoyed *Titurel* very much, since the fragments have survived in only three manuscripts.[7] No one likes an open end, people both then and today have preferred a good closure, an answer to critical questions, or the revelation of the secret behind it all. But Wolfram obviously enjoyed teasing his audience and to provoke it with observing the secret as sacred phenomenon that would not need to be pursued to the very end. Some secrets just deserve to be respected as such, and Wolfram was certainly not the last to tantalize his audience deliberately, maybe in the awareness that life is not always straightforward, that love and death are intricately interwoven with each other, and that we really do not know what either one is as such.[8]

We cannot fathom all the reasons for this lackluster outcome, but it is certain that Wolfram intentionally operated with the notion of the fragment, or rather the secret, which was obviously not really pleasing for his listeners or readers, apparently dumbfounded by the unresolved mystery of this most unusual method of writing down the beginning of a romance about love, life, and death. Many times, when a romance did not reach a conclusive outcome, subsequent authors jumped into the void and developed lengthy continuations, finishing up with what had been left open-ended.[9] Wolfram was consequently followed up by a successor poet, Albrecht (von Scharfenberg), who created a huge romance loosely based on the *Titurel* fragments, the *Jüngere Titurel*, which is determined by a strong sense of a utopian projection.[10] Both Sigune and the audience, however, are left with a deep sense of frustration, at least in Wolfram's poem, because there is no full answer as to the meaning of the text on the leash, which remains, after all, an epistemological secret. However, this does not happen by accident, and it is not the result of the poet's failure to conclude his work properly.

Instead, as I would like to argue, Wolfram operated deliberately with the concept of the secret as a key for the full comprehension of this world, yet a key which hardly anyone can fully grasp or gain access to, and only mystical revelation would finally throw some light on the phenomenon. As we will see below, there are intriguing connections between this dog leash and the Grail as discussed in his *Parzival*. We thus face important reflections on medieval epistemology at large, that is, on the examination of the correlation between sensuous perception and intellectual understanding, or between *ratio* and *intellectus*, as theorized, for instance, by scholars such as Hugh of St. Victor (*Didascalicon*, 1, 3), Thomas de Cantimpré (*Liber de natura rerum*, 1, 2), and William of Conches (*Philosophia*, 4, 21, 37).[11]

Considering the extensive remarks offered by the narrator about the story embossed on the leash, it seems highly unlikely that the words could have actually all fit on that leash, and the weight of the gemstones to make up the individual letters would have made it truly impossible for the dog even to move, let alone run so fast after its prey. The dog and the leash had been sent by a queen of Kanadic to her lover, Ilinot the Briton. She is identified as Florie. Tragically, in wooing her, he took it upon himself to carry out knightly adventures, and thus died in a joust. His beloved then died out of grief as well (stanzas 147–48), a phenomenon we often hear in medieval literature, such as in the case of the *lai* "Deus amanz" by Marie de France, which I have discussed above.

Florie was survived by Clauditte, who took over the rule of the country, but the lords then demanded from her to choose a husband who could ascend to the throne. Clauditte had already fallen in love with Duke Ehkunat of Salvasch Florie (Ehkunat of the Wild Flower) and so she sent him, as Wolfram formulates it, a "wild" letter:

> Since he took his name from the wilderness, into the wilderness she sent him this wildish letter, the bercelet, who kept to the trail in forest and field, as he ought to by nature. (365–66; stanza 153)

Yet Gardeviaz, the untrammeled dog, did not stay with its new master; instead, he had run away from Ehkunat before, and we are left with wondering what might have happened with Ehkunat and his beloved. We know, as already stated, that Schionatulander will die in his effort to retrieve the dog, which would guarantee him Sigune's love. But knighthood appears, as we already had heard at the beginning of Wolfram's *Parzival*, as the source of continuous sorrow and pain, devouring the best knights who are killed in jousts or in warfare (Gahmuret). Although Schionatulander tries his best to follow the dog and to retrieve it, that is, the leash and the text, he fails because he is barefoot again and cannot make his way through the brushwork and thorns blocking his way. When he returns to the camp empty-handed, his bloodied feet and legs speak a symbolic language: "His white feet met with their share of wounds, too, from running through the thorns. His wounds were more apparent than those of the speared beast" (366, stanza 161). Simultaneously, Sigune's palm are badly scratched, and her wounds equally speak prophetic words: "The palms of her hands were grey, as if hoar-frosted, like a jouster's hands whose shaft slips in the counter-charge, scraping, grazing the bare skin. In just that way the leash had run through the duchess's hands" (366–67, stanza 162).

The narrator thus challenges us to read what cannot be understood and which yet speaks an obvious language. Wounds and blood mark the path through this world, and the secret behind it all rests in the individual's ability to understand their meaning. Obviously, however, neither Sigune nor Schionatulander can comprehend what their bodies are telling them, so they allow the bloody trail to pull them along further into the physical and metaphysical wilderness, which will result in both their premature death.[12] The answer for all the secrets indicated in this short episode might rest in the dog, especially because it carries the name "Gardeviaz," that is, guard the way, but none of the young lovers are strong enough to observe this message and thus fall victim to their emotions and passions. The secrets of love, death, and life thus remain hidden, which might have left the medieval audiences rather frustrated, particularly because they are openly inscribed into the leash and ready to be studied, if the text then would not have escaped, physically and metaphorically. Since Wolfram left his *Titurel* behind as a fragment, he obviously intended it to remain a literary secret, appreciating the secret as such for its hermeneutic function, and until today we cannot tell fully what he might have had in mind with this noetic challenge. But it is an essential challenge and as such an important barrier for our understanding of the text and hence even of life at large.

However, in his *Parzival*, much discussed and examined by scholarship for the last two hundred years or so,[13] Wolfram incorporated an even much bigger secret, which scholars have examined already for a long time, the Grail. Indeed, there is no shortage of critical studies invested in this mysterious object, its properties, origin, and meaning. I do not intend here to revisit all those issues, many of which are closely associated with speculation, both medieval and modern. There are, to be sure, many fascinating theories regarding the Grail, either religious or historical in nature, or linguistic and art-historical. As much as the Grail is indirectly connected with the world of King Arthur, it certainly supersedes it and constitutes a new spiritual dimension, blending the secular with the sacred, an almost perfect formulation for the emergence of a secret.[14]

The word itself does not constitute anything secretive; instead, it can be found a number of times already in early (718) and high (1200) medieval Latin documents, such as in Hélinand of Froidmont's chronicle, *Chronicon* (1211–1223), or in household inventories, representing a valuable serving dish or vessel. Precious food is placed in that bowl or on that plate with the pieces arranged gradually (*gradatim*) or in patterns (in the vernacular French, *graalz*). In the *Roman d'Alexandre* (twelfth century, ca. 1165–1170), the protagonist refers to the *grāal* from which he had eaten the night before. Famous Chrétien de Troyes was one of the first to introduce the term into the contemporary literary discourse, when he describes in his *Perceval* (ca. 1180) the procession during a festive dinner when the *graaus* is carried by a maiden. Interestingly, in clear contrast to most other Grail narratives, here the procession does not end at the dinner table, but moves on to another room, so the Grail does not specifically serve food. In the successor story to Chrétien's version, Robert de Boron (fl. 1190–1210) pursued this motif further, identifying it as the vassal which Joseph of Arimathia had used to catch Christ's blood flowing from his side wound after the deposition. This transformed the Grail into a holy object, hence the "Holy Grail." For Robert, the Grail was a cup fitting for the religious reference to the event during Christ's Passion, but for Wolfram von Eschenbach, it was a stone (*lapsit exillis*) or tablet which produces exquisite foods and drinks for the feast at court. Then the Grail figures prominently in the *First Continuation* of the *Perceval*, where Gawain becomes one of the Grail questers, and in the *Second Continuation*, where it turns into a medium for personal atonement. In both versions, we also hear of the Bleeding Lance, now associated with the spear of Longinus, which Robert had ignored. In the *Continuation* by Manessier and Gerbert de Montreuil, it is an object carried by a maiden, as is also the case in Wolfram's work. In the Welsh *Peredur*, two maidens carry the vessel in which a man's decapitated head is swimming in blood. In *Perlesvaus* (first decade of the thirteenth century), the Grail refers once again to the vessel used to catch Christ's blood, which brings about rejuvenation. In the *Prose Lancelot*, the Grail is a chalice; in the *Queste del Saint Graal* (ca. 1230–1250), the Grail represents, as an object, the quest performed by Bors, Perceval, and Galahad. Once that has been achieved, an angelic arm extends from the sky and removes the Grail for good from its sinful earthly abode.[15]

As Rupert T. Pickens notes, "The Grail is simultaneously an ordinary and a mysterious object. Mystery arises, in fact, because it behaves or is treated in unexpected ways." And he summarizes the essential properties of the Grail as follows: "The Grail as a source of plenty is one characteristic that brings its literary manifestations into contact with mythic and folkloric themes and motifs."[16]

In Wolfram's *Parzival*, the Grail matters centrally, just as in Chrétien's *Perceval*, and the many other continuations and adaptations. What then constitutes the secret of the Grail in his version? We need first to gain an understanding of the narrative context before we can tackle Wolfram's approach to the ultimate secret in all of medieval literature.

Parzival is already well established when we encounter him in Book V, having not only acquired the standard accolades of knighthood, but having won the love of his future wife, Condwirmaurs. Both enjoy each other's company, and they form a happy couple. But Parzival now remembers his mother and requests from his wife the approval to leave her for a while to visit Herzeloyde, who has, actually, died a long time ago upon her son's abrupt departure. Parzival does not know anything about it, so this plan seems to be appropriate for both. Nevertheless, as soon as the protagonist is out of his wife's sight, he feels deep longing for her. In fact, we might even go so far as to claim that the true and only secret in the entire romance consists of this pure and honest love, which is so esoteric and yet so firm, bonding these two people closely together, even though they do not see each other for many years after he has left her. But in pragmatic terms, we can concentrate on the Grail which is situated on castle Munsalvaesche, inaccessible to all who are not qualified and not permitted to enter.[17]

Parzival at first crosses a huge distance which amazes even the narrator. Then he reaches a lake where a group of men are trying to catch fish from a boat, which might be a relevant connection to the situation in *Titurel*. Whether Wolfram had one of the central metaphors of the New Testament in mind, of Christ being a fisherman who is making every effort to catch good souls, cannot be determined here. In Matthew 4:19, Jesus encounters encountered the fishermen Simon Peter, and Andrew and calls upon them to join him, leaving behind their traditional profession and to turn to the task of missionaries: "Come, follow me," Jesus said, "and I will send you out to fish for people."[18] But when we closely trace the exchange between Parzival and the richly clothed leader of the band of men—the Grail King Anfortas, here not yet mentioned by name—we could imagine that Wolfram had some of those words in mind:

> Sir, to my knowledge neither water nor land within these thirty miles is inhabited, except for one castle that lies nearby. By my loyalty, I advise you to go there. Where else could you go before the day is out? There, at the cliff's edge, take a right turn. When you come up to the moat, I expect you'll have to halt there. Ask for the drawbridge to be let down for you and for the road to be opened to you. (p. 95–96, Book V, ch. 225).

While Jesus collected his disciples and then sent them out into the world, Wolfram the narrator projects the opposite, and yet parallel development, with the protagonist arriving from the outside and then joining the inside group so that in turn he, that is, the Grail, can dedicate himself to the world badly in need of leadership. Many issues within the Arthurian world have become muddled, confusing, or simply confused, and there is a great need for Parzival to step in and assume the throne of Munsalvaesche. It remains, of course, rather unclear why he fails so badly the first time he is allowed to visit that castle and its company, but we can be certain that Wolfram intended to criticize the traditional courtly society and actually blamed it for fundamental failures to maintain or observe its own ideals and values. Parzival operates in the way of how he has been taught by the knight Gurnemanz, but those lessons are no longer valid in the new context, which makes the young man fail, tragically.

At stake, then, is a major secret which no one at King Arthur's court fully understands; they all have heard about it, so it seems, and many go on a quest to find the Grail, though no one except for Parzival are privileged to achieve that goal. That means, traditional society has failed to address the most urgent issues, and only one individual, the young protagonist, can overcome the barriers and transcend the limitations. Why that is so, basically remains a secret we have to live with, but this is a standard feature in all of Grail literature, as outlined above.

Ultimately, of course, every secret follows, in one way or the other, the same model because it is, ultimately, visible to spectators, questers, or heroes from the outside, but it withdraws from them and leads them on into some spiritual depths, without necessarily revealing itself. Once the solution has been found, the secret itself disappears and becomes almost meaningless, unless the revelation then leads over to a new model of community, social life, ethics, and ideals. The conclusion of *Parzival*, as fragmentary as it might be,[19] underscores that the poet did not intend to answer all questions, and the narrative development in *Titurel* also indicates that the secret was a universal epistemological phenomenon he wanted to subscribe to in a variety of ways, some subtle, others more explicit.[20]

This then takes us back to the Grail in *Parzival* where the young man is completely unprepared for what is expecting him there. It begins with the description of the castle as being undefeatable, as a perfect defense construction that no army in the world would ever be able to break through: "If all armies on earth were to attack them, they wouldn't yield a single loaf under such pressure, not in thirty years" (96, Book V, ch. 226). Not only is Munsalvaesche a most isolated castle, it also proves to be a building almost out of this world. However, despite its splendid architectural design and materiality, sorrow has come down to it; all knighthood has come to a sad ending, and society is no longer working properly because chaos has replaced traditional order.[21]

Even the Grail world appears to be in shambles, although the material dimension continues to exceed all expectations, especially for the protagonist who does not grasp the meaning of all those dazzling phenomena in front of his eyes. His royal treatment by squires and knights almost leaves him speechless, and the less he comprehends the more the secret of the Grail society presses itself upon him. The narrator makes greatest efforts to describe in astounding detail the fabulous arrangements in the dining hall, in the guest's sleeping room, and elsewhere. But all those objects do not present secrets; they are only attributes of the actual secret to emerge as soon as the host and Parzival have sat down. First, it is the mysterious lance:

A squire leapt in at the door, carrying a lance—a custom that furthered grief. From its blade blood gushed forth, running down the shaft to his hand, stopping at his sleeve. Then there was weeping and wailing all over the wide hall. The populace of thirty lands would be hard put to exact so much from their eyes! He carried the lance in his hands round to all four walls, and back again to the door. The squire leapt out through it. (98, Book V, ch. 231)

This much discussed lance, like the other symbolic objects, constitutes, at least for the protagonist, a secret which he cannot comprehend. But he notices, at least, as the narrator signals, that the lance with its blood caused profound pain. Once it has disappeared from view, four maidens arrive, who dazzle the observers and the modern audience alike. But we are not given any specific explanations and thus left with a sequence of secrets within a procession. However, none of the maids come close to the beauty and brilliance associated with Herzeloyde, who actually carries the grail Itself, which the narrator identifies as "earth's perfection's transcendence" (100, Book V, ch. 255).

The entire setting is determined by light in many forms, by balsam burning in vessels, all very much in line with a Catholic service. Parzival, as the narrator hastens to emphasize, is struck by the extraordinary beauty displayed by all the maidens, who perform meticulously their ceremonial roles. Female aesthetics and religious features merge here perfectly, which stuns the protagonist to the extreme because the entire setting proves to be a secret he can only marvel at but is not capable of understanding. Almost ironically, Parzival has arrived at the center of a stage and is seemingly the center of all attention, but he does not know the role he is supposed to play and has not received any script to respond in kind. But we do not know either and are kept outside of the secret, which evolves right in front of our eyes:

All the knights seated throughout the great hall had chamberlains assigned to them, with heavy golden basins, one for every four knights, and also a well-favoured page, carrying a white towel. Opulence was seen there in plenty. There must have been a hundred tables carried in through the door. (100, Book V, ch. 236–37)

As much as Parzival is fully integrated into the ceremony of the Grail, being the king's personal guest, he can only stare at the events, enjoy the individual treatment (washing the hands, taking food and drinks, etc.), but he does not penetrate the secret itself which displays itself in front of his eyes. The real miracle then takes place because the food on the table, which constitutes the Grail, never becomes exhausted. This finds its parallel to the German fairy-tale motif of "Tischlein-deck-dich" (dinner table, set yourself), and it adds considerably to the synesthesia of the entire scene, combining the visual, auditory, haptic, and culinary elements. The narrator then summarizes it in short but specific terms: "the Grail was bliss's fruit, such sufficiency of this world's sweetness that it almost counterweighed what is spoken of the Heavenly Kingdom" (101, Book V, ch. 238). As we are then informed, "The noble company was entertained at the Grail's expense" (101, Book V, ch. 239).

As much as Parzival enjoys the spectacle, it remains just that for him, and he does not know how to penetrate the riddle or secret itself. This continues even when the Grail king graces him with an extraordinarily precious sword which he himself can no longer wield in battle because his body is no longer capable of performing its traditional duties: "before God afflicted my body" (101, Book V, ch. 239). There is no direct invitation to Parzival to inquire about the cause of his suffering, although this is the ultimate purpose of the entire ceremony. The secret is waiting for Parzival to respond, it wants him to speak up, to ask the long-awaited question, it cajoles him with all human senses to turn to his host's physical ailment and express his empathy. This will happen, of course, at the very end of the Wolfram's romance, but then Parzival has matured so much and learned deeply from much suffering. However, it remains a large question which scholarship does not seem to have addressed yet whether the protagonist has really acquired a full understanding of the Grail, whether he has discovered the meaning of the secret. Does the Grail even want to be understood, or is its very nature to be a secret, representing the numinous in human existence? We could also extend the inquiry to King Anfortas and the Grail society. They all perform according to their expectations, but do they really know what the Grail is? As much as all the members of the court perform their roles well, there is no specific explanation here about its true property, origin, or function. All the attendees can eat to their fill what the mystical table offers, but the entire drama of this court festival serves only one purpose, to make Parzival open his mouth and ask the crucial question regarding Anfortas's suffering.

Tragically, however, he does not do that, so his destiny takes its course, and after a night filled with bad dreams, he wakes up, completely alone, and then leaves the castle deeply puzzled because no answer has been provided to many of his questions. The secret of the Grail withdraws from Parzival as soon as possible, and the forlorn man finds himself at a loss of what to do since there is no one left early in the morning to offer him any instructions. As important as the Grail certainly is for all member of the court and later for Parzival and his half-brother Feirefiz, we are never fully enlightened as to its full nature and role within the Arthurian world. It certainly applies some criticism, but also encouragement to observe the rules set up by the Grail itself, perhaps an entity or agency all by itself.

Both in *Titurel* and to some extent also here in *Parzival* does the poet indicate some connections with the origin of the dynasty. During Parzival's first visit at Munsalvaesche, he has also the opportunity to gaze briefly into a distant chamber, where he espies "the most handsome old man of whom he ever gained knowledge. I may indeed say, without exaggeration, that he was even greyer than the mist" (102; Book V, ch. 240). Old age receives great acknowledgement because it refers to the origin of the Grail, and we will learn later that the old man is Titurel, the founder of the Grail family (*Titurel*, stanza 1), or rather as the earthly representative of the divine power: "When I received the Grail by the message which the exalted angel sent me, by his high authority, there I found written all my order. That gift had never been given, before me, to human hand" (*Titurel*, stanza 6). But the Grail family has grown old, its members have died away, and there is only Sigune left who could continue with the tradition, but she also experiences a tragic death, brought about, so to speak, by her own actions, her haste, lack of spiritual understanding, and excessive anxiousness to unravel the secret. She then sends her lover to his death, which she did not intend, and ultimately dies out of grief. The Grail, however, does not reveal itself, does not explain the meaning of these events; and the members of the Grail family are left behind as innocent victims not able to uphold the ideals and values embedded in the Grail.

Young Parzival, to be sure, is the last one who might be able to decode the Grail, although he himself had partaken in the feast offered by this mysterious table, or mobile altar. Every possible attempt had been made by the community of Castle Munsalvaesche to make him feel comfortable, but also to signal to him indirectly some of the mysteries at play there, hence, of the suffering and sorrow, to which he was supposed to react. Tragically for them, however, by then Parzival has learned already too much the lessons of courtliness, so he refrains from asking any question, which terminates all possibilities of solving the secret, of creating new bonds between the Grail and the outside world, and to re-establish empathy and communication. The entire romance from then on mirrors this drastic downfall, the sense of hopelessness, and the realization that the secret remains what it is, a secret.

While Parzival continues to seek for the Grail castle after he had been expelled from there, and while his friend Gawan also pursues that goal on his own, the narrator never forgets about the secret and occasionally reminds us of it by way of offering more glimpses into its actual origin and possible meaning. This thus shifts the attention away from the intradiegetic discourse to an extradiegetic mode of conversation, since the narrator increasingly makes attempts to incorporate the audience and to take them with him on a path to discover and understand the secret of the Grail.

Several times, the narrator gives us more specific information about the origin of the Grail, but the more he discusses it, the more mysterious it becomes, as scholarship has confirmed already for a long time.[22] There is almost universal consensus that Wolfram created a unique literary fiction here, and has thus mostly abandoned the search for the 'historical' Grail.[23] According to the narrator, the Provencal master Kyot found the story of Parzival in the Spanish city of Toledo in a fragmentary Arabic manuscript, which he then translated into French, which required from him to learn the secret code in which this text had been written. Only a Christian would be able to decipher it—all elements typical of secrets in religious or necromantic disciplines. The text itself had been written down by the Syrian Flegetanis who possessed extensive astronomical knowledge and had been able to discover the Grail story written into the stars. Kyot was then able to translate Flegetanis's report, and by way of searching further in other Latin chronicles, he had then discovered the entire history of the Grail dynasty, of the Anjou family down to King Anfortas and Queen Herzeloyde. Parzival is thus the direct descendent of this graced family tree and hence privileged to take over the Grail throne from Anfortas, once he would have achieved the necessary level of maturity, intellect, and human compassion, which ultimately is the case at the end of the romance. Wolfram here proves to be a master poet who drew extensively from Chrétien and other sources and embellished them extensively, expanding the entire account with this reference to the mysterious Grail and its translation from Flegetanis to Kyot, and then to Wolfram as the master narrator.[24]

Even though scholarship has mostly agreed that the references to Kyot and Flegetanis would have to be seen as the results of Wolfram's poetic imagination, the question of why he incorporated this whole mysterious scenario remains unanswered until today, and the poet probably injected this entire account not simply out of pure fantasy, or enjoyment with imaginary figures of exotic origin, but because he wanted to mystify his narrative to a point at which the audience could only guess or simply gave up questioning the authenticity of these two figures.[25]

The narrator explicitly emphasizes that the Grail constitutes a secret which should not be divulged to the masses; only the few initiates, members of the courtly elite, such as the descendants of the Grail family itself, would be entitled to learn about the phenomenon itself and understand, to some extent, its meaning:

Whoever asked me about this before and squabbled with me for not telling him about it has won infamy by it. It was Kyot who asked me to conceal it, for the adventure commanded him that no-one should ever think of it until the adventure took it, through words, to meet the stories' greeting—so that now it *has*, after all, to be spoken of. (191, Book IX, ch. 453)

Kyot appears to have been a converted Jew since the narrator emphasizes with praise his baptism. Wolfram expresses great respect for this learned man who had managed to read the Arabic, but not with the help of necromancy; instead, on the basis of his thorough education. After all, the Grail represents the greatest secret of them all, understandable only to a select few: "No heathen cunning could avail us to tell about the Grail's nature—how its mysteries were perceived" (191, Book IX, ch. 453). Flegetanis is also identified as a Jew, but he never converted to Christianity because he had lived before the time of Christ. Nevertheless, the poet calls him a "fisîôn" (ch. 453, 25; "visionary"), who had descended from the house of Solomon. Although the narrator laments his adherence to a wrong faith, he still praises him greatly for his profound learning: "Flegetanis the heathen saw with his own eyes . . . occult mysteries in the constellation. He said there was a thing called the Grail, whose name he read immediately in the constellation" (192, Book IX, ch. 454). We can thus trace the origin of the Grail backwards, via Kyot to Flegetanis, and from him to the stars. Wolfram as the narrator places himself within the chain of transmitters and thus claims high authority regarding this secret, which is ominously associated with the Grail family: "A true account of all his lineage was written there, and how, on the other side, Titurel and his son, Frimutel, bequeathed the Grail to Anfortas, whose sister was Herzeloyde, by whom Gahmuret gained that son of whom these tales tell" (192, Book IX, ch. 455).[26]

We never learn whether Parzival or anyone of his family and friends fully understands the meaning of the Grail. The narrator's explanation addresses only the audience and invites them to join the group of the initiates, but even under those circumstances, almost everything remains baffling and stupefying because the ultimate mystery, as recorded in the star constellations, never reveals itself fully to human readers. Flegetanis read the family story, and handed that down in writing, which made it possible for Kyot to discover and translate the account. But when Parzival is finally allowed to return to castle Munsalvaesche, he has not truly learned the secret and only welcomes with great joy that the Grail had identified him through enigmatic writing as the predestined success to the throne.

When the Grail messenger Cundrie returns to King Arthur's court, after Parzival and Feirefiz have already recognized each other as being half-brothers, she makes the astounding announcement: "The epitaph has been read: you are to be the Grail's lord" (327, Book XV, ch. 781), which is combined with the revelation that his wife Cundwiramurs and her two sons have been called in to the Grail court. Parzival learns only at that moment of his children since they were born long after his departure to visit his mother, and Cundrie then associates this change in the protagonist's life with the revolution of the stars, which she lists by their Arabic names: "All that the planets' journey encompasses and that their radiance covers are goals staked out for you to attain and win. Your grief must perish . . . the Grail and the Grail's power forbid you fellowship with such false company" (527, Book XV, ch. 782). Consequently, Parzival is finally entitled and invited to return to Munsalvaesche to the suffering king and to formulate the long-awaited question, which solves all issues, frees the king from his pain, and designates Parzival as his successor. It is a very simple formulation, cast in the form of a question, and it is the code by which the secret is solved: "Uncle, what troubles you?" (333, Book XVI, ch. 795). Parzival has thus found the key for all of human communication, has established the fundamental bond between himself and his relative, and thus overcome the global conflict and tensions that have prevented the world, that is, courtly society, to find a way back to its own ideals and values.[27]

We could, following Fritz Peter Knapp and others, assume that Wolfram simply played with the phenomenon of the miraculous, the wondrous, or the magical in his treatment of the Grail and tried to establish a middle course between *historia* and *fabula*, that is, between pure imagination and chronicle accounts, or, between fact and fiction.[28] But there is healing at the end of *Parzival*, which has been brought about because the protagonist has been selected after all as the successor to Anfortas as the ailing and suffering king. This might be a form of miracle, but this would not lead us to a real explanation or understanding, since the term "miracle" only postpones the further question. There are forces in the background that look over Parzival and the Grail family, and the young Wolfram obviously harbored considerable optimism regarding the possibility that the fundamental shortcomings of this world could be healed. In *Titurel*, that optimism turned into pessimism, maybe as a result of Wolfram's own sense of his oncoming death.[29] The narrator indicates his grave doubts that people can actually achieve the desired goal of deciphering the world, to translate the words written down, and to establish effective forms of communication.[30]

However, all that does not change anything regarding the presence of the great secret, the Grail, which clearly operates as the ultimate engine that drives this world, spiritually and materially. Once Parzival has fully submitted under its force, has subscribed to the principles of ethics, morality, and faith, the Grail allows him to return to Castle Munsalvaesche to ask the long-awaited question, and thus absolve his uncle from his suffering. We clearly notice the religious dimension behind this secret, and hence the merging of the profane (knighthood) with the sacred (the Grail/the divine/God), as Parzival's other uncle, Trevrizent, who had helped him to learn his last lesson and who had taken upon himself to carry Parzival's sins to free him from that burden, formulates: "Greater miracles has seldom happened, since your defiance has caused God's endless Trinity to be acquiescent to your will" (334, Book XVI, ch. 798).

The secret as it ultimately unfolds is two-sided; for the Grail company and for Trevrizent, it is God's working here in this world. Parzival closely follows that concept, but he is also determined deeply by his love for his wife whom he has not seen for five years: "When we were together, she was dear to me—as she still is. . . . I wish to ride to meet my wife" (335, Book XVI, ch. 799). We can thus conclude that for Wolfram, the secret he dealt with both in his *Parzival* and in his *Titurel* consisted of the realization that the final purpose of life consists of finding love for the marriage partner and finding love for God. Wolfram's greatest accomplishment might thus well be the merging of both dimensions in a harmonious union, as the outcome at least of his *Parzival* indicates. This happiness then also finds its expression in Parzival's half-brother Feirefiz privilege of loving and marrying the Grail maid Repanse de Schoye, with whom he moves back home to his eastern countries, that is, India, where their future son, the Prester John, then become the cornerstone of a new Christian empire. Feirefiz himself, however, initiated that process of missionary activities: "Feirefiz had letters sent all over the land of India, telling them about the Christian way of life" (344–45; Book XVI, ch. 822). There is no longer any word about the Grail, which would also not be necessary. Parzival and his half-brother have found each other, King Anfortas has been healed, Parzival has reunited with his wife and children, and happiness rules the world under the newly appointed Grail king. The Christian message does not need any further elaboration, but we still have to confirm that the poet himself operates with an epistemological challenge of the Grail which I call a secret because it does not conform with the biblical teachings and pursues a spiritual independence which has provoked readers or listeners of Wolfram's romance ever since he had completed it.

Of course, there is a bit of magic (Clinschor) involved in this Grail account, and there is much Christian religion (Sigune, Trevrizent, etc.), but the ultimate purpose appears to be to challenge audience with a secret that hovers large on the horizon and yet remains mysterious to the very end. Granted, the protagonist and his family are presented as happy individuals, and the Grail community joins them in that happiness, but does anyone here really know what the Grail entails? Our ignorance is the same as that of the protagonists, and it represents the secret of human life within a larger, spiritual dimension. Undoubtedly, Wolfram had the relationship between the microcosm and the macrocosm in mind when he developed his narrative, as the learned Cundrie indicates when she displays her arcane knowledge at the end shortly before the Grail's redemption. Yet, it would be too simplistic to assume that the mystery of the Grail would be exhausted with a reference to that broad worldview. Rather, behind the Grail, that is, behind the secret itself, rests the large question what constitutes human life, and what provides the individual with the right direction to make his/her way through this short-term existence here on earth. The trail is the ultimate symbol, from the sylvan island in Parzival's youth to the wild mountain castle Munsalvaesche: the Grail is constantly calling him, yet he has to wait many years until he has reached the necessary maturity and spiritual sophistication.[31] He cannot track down the secret until it has revealed itself voluntarily.

NOTES

1. Marianne Stauffer, *Der Wald: Zur Darstellung und Deutung der Natur im Mittelalter*. Studiorum Romanicorum Collectio Turicensis, X (Bern: Francke Verlag, 1959); Christian Schmidt-Cadalbert, "Der wilde Wald: Zur Darstellung und Funktion eines Raumes in der mittelhochdeutschen Literatur," *Gotes und der werlde hulde: Literatur in Mittelalter und Neuzeit. Festschrift für Heinz Rupp zum 70. Geburtstag*, ed. Rüdiger Schnell (Bern and Stuttgart: Francke Verlag, 1989), 24–47; Mireille Schnyder, "Der Wald in der höfischen Literatur: Raum des Mythos und des Erzählens," *Das Mittelalter* 13.2 (2008): 1220–35; Jens Pfeiffer, "Verirrungen im Dickicht der Wörter: die Wälder der Ritter und der Wald Dantes," *Der Wald im Mittelalter* (2008): 136–51; Albrecht Classen, *The Forest in Medieval German Literature: Ecocritical Readings from a Historical Perspective*. Ecocritical Theory and Practice (Lanham, Boulder, et al.: Lexington Books, 2015), 81–101, esp. 96–100; for the role of the forest in economic and political terms, see Charles R. Young, *The Royal Forest of Medieval England* (Leicester: Leicester University Press, 1979); Roland Bechmann, *Trees and Man: The Forest in the Middle Ages*, trans. Katharyn Dunham (1984; New York: Paragon House, 1990).

2. Wolfram von Eschenbach, *Titurel*, ed. Helmut Brackert and Stephan Fuchs-Jolie. With a [German] trans., commentary, and materials (Berlin and New York: Walter de Gruyter, 2002).

3. Wolfram von Eschenbach, *Parzival* and *Titurel*, trans. and notes by Cyril Edwards. Oxford World's Classics (Oxford: Oxford University Press, 2004/2006). *Parzival* is divided into books, or chapters, of each thirty lines, so I will quote here the page first and then the book. *Titurel* consists of stanzas only, so here I refer to the page and the stanza when I quote a passage. For a historical-critical edition, see Wolfram von Eschenbach, *Parzival*. Studienausgabe. Mittelhochdeutscher Text nach der sechsten Ausgabe von Karl Lachmann. Übersetzung von Peter Knecht. Einführung zum Text von Bernd Schirok (Berlin and New York: Walter de Gruyter, 1998). For a recent summary of the relevant research, see, above all, Joachim Bumke, *Wolfram von Eschenbach*. 8th completely rev. ed. (Stuttgart and Weimar: Metzler, 2004); cf. also Heiko Hartmann, *Einführung in das Werk Wolframs von Eschenbach*. Einführungen Germanistik (Darmstadt: Wissenschaftliche Buchgesellschaft, 2015). For a solid number of introductory or interpretive studies in English, see *A Companion to Wolfram's Parzival*, ed. Will Hasty. Studies in German Literature, Linguistics, and

Culture (Columbia, SC: Camden House, 1999). I myself contributed an article here on "Reading, Writing, and Learning in Wolfram von Eschenbach's *Parzival*" (189–202); for a recent critical overview, though more directed at the general reader, see Joachim Heinzle, *Wolfram von Eschenbach: Dichter der ritterlichen Welt: Leben, Werke, Nachruhm* (Basel: Schwabe Verlag, 2019). The body of Wolfram research is legion; the Wolfram-von-Eschenbach Society publishes on a regular basis its yearbook, which often includes also bibliographical summaries.

4. For the latest edition of Wolfram's dawn songs, see *Die Lieder Wolframs von Eschenbach*, ed., trans., and commentary by Joachim Heinzle (Stuttgart: S. Hirzel Verlag, 2021).

5. Larissa Schuler-Lang, *Wildes Erzählen—Erzählen vom Wilden: "Parzival," "Busant" und "Wolfdietrich D."* Literatur – Theorie – Geschichte, 7 (Berlin: Akademie Verlag/De Gruyter, 2014), 191–99. She emphasizes correctly that the secret with which Parzival is invited to play with in the eponymous romance turns into deadly seriousness in *Titurel*. The poet's criticism is directed, as she points out, against the social construct of courtly wooing, which results, at least in *Titurel*, in a deadly constellation from which neither Sigune nor Schionatulander can extricate themselves. See also Astrid Lembke, *Inschriftlichkeit: Materialität, Präsenz und Poetik des Geschriebenen im höfischen Roman*. Deutsche Literatur, 37 (Berlin and Boston: Walter de Gruyter, 2020), for a discussion of the role of the written text, a secret by itself which Schionatulander obviously does not understand how to read critically.

6. Albrecht Classen, *Utopie und Logos. Vier Studien zu Wolframs von Eschenbach Titurel*. Beiträge zur älteren Literaturgeschichte (Heidelberg: Carl Winter Universitätsverlag, 1990); Alexander Sager, *Minne von maeren: On Wolfram's Titurel*. Transatlantische Studien zu Mittelalter und Früher Neuzeit, 2 (Göttingen: Vandenhoeck & Ruprecht, 2006); Larissa Schuler-Lang, *Wildes Erzählen – Erzählen vom Wilden: "Parzival," "Busant" und "Wolfdietrich D."* Literatur—Theorie—Geschichte, 7 (Berlin and Boston: Walter de Gruyter, 2014); see also the insightful studies by Walter Haug, "Erzählen vom Tod her: Sprachkrise, gebrochene Handlung und zerfallende Welt in Wolframs 'Titurel,'" id., *Strukturen als Schlüssel zur Welt: kleine Schriften zur Erzählliteratur des Mittelalters*. Kleine Schriften, 1 (1980; Tübingen: Max Niemeyer, 1989), 541–53; id.,"Vom Tristan zu Wolframs *Titurel* oder die Geburt des Romans aus dem Scheitern am Absoluten," *Deutsche Vierteljahrsschrift für Literaturwissenschaft und Geistesgeschichte* 82.2 (2008): 193–204; most recently, see Astrid Lembke, *Inschriftlichkeit: Materialität, Präsenz und Poetik des Geschriebenen im höfischen Roman*. Deutsche Literatur. Studien und Quellen, 37 (Berlin and Boston: Walter de Gruyter, 2020), who examines the material culture of the written word in courtly romances, and so also in Wolfram's *Titurel*.

7. https://handschriftencensus.de/werke/439 (last accessed on May 29, 2022).

8. Jutta Eming, "Evokation und Episteme: Zu Wissensmodi des Wunderbaren im späthöfischen Roman," *Darstellung und Geheimnis in Mittelalter und Früher Neuzeit*, ed. Jutta Eming and Volkhard Wels. Episteme in Bewegung, 21 (Wiesbaden: Harrassowitz, 2021), 25–47; the entire book is available free of charge at: https://www.harrassowitz-verlag.de/pdfjs/web/viewer.html?file=/ddo/artikel/81693/978-3

-447-11548-3_Kostenloser%20Open%20Access-Download.pdf#pagemode=thumbs (last accessed on May 30, 2022).

9. Monika Schausten, *Erzählwelten der Tristangeschichte im hohen Mittelalter: Untersuchungen zu den deutschsprachigen Tristanfassungen des 12. und 13. Jahrhunderts*. Forschungen zur Geschichte der älteren deutschen Literatur, 24 (Munich: Wilhelm Fink, 1999), 201–17.

10. See, for instance, Thomas Neukirchen, *Die ganze aventiure und ihre lere: der "Jüngere Titurel" Albrechts als Kritik und Vervollkommnung des "Parzival" Wolframs von Eschenbach*. Beihefte zum Euphorion, 52 (Heidelberg: Universitätsverlag Winter, 2006); see also the contributions to *Der "Jüngere Titurel" zwischen Didaxe und Verwilderung: neue Beiträge zu einem schwierigen Werk*, ed. Martin Baisch, Johannes Keller, Florian Kragl, and Matthias Meyer (Göttingen: V&R unipress, 2010); Britta Bußmann, *Wiedererzählen, weitererzählen und beschreiben: der "Jüngere Titurel" als ekphrastischer Roman*. Studien zur historischen Poetik, 6 (Heidelberg: Universitätsverlag Winter, 2011). As to the fragment as a literary phenomenon, see Albrecht Classen, "Die Suche nach der Utopie in der Gralswelt. Albrechts (von Scharfenberg) *Der jüngere Titurel*," *Parzival. Reescritura y Transformación*, ed. Berta Raposo Fernández (Valencia: Universitat de València, 2000), 133–56; id., "Der Text der nie enden will. Poetologische Überlegungen zu fragmentarischen Strukturen in mittelalterlichen und modernen Texten," *Zeitschrift für Literaturwissenschaft und Linguistik*, vol. 99: *Anfang und Ende*, ed. Wolfgang Haubrichs (1995), 83–113.

11. Armin Schulz, *Erzähltheorie in mediävistischer Perspektive*. Studienausgabe. 2nd rev. ed., ed. Manuel Braun, Alexandra Dunkel, and Jan-Dirk Müller (Berlin and Boston: Walter de Gruyter, 2015), 39–43.

12. I have recently investigated this metaphorical language at great length in *Tracing the Trails in the Medieval World: Epistemological Explorations, Orientation, and Mapping in Medieval Literature*. Routledge Studies in Medieval Literature and Culture (New York and London: Routledge, 2021). See also Joachim Bumke, *Die Blutstropfen im Schnee: Über Wahrnehmung und Erkenntnis im 'Parzival' Wolframs von Eschenbach*. Hermaea. Germanistische Forschungen, Neue Folge, 94 (Tübingen: Max Niemeyer, 2001).

13. See, for instance, Evelyn Meyer, "Wolfram von Eschenbach's *Parzival*: A Complex Reshaping and Expansion of a Source," *A Companion to World Literature*, ed. Ken Seigneurie. Vol. 2: *601 CE to 1450 CE*, ed. Christine Chism. Blackwell Companions to Literature and Culture (Hoboken, NJ, and Chichester, West Sussex, 2020), 967–77. I myself have written on Wolfram numerous times, see, for instance, "Wolfram von Eschenbach," *Medieval Folklore. An Encyclopedia of Myths, Legends, Tales, Beliefs, and Customs*, ed. John Lindow, John McNamara, and Carl Lindahl (Santa Barbara et al.: ABC-CLIO, 2000), 1062–63; id., "Wolfram von Eschenbach," *Arthurian Writers: A Biographical Encyclopedia*, ed. Laura Cooner Lambdin and Robert Thomas Lambdin (Westport, CT, and London: Greenwood Press, 2008), 70–80; see further Marion E. Gibbs, "Parzival," *The Literary Encyclopedia*. First published 09 January 2004 [https://www.litencyc.com/php/sworks.php?rec=true&UID=13213, last accessed on May 29, 2022). She also published the introductory article looking at Wolfram at large. For an extensive bibliographical overview with commentary, see

Albrecht Classen, "Wolfram von Eschenbach," *Oxford Bibliographies*, online (an extensive commented bibliography on this poet): http://www.oxfordbibliographies .com/view/document/obo-9780195396584/obo-9780195396584-0163.xml?rskey =JnnNsa&result=1&q=Wolfram#firstMatch (last accessed on May 29, 2022).

14. Albrecht Classen, "Introduction: The Authority of the Written Word, the Sacred Object, and the Spoken Word: A Highly Contested Discourse in the Middle Ages, With a Focus on the Poet Wolfram von Eschenbach and the Mystic Hildegard von Bingen," *Authorities in the Middle Ages: Influence, Legitimacy, and Power in Medieval Society*, ed. Sini Kangas, Mia Korpiola, and Tuija Aionen. Fundamentals of Medieval and Early Modern Culture, 12 (Berlin and Boston: Walter de Gruyter, 2013), 1–24; see also the contributions to *Sacred and Profane in Chaucer and Late Medieval Literature: Essays in Honour of John V. Fleming*, ed. Robert Epstein (Toronto: University of Toronto Press, 2010). Cf. also Barbara Newman, *Medieval Crossover: Reading the Secular Against the Sacred* (University of Notre Dame Press, 2013). See also the contributions to the exhibition catalog, *Secular Sacred: 11th–16th Century Works from the Boston Public Library and the Museum of Fine Arts*, ed. Nancy Netzer (Chicago: University of Chicago Press, 2006). Very insightful proves to be also Jane L. Mecham, "Cooperative Piety Among Monastic and Secular Women in Late Medieval Germany," *Church History and Religious Culture* 88 (2008): 581–611; see also Gabriele Signori, "Wanderer zwischen den 'Welten': Besucher, Briefe, Vermächtnisse und Geschenke als Kommunikationsmedien im Austausch zwischen Kloster und Welt," *Krone und Schleier: Kunst aus mittelalterlichen Frauenklöstern, Ruhrlandmuseum, die frühen Klöster und Stifte 500–1200. Kunst- und Ausstellungshalle der Bundesrepublik Deutschland, die Zeit der Orden 1200–1500*, ed. Jutta Frings and Jan Gerchow (Munich: Hirmer, 2005), 130–41; *The Sacred and the Secular in Medieval Healing: Sites, Objects, and Texts*, ed. Barbara S. Bowers and Linda Migl Keyser. AVISTA Studies in the History of Medieval Technology, Science and Art, 10 (London: Routledge, 2016).

15. Richard O'Gorman, "Grail," *The New Arthurian Encyclopedia*, ed. Norris J. Lacy. Updated Paperback Ed. (1991; New York and London: Garland Publishing, 1996), 212–13.

16. Rupert T. Pickens, "Grail and Grail Romances," *Medieval France: An Encyclopedia*, ed. William W. Kibler and Grover A. Zinn (New York and London: Garland Publishing, 1995), 409–10. See also the classical study by Roger Sherman Loomis, *The Grail: From Celtic Myth to Christian Symbol* (1963; Princeton, NJ: Princeton University Press, 1992; 2018); *The Grail, the Quest and the World of Arthur*, ed. Norris J. Lacy. Arthurian Studies, 72 (Cambridge: D. S. Brewer, 2008); Ben Ramm, *A Discourse for the Holy Grail in Old French Romance* (Cambridge: D. S. Brewer, 2012). There are many intriguing but also rather speculative studies that try to associate the ancient and medieval grail (as a cup) with specific vessels in various major churches or cathedrals. There might be some value to those endeavors, but they do not take us very far because the Grail has always been an ideological, mythical, and religious symbol which should not be confused with material aspects. There exist, however, indeed, specific references to the Grail in the Catalan world, both linguistically and materially, which has inspired some scholars to associate that region with

the origin of the Grail account; see, for instance, André de Mandach, *Auf den Spuren des Heiligen Gral: die gemeinsame Vorlage im pyrenäischen Geheimcode von Chrétien de Troyes und Wolfram von Eschenbach*. Göppinger Arbeiten zur Germanistik, 596 (Göppingen: Kümmerle, 1995).

17. Maximilian Benz, "Verrätseltes Erzählen vom Mysterium: Wer nimmt was auf Munsalvæsche wahr?," *Darstellung und Geheimnis in Mittelalter und Früher Neuzeit*, ed. Jutta Eming and Volkhard Wels. Episteme in Bewegung, 21 (Wiesbaden: Harrassowitz, 2021), 125–40.

18. https://www.biblegateway.com/verse/en/Matthew%204:19 (last accessed on May 29, 2022).

19. Horst Brunner, "*Von Munsalvaesche wart gesant / der den der swane brahte*: Überlegungen zur Gestaltung des Schlusses von Wolframs Parzival," *Germanisch-Romanische Monatsschrift* 41.4 (1991): 369–84.

20. Ulrike Draesner, *Wege durch erzählte Welten: intertextuelle Verweise als Mittel der Bedeutungskonstitution in Wolframs Parzival*. Mikrokosmos, 36 (Frankfurt a. M., Bern, et al.: Peter Lang, 1993); see also the illuminating study on the functioning of fictionality in Wolfram's work by Gertrud Grünkorn, *Die Fiktionalität des höfischen Romans um 1200*. Philologische Studien und Quellen, 129 (Berlin: Erich Schmidt Verlag, 1994).

21. Elizabeth Archibald, "Questioning Arthurian Ideals,"*The Cambridge Companion to the Arthurian Legend*, ed. eadem and Ad Putter (Cambridge: Cambridge University Press, 2009), 139–53; see also the contributions to *The Rusted Hauberk: Feudal Ideals of Order and Their Decline*, ed. Liam O. Purdon and Cindy L. Vitto (Gainesville, Tallahassee, et al.: University Press of Florida, 1994); and to *La matière arthurienne tardive en Europe: 1270–1530*, ed. Christine Ferlampin-Acher (Rennes: Presses universitaires de Rennes, 2020).

22. Herbert Kolb, *Munsalvaesche: Studien zum Kyotproblem* (Munich: Eidos-Verlag, 1963); Albrecht Classen, "Noch einmal zu Wolframs 'spekulativer' Kyôt-Quelle im Licht jüdischer Kultur und Philosophie des zwölften Jahrhunderts," *Studi Medievali* XLVI (2005): 281–308; Michael Stolz, "Kyot und Kundrie: Expertenwissen in Wolframs 'Parzival,'" *Wissen, maßgeschneidert: Experten und Expertenkulturen im Europa der Vormoderne*, ed. Björn Reich, Frank Rexroth, and Matthias Roickh. Historische Zeitschrift, Beiheft, N.F., 57 (Munich: Oldenbourg, 2012), 83–113.

23. Hartmann, *Einführung in das Werk* (2015), 20–25.

24. Eberhard Nellmann, *Wolframs Erzähltechnik: Untersuchungen zur Funktion des Erzählers* (Wiesbaden: Steiner, 1973), 57 et passim; id., "Wolfram und Kyot als 'vindære wilder mære," *Zeitschrift für deutsches Altertum und deutsche Literatur* 117 (1988): 31–67; as to the family structure, see Martin Przybilski, *sippe und geslehte: Verwandtschaft als Deutungsmuster im "Willehalm" Wolframs von Eschenbach*. Imagines medii aevi, 4 (Wiesbaden: Reichert, 2000).

25. For a convenient summary of this complex, see Hartmann, *Einführung in das Werk Wolframs von Eschenbach* (2015), 24.

26. Elisabeth Schmid, *Familiengeschichten und Heilsmythologie: die Verwandtschaftsstrukturen in den französischen und deutschen Gralromanen des 12. und 13. Jahrhunderts*. Beihefte zur Zeitschrift für romanische Philologie, 211 (Tübingen:

Max Niemeyer, 1986); Rolf E. Sutter, *Mit saelde ich gerbet han den gral: genealogische Strukturanalyse zu Wolframs von Eschenbach Parzival*. Göppinger Arbeiten zur Germanistik, 705 (Göppingen: Kümmerle, 2003).

27. I have addressed this issue already a while ago at great length, Albrecht Classen, *Verzweiflung und Hoffnung. Die Suche nach der kommunikativen Gemeinschaft in der deutschen Literatur des Mittelalters*. Beihefte zur Mediaevistik, 1 (Frankfurt a. M., Berlin, et al.: Peter Lang, 2002). See also my very condensed article "Communication in the Middle Ages," *Handbook of Medieval Studies: Terms—Methods—Trends*, ed. Albrecht Classen (Berlin and New York: Walter de Gruyter, 2010), vol. 1, 330–43. For a more linguistic approach to the same issue, communication, see Andreas Urscheler, *Kommunikation in Wolframs "Parzival": Eine Untersuchung zu Form und Funktion der Dialoge*. Deutsche Literatur von den Anfängen bis 1700, 38 (Bern, Berlin, et al.: Peter Lang, 2002).

28. Fritz Peter Knapp, "Der Gral zwischen Märchen und Legende," id., *Historie und Fiktion in der mittelalterlichen Gattungspoetik: Sieben Studien und ein Nachwort* (Heidelberg: Universitätsverlag C. Winter, 1997; orig. 1996), 133–51; he relies also on the theoretical concepts of John Stevens, *Medieval Romance: Themes and Approaches*. The Norton Library (London: 1973), 99–102 et passim.

29. Walter Haug, "Erzählen vom Tod her: Sprachkrise, gebrochene Handlung und zerfallende Welt in Wolframs 'Titurel,'" *Wolfram-Studien* VI, ed. Werner Schröder (Berlin: Erich Schmidt Verlag, 1980): 8–24; id., "Lesen oder Lieben? Erzählen in der Erzählung: vom 'Erec' bis zum 'Titurel,'" *Beiträge zur Geschichte der deutschen Sprache und Literatur* 166 (1994): 302–22.

30. See now the contributions to *Communication, Translation, and Community in the Middle Ages and Early Modern Period: New Socio-Linguistic Perspectives*, ed. Albrecht Classen. Fundamentals of Medieval and Early Modern Culture, 26 (Berlin and Boston: Walther de Gruyter, forthcoming).

31. Albrecht Classen, *Tracing the Trails* (2021), 140–64, esp. 153–54.

Chapter Four

Heldris de Cornuälle's *Roman de Silence*

The Secret of Gender Identity and the Secret of the Self—Nature versus Nurture, a Debate Raging Already in the Thirteenth Century

To gain a solid foundation for this chapter, we first need to reflect one more time on the ordinary definition of secrets in epistemological terms before we approach this phenomenon in terms of a person's peculiar identity, as it was already addressed in some medieval texts, such as Heldris de Cornuälle's *Roman de Silence*—he is also known as Heldris of Cornwall. Normally at least, we identify secrets with hidden, very important, highly sensitive, even elusive knowledge or data, that is, with mysterious objects or texts that point the way toward a sacred dimension, and this with special words that amount to a riddle or a magical formula with which the material world or personal relationships can be transformed. Secret codes or elusive keys serve some unique individuals to exclude most other people and thus to protect a mysterious truth, entity, location, or power; that is, a person or a tiny elite group protects a secret from being spoiled, abused, vandalized, or trivialized by the crowd or the masses for a number of good or bad reasons.

As I have already indicated in the introduction to this volume, much of human epistemology is limited, although we know of the existence of countless secrets and are painfully aware of our lack of knowledge or comprehension of the larger world. Countless late medieval philosophers already embraced this notion in their assessment of this world and its relationship with God. The simplest term for this phenomenon would be the "secret" that most people can ever comprehend. But this secret can also rest in the individual and forces him/her to wrestle with this issue for the rest of his/her life. In other words, our awareness or understanding of this existence in its material dimension proves to be rather limited, perhaps because we are only part of the microcosm, and possess nothing but a hunch of the macrocosm, as medieval thinkers would have argued. Hence, we might say that we really live in a world filled with secrets, and the more we study and learn about the universe, the less we seem to know because one secret is piled on another, and when we grasp finally one secret, or open one door, countless other rooms and doors appear hiding further secrets.

There are magical, scientific, medical, mechanical, artistic, and musical, but then also personal or social secrets. Maybe a little facetiously or imaginatively, we could claim that all of life actually consists of secrets and give us purpose, like doors and walls create subdivisions in a house; removing those would make our world simply flat and boring, perhaps even meaningless. One of many reasons why the Middle Ages as a cultural period continue to appeal to us, or once again within the framework of post-modernity, might really be the realization that many medieval people operated with secrets and did not voluntarily share their knowledge, whether we think of architects (building masters), pharmacists, composers, but then also of cooks and bakers, brewers and wine producers, painters and sculptors, magicians and musicians. If we think, for instance, of the rich tradition of medieval bestiaries, which did not really intend to present the concrete animal world as it was known then but offered instead allegorical messages and symbols of human vices and virtues, then we gain a hunch of the profound importance of secrets as epistemological vehicles.[1] In fact, the entire world of medieval manuscript illuminations appears as predicated on the notion of secrets insofar as only the learned individuals would be able to decipher the text, to comprehend its meaning, and hence to understand the secret hidden behind the words or the images.[2]

Secrets thus assume a critical role in all of human intellectual life, not so much because they might hide specific aspects, which would take on the active role of a demiurge behind or underneath all existence. Instead, they simply represent the next dimension, the depth, or the height, the unknown, the sacred, or the mysterious. Of course, Christians always believed that true or full knowledge of God was impossible because He is, epistemologically speaking, a secret.[3] We can, however, also perceive a rather trivial concept of medieval—or universal—secrets, which continue to be so attractive to us as something magical or even unbelievable.

Secrets both then and today inherently attract people's attention, just as a key for a locked door, whether there is anything hidden behind the closure or not. As we saw, for instance, Gawein in Heinrich von dem Türlin's *Diu Crône* also faced such a symbolic door, but when he finally pushed it open, there was nothing behind it, neither people nor furniture, and so no secret at all. However, the door itself proved to be the secret itself, as is often the case in life, or rather, the key to a secret that evades the protagonist's investigative grip. The question proper what something might mean in all of its cosmic, spiritual, or magical dimensions underscores the very nature and meaning of the secret, which is always elusive and yet present at the same time. Moreover, the further one seeks answers, the more new levels of meaning open up and challenge the individual to continue with this quest.

One of the greatest secrets of them all might well be the human being him/herself, apart from God or death. All our soul-searching might take us only so far, and then we stumble upon the next secret within our individuality. Whereas before we have examined cases of secrets that pertained to the domain of religion, or knowledge, here the focus will rest on secrets that are the inner core of the human being, whether we are talking about the soul, the brain, the heart, or the character, and so also about our own self, which is so easily challenged in the face of the divine, for instance. Medieval mystics had much to say about this, irrespective of the question of whether they understood this Godhead or not, whether they could comprehend the divine voices and visions or not.[4] Mysticism by itself could hence be identified as the experience of the soul with the divine secret.[5] Of course, all religions engage with the same phenomenon and could be identified as an esoteric strategy to come to terms with the *numinous*. But mysticism itself constitutes a direct, personal entrance into the secret world of the divine.

From here we can now turn to a different dimension of the secret, one closely associated with the human existence in its physical appearance. Not surprisingly, both our individual gender and our social standing are matters of intense debate and investigation particularly today, especially if we think of the LGBTQ discourse and related topics. Not even medically is it possible to solve the ultimate secrets behind our being; who would be able to determine immediately after conception whether the future baby will be male or female? Maybe medical research has already crossed the threshold of this secret and will be able in the near future to predict, if not even produce, the fetus' gender. The issue itself, however, consists of the fundamental observation that we as human beings are constructed, shaped by many different social and natural forces, and emerge from a host of different sources of influence to become ourselves. Who is to say what factors matter in that whole process?

Surprisingly, already the late Middle Ages witnessed the exploration of those secrets that predict our own future. I know of at least several cases when an individual undergoes at least a formal transformation. Here the focus will rest on gender conflicts brought about by some protagonists who use cross-dressing as a strategy to hide their true identity and to realize a particular agenda. Hiding behind a mask makes it possible for those characters to achieve their goals without being hampered by social stereotypes and prejudice.[6] The most important example is the thirteenth-century romance *Le Roman de Silence* by Heldris de Cornuälle, the focus of this chapter, where the secret of the gendered body assumes critical importance.

PARALLEL CASES OF CROSS-DRESSING: STRATEGIES OF GENDER SECRETS

But let us first examine a fourteenth-century Middle High German verse narrative, "Der Borte," by an otherwise virtually unknown poet, Dietrich von der Glezze. Here as well the secret of the female body in the disguise of a male knight matters centrally and invites us to reconsider the impact of the secret in social terms. Here, the mask serves the female protagonist to assume power within a patriarchal society and to defeat even her own husband and to expose his inner weakness. This verse narrative was created sometime in the second half of the thirteenth century, but we cannot say much more in definitive terms about the poet and his literary intentions. No other works by Dietrich seem to have survived, and we are facing a real mystery, as much as recent research has endeavored to investigate this brief text.[7]

The narrator presents at first a happily married couple, but the husband, Conrad, feels deeply frustrated with his low social status, maybe due to his youth, maybe due to his lack of masculinity. One day, he decides to join a tournament to improve his knightly esteem, so he leaves his wife behind, who has happily agreed with his plan. While she is enjoying her time in an enclosed garden, a stranger knight appears who immediately falls in love with her and tries to coax her into making love with him. First, he offers her a highly valuable goshawk that has the magical power of catching every bird it might be sent out to hunt. However, the lady flatly refuses this offer and does not want to be made a prostitute by him. He then adds his two greyhounds to the deal, and again we learn that those would be able to catch and kill any animal. Because she is refusing even this offer, he promises to grant her his horse which can run faster than any other animal. Again and again, the lady observes her honor and dignity and rejects all those valuable "attributes" of a worthy knight. Finally, when he promises even his belt which would guarantee its owner complete honor, she can no longer resist, takes all the animals and the belt, and allows the knight to make love to her. As he emphasizes, "Whoever wears the belt into which the stone is embossed will never lose honor and will always enjoy happiness; he will never be slain; he will never despair; he will always win the victory whenever he enters a fight. The stone helps against fire and water" (23).

The lady finally submits, takes all the gifts, and grants the knight her body. Unfortunately, they are secretly observed by one of her husband's servants, who promptly reports to his master what he has witnessed. Realizing that his wife has committed adultery, Conrad is so distressed that he immediately departs for Brabant (Flanders) to be as far away from his wife as possible, without communicating with her or returning home. Eventually, she takes charge of the entire situation, and embarks on a voyage to Brabant, but changes her appearance to a knight, calling herself Heinrich. At the court in Brabant, s/he demonstrates her/his superior knightly skills, being in command of those magical animals, which make it very easy for her to win every competition. She also enjoys the highest honor, which eventually makes her husband, who does not recognize him/her, beg for a gift so that he as well could gain some public respect. Either one of those superior animals would help him specifically to acquire some public fame (27). Heinrich, however, at first refuses, as s/he has done before, but then yields on the condition that his/her wish be fulfilled: "I love men, I have never loved women. If you do whatever I wish, I'll gladly give you the greyhounds and the bird of prey. But this has to happen secretly" (27). Of course, Conrad agrees, as much as he laments the fact that this worthy knight Heinrich is a homosexual: "I will have to lament this forever that you, wonderful knight, love men and not women" (27), and: "I will suffer everything and not refuse anything, whatever you desire from me. I want to and have to accept it all in return for the greyhounds and the bird of prey" (27).[8]

Only in the last minute, just after Conrad has placed himself on the floor to receive Heinrich as a sexual partner, does the latter reveal her true identity, lambasting her husband for his low morality and willingness to prostitute himself even in an act of homosexuality just in return for a bird of prey. She herself had committed this act of prostitution only under heavy duress and then not for herself, but for his sake, and certainly not in a homosexual context. Conrad is shocked and humiliated, but when he asks for forgiveness, she grants it to him, and the couple then reestablishes their mutual happiness.

As we can observe clearly, by employing the strategy of disguising her true sexual identity, making it a secret, the lady succeeds in demonstrating to her husband that she had sacrificed herself and should not be blamed so much, whereas he had thought only about himself and pursued the deal with Heinrich out of purely selfish reasons, or because he suffered from a profound character weakness. The secret itself was well guarded; not even the lady's servants were informed about her change of role-playing and once she had transformed into a knight, at least on the outside, she managed to play her new role perfectly, winning all the honors her husband was so desirous of and could never achieve. Ironically, she becomes more masculine than Conrad by means of those mysterious animals, which puts him, in the grander schema of things, into an even weaker position, but his wife prevents his complete falling down by handing over those magical creatures, which thus provide him what he essentially needs.

In fact, she knew exactly that she could not confront her husband directly, and she had to create a facade of a worthy and even admirable knight in order to undermine and destroy his pretense of moral superiority. She herself then reveals the secret and can thus triumph over him, but not at all in hostile terms. Instead, her effort with the disguise served the exclusive purpose of regaining him as her marital partner by way of demonstrating to him the tendency of all people to fail in difficult circumstances, particularly when the intention was a worthy one.[9]

Before we turn to *Silence*, where the hiding of the true gender assumes a particularly significant role, functionalizing the secret of Silence's true sexual identity for political purposes, let us also consider the charming *chantefable* of *Aucassin et Nicolette*, a prosimetric narrative from the middle of the thirteenth century where the young prince Aucassin falls in love with the former Muslim slave girl Nicolette, and against his father's angry attitude the two manage to escape from their imprisonments and flee into the world of fancy and even utopia.[10] Unfortunately, after a series of adventures, they are captured by pirates and taken in very different directions, though he can eventually return home, while she reaches her father's kingdom where they recognize and welcome her again. But their suffering is not over yet at all; while he laments the loss of his Nicolette, she is in danger of being forced to marry a Saracen king, which she refuses since she loves only Aucassin.

In that situation, Nicolette resorts to the same strategy as the lady in Dietrich's "Borte," disguising herself and assuming the role of a minstrel, although both lovers are filled with the same feelings for each other and suffer because of their involuntary separation. In the German verse narrative, Conrad had left his wife out of deep anger and frustration, and never makes an attempt at a rapprochement, which requires from her ultimately to pick up the baton and pursue her foolish husband and to bring him to reason.

When Nicolette realizes that her family intends to arrange a marriage for her without any consultation, she transfigures herself into a minstrel, first learning how to play the viol masterfully, then transforming her physical appearance into a male. She uses a potent herb which achieves the desired effect, and with the help of male clothing the disguise is perfect: "And she had a jacket, cloak, shirt and breeches made, then dressed in the guise of a minstrel. She took her viol, came to a mariner and charmed him so much that he allowed her on his ship" ("Et ele fist faire cote et mantel et cemisse et braies, si s'atorna a guise de jogleor. Si prist se viële, si vint a un marounier, se fist tant vers lui qu'il le mist en se nef").

Nicolette thus reaches the harbor city of Biaucaire where Aucassin resides—his parents have died already three years ago—and converses with him, pretending all the time to be a male minstrel. Once s/he has realized how much the prince is longing for his beloved, s/he promises to arrange a meeting, changes her appearance back to a woman, and can thus welcome her lover, which fills both with tremendous joy.

Just as in Dietrich's *Belt*, the cross-dressing is only temporary and serves exclusively for the purpose of allowing for some private space for both women in which they can operate as men—as a glorious knight or as an excellent minstrel. Once the male lover has been tested—in a way, Conrad really fails the test—the female figure changes back into her original appearance and solves the riddle for the male partner. Only because these two women have slipped into a secret existence, do they gain the inner freedom to orchestrate a major strategy either to teach the husband a lesson about human frailty and humility or to test and confirm the honesty of the feelings of the beloved. There are a good number of other such cases, often within the context of hagiography and martyrdom, and each time the narrative focus is predicated on the existence of a secret that functions as the critical key to making it possible for the love affair to revive or to develop further.

It is also worth considering briefly Ulrich von Liechtenstein's famous *Frauenbuch* from ca. 1270 in which this Styrian poet created a female image of himself, dressing up as Lady Venus and organizing and participating in tournaments in that role while traveling around in his region. Everyone saw through his mask, of course, but it still served him as a unique secret to play a double role as a knight and as a courtly lady.[11] As to be expected, everyone in his social environment is fully aware of the ploy utilized by this famous figure, and they all join in his theater production of late medieval knighthood, certainly great fun for them all because Ulrich had put on a mask and pretends to be a woman and yet fights like a man, and this very successfully.[12] As much as the protagonist pretends to wear a mask and thus to hide his sexual identity, as much everyone among his audience—Ulrich really transforms his entire knightly journey into a protracted theater stage—admires his costume, knowing full well that a man hides behind the woman's clothing: "They'd only come to look at us. / I had a servant question thus, / 'Are there no jousters hereabout?' / They answered, 'Lady, yes. No doubt / there are at least a thousand here / who would most gladly break a spear / with you but jousting in this state / is outlawed by the magistrate' (stanza 490). It is all a 'masquerade' (stanza 473, 2), but certainly a delightful one."[13]

And in "her" letter, the Queen Venus informs all the knights in the various parts of the Habsburgian empire of her arrival and her intention of teaching them the principles of love (p. 100). The secret of her true identity is seemingly very important, but the facetious nature of this entire game remains rather obvious: "She decrees that on the eighth day after the end of her journey there shall be a tournament at Korneuburg. Whichever knight hears of her journey and does not come against her she places under the ban of love and of all good women" (p. 100). As much as Ulrich operates with a secret, as much it also proves to be an open secret everyone acknowledges and understands, which actually heightens the intensity of this operetta, as we might call the entire *Frauendienst*. The more Ulrich pretends to rely on his secret mask, the less it really covers his true identity, which puts this work into a clear contrast to the other examples of cross-dressing.[14]

HELDRIS DE CORNUÄLLE

This now invites us to turn to the most amazing *Romance de Silence* (ca. second half of the thirteenth century), which has come down to us in only one manuscript, originally kept in Wollston Hall, Nottinghamshire, first rediscovered in 1911 by W. H. Stevenson when he created a report of the manuscripts of Lord Middleton (1911), and now kept in the University of Nottingham Library under the shelf mark of Mi.LM.6.[15] This manuscript also contains the following works: *Le roman de Troie, Ille et Galeron, Le roman d'Alixandre* (at least 4000 verses of the complete text), *La chanson d'Aspremont*, most of *La Vengeance Raguidel*, four anonymous fabliaux, six fabliaux by Gautier li Leus, and *Li dis Raoul de Hosdaing*.[16] But scholarship cannot proceed fully until a reliable edition of a text has been produced, which was finally published by Lewis Thorpe in a serial fashion in the *Nottingham Mediaeval Studies* from 1961 to 1967, and then, in book form, in 1972.[17] Quite uniquely, at least for his time, Heldris discussed the basic issue of gender construction, which he cast in the dialectical tension between nature and nurture. In practical terms, the romance relates the story of the female character Silence who is forced to be brought up as a male because the king of England has banned all females from inheriting their fathers' lands as a result of unfortunate circumstances involving twin sisters and their lovers who fight against each other and succumb to death.[18]

This richly illustrated manuscript (eighty-three miniatures) did not attract much attention at first, and the realization that it actually contained this most curious *Roman de Silence*, which does not conform to the standard features of Arthurian or Grail romance at all, did not occur until 1928.[19] As Psaki emphasizes, this narrative falls neither into the category of *romans réalistes* nor into the one of *romans merveilleux*; there are virtually no references to magic, to King Arthur, no allusions to archetypal themes, and no remarks about fanciful or imaginary locations. Instead, as creative as this *Roman de Silence* proves to be, it is still squarely situated in the here and now, reflecting specific historical and political events, and yet yanks us out of reality.[20] Only fairly recent scholarship has recognized the enormous potential of the themes included in this text, that is, primarily the conflict between nature and nurture, the identification of gender, identity and gender, the role of females as feudal rulers, sex and violence, cross-dressing, silence and speaking, words and power, and the significance of names for one's social and gender identity.[21]

He was deeply grieved over the death of two knights who had married twin sisters and had then fought to their mutual death over the issue of who would be entitled to take over the inheritance from their wives (the heirs). Silence's parents (Cador and Euphemie) are fully aware of this political and legal restriction, but since they have only one child, a daughter, they try secretly to subterfuge the king's order by pretending throughout their whole life that their daughter is male. This then leads to many conflicts between the boy-maiden and her social environment, but Silence proves to be strong, resolute, intelligent, brave, and smart and can thus maintain the deception until Merlin appears who reveals not only the truth of her gender identity but also the false roles played by the queen and her male lover, disguised as an abbess. Despite the protagonist's long-term pretense, which works surprisingly well considering her strength and power to act out the role of a male within a knightly society—or also as a jongleur or rather minstrel—in the end, she is happy to return to her own biological gender and shed her male appearance.[22]

At the same time, which even recent research has not yet fully recognized, so it seems, there are numerous highly important topics concerning the basic political and legal structure in late medieval Europe, such as a wise king, the reliance on trustworthy counselors, the lack of legal procedures, falsification of letters, communication, the significance of rituals and gestures, especially with regard to the kiss,[23] the conflicts between a king and his vassals/barons, the relationship between parents and their children, the meaning of masculinity, and others.[24]

Significantly, Heldris did not compose a courtly narrative in the tradition of Arthurian romance, although one of the main figures, King Ebain, is identified as the king in England next to King Arthur (107–111). However, at the end of the romance, the *deus ex machina* is Merlin who, through his prophetic abilities, succeeds to reveal all secrets and thus to solve all major conflicts. Heldris drew here directly from one of his sources, *L'Estoire Merlin*, and thus incorporated a major narrative key to solve the issue addressed in this intriguing romance. As the literary tradition relates, Merlin would not allow any male to catch him and to take him prisoner. Only a female would be entitled to do that, and since Silence is really a woman, Merlin makes this miracle happen, which then exposes all the masks at the king's court and leads to the happy end, where nature and nurture find themselves together again in a harmonious union.[25]

Nevertheless, Merlin here appears almost like personified secret himself because he might well operate in a double configuration. Forlorn Silence does not know how to find Merlin and thus to accomplish his/her task set by the king, who really does not want him/her to return ever in response to his wife's charge against the young "man" that he tried to kill her due to her unwillingness to grant her love to him. Suddenly, however, a wise old man appears and reveals to the young woman/man the specific trick or trap by which Merlin could be caught (cooked meat, drinks, etc., hence, human cuisine and culture). Some scholars have gone so far as to equate the actual Merlin with this old man because it would make good sense to assume that the mysterious magician might want to return to society and to expose finally all the secrets, including Silence's own identity, especially because that man knows so much about Merlin and assures the protagonist that he will catch him (5925–28).[26] This would suggest from the start that the poet Heldris intended to reflect on the very nature of human identity, the structure of society, and the role of the individual within his/her world. The ultimate purpose of this romance would hence be to explore the fundamental epistemology of human existence which tends to remain hidden for most people who struggle throughout life to comprehend themselves and to solve the riddle of who they are.

In his prologue, the narrator vehemently laments the decline of ethics and morality among the aristocracy, bemoaning the fact, above all, that money matters much more than honor in public life and that consequently, people seem to have lost a sense of their own values and ideals, that is, knowledge about themselves. He also includes several times rather negative comments about women at large and also presents truly evil female characters, such as King Ebain's wife, Eupheme. However, by the same token, Heldris also idealizes the female protagonist, presents her mother Euphemie in highly positive terms, and so seems to contradict himself either deliberately or unconsciously. Moreover, he emphasizes himself or has one of the male figures state that women ought to stay quiet, hence, ought to submit themselves completely under patriarchal rule—in a direct allusion to the meaning of Silence's name. They could not be trusted and would have to be regarded as irrational beings easily subject to their erotic desires without any self-control.

However, at closer analysis, we easily discover that the poet actually demonstrates great respect for his female protagonist who performs major feats of chivalry and knighthood and knows exceedingly well how to formulate his thoughts and to communicate with her social environment. Ironically, Merlin actually acts out the role of the silent one, laughing out loudly about the various people whom he encounters at court due to their deceptions or self-illusions. In other words, Merlin constitutes a secret, both here in *Silence* and in many other Arthurian narratives. As William W. Kibler summarizes concerning all of the medieval traditions, "Merlin is constantly at the center of the action, predicting events and using his magical powers to control history. He is puckish and benevolent and constantly makes us of his shapeshifting powers to aid and befuddle."[27] For a long time, he refuses to speak, and only laughs, which irritates the king to no end, so he needs to threaten Merlin in most severe terms to reveal what he knows truly. Silence (here the absence of words) as a shroud to keep a secret thus proves to be a key component of the entire romance, while the protagonist Silence keeps silent about her true identity.

The real culprit in the entire narrative set-up, if that is the proper term, proves to be King Ebain because he had imposed the law that women would no longer be entitled to their parents' inheritance. From this followed a whole sequence of events mostly predicated on the workings of secrets. Not only does Silence face almost two decades in the disguise of a male person before everything is solved, but s/he is also erotically pursued by the Queen Eupheme who has fallen madly in love with him/her—certainly not an indication of any homosexual inclinations since she fully assumes Silence to be male—and then, since the boy-maiden rejects all of her efforts to seduce her/him, tries her hardest to get him executed, first immediately at their court, subsequently by sending him to the king of France with the request to have him killed without delay. Later, since her plot by means of a falsified letter had failed, she makes her husband send him away from the court with the task of catching Merlin. However, we might assume that Merlin is already waiting for Silence and just makes her/him struggle hard for a long time to find him. Once the *deus ex machina* has allowed (!) Silence to set up the trap, he becomes instrumental in solving the many secrets at court.

This then leads over to another major thematic involving the French king, whom Ebain allegedly had asked to execute the young man, although it had been the queen who had replaced the original letter with her own—a topos which traditionally victimized innocent women have to suffer, such as in the Middle High German *Mai und Beaflor*.[28] Other literary parallels can be found in *Huon de Bordeaux*, *L'Estoire Merlin*, and in *Tristan de Nanteuil*.[29] Silence immediately impresses everyone at the court—maybe because of her feminine appearance within a male guise—and the king likes him/her so much that he embraces and kisses him, which represents a definite guarantee of his personal safety. The king's kiss represents a public pledge, but he is caught in a dilemma because Ebain is his loyal friend to whom he is committed in many ways, so he cannot really afford to carry out the request of having Silence executed on the spot. Hence, he turns to his baronial counselors who reflect intensely on how to decide in this case. One of them emphasizes that the kiss provides Silence at least with a guarantee of forty days of safety.[30] Another questions, however, is whether Ebain had really dictated that letter, so they finally recommend inquiring with King Ebain about this situation before they proceed with any actions. Ebain soon learns the truth because his Chancellor, who had written the original letter, finally realizes that the queen had replaced that one with her own.

Surprisingly, however, Ebain covers for his wife and pretends that all is good at his court. Since he then finds a major uprising by one of his barons, he asks for Silence's return, who then proves to be the most valiant fighter and secures the victory. However, the queen then seeks further the demise of the obstinate youth and can convince her husband, on the pretense once again that Silence had tried to rape and/or kill her, to send the young man on a quest to catch the wild Merlin, without whom he would never be allowed to return. Silence succeeds despite all odds because an old man shows him a trick of how to trap the wizard. This then leads to the conclusion because Merlin, though a prisoner, laughs loudly and uncontrollably when he recognizes the truth behind all the masks carried by various people or their ignorance about their destiny. This laughter indicates that the revelation of the secrets is near, the resolution of the entire romance is about to happen because from the laughter results enlightenment, so the secrets will be revealed.

What makes the *Roman de Silence* stand out so much in comparison with most other courtly narratives from across medieval Europe thus can be identified as the poet's brilliant strategy to combine various narrative strategies and motives, at times almost contradictory in their orientation (women are supposed to be quiet, and yet women need to speak out for themselves). As much as Heldris created a fictional work, as much he situated it within a concrete historical context. There are elements borrowed from the genre of "mirrors for princes" and political didacticism (prologue); there are allusions to King Arthur (Merlin) and the *Tristan* tradition (Cador's love for Euphemie).[31] Further, he experimented in a most innovative manner with the gender issue (nature versus nurture), and he reflected on the legal, political, and financial aspects determining Silence's destiny.

Although this romance has survived only in one manuscript, we are on solid ground to identify it as one of the major thirteenth-century French literary masterpieces because of the complexity of the narrative development, the individual figures' characters and motives, and because of the combination of many different political, ethical, moral, and gender topics. We are also informed much about the contemporary music scene when young Silence runs away from home and joins two minstrels whose art s/he learns quickly and then outdoes easily, which makes them to hate the young "man," whom they try to kill but fail, without any consequences for either side.

Of course, the poet drew from a variety of sources (biblical, classical, and medieval), but the entire romance emerges as a most unique work which finds no real parallel in medieval and even modern literature. we find parallel cases of a queen trying to seduce a young knight who flatly rejects all of her pursuits, which in turn makes her an enraged enemy, then attempting to get him executed because of his alleged rape attempt (motif borrowed from the Old Testament, story of Joseph and Potiphar's wife, *Genesis* 39 (see Marie de France, "Lanval," ca. 1190).[32] Altogether, however, the *Roman de Silence* stands on its own and deserves greatest respect for its innovative contributions to medieval French literature. This very innovative character, however, probably prevented it from experiencing any significant reception or popularity. Only through our modern critical perspectives have been able to realize its true literary quality.

The purpose of this chapter, of course, cannot be to offer an in-depth reading of this thirteenth-century romance, which contains so many different topics, issues, themes, and motifs of great significance in military, political, economic, communicative, and social terms, not to speak of gender. As Julia Rüthemann has recently indicated once again, the *Roman de Silence* constitutes really a literary reflection of the nature of human language, its potentiality, its transformative power, and the danger of changing material reality.[33] By contrast, and as a direct reflection on the eponymous protagonist's experiences and actions, the entire romance is actually predicated on the sense of the secret, here concerning Silence's true gender. But the poet also engaged with the notion of language as a secret, pitting words against silence, behind which rests the true secret of Silence's actual identity.

We would not need to go much further in our discussion about Silence's gender role as a secret, since this is very apparent throughout the text, and which scholarship has discussed almost *ad nauseam*. More important, however, seems to be the phenomenon that the entire romance consists of many different layers of secrets, which do not all concern the protagonist. Let us examine some of those more carefully in order to gain a better insight into the epistemological function of secrets as they determine many different aspects in this narrative. Although the author/narrator does not address the secret as such in the prologue, he certainly points out a major discrepancy among his contemporaries who pretend to pursue the ideals of nobility but in reality have subscribed entirely to the acquisition of money. Traditional courtly values have been replaced with financial interests: "Courting, jousting and tourneying, / carrying sleeves as favors, wooing ladies, / all this they have changed into piling up manure" (43–45). True manure would at least fertilize the ground (49), whereas money "shames the one who hoards it" (51). Flattery has become the common strategy in the courts, whereas honest words are no longer appreciated (71–72) both comments certainly belonging to an old tradition of rhetorical complaints about the downfall of the world in ethical and moral terms. However, Heldris thereby sets the stage for his criticism of his world where the truth has been lost and deception rules. Remarkably, he posits this profound insight: "and honest poverty is worth much more / than a thousand marks without joy and celebration; / and a free and noble will is worth more / than to be avaricious and the king of France" (97–100; with line 99 specifying in the original: "gentils et france"). External appearance trounces the hidden truth and value, so a mask has been put on by most members of courtly society who no longer live by the ideals of the past. Of course, his laments do not address a secret, quite on the contrary. But the narrator thus sets the tone for the entire romance in which reality often seems to be divorced from the pretenses embraced by many individuals.

When we learn about the love relationship between Cador and Euphemie, who later become Silence's parents, we recognize a different kind of secret, this one identified as love per se which both feel strongly for each other but cannot reveal. The entire conversation between both is a delightful play with words, rhetorical exchanges, alluding to the secret of erotic passion, pretending, and probing at the same time. As the narrator emphasizes: "She loved him much, but he did not know it" (555), while describing his great hesitation to ask her about her feelings for him: "He wanted to tell her without delay / . . . / but then he thought that he would not dare / just yet, but would wait awhile longer" (571–74). Although she is able to heal his physical sickness resulting from the dragon's toxic fumes, lovesickness then overpowers him, and yet he does not dare to reveal his passion to Euphemie. The same applies to her, so both are actually stuck in their own feelings and cannot address the secret shared by both, their love for each other. Moreover, Cador does not reveal to his uncle, King Ebain, what he ails from, transforming his feelings for Euphemie into a special secret that tortures him increasingly without any release. The same, however, is the case with her: "On account of the pain which bound her / and the love which preoccupied her" (775–76). In an ironic twist, she laments that she has healed many people with her various medicines but cannot help herself in this situation (789–91). Tragically for her, the king had, of course, promised to Cador that he could choose any woman in the kingdom still available as his future wife, and Euphemie is now scared that he might have already made up his mind, but against her (798–804). However, she herself has been given by the king the privilege to choose her own marriage partner in return for healing Cador from his mortal sickness. In short, the plot thickens tremendously, the secret between them is that there is no secret, only love shared by both. The narrator virtually smiles about both since they are truly destined for each other, pine for each other, and yet remain distanced out of fear of rejection. For example: "And if Euphemie for her part had been aware / that he had suffered such pain for her, / she would hardly have refused him, I think" (833–35). Both here and throughout the entire narrative, the poet has deeply invested in the exploration of the relationship between speaking/language and silence, and the secret itself, either the love between Cador and Euphemie or Silence's true gender identity, looms large on the narrative horizon.[34]

In a most intricate strategy, early the next morning she enters his room and utters the phrase, "Ami, speak, alas!" (882), which reveals what she means and yet hides it as well, as the narrator then elaborates through a complex reflection her use of words and the deliberate abstinence of resorting to the pronoun "to me" (885). Linguistically, as we could say, the secret of their love experiences a tremendous rapprochement in that situation, but it still takes many thoughts, comments, and reflections until both finally get so close that they cannot help but to reveal their love for each other, which thus breaks the secret and makes it to a shared experience. Yet, both linger on, still stuck in that secret which makes them believe that the other one has a specific marriage partner in mind, which would make their love impossible: "But Euphemie was jealous of that person" (987). Cador even reflects on the "secret" that "You will take a lord as soon / as I, *amie*, shall take a wife" (1003–04). In the original, it says: "Que jel vos di tolt a larron," which certainly carries the same meaning of secrecy. He even envisions the moment when she will marry someone else, which would create great pain for him (1012), which then leads over to his admission that he is suffering from love sickness, at least according to his description of his physical manifestations (1015–23).[35]

After more back and forth, both finally realize that they carry the same secret, and that the time has come for them to reveal it to each other, but this in greatest secrecy: "And let us promise here / to keep the secret; you / will not tell me unless I permit you; / nor will I tell you unless you allow, by faith" (1079–82). Cador agrees to tell the full truth to her, but he insists that neither one holds anything back (1088–89) because the secret that still separates them proves to be too sacred or powerful to let it be defiled. Ironically, when they then both touch each other's hand for the oath-taking, the physical contact infuses them with so much passion that their words fail them, and instead of talking about their feeling, they begin to kiss uncontrollably, which the narrator comments in highly respectful and admirable terms: "They acted without speaking, it seems to me, / a very clear sign of noble love, / for the kiss taught them well" (1094–96).

This kiss constitutes the open confession of their love since it is not the kiss exchanged between a mother and a son, or a father and his son (1100); instead, it is the kiss of love, just as in the famous case of Paolo and Francesco in Canto V of *Inferno* by Dante Alighieri (ca. 1320).[36] We could also think of the kiss exchanged between Tristan and Isolde in Gottfried von Straßburg's eponymous romance (ca. 1210), where the crucial scene is preceded by an equally opaque exchange of words that threaten to confound Tristan, although he himself is filled with strong feelings of love for Isolde, his uncle King Mark's future bride back in Cornwall.[37] The kiss creates a new space for the two young people, and this both in this and in many other medieval narratives, a space that is preserved only for them and constitutes a physical secret, just as the love cave in Gottfried's *Tristan* identifies a secret love which only the two of them can share. Of course, what Heldris and Gottfried describe in their respective romances, constitutes a universal, archetypal experience; the secrecy of the erotic encounter. In a way, I am not really observing anything dramatically new here. However, continuing with the overall observation that life constitutes a secret, we would be allowed, I think, to claim that Heldris, above all, elaborated on the secretive nature of the feeling of love in most specific terms, confirming that love, as the apogee of life, is hence a secret and needs to be acknowledged as such.

Almost as a side note, the two lovers then even reflect on secrecy in case they might have to go into exile if their wishes would not be approved by the king and his council to let them marry: "Tolt a laron, sans faire noise" (1350; "secretly, without any fuss"). Both had received the king's pledge to fulfill their wish of a marriage partner, but the final decision is here prolonged, which makes the couple deeply worried. But in this case, secrecy proves to be only temporary since the council simply takes some time to deliberate with the king. And this delay provides the opportunity for the two young people to express more specifically the true character of their love for each other. Even if they owned everything in the world, they would not be happy without love (1372–73). As Cador says explicitly, thus divulging the deepest secret in his heart: "And if anyone took your love from me / he could not console me with all the world" (1383–84).

These verbal exchanges remain, however, secrets to the outside world because the two people only whisper into each other's ears afraid of revealing their feelings to the public. Nevertheless, the Count of Chester, who is sent by the council to confer with them and to urge them to accept each other in marriage because they would fit together so well, then recognizes by their gazes and postures that they are actually deeply in love, which means that both sides actually pursue the same wishes. In other words, the secret that Cador and Euphemie still try to maintain is suddenly no longer one, and this revelation constitutes the major breakthrough in their relationship, which then leads over to their publicly approved union in marriage.

Heldris develops the entire scene in a delightfully entertaining fashion, with the count arriving, watching the two from some distance, understanding their feelings—he himself had once been deeply in love and so knows clearly what is going on here at this moment—as displayed in their bodily presence, and alerting them about himself by making a coughing sound ("Ahem," 1405), "for he was courteous, and wished to alert them" (1406). In this situation secrecy is no longer of any use, so he requests Cador to be open about his love because his feeling for Euphemie is exactly what the council would actually like to see. Of course, as he knows, and as the narrator confirms, "and he knew well that in love there is shame" (1413), which thus leads to secrecy. Accordingly, as soon as the count has spoken and indicated that he knows about their secret love for each other, the color of their faces changes dramatically as a result of their embarrassment (1428–32). The secret thus reveals itself, and since it meets with the king's and his counselors' full approval, it is no longer necessary to preserve a cover for their love.

Nevertheless, already in the next stage of the narrative, with the birth of their daughter, they resort to the strategy of relying on a secret once again in order to protect the inheritance for Silence, and raise her as a boy, which leads to all kinds of complications, as I have discussed already above. The entire episode with Cador and Euphemie falling in love with each other serves particularly well to indicate the significance of the secret, that is, the distance between inside and outside knowledge. In their case, things turn out well with complete happiness for both and their families, for the king, and for his council. The opposite, however, occurs later when Ebain's wife Eupheme lusts for Silence and does not understand that he/she is of a different gender than publicly assumed. As the narrator underscores: "who was so misled by appearances" (4722). Of course, we often hear how much people who encounter Silence find him/her very attractive, whether jongleurs or the king of France and his court, none of them knowing anything about the young man's actual gender identity. But the queen goes one step further and wants to possess Silence's body sexually, which the narrator characterizes as "disloyalty" (3696), "misfortune" (3697), and "madness" (3698).

She resorts to secrecy as well and calls Silence into her private chamber: "she wanted to tell her love in secret" (3728). She pretends to be ill, suffering from a bad case of migraine, asks all her servants and maids to leave, and requests the young man to soothe her with his harp playing, which carries, of course, deeply symbolic meaning, apart from the direct allusion to the biblical harpist, David who was called in by King Saul to help him with his music to ease his pains (1 Samuel 16:14–23). The queen fails, however, in all of her attempts to seduce the young man "since his nature did not allow it" (3824), that is, because s/he keeps her own secret well- hidden and cannot be swayed by the queen. In fact, Silence then experiences horrible sexual harassment, but s/he cannot afford to reveal her true gender if she does not want to lose all of her inheritance.

The more the queen feels passion for him, the more his/her heart is filled with hatred (3878), but the entire conflict, which would have almost cost his life, is resolved only at the very end with the help of Merlin who reveals not only Silence's true identity but also the queen's secret love affair with a man under the guise of an abbess. One secret is thus balanced by another secret, and only once the mysterious man has stopped laughing and begun telling the court what he knows about them all, that is, their secrets, does the narrative reach its conclusion.

Intriguingly, throughout the entire romance, Silence is struggling with him/herself whether s/he should accept the role given him/her by nature or nurture, and at one point, having weighed both options for male or female, s/he decides to keep it all a secret: "I will not reveal my secret" (2656). But the narrator also acknowledges that the human heart often pursues its own path and does not readily reveal its secrets, vacillating and turning this or that way depending on many different circumstances (2667–72). Consequently, Silence finds him/herself caught in a secret, that is, an existential dilemma from which there does not seem to be an easy way to extricate him/herself from. But when s/he runs away with the minstrels, s/he resorts to the same strategy as his/her parents had done, disguising their child as a male. In this situation, Silence puts on the mask of a simple person, hiding his/her aristocratic origin (2909–12). As much as there is deep doubt about his/her gender identity, s/he plays with the secret strategy of changing his/her appearance and also name (then Malductus) and proves to be quite successful in that, which allows her/him to learn the trade of a minstrel and to acquire mastery in playing the harp and vielle accompanying it with his/her voice, and this so much that the two jongleurs even plot to assassinate him out of jealousy, though this fails because Silence simply stays behind at a duke's court and sends the two men off.

Finally, to reflect on the role played by Merlin once again, we can recognize clearly the typical narrative strategy to cast this mysterious person as a living secret who does not allow any man to catch him; only a woman would be entitled to succeed in that, which could be a direct allusion to the symbolic unicorn putting down its head in the Virgin Mary's lap.[38] In a way, Merlin's own identity remains mysterious, it is just as much a secret as is that of Silence, although in the end the magician and prophet in one person reveals all the secrets of the protagonist, the queen, and the abbess. But he also admits to the king that he himself had been deceived by Silence, just as the king had been, and so all other people whom the boy-maiden had encountered throughout her/his life. By means of his prophesying power Merlin can thus solve all the riddles, reveal the secrets, and return order to the world, allowing nature to regain its right over Silentius—here in the Latinized version—and transform him back into a female, as Silentia (6664–68).[39]

The king revokes his own rule excluding women from inheritance (6643), acknowledges both Silence and women at large in their own strength and honor, and entirely rejects the traditional misogyny voiced so many times throughout the Middle Ages, and so as well in this romance: "There is no gem or treasure / so precious as a good woman. / No man can value enough / a woman who refuses to deceive" (6633–35). The greatest secret thus proves to be not just Silence and his/her disguise, but womanhood at large which men have misunderstood, despised, belittled, and rejected for so long.[40] Although we hear repeatedly that women's greatest quality would be to observe silence (6398–406), King Ebain has his wife Eupheme executed brutally (drawn and quartered), and soon after marries Silence, which thus brings about harmonious closure to a world determined by many secrets.

There are, of course, as scholars have pointed out repeatedly, many earlier cases of cross-dressed women such as the saints Marina, Eugenia, Apollinaris, Euphrosyne, Pelagia, Theodora, etc.[41] But Silence represents much more than a martyr, far from it. Instead, she struggles for the first two decades of her life to find herself and to gain acceptance as an independent person who is entitled to inherit her father's lands and title. Silence does not only stand in, just as Merlin does for a long time, for the function of the human language in revealing and hiding truths[42]; she emerges as the core of the secret itself, she is the secret, as a woman in a man's physical appearance, and thus mirrors the deceptiveness of human epistemology, language, and understanding at large. Little wonder that it took so incredibly long for modern scholarship[43]—not even to talk about the medieval audience (middle or late thirteenth century), which apparently mostly ignored Heldris's romance—to recognize the intricate meaning of this highly unusual romance. Most uniquely and intriguingly, this literary masterpiece is fundamentally predicated on the exploration of the secret as such as a life-supporting instrument, obviously much more than almost all other similar cases in medieval literature. Silence's true gender identity, though at the end revealed as being female, proves to be rather hybrid, which even the female clothing donned at the end cannot hide. Within her masculine garb, Silence was certainly one of the most competent knights of her time and the critical military supporter safeguarding the king's survival. In a way, Heldris suggested that gender might not necessarily be the best category to provide people with a specific identity; the secret consists in the gender fluidity and hence in the observation that the individual does not know that much about him/herself in the first place. Just as we today are beginning to realize the degree to which gender is socially constructed (Judith Butler and others) this Old French romance author already realized through his romance a remarkable literary testimony of the most burning secret, that is, ourselves.

There is no doubt that Silence operates most effectively as a knight, and s/he can outdo many men at court and on the battlefield. But once s/he has been exposed by Merlin, she easily transforms into a woman and performs in that role very well. In a way, Heldris leaves us guessing as to what determines really gender since his protagonist can carry out both male and female roles without difficulties, depending on the circumstances.

NOTES

1. See, for instance, Florence Mcculloch, *Medieval Latin and French Bestiaries*. North Carolina Studies in the Romance Languages and Literatures (Chapel Hill, NC: University of North Carolina at Chapel Hill Department of Romance Studies, 2017); Christian Heck and Rémy Cordonnier, *The Grand Medieval Bestiary: Animals in Illuminated Manuscripts* (New York: Abbeville Press, 2012); Meredith T. McMunn and Willene B. Clark, *Beasts and Birds of the Middle Ages: The Bestiary and Its Legacy*. The Middle Ages Series (1989; Philadelphia, PA: University of Pennsylvania Press, 2016); Debra Hassig, *Medieval Bestiaries: Text, Image, Ideology* (Cambridge: Cambridge University Press, 1995); Stephanie Mühlenfeld, *Konzepte der "exotischen" Tierwelt im Mittelalter* (Göttingen: V&R unipress, 2019).

2. There are numerous studies on medieval manuscript illuminations; and one of the most intriguing examples would be the *Book of Kells*; see Albrecht Classen, "The Book of Kells—The Wonders of Early Medieval Christian Manuscript Art Within a Pagan World," *Mediaevistik* 32 (2019; appeared in 2020): 55–69.

3. Bee Yun, *Wege zu Machiavelli: Die Rückkehr des Politischen im Spätmittelalter*. Beihefte zum Archiv für Kulturgeschichte, 91 (Vienna, Cologne, and Weimar: Böhlau, 2021), 155, illustrating this argument in light of Coluccio Salutati's (1331–1406) political and theological theses. Yun cites, for instance, "Scimus Deum necessarium quidam esse, necessaria cuncta necessitans, et cum certisimum sit quod sit, impossibile tamen scire quit sit" (impossible to know what He is).

4. This finds a beautiful expression in the book title chosen by Hildegard Elisabeth Keller for her study *My Secret is Mine: Studies on Religion and Eros in the German Middle Ages*. Studies in Spirituality, Supplement 4 (Leuven: Peeters, 2000). She examines, above all, the erotic relationship between the medieval mystic and the divine bridegroom, the Godhead.

5. Joanna Maria Godlewicz-Adamiec and Paweł Pisczatowski, "Mystisches Geheimnis zwischen Sprachschöpfung und bildhafter Aussage," *Geheimnis und Verborgenes im Mittelalter: Funktion, Wirkung und Spannungsfelder von okkultem Wissen, verborgenen Räumen und magischen Gegenständen*, ed. Stephan Conermann, Harald Wolter-von dem Knesebeck, and Miriam Quiering. Das Mittelalter: Perspektiven mediävistischer Forschung, 15 (Berlin and Boston: Walter de Gruyter, 2021), 89–106; see also Hans-Peter Kampfhammer, "Das Geheimnis mystischer Zustände: Klinische und neurobiologische Aspekte," *Das Geheimnis: Psychologische, psychopathologische und künstlerische Ausdrucksformen im Spektrum zwischen Verheimlichen und Geheimnisvollem*, ed. Daniel Sollberger, Jobst Böning, Erik Boehlke, and Gerhard Schindler. Schriftenreihe der Deutschsprachigen Gesellschaft für Kunst und Psychopathologie des Ausdrucks e.V., 35 (Berlin: Frank & Timme, 2016), 103–32.

6. Erika E. Hess, *Literary Hybrids: Cross-Dressing, Shapeshifting, and Indeterminacy in Medieval and Modern French Narrative*. Studies in Medieval History and Culture, 21 (New York: Routledge, 2004); *Riddles, Knights and Cross-Dressing Saints: Essays on Medieval English Language and Literature*, ed. Thomas Honegger. Collection Variations, 5 (Bern, Berlin, et al.: Peter Lang, 2004); Valerie R. Hotchkiss, *Clothes Make the Man: Female Cross Dressing in Medieval Europe*. Garland Reference Library of the Humanities. New Middle Ages, 1 (New York: Routledge, 2012). See also the contributions to *Körper—Kultur—Kommunikation: Corps—Culture—Communication*, ed. Alexander Schwarz, Catalina Schiltknecht and Barbara Wahlen. Tausch, 18 (Bern: Peter Lang, 2014).

7. The latest research was summarized by Anne and Matthias Kirchhoff in the commentary to the tale, as no. 43, in *Deutsche Versnovellistik des 13. bis 15. Jahrhunderts*, ed. Klaus Ridder and Hans-Joachim Ziegeler. Vol. 2 (Berlin: Schwabe Verlag, 2020), 103–26. For an English translation, see Sebastian Coxon, vol. 5 (ibid.), 126–33; here I draw from *Erotic Tales of Medieval Germany*, selected and trans. by Albrecht Classen. Sec. ed., rev. and expanded. Medieval and Renaissance Texts and Studies, 328 (2007; Tempe, AZ: Arizona Center for Medieval and Renaissance Studies, 2009), no. 3, 19–28.

8. Petrus W. Tax, "Zur Interpretation des 'Gürtels' Dietrichs von der Glezze," *Zeitschrift für deutsche Philologie* 124.1 (2005): 47–62; Brikena Ribaj, "Economics of Virtue in Dietrich von der Glezze' 'der borte': A Wife Errant and a Husband Caught," *Neohelicon* 93.4 (2009): 647–57; Albrecht Classen, "Disguises, Gender-Bending, and Clothing Symbolism in Dietrich von der Gletze's *Der Borte*," *Seminar* XLV.2 (2009): 95–110; id., "Der Gürtel als Objekt und Symbol in der Literatur des Mittelalters. Marie de France, *Nibelungenlied, Sir Gawain and the Green Knight* und Dietrich von der Glezze," *Mediaevistik* 21 (2008, appeared in 2010): 11–37; Jacob Klingner, "Der Sündenfall als Glücksfall?: Zur Deutung des Gürtels in Dietrichs von der Glezze 'Borte,'" *Liebesgaben: kommunikative, performative und poetologische Dimensionen in der Literatur des Mittelalters und der Frühen Neuzeit*, ed. Margreth Egidi, Ludger Lieb, Mireille Schnyder, and Moritz Wedell. Philologische Studien und Quellen, 240 (Berlin: Erich Schmidt Verlag, 2012), 163–79; Albrecht Classen, "Contracting Love Versus Courtly Love: Jans Enikel's 'Friedrich von Auchenfurt,' the Anonymous *Mauritius von Craûn*, and Dietrich von der Gletze's 'Der Borte,'" *Neohelicon* 46.1 (2019): 159–81, https://doi.org/10.1007/s11059-019-00476-3; "The Agency of Female Characters in Late Medieval German Verse Narratives: Aristotle and Phyllis," Dietrich von der Gletze's "Der Borte," "Beringer," and Ruprecht von Würzburg's "Die zwei Kaufleute," *Totius mundi philohistor: Studia Georgio Strzelczyk octuagenario oblata*, ed. Małgorzata Delimata-Proch, Adam Krawiec, and Jakub Kujawiński (Poznań: UAM/Adami Mickiewicz University Press, 2021), 227–42.

9. I have explored this topic already before in light of some other narratives, see Albrecht Classen, "Angst vor dem Tod: Jämmerliche Männerfiguren in der deutschen Literatur des Spätmittelalters (von *Mauritius von Craûn* zu Heinrich Kaufringer und *Till Eulenspiegel*)," *Jenseits: Eine mittelalterliche und mediävistische Imagination: Interdisziplinäre Ansätze zur Analyse des Unerklärlichen*, ed. Christa Agnes Tuczay. Beihefte zur Mediävistik, 21 (Frankfurt a.M.: Peter Lang, 2016), 213–31.

10. Roger Pensom, *Aucassin et Nicolete: The Poetry of Gender and Growing Up in the French Middle Ages* (Bern, Berlin, et al.: Peter Lang, 1999); Albrecht Classen, "Aucassin et Nicolette," *Encyclopedia of Medieval Literature*, ed. Jay Ruud (New York: Facts on File, 2005), 44–46; *Aucassin and Nicolette: A Facing-Page Edition and Translation* by Robert S. Sturges (East Lansing, MI: Michigan State University Press 2015); see also *Aucassin et Nicolette*, ed. critique. 2nd rev. and corrected ed. by Jean Dufournet (Paris: GF-Flammarion, 1984). See also *Aucassin et Nicolette*, trans. and photo-ill. by Katharine Margot Toohey (2017), online at: https://quemarpress .weebly.com/uploads/8/6/1/4/86149566/aucassin_and_nicolette_-_translation_by_k .m._toohey.pdf (this has the advantage of providing both the Old French and the English translation, but Toohey accompanies her text with utterly foolish photos; for further links to older editions; last accessed on March 30, 2022); see further June Hall Martin *Love's Fools: Aucassin, Troilus, Calisto and the Parody of the Courtly Lover*. Colleción Tamesis, A, 21 (London: Tamesis Books, 1972); Barbara Sargent-Baur, *Aucassin et Nicolete: A Critical Bibliography*. Research Bibliography & Checklists, 35 (London: Grant & Cutier, 1981). See also Albrecht Classen, "Imagination, Fantasy, Otherness, and Monstrosity in the Middle Ages and the Early Modern Age," *Imagination and Fantasy in the Middle Ages and Early Modern Times: Projections, Dreams, Monsters, and Illusions*, ed. Albrecht Classen. Fundamentals of Medieval and Early Modern Culture, 24 (Berlin and Boston: Walter de Gruyter, 2020), 1–229; here 157–61.

11. Alan V. Murray, "Tourney, Joust, Foreis and Round Table: Tournament Forms in the Frauendienst of Ulrich von Liechtenstein," *Pleasure and Leisure in the Middle Ages and Early Modern Age: Cultural-Historical Perspectives on Toys, Games, and Entertainment*, ed. Albrecht Classen (Berlin and Boston: Walter de Gruyter, 2019), 365–94; Ulrich von Liechtenstein, *Frauendienst*, trans. Franz Viktor Spechtler. Göppinger Arbeiten zur Germanistik, 485 (Göppingen: Kümmerle, 1987); Ulrich von Liechtenstein, *The Service of Ladies*, trans. J. W. Thomas (Woodbridge: Boydell & Brewer, 2004); see also the contributions to *Ulrich von Liechtenstein: Leben—Zeit— Werk—Forschung*, ed. Sandra Linden and Christopher Young (Berlin and New York: Walter de Gruyter, 2010); *Ich—Ulrich von Liechtenstein: Literatur und Politik im Mittelalter. Akten der Akademie Friesach "Stadt und Kultur im Mittelalter" 1996*, ed Franz Viktor Spechtler and Barbara Maier (Klagenfurt: Wieser, 1999). Cf. also the valuable study by Christiane Ackermann, *Im Spannungsfeld von Ich und Körper: Subjektivität im 'Parzival' Wolframs von Eschenbach und im 'Frauendienst' Ulrichs von Liechtenstein*. Ordo, 12 (Cologne, Weimar, and Vienna: Böhlau, 2009).

12. Andrea Sieber, "Paradoxe Geschlechterkonstruktionen bei Ulrich von Liechtenstein," *Ulrich von Liechtenstein: Leben—Zeit—Werk—Forschung* (2010), 261–304.

13. The word itself appears only in Thomas's translation and is not contained in the original Middle High German text. But the entire context here is determined by references to female clothing being made for Ulrich and his many squires.

14. See now the contributions to *Kulturelle Inszenierungen von Transgender und Crossdressing: grenz(en)überschreitende Lektüren vom Mythos bis zur Gegenwart*, ed. Anne-Berenike Rothstein. GenderCodes - Transkriptionen zwischen Wissen und Geschlecht, 20 (Bielefeld: transcript, 2021).

15. Heldris of Cornwall, *Silence: A Thirteenth-Century French Romance*, newly ed. and trans., with intro. and notes by Sarah Roche-Mahdi (East Lansing, MI: Colleagues Press, 1992); Heldris de Cornuälle. *Le Romanc de Silence*, trans. Regina Psaki. Garland Library of Medieval Literature, Series B, 63 (New York and London: Garland Press, 1991); W. H. Stevenson, *Report on the Manuscripts of Lord Middleton, Preserved at Wollaton Hall, Nottinghamshire*. Historical Manuscripts Commission (London: Stationery Office, 1911); Lewis Thorpe, "*Le Roman de Silence*," *Nottingham Mediaeval Studies* 5 (1961): 33–74; 6 (1962): 18–69; 7 (1963): 34–52; 8 (1964): 35–61; 10 (1966): 25–69; 11 (1967): 19–56; the complete work was then published as *Le Roman de Silence: A Thirteenth-Century Arthurian Verse-Romance by Heldris de Cornuälle*, ed. Lewis Thorpe (Cambridge: W. Heffer and Sons, 1972).

16. See the introduction to Heldris de Cornuälle, *Le Roman de Silence*, trans. Regina Psaki (1991), XII–XIII. Cf. also the introduction and notes by Sarah Roche-Mahdi in her edition, *Silence* (2007).

17. Michèle Perret, "Travesties et transsexuelles: Yde, Silence, Grisandola, Blanchandine," *Romance Notes* 25.3 (1985): 328–40. For a criticism of Thorpe's 1972 edition, see Roche-Mahdi, ed., *Silence* (1992), xxiii–xxiv; Inci Bozkaya, "Illuminiertes Schweigen. Zur Überlieferung des »Roman de Silence« im Codex WLC/LM/6," *Der Ritter, der ein Mädchen war: Studien zum Roman de Silence von Heldris de Cornouailles*, ed. Inci Bozkaya, Britta Bußmann, and Katharina Philipowski. Aventiuren, 13 (Göttingen: V&R unipress, 2020), 75–114.

18. Roberta L. Krueger, "Questions of Gender in Old French Courtly Romance," *The Cambridge Companion to Medieval Romance Cambridge*, ed. eadem (Cambridge and New York: Cambridge University Press, 2000, 132–49; Katherine Terrell, "Competing Gender Ideologies and the Limitations of Language in *Le Roman de Silence*," *Romance Quarterly* 55.1 (2008): 35–48; Heather Tanner, "Lords, Wives and Vassals in the *Roman de Silence*," *Journal of Women's History* 24.1 (2012): 138–59; Emma Campbell, "Translating Gender in Thirteenth-Century French Cross-Dressing Narratives: *La Vie de Sainte Euphrosine* and *Le Roman de Silence*, " *The Journal of Medieval and Early Modern Studies* 49.2 (2019): 233–64; Masha Raskolnikov, "Without Magic or Miracle: The Romance of Silence and the Prehistory of Genderqueerness," *Trans Historical: Gender Plurality before the Modern*, ed. Greta LaFleur, Masha Raskolnikov, Anna Kłosowska (Ithaca, NY, and London: Cornell University Press, 2021), 178–206.

19. William Henry Stevenson, *Report on the Manuscripts of Lord Middleton, preserved at Wollaton Hall, Nottinghamshire* (1911); Heinrich Gelzer, "Der Silenceroman von Heldris de Cornualle," *Zeitschrift für romanische Philologie* 47 (1927): 87–99; Frederick Augustus Grant, "Origins and Peregrinations of the Laval-Middleton Manuscript," *Nottingham Medieval Studies* 3 (1959): 3–18.

20. Psaki, ed., Heldris de Cornuälle (1991), xviii.

21. Erin F. Labbie, "The Specular Image of the Gender-Neutral Name: Naming Silence in *Le Roman de Silence*," *Arthuriana* 7.2 (1997): 63–77; *Sign, Sentence, Discourse: The Ambiguity of Silence*, ed. Peter Allen, Jennifer Wasserman, and Lois Roney (New York: Syracuse University Press, 1998); Florence Ramond Jurney, "Secret Identities: (Un)Masking Gender in *Le Roman de Silence* by Heldris

de Cornouaille and *L'enfant de sable* by Tahar Ben Jelloun," *Dalhousie French Studies* 55 (2001): 3–10; Katherine Terrell, "Competing Gender Ideologies and the Limitations of Language in Le Roman de Silence," *Romance Quarterly* 55.1 (2008): 35–48; see now the contributions to *Der Ritter, der ein Mädchen war: Studien zum Roman de Silence von Heldris de Cornouailles*, ed. Inci Bozkaya, Britta Bußmann, and Katharina Philipowski (2020). It deserves to be mentioned that Lewis Thorpe, in the introduction to his edition from 1972, had already explored many of the critical aspects relevant for this romance, that is, not only the manuscript itself, but the author, the date of the composition, the plot, the geographical and historical background, the sources (murky situation), and the poem's language.

22. It seems absurd to claim, as Julia Rüthemann, "Silence als narratives Prinzip und poetologische Figuration. Oder: haben wir es mit einem weiblichen Merlin zu tun?," *Der Ritter, der ein Mädchen war* (2020), 233–66, does, that at the end Silence, who then marries King Ebain, "verschwindet in die Gemächer des Königs, so dass ihre Geschichte bzw. der Roman endet" (261; disappears in the king's chambers so that her story, that is, the romance, can conclude). She calls this marriage her imprisonment (ibid.). There is no indication in the text that Silence transfers her inheritance to the king (cf. 263) or that she is engulfed by patriarchal society and disappears in the dust of history. The romance simply concludes there, and we also do not hear anything else about her husband.

23. Horst Wenzel, "Boten und Briefe: Zum Verhältnis körperlicher und nicht-körperlicher Nachrichtenträger," *Gespräche—Boten—Briefe: Körpergedächtnis und Schriftgedächtnis im Mittelalter*, ed. id. together with Peter Göhler et al. Philologische Studien und Quellen, 143 (Berlin: Erich Schmidt Verlag, 1997), 86–105; Nancy B. Black, *Medieval Narratives of Accused Queens* (Gainesville, Tallahassee, Tampa, et al.: University Press of Florida, 2003), 10–11; 104–05.

24. Gerhild Scholz Williams, "Konstruierte Männlichkeit: Genealogie, Geschlecht und ein Briefwechsel in Heldris von Cornwalls 'Roman de Silence,'" *Gespräche—Boten—Briefe: Körpergedächtnis und Schriftgedächtnis im Mittelalter*, ed. Horst Wenzel. Philologische Studien und Quellen, 143 (Berlin: Erich Schmidt Verlag, 1997), 193–211. As to the communicative function of the kiss, see Albrecht Classen, "The Kiss in Medieval Literature: Erotic Communication, with an Emphasis on *Roman de Silence*: Erotic Communication, with an Emphasis on *Roman de Silence*," *Journal of Humanities, Arts and Social Science* 6.2 (2022): 227–32, chrome-extension://efaidnbmnnnibpcajpcglclefindmkaj/https://www.hillpublisher.com/UpFile/202206/20220609154525.pdf; DOI: 10.26855/jhass.2022.06.009.

25. Howard R. Bloch, "Silence and Roles: *The Roman de Silence* and the Art of the Trouvère." *Yale French Studies* 70 (1986): 81–90; cf. now the contributions to *Der Ritter, der ein Mädchen war* (2020).

26. Psaki, "Introduction," Heldris de Cornuälle, *Le Roman de Silence* (1991), xxxv.

27. William W. Kibler, "Merlin," *The New Arthurian Encyclopedia*, ed. Norris J. Lacy. Garland Reference Library of the Humanities, 931 (New York and London: Garland, 1996), 319–21; here 321; see also Aileen Ann Macdonald, *The Figure of Merlin in Thirteenth Century French Romance*. Studies in Medieval Literature, 3 (Lewiston, Lampeter, and Queenston: Edwin Mellen Press, 1990); the contributions

to *Merlin in der europäischen Literatur des Mittelalters*, ed. Silvia Brugger-Hackett. Helfant-Studien, 8 (Stuttgart: Helfant, 1991); Stephen Knight, *Merlin: Knowledge and Power through the Ages* (Ithaca, NY, and London: Cornell University Press, 2016); Laura Chuhan Campbell, *The Medieval Merlin Tradition in France and Italy: Prophecy, Paradox, and Translatio*. Gallica, 42 (Cambridge: D. S. Brewer, 2017). She observes that Merlin emerges as a translator, as the one who renders the secret or hidden words into spoken, audible words, revealing the truth (67).

28. *Mai und Beaflor*. Herausgegeben, übersetzt, kommentiert und mit einer Einleitung von Albrecht Classen. Beihefte zur Mediaevistik, 6 (Frankfurt a. M.: Peter Lang, 2006); see also Nancy B. Black, *Medieval Narratives of Accused Queens* (2003).

29. Psaki, trans., *Roman de Silence* (1991), xxxiii.

30. Albrecht Classen, "The Kiss in Medieval Literature" (2022).

31. Britta Bußmann, "*l'amer amer* – 'Tristan'-Referenzen und ihre Funktion im 'Roman de Silence,'" *Der Ritter, der ein Mädchen war* (2020), 155–82. As she observes, true love, as experienced by Tristan and Isolde, or Cador and Euphemie, is determined by its coupling with bitterness, which is strikingly absent in Queen Eupheme's admission of "love" for Silence.

32. Manfred Tiemann, *Josef und die Frau Potifars im populärkulturellen Kontext: transkulturelle Verflechtungen in Theologie, bildender Kunst, Literatur, Musik und Film* (Wiesbaden: Springer, 2020); John D. Yohannan, *Joseph and Potiphar's Wife in World Literature: An Anthology of the Story of the Chaste Youth and the Lustful Stepmother* (New York: New Directions, 1968); Monia Merzetti, *I volti della moglie di Putifarre nella letteratura francese (sec. XII–XX)* (Pisa: Edizioni ETS, 2010); most recently, Dinah Wouters, "Revisiting Potiphar's Wife: A European Perspective on a Character in Early Modern Drama," *Medievalia et Humanistica* New Series, 47 (2022): 81–106.

33. Julia Rühtemann, *Die Geburt der Dichtung im Herzen: Untersuchungen zu Autorschaft, Personifikation und Geschlecht im Minnesang, im "Parzival," in "Der Welt Lohn" und im "Roman de Silence."* Philologische Studien und Quellen, 283 (Berlin: Erich Schmidt Verlag, 2022), 313–39.

34. Julia Rüthemann, "Silence als narratives Prinzip und poetologische Figuration" (2020), 233–66.

35. Bernhard Dietrich Haage, "Liebe als Krankheit in der medizinischen Fachliteratur der Antike und des Mittelalters," *Würzburger medizinhistorische Mitteilungen* 5 (1987): 173–208; see also the contributions to *Liebe als Krankheit*, ed. Theo Stemmler. Kolloquium der Forschungsstelle für Europäische Lyrik des Mittelalters, 3 (Tübingen: Narr, 1990); Mary Frances Wack, *Lovesickness in the Middle Ages: The Viaticum and Its Commentaries*. Middle Ages Series (Philadelphia, PA: University of Pennsylvania Press, 1990). However, she does not include this powerful scene in the *Roman de Silence*. See now also Julie Orlemanski, *Symptomatic Subjects: Bodies, Medicine, and Causation in the Literature of Late Medieval England*. Alembics: Penn Studies in Literature and Science (Philadelphia, PA: University of Pennsylvania Press, 2019). For love sickness in the early modern age, see also Lesel Dawson, *Lovesickness and Gender in Early Modern English Literature* (Oxford: Oxford University Press, 2008).

36. Dante Alighieri, *The Divine Comedy*. Vol. I: *Inferno*, trans. with an intro., notes, and commentary by Mark Musa (1971; London: Penguin, 1984). Cf. Yannick Carré, *Le baiser sur la bouche au moyen âge: rites, symboles, mentalités, à travers les textes et les images, XIe–XVe siècles* (Paris: Le Léopard d'Or, 1992); Christine Axen, "Kissing in the Middle Ages," *Medievalists.net*, online at: https://www.medievalists.net/2022/02/kissing-middle-ages/ (last accessed on May 16, 2022). Older, but still valuable, proves to be Krystoffer Nyrop, *The Kiss and Its History*, trans. William Frederick Harvey (1901; Detroit, MI: Singing Tree Press, 1968); for the political kiss, see Kiril Petkov, *The Kiss of Peace: Ritual, Self, and Society in the High and Late Medieval West*. Cultures, Beliefs and Traditions, 17 (Leiden and Boston: Brill, 2003). The best researched study, however, is Klaus Schreiner, "'Er küsse mich mit dem Kuß seines Mundes' (Osculetur me oscuto oris sui, Cant 1,1). Metaphorik, kommunikative und herrschaftliche Funktionen einer symbolischen Handlung," *Höfische Repräsentation: Das Zeremoniell und die Zeichen*, ed. Hedda Ragotzky and Horst Wenzel (Tübingen: Max Niemeyer, 1990), 89–132; see now Albrecht Classen, "The Kiss" (2022).

37. Gottfried von Strassburg, *Tristan and Isolde* with Ulrich von Türheim's *Continuation*, ed. and trans., with an intro. by William T. Whobrey (Indianapolis, IN, and Cambridge: Hackett Publishing, 2020). There is much research on Gottfried's work; but one of the best close readings was presented by Hugo Bekker, *Gottfried von Strassburg's* Tristan: *Journey Through the Realm of Eros*. Studies in German Literature, Linguistics, and Culture (Columbia, SC: Camden House, 1987), 171–79.

38. Hillary Smith, "The Unicorn Myth," *World History Encyclopedia* (Oct. 23, 2020), online at https://www.worldhistory.org/article/1629/the-unicorn-myth/. For great illustrations, see also https://blogs.getty.edu/iris/the-little-known-tale-of-the-medieval-unicorn/. See also https://bestiary.ca/beasts/beast140.htm (both last accessed on May 16, 2022); cf. also Christoph Wetzel, *Das Grosse Lexikon der Symbole*. Sec. ed. (2008; Darmstadt: Primus Verlag, 2011), 72, 82–83.

39. Gloria Thomas Gilmore, "*Le Roman de Silence*: Allegory in Ruin or Womb of Irony?," *Arthuriana* 7.2 (1997): 111–23; here 111: "The delivery of Merlin into the hands of society implies the delivery of meaning to the understanding of men."

40. For an excellent collection of relevant text passages, though without reference to Heldris's romance, see *Woman Defamed and Woman Defended: An Anthology of Medieval Texts*, ed. Alcuin Blamires with Karen Pratt and C. W. Marx (Oxford: Clarendon Press, 1992); see also Alcuin Blamires, *The Case for Women in Medieval Culture* (Oxford: Clarendon Press, 1997), again without any comments on the *Roman de Silence*.

41. Roche-Mahdi, ed., *Silence* (1992), xvi–xvii. See also Bloch, "Silence and Roles" (1986). Rüthemann, *Die Geburt der Dichtung im Herzen* (2021), 338–39, erroneously claims that a woman in a medieval narrative can assume the role of a protagonist only as a male knight or as an allegorical figure. When she specifies that this romance reveals "*ex-negativo*, de-figurierend und das heißt sprechend-schweigend bzw. ent- und verhüllend sprach-reproduktive Logiken des Erzählens" (339; ex-negativo reveals, in a de-figurizing, that is, speaking and covering up, exposing and disguising, language-reproductive logics of narration), she really means the

operation of secrets, of epistemological strategies pursued by Count Cador and his daughter/son Silence, but then also by the Queen Eupheme. They all try, each in his/her own way, to manipulate reality to their personal advantage and to hide their purposes behind a secret mask.

42. Rüthemann, *Die Geburt der Dichtung im Herzen* (2021), 335.

43. To mention another example, the *Encyclopedia of Medieval Literature*, ed. Jay Ruud (New York: Facts on File, 2006), does not even include a reference to Heldris and his work. The same applies to the four-volume *The Oxford Dictionary of the Middle Ages*, ed. Robert E. Bjork (Oxford: Oxford University Press, 2010). But who would blame these editors for this lacuna when even the famous *Lexikon des Mittelalters*, vol. IV (Munich and Zürich: Artemis Verlag, 1989) deemed Heldris not worthy of an entry (neither under the poet's name nor under the title of the romance) or simply did not know his name?

Chapter Five

Secrets and Mysteries in the World of Heinrich von dem Türlin's *Crône*

The Transformation of the Arthurian and the Grail Romance

Anyone familiar with medieval courtly romances, with any of the countless adventures which the knights of the Round Table normally seek out or experience, with the famous figure of King Arthur, and so forth, will feel rather disturbed and confused by many of the events as they evolve in Heinrich von dem Türlin's Middle High German *Diu Crône* (The Crown) from ca. 1225–1230. It is a complex romance, with many different figures, operations, threats, monsters, and then some of the most curious mysteries ever told in medieval literature. King Arthur receives the highest praise, of course, but he really plays only the second fiddle behind his nephew Gawein.

This Austrian poet, maybe originating from Carinthia in the south near the Alps, obviously endeavored to transgress all of our expectations and to embark on a new literary strategy that has left all interpreters until today rather baffled. This chapter will examine some of the most unusual scenes presented here which I would identify as truly arcane, almost shocking secrets which never find any good explanation and yet challenge both the protagonist and the audience until today.[1] There is certainly some meaning implied, but it remains very difficult to come to terms with the experiences witnessed by the protagonist who watches them with amazement, but who is also helpless in coming to terms with them, often because emotionally he would like to intervene, but is sternly advised to abstain from it. As we will observe, Heinrich von dem Türlin did not simply drop some strange comments into his account about Gawein's adventures. Instead, the so-called "Wunderketten" (narrative chains of marvels) form a critical component of *Diu Crône* and deeply challenge us in epistemological terms.² If we ever have looked for secrets in medieval literature, here we encounter them in an intensive fashion.

Many aspects of this romance prove to be extraordinary, to say the least. For instance, we observe King Arthur (Artus) being challenged by his wife Guinevere (Gyneuer) to meet a knight outside in the wintry landscape who seems not to feel any cold and who sings songs of love dedicated to her, challenging King Arthur as his competitor for the woman he wants to woo, if not steal from the side of her husband. The latter is thus forced to arm himself and to meet that unusual foreigner, along with three of his knights, but all of them feel the bitter cold and cannot understand why the stranger seems so unaffected by the low temperature.³ The cold weather also brings it about that Arthur's companions, among them the notorious court steward Keie, simply fall asleep and are thus caught by surprise when the young man appears, named Gasozein de Dragoz, who can thus belittle and shame them. The joust between Arthur and the stranger remains undecided, and they agree on a continuation at a later moment.⁴

The reason for Arthur's particular situation is also unusual since the entire court of knights has secretly departed very early in the morning for a tournament in Jaschune, leaving the king behind in his sleep, with all of them assuming that he would prevent them from attending that tournament if he were to hear about it. When Arthur realizes all this too late, he is rather irritated, but there is nothing left for him to do but to go hunting with the three remaining knights, and when they return home, they are all very cold. When Guinevere observes how her husband is trying to warm himself at the fire, she mocks him and dares him to meet that foreign knight whom she seems to fancy as a wooer, although we are not clearly informed about her emotions.

Later, however, which also proves to be a major transgression of virtually all of the traditional Arthurian ideals, Gasozein attempts to rape the queen, which is described in most graphic terms despite, or just because of the use of military siege terminology, which finds some parallels in the conclusion of the second part of the Old French allegorical romance, the *Roman de la rose*, by Jean de Meun.⁵ In the nick of time, Gawein appears in the forest location and rescues the queen, but in the subsequent fighting, both knights become so badly wounded that they barely survive and later need a whole year to recover their health. But this entire situation is extremely complicated because Gasozein had invited Guinevere to choose between himself and her husband Arthur, as if he were the most attractive man in the world. She decides, however, to stay with the king, which does not convince her own brother of her innocence and lack of any guilt. Hence, he kidnaps her and tries to kill her to redeem the shame that her "misbehavior" has brought upon their family, very similar to modern-day honor killing within some sections of Islamic society. Gasozein, however, who had followed them, can prevent this crime in the last minute. Yet, he himself then attempts to rape her, which casts a rather grotesque light on all of his claims to woo this lady according to the highest standards of the court.[6] Heinrich thus presents a world of crime, violence, and marvels, where the Grail also plays a significant role and yet then vanishes. The audience is thus invited into a literary world of stunning events, figures, experiences, and marvels, and those then suddenly disappear, leaving us behind with more questions than answers. If at all, then the term "secrets" makes the best sense here since the circumstances lend themselves specifically to questions pertaining to the comprehension of the world and its deliberate obscuring on the part of the narrator. The latter is completely in control of the events and sets up many roadblocks for our efforts to come to terms with what is being presented here.

In the course of the subsequent events, the narrator builds in many additional situations that defy the common expectations of a courtly knight, even though Gawein, who assumes the central position, demonstrates his usual bravery and excellence in every possible regard. For instance, he liberates a young woman from a wild man, but is himself overpowered and abducted by a wild woman. In the nick of time, he can free his hands and get to his sword, and thus hurt her so badly that he manages to free himself—a motif borrowed by the poet from the genre of heroic epic poetry, such as *Wolfdietrich B*.

Later on, Gawein has to fight against giants, and lions, and achieves many triumphs, but news about him gets lost and it is then announced that he has died, which casts the entire court into deep sorrow, in accord with the emotional and ethical framework of this genre. In the meantime, Gawein has received the gift of eternal youth from Queen of Virgins and is charged with the quest for the Grail. This then leads to many new adventures, which appear to be closely modeled after Wolfram von Eschenbach's *Parzival* (ca. 1205).[7] The Arthurian company comes together again, and they all have to pass a test concerning their virtues by means of a magical glove, but only Arthur and Gawein arise triumphantly, as to be expected according to a long literary tradition.

Gawein then continues with his quest and actually succeeds in finding the mysterious castle, where he raises the expected question, thus liberating the entire Grail society—in *Parzival*, this is possible only after the protagonist's many years of searching, once he had failed in his youth to ask that very question. Thereafter, the Grail castle disappears, and Gawein returns to King Arthur, who organizes a huge feast in his honor.[8] As Ernst S. Dick has poignantly commented about the poet, "No longer committed to the aesthetics of his predecessors, he redefines the genre by striking a precarious balance between the literary conventions, on the one hand, and an original blend of fairy-tale stereotypes and unprecedented projections of the fantastic, on the other."[9]

Let us first explore briefly what little we know about the poet, Heinrich von dem Türlin, and the success of his major Arthurian romance (ca. 1215–1230). The text has survived in only one complete manuscript, Heidelberg Cpg 374 from 1479. Half of the work has also come down to us in the Vienna Österreichische Nationalbibliothek Hs. 2779 from the first quarter of the fourteenth century, which appears to be relatively close to the original in content and form. Then there are four fragments, one of which dates from the late thirteenth century (Linz; see also the fragments in Berlin, Kiel, and Schwäbisch-Hall).[10] The poet, who might have originated from Carinthia or South Tyrol, was a highly learned person who was thoroughly familiar with the tradition of courtly literature, especially in Middle High German. We can also identify Old French romances such as *La Vengeance Raguidel*, Chrétien de Troyes's *Le Chevalier de la Charrette* and *Le Conte du Graal*, the *Première Continuation du Conte du Graal*, then *La Male sans Frein* by Paien de Maisières, and *Le Chevalier à L'Épée*, *Lanval*, *Graelent*, *Le Bel Inconnue*, and parts of the *Graal* prose romance as those texts he obviously drew inspiration from.[11] Altogether, Heinrich von dem Türlin must be associated with an international court with a high interest in literary texts from France and Germany, such as the House of Andechs-Meran in Bavaria with its strong dynastic ties to Burgundy.[12]

He intended to produce the crowning achievement (The Crown) with his work originally scheduled to consist of exactly 30,000 verses, in which we encounter many different Arthurian adventures, with Gawein being the perfect protagonist who curiously once loses the memory of himself due to a magical potion, which is an indirect allusion to a fairly similar experience by Iwein in Hartmann von Aue's eponymous romance (ca. 1190). This protagonist is not experiencing any crisis, and he is also not characterized as the typical womanizer of previous romances since he faithfully observes his marital bond with the lady Amurfina. God plays a rather minor role in this massive literary account, whereas Fortuna assumes central importance, though her allegorical wheel stops turning when Gawein enters the stage since the goddess promises him eternal bliss and happiness (15870–908).[13]

Scholarship has made numerous efforts to come to terms with *Diu Crône*, but we can only agree with Max Wehrli's assessment that this romance exhausts the reader/listener with its endless sequence of adventures involving knights, giants, fairies, monsters, and marvels of all kinds, finds confirmation even in the narrator's own admission: "Daz ez übel ze glouben ist, / Daz sölh chvnst vnd ir list / Jmmer möht fvnden sein" (8512–14; It is hard to believe that one could ever discover such art and skill).[14] Wehrli goes so far as to claim that the many different adventures described here no longer serve an ideal or symbolic function, which ultimately prevents the poet from concluding his work in a meaningful way, or at least in a way we would normally expect medieval courtly authors to do.[15]

The name of the poet is recognizable through an acrostic in *Diu Crône*, verses 183–200; however, we cannot say much about Heinrich in biographical terms, although it is obvious that he had access to an excellent library with many French, German, Latin, and maybe also Italian manuscripts. A Heinrich von dem Türlin testified in a document for Count Albert I of Görtz and Tyrol in 1229; around 1230 or 1240, Rudolf von Ems refers to Heinrich by name in his *Alexander* romance, but we cannot say anything definitive about him beyond those sparse references. The laudatory mentioning of Hartmann von Aue, who passed away around 1200, and comments about or the use of Wolfram von Eschenbach's *Parzival* (ca. 1205) and Wirnt von Gravenberg's *Wigalois* (ca. 1202–1205) provide us with a specific *terminus post quem* (date after which). The narrator specifies his own work as a crowning achievement (vv. 29916–21; 29966–90), which has justified the establishment of the title *Diu Crône*. To be sure, as Lewis Jillings has confirmed, here we encounter a secular author with little interest in religious symbolism and a great fascination with experimenting with the rich reservoir of literary tradition.[16] The audience is often invited to laugh about the various figures, especially the court steward Keie, but then also King Arthur, who does not cut a particularly impressive figure.[17]

In the fifteenth century, the Bavarian court poet Ulrich Fuetrer (before 1450–1496/1500) picked up the narrative part pertaining to the knight Gasozein and included it in his *Buch de Abenteuer* (1473–1478), but otherwise, Heinrich von dem Türlin appears not to have enjoyed major popularity. Modern research since the second half of the twentieth century has, by contrast, recognized the considerable literary quality of *Diu Crône*, discussing it from many different perspectives, including the gender issue, the complex narrative structure, the reception of many of the previous courtly romances, and Heinrich's intertextual strategies—all rather difficult to come to terms with.[18]

For our purposes, we can focus on the "Wunderketten" alone, which appear three times in this romance; first, on his way to Lady Saelde (Fortune), vv. 14110–409; second, on his return trip to King Arthur's court, vv. 16000–16496; and third, on his journey to the Grail castle, vv. 28608–990.[19] There is much fantasy behind those mostly grim and hellish scenarios, but they also underscore the extent to which the poet experimented with many different narrative materials borrowed from a variety of sources and as a result of his own imagination.[20] As Nicola Kaminski observes, throughout the entire romance, deep secrets are hidden, which might explain why scholarship has had such a difficult time coming to terms with *Diu Crône*. It is not evident that Kaminski has lifted the veil from this romance, but we can agree with her that Heinrich operated with a mystifying strategy throughout his entire work.[21]

This chapter does not want to add yet another level of interpretation to this massive romance *in toto*, and it also does not want to isolate a particular theme or motif of significance, although *Diu Crône* truly invites many different scholarly approaches to it.[22] Instead, the focus rests on those "Wunderketten" and their epistemological challenge both for the protagonist and the audience. There are certainly many opportunities to correlate individual scenes or figures with biblical sources, literary models, and apocalyptic imaginations.[23] There is no question that Gawein, who witnesses all of those horrifying scenes, is entirely baffled and confused, often filled with empathy, sorrow, pity, and fright, but he always remains nothing but an observer who cannot intervene and is so to speak shut out of the events passing by his eyes.

Johannes Keller can be credited with having made the most extensive effort to unravel the secret of these "Wunderketten," correlating them with older literary motifs and with events related in the earlier parts of *Diu Crône*. He reaches, however, no fully convincing conclusion, apart from pointing out the connection of those mysterious scenes with death, with the role of the Grail—a rather vague interpretation—and with secrets behind all literary creations.[24] The narrator himself appeals to his audience to probe the meaning of his many accounts, some "zam" and some "wilde" (29985; tame, wild), whereby he acknowledges the paradoxical nature of his romance, that is, of the "Wunderketten." In Keller's words, "[p]aradox erscheinen die Bilder den 'tumben' wie den 'guoten' als 'wild.' Sehen aber die Törichten nur die Oberfläche, nehmen die Verständigen auch die verborgenen Zusammenhänge wahr. Die 'wildekeit' der Oberfläche ist nicht identisch mit der sich im Verborgenen zeigenden 'wildekeit'" (425; for the fools and the wise ones the images appear as "wild." But while the fools perceive only the surface, the wise ones also recognize the "wildness" which reveals itself in the hidden space). Keller accepts that these "Wunderketten" represent secrets, but he correlates those with the Grail exclusively, which disappears at the end and allows Gawein to return to the Arthurian court. At that location, however, no more adventures are to be expected because they have all been told, and the world of narration has reached its completion, as expressed by the metaphor of the crown which concludes all courtly romances.[25]

If we treat the scenes that Gawein witnesses as what they are, both on the surface and in their inner core, that is, as secrets that contain some message which not even the best representative of the Arthurian court can really grasp, then we have a solid epistemological tool in our hands to probe more deeply what they might mean not so much within the fictional framework but as expressions of the binary opposition of death and life, of meaning and lack thereof within human life. That appears to be the shared experience in the other examples studied in this book, and all we need to confirm at first is that Heinrich thus emerges as a poet of secrets. He draws from both the Arthurian and the Grail background, but he certainly supersedes both dimensions and embarks on a more existentialist exploration in light of death and life which Gawein has to reflect upon, and which we as the audience are encouraged to take into consideration as well.

Most significantly, Gawein encounters the first "Wunderkette" after he has veered off the road, he is traveling together with his companions without noticing this sudden change—a powerful medieval and early modern metaphor for the passage of human life. While he was too much in deep thought to realize the change, the others are too much in a haste to notice his disappearance (13935ff.). Due to the emergence of a new trail, both concretely and metaphorically, the protagonist must reflect on his life in a new way.[26] This situation suddenly makes him confront a series of secrets that he observes with deep concern, but without comprehension, a pattern that will be repeated throughout the entire romance. First of all, Gawein perceives considerable noise in some distance which seems to come from a tournament, but he cannot get close enough to figure out what is really going on because the faster he rides, the further away the sound appears to be. Only then does the protagonist notice that he is all alone (159; from here on I will mostly refer to the English translation by page number/s; only at critical passages will I engage with the original and offer more detailed translations to get to the bottom of the issue/s).

Suddenly he comes across a maid on a white Castilian horse holding a corpse of a dead man in her lap. She bitterly weeps and complains about Parzival because he had failed to ask the crucial question which would have liberated the Grail and would, in turn, have fulfilled the duties expected of an Arthurian knight to have compassion and display bravery in combat (161). Gawein himself remains quiet and does not ask her about the cause of her sorrow, or why the knight had died, and thus he repeats the same failure that Parzival had been guilty of, as problematic as this charge might be in the first place. Curiously, however, as soon as Gawein has decided to probe this issue further, he can never come close to the lady, who always rides far away from him, which proves to be the same phenomenon as discussed in the Welsh *Mabinogi*, that I will discuss in the following chapter.

Gawein then gives up his hope to overtake the lady and returns to his pursuit to find out what the knights might be doing in the distance. At first sight, the entire group of 600 men, all nicely decked in festive tournament armor, appears to perform very well as a group, but the poor observer suddenly realizes that they are all attacked by a mysterious sword and a long spear suspended somehow in the air, mercilessly striking down the knights one group of thirty of them at a time: "he saw that blood was dripping from the spear and that even the ornate hilt of the sword was red" (160). The protagonist watches the horrible scenario, but he cannot intervene, he does not have a stake in this uneven battle, and witnesses then the death of even the last knights.

Although he is determined to learn the truth behind this infernal scenery, and although he does not display any fear himself, the deadly weapons are then quickly transported away, and the pile of dead knights becomes ignited spontaneously, the glare of the fire being so intense that the night is completely lit up.

Despite his best efforts, Gawein achieves nothing and only reaches a desolate land the next morning where everything has burnt down, with not even grass left for his horse to feed on. Undaunted, the protagonist rides on and then encounters another hellish scene: "He saw a beautiful, nude maiden with a cloven stick trying to drive large birds away from the fresh wounds of an ugly, chained giant" (161). Of course, she is helpless, so the giant dies, and his flesh is eaten by big birds: "they stripped off his flesh with such ravenous fury that they soon tore him open, gnawed away at his heart, and divided his entrails between them" (161). Again, as will become a standard response by Gawein, he passively takes note of it, does not ask a question, and moves on to continue with his quest for the Grail. But he no longer sees the forest for all the trees, so to speak, but this does not make the chain of monstrous phenomena go away.

The next scenario involves a green beast with a sharp horn on its forehead. An old lady is seated on it, and with a whip she is constantly beating a naked black man running next to her. There is no explanation given for anything Gawein witnesses, but he feels pity for the poor man; he "would gladly have aided him, but he couldn't very well stop and he also didn't want to get into a conflict a woman" (161–62). The issue always proves to be that the protagonist is determined to follow his original adventure, and so he stays away from all "temptations" to get involved in another one. After all, the individual scenes just flash by him, one more frightful than the next, and yet each one inviting him to rush to the aid of a person, or to inquire about the meaning.

Two knights, for example, pass in front of him, one carrying the decapitated head of a woman in his hand by the braids, with the other chasing him, entreating him to stop and to face him. Gawein is stunned by what he witnesses, but the two knights never come to a stop and quickly disappear from his view. This leaves him behind rather disappointed "that he was not to see and could not tell anyone how it turned out" (162). At the same time, we are left with the big question whether Gawein might feel anything else but curiosity, or whether he realized that he had seen nothing but an illusion. Why would such horrible adventures be fascinating for the knight protagonist to report about them to an inquisitive audience?

Does Gawein witness, by chance, the equivalent of a horror movie almost in the modern sense of such spectacle? Is it even reality that he is confronted with? After all, the next scene strongly suggests that he witnesses nothing but pictures, sounds, and stage props, so to speak, and not reality, such as in the next moment when he comes across a curious setting with all the trappings that a knight would expect to have, and all of the objects covered in blood. On the top of a banner, there is stuck the head of a knight, and Gawein hears much wailing by maidens, but no living creature comes out to the stage in front of him (162).

When the protagonist is pleased with the sight of a most fanciful castle surrounded by a delightful wall out of crystal, he is soon forced to witness its complete destruction. A huge naked and black peasant emerges from the forest, approaches the castle, and destroys it with his humongous club. The debris immediately catches fire, and the maids who had entertained themselves within simply collapse and catch fire. The narrator then remarks "the peasant went in and, with the handle of his club, pushed many of the maidens, one on top of the other, into the fire" (163). Although Gawein is deeply troubled by what he is witnessing, nothing seems to affect him further, there are no actions taken by him; instead, he keeps riding along throughout the night until he reaches a delightful valley filled with the most beautiful flowers. Their fragrance restores all of his energy, so he can continue on his journey, but this is immediately interrupted again by yet another horrible scenario, and it would be hard to evaluate which one might be worse than the others. Terrible torture, pain, and death dominate all the scenes, the victims are screaming, they collapse, die, and go up in flames. The narrator emphasizes repeatedly that Gawein "was strongly affected by per he had seen and did not forget it" (164), but we must wonder whether this is meant just superficially or whether there is a rreal meaning hidden behind the events as the knight observes them.

He himself then gets into deep trouble because he needs to cross a river in pursuit of knights who are able to traverse the water without any problems. Gawein, on the other hand, when he finally dares to enter the water, would have almost drowned together with his horse, when suddenly a lady arrives sent by her mistress, Lady Fortune. She promises him all the help he needs, in return for his promise to carry out her bid. With some magical potion, she then makes the water turn into glass, which then makes it possible for the protagonist to save himself and his beast. But then, right afterward, he encounters yet another strange scenario, this time a surcoat pierced by a spear. Letters on the surcoat inform him that a knight was killed with that spear and that he who would pull out the spear would be required to avenge the slaughter.

When Gawein is about to accept this adventure, the lady insists that he refrain from it, and then she tells him, at least in fragments, the name of the dead man and the reason for his death at the hand of the lady's brother. Details are missing, and nothing is explained; but since Gawein had promised to carry out the lady's wishes in return for her help, he lets it all stand as is and moves on in his journey, while the lady quickly disappears as well.

This is then followed by Gawein's experiences at a mysterious castle that seems very similar to Castle Munsalvaesche, the Grail castle, in Wolfram von Eschenbach's *Parzival*. Religious mysteries abound, although strange noises peel throughout the building, and we are told, for instance, "A voice now cried out three times in distress" (167). Religious symbolism abounds, but this does not mean at all that Gawein is in a position to understand what is happening around him. Nor are we, as the audience, allowed to comprehend the mysteries which he witnesses, probably because their meaning consists of the secrecy itself and the obscurity of the elements, voices, actions, and images determining this scene. As to be expected, one of the maidens, superior to the others, carries the Grail, a vessel filled with blood, which might underscore the correlation between life and death, body and mind.

Gawein is forced to think deeply about what he is witnessing, but there is never any indication that he might gain real understanding: "Gawein therefore sat there pondering the affair for half the night, until he was sure that it was a waste of time; they would not return" (168). Significantly, the narrator himself admits not comprehending fully what is going on or who had done what for Gawein: "I don't know by whom" (168). Next to his horse, there are also two white horses, and again we learn that the protagonist is challenged: "which gave the knight cause for reflection" (168). The original reads just as innocently: "Da von gewann er manigen gedang" (14870; This gave him many thoughts), but the meaning behind it proves to be rather ominous and secretive. After all, Gawein can think about all those phenomena as much as he likes, but there is no constructive outcome, no result. Although he hopes to get to the bottom of things by the next morning, he is badly disappointed because he wakes up and finds himself in nature, with the mysterious castle having disappeared completely. Only his horse is well taken care of, whereas all of his knightly trappings are covered by the morning dew, which indicates that much must have happened during the night.

Once Gawein has saddled and mounted his horse and departed, he "began to follow an old trail he found close by that led into a forest where there were many paths, which brought him both pleasure and pain" (169). All the secrets he had encountered are then left behind, and there are then more questions than answers, or rather, there are absolutely no answers because the secrets, as presented by figures, sounds, weaponry, armor, horses, and colors remain just that, secrets. The narrator seems to relate those secrets from a book that he has read. Referring to the image of a dead virgin, to whom a strange boy fans some fresh air—his eyes are shot through with an arrow, and his legs are tightly bound to a board—the narrator comments: "NÛ sagt das büch, sie were dot" (14378; Now, the book says that she was dead). We thus find ourselves in the curious situation that we learn through this manuscript the story as told by Heinrich von dem Türlin, who has his narrator say that he read about all those events in a written source. Moreover, Gawein himself turns to reading, thus after he has crossed the river, having been saved by the fairy, or Lady Fortune, he studies a precious coat covered with golden letters: "I was killed with this spear, and whoever draws it out must avenge me. He should therefore consider the matter carefully" (165).

However, the written text itself defies the reader and remains a mystery, almost as in the case of Wolfram von Eschenbach's *Titurel*, although there the young woman Sigune knows very well how to read but is then too anxious to find out the events in the lives of tragic lovers, which then makes herself into a tragic figure, as I have discussed in the previous chapter. Ironically, the narrator subsequently alerts his audience to consider all matters very carefully, drawing advice from Proverbs in the Old Testament: "As is often heard in the proverbs of the sages, one should praise the man who gets to know a matter well rather than blithely throwing caution to the wind and believing it before he gets to the end of it" (168).

The second "Wunderkette" sets in when Gawein has embarked on his journey again about thousand verses later. But he has hardly left a castle called Amontsus to which a knight called Aanzim, Fortuna's brother, had invited him, when the forest behind him becomes subject to a catastrophic hailstorm destroying all trees (181). As soon as that is over, the poor knight faces a rainstorm "that boiled and burned as frightfully as if it were constantly heated by a mighty fire, and with it fell a shower of rocks, colarge and small" (181). Of course, as before, Gawein is saved by Luck, and so even the subsequent heavy snowfall cannot affect him in a life-threatening way. However, the slow flakes are not soft and puffy; instead, they come down like metal bullets and "crushed his armor and bruised his flesh wherever they touched him, causing great pain" (181). The snow is then replaced by a firestorm, but even this leaves the protagonist unscathed.

At this point, a knight comes up from behind to challenge him to a joust, while a maid arrives exiting from the forest. She holds the head of her dead lover, whom the other knight had killed while he had been asleep, that is, whom he had murdered. However, as much as the situation normally would require Gawein to take side of the maid and to avenge the death of her lover, he had been advised by Aanzim to abstain from all knightly combat for whatever reason because this would endanger his goal to accomplish his real adventure (180). However, both persons appeal to him to do their bidding and try to dare him by calling him a "coward" (182).

Next, nature strikes again, this time with a whirlwind that makes the maid and the knight disappear in a swoop; instead, a sorrowful mother now arrives whose son has been killed with an arrow shot through his heart. Again, Gawein is challenged to live up to his emotional and ethical ideals, but he refrains from getting involved here as well despite the heart-rendering appeals by the various victims of unmentionable violence against their loved ones.[27] Both nature and these people appear as allied forces to make Gawein turn away from his predestined path, to distract him, either through emotional appeals or terrifying storms and fires. The next scenes repeat the same challenges, either a knight who insists on jousting with Gawein, or people grieving the death of an innocent victim. As the narrator indicates, the hero's resolve is severely tested: Gawein became troubled and undecided. He would gladly have consented if he had not been counseled not to do so. Moreover, it pained him to refuse" (184).

Miraculously, Gawein is rescued at the last minute before he would have engaged in a joust with the hostile knight when a maid arrives, tries to stop the two men from fighting, and since she cannot do so, she cuts down a tree with her mace which creates yet another storm of incredible strength, which makes both the knight and the bier with the dead maid disappear, which thus proves that all of those figures are nothing but delusional imaginations, maybe the outcome of Gawein's inner feelings, hence certainly not real, but rather mirroring secrets—actions, figures, events, etc.—operating in the background. Even when they encounter a whole band of knights fuming with anger and fury about some alleged wrongdoings committed by the protagonist, the magical maid prevents him from engaging in any joust: "She left him no power over his spirit or strength and would not allow him to accept any challenges, although he heard others before they left the great forest" (186).

We could claim that Gawein's inner self has turned outside, as both the natural phenomena and the individual figures addressing him with hostility or grief appear to be nothing but mirrors of his own soul. We might call all those weeping women and angry knights manifestations of his own inner turmoil and reflections of his values, ideals, and concerns. But the poet refuses to explain all of that and assumes that the audience would be intelligent enough to decipher those secrets. Just because all of those appearances remain cryptic and mysterious, they challenge both the protagonist and the audience in their serious attempt to comprehend what is going on in that fearsome land, where nature fights with the greatest fury against the knight, where infernal scenes horrify him, and where other knights challenge him with the greatest intensity. But both here and in the other settings, Gawein remains steadfast and steers through this space of secrets and threats, never fully understanding what those mean and why he is not allowed to engage in them. However, since he obeys the instructions, he succeeds in getting out of those hellish settings unscathed and can thus pursue his charge as before. The secrets stay behind, as puzzling and confusing as they all prove to be.

Intriguingly, they are derived from the tradition of medieval literature, with many motifs borrowed from French and German romances. At the same time, we could easily draw from medieval art history to recognize numerous apocalyptic visions and could from here move to the world of sermons and preaching. But behind these possibly religious or prophetic aspects, there are more profound epistemological issues at stake because the protagonist has to make his way through a challenging world that seems so familiar and yet is entirely alien. As the protagonist realizes, and as the audience is to learn, the world as we all know is only the screen for a very different one which awaits the individual behind the material dimension. The key to the solution to those secrets is, however, not provided, which makes the reception of this romance to such an extraordinary challenge. We are only told that if Gawein had not found help from the fairy maid sent by Lady Fortune, if he had disregarded her brother Aanzim's advice and had engaged with those mysterious phenomena, it "would have been a serious mistake that would have brought about the downfall of the court" (186). In other words, there are deeply hidden secrets of existential importance, although most people cannot solve them. Without the assistance of those magical forces, Gawein would have committed the worst-possible mistakes, which then would have destroyed the world as he knew it.

When Gawein approaches the Grail, he runs into the third "Wunderkette," and again he has to cross a country that is virtually barren of all nourishment for himself and his horse as a result of warfare or other kinds of conflicts (319). The narrator does not go into details, though he laments the protagonist's suffering, though he uses this setting one more time to confirm Gawein's determination and resolve: "This dearth made the journey seem long, but it did not make him turn aside from his path" (319).

This time, the scenario turns even more infernal, with a red man in flames driving a group of naked women with a whip; the enormous pain makes them all scream miserably, and again Gawein feels deeply urged to intervene and help them. However, things quickly change, the ghost-like figures approach him, the red man kissing his leg and feet paying his respect, whereas the naked women approach and greet him. Once that has happened, they all rush away, and the women simply disappear into the ground (320). Gawein is deeply grieved, especially because no one is there to enlighten him about the meaning of this entire setting, as if that would have helped him in any particular way. But profound pity fills his heart because of their suffering, and he is horrified about the burning man.

Immediately following, he encounters another scene, this time with a knight on a horse to whom a woman clings tightly. Both are chased by an old lady, who has no other weapon but a glass which she finally tosses against a tree, which makes the entire forest go up in flames. The old lady has left the stage in time, but the couple burns away to nothing, an outcome which is exceedingly distressing for Gawein, especially because he is filled with empathy and yet does not know what to make out of all those scenes. We might argue that the glass represented time as such—an hourglass—but we cannot be certain about that at all—which would hence explain the complete disappearance of the knight and the pursuit by the old woman. Nevertheless, although the protagonist does not understand what he just has witnessed, he is said to take "careful note of what had transpired" (320; "als er wol marckte das," 28699). These visions are all nothing but images, maybe reflections of his own fantasy, and they challenge him and us to penetrate deeper into their secret character, although they all consistently defy this very effort.

The next scene involves a monster bound to a branch and an old man sitting on its back, also tied, but to his steed. The latter holds a salve box the content of which exudes such a sweet perfume that Gawein forgets all of his trouble and recovers his strength. The narrator, however, hastens to add, as is his habit, of course, that he does not know its properties: "Die mir die Auenture nit enseite" (28721; that the Muse has not revealed to me). Although Gawein realizes that both the monster and the old man are alive, he does not engage in a conversation with him and after a while simply rides on, only paying brief respect by bowing in front of them (321). Does he understand, perhaps, that these are nothing but visions?

The following scene underscores this character because when he discovers a group of knights and follows them toward a castle, he can never overtake them, and thus enters the castle when they have already arrived there well before him. Curiously, however, Gawein then does not discover one living soul, no matter how hard he is searching throughout the entire castle. The mystery becomes even more intensified when he reaches closed door and believes that the entire group might be hidden behind it. But the protagonist does not hear any sound, and when he finally pushes his way into the room behind the door, he finds it to be empty (321). Neither spatial nor chronological criteria assist him to figure out the context, the secret events, and the mysterious figures. He wanders through an obscure world, certainly well lit, but dark in its meaning. Although the protagonist is trying to investigate what the matter might be, as represented by his long listening at the closed door, all his attempts fail because he ends in the void.

The contrast between the material splendor of the entire castle and the absence of all people leaves him stunned, as much as he is reflecting upon this strange phenomenon: "Manigerhand gedoht er vnd sprah / Nach disem groszen wonder" (28845–46; Gawein thought and said all sorts of things about this most unusual state of affairs). In contrast, the somewhat later

Partonopier und Meliur by Konrad von Würzburg (ca. 1280) also operates with the idea of the invisibility of all people in the palace of the Byzantine princess, but the phenomenon is quickly revealed to be the result of her magic trick she has utilized to test her still too young lover. Unfortunately, under his mother's and a bishop's influence, he then overcomes her magic with the help of a countermeasure provided by his mother, which then destroys both of their happiness.[28]

By contrast, in *Diu Crône*, there is no explanation for this strange absence of all people, there are no responsible individuals who produce this strange effect, and there is no end in sight for this secret to be explained, irrespective of how long Gawein might wait outside of the castle gate for anyone to come by and help him understand the situation: "he would have observed nothing if he had stood there forever" (322t At last once there is a lone voice by a maiden who calls out to him when he is about to depart, entreating him to trust the lady who had provided him with so much hospitality. But Gawein does not catch a glimpse of the maid and is thus forced to leave without ever having received any answer to all of his questions.

Thereafter, the protagonist travels for a long time and can enjoy much of the plenitude available in another country, recovering from his previous suffering and deprivations. However, even there he encounters inexplicable phenomena, such as a castle made of glass in front of which a sword of fire guards the road. Gawein can look into the castle, but it is likewise completely deserted. The narrator offers the suggestion that it might have been a secret beyond human comprehension. While the English translator J. W. Thomas resorts to the term "enchanted castle" (323), the original is considerably more poignant—see then my own translation:

> Gaweinen duhte die mere
> Fremde sin vnd seltzame.
> Als ich mich wol verwane,
> Das was kein vnbild,
> Wann die geschiht was gnüg wild. (28985–89)

> [Gawein thought that these events
> were strange and curious.
> As far as I can tell,
> this was not a monstrous feature,
> since the story was wild enough.]

There is no way for the protagonist or the narrator to solve the riddles; those are there to stay and defy all interpretive efforts.

We are, in fact, left alone with these references and do not receive any help in deciphering those secrets. Gawein encounters two of his companions, joins them, and they are then welcomed by a very hospitable lord of a splendid castle, and then the Grail returns, which allows Gawein to ask the long-awaited question and to solve the Grail problem. In other words, the narrative then returns to the traditional path and leaves all secrets behind. Those cannot be addressed further and remain what they are. Heinrich von dem Türlin deserves considerable credit for this unusual strategy, unless one would want to call it a literary failure, to project a host of secrets and to refuse revealing their meaning. Gawein has to face them, has to observe them with a steadfast mind, but he is never allowed to engage with them, so he simply leaves them behind, which allows the romance to reach a respectable, that is, traditional conclusion.

Nevertheless, even at that final point in this long narrative, we are alerted one more time to the great importance of secrecy, especially with regard to the Grail: "this miracle of God must not become common knowledge: it must be kept secret" (328). The poet engineers a very different explanation of the Grail and the role which Parzival had played, or rather failed to do so, leading to many calamities (328). Gawein, on the other hand, had asked the question, had demonstrated public empathy, and had thus fulfilled the long-awaited challenge. His host then reveals even more secrets, pointing out that he is actually dead, and so are the men of his retinue; only the maids are alive and not ghosts of themselves (329).

The old lord offers even further insights into the Grail, the most secret object of them all. It is, as he emphasizes, a divine secret that should not be divulged to ordinary people. Once Gawein has healed the Grail (found it), it "would never again be seen to publicly . . . no one should reveal anything about the Grail; to do so would harm the divine mystery" (329). Talking about the Grail would be a transgression and exploring its meaning would be a danger that could not be permitted. This thus sheds more light on all the previous secrets, which the protagonist was granted to witness, but could not get engaged with. Secrets in *Diu Crône* are beyond the reach of people, and even the narrator refuses to provide any explanations.[29]

Not surprisingly, as soon as the old man has explained the external circumstances of the Grail, he disappears along with the Grail itself and the entire company, except for the lady and her maidens. Death has taken the dead back, and only the living remain on the narrative stage. Gawein's deed is finally explained as the ultimate solution, freeing the land and the people from their suffering, and hence the "dead were relieved of life; the living of all their sorrow, and everyone was happy" (330). It remains rather mysterious how the Grail is associated with Lady Fortune, how she is to be understood in relationship with God, and how the destiny of the Grail was predicated on the well-being of humanity. We are simply assumed to accept it, although it seems to fly in the face of traditional Christian teachings.

It might be useful to draw specific connections between the various motifs employed by Heinrich and by his various predecessors, but this would not address the critical issue of the secret a such as it emerges regularly and challenges the protagonist to engage with it—certainly a dangerous invitation which would distract him from his path toward his life's goal and which would make him a victim of obviously nothing but visual projections of apocalyptic fantasies. We could also conceive of significant parallels between Heinrich's *Diu Crône* and the visual world of Hieronymus Bosch (ca. 1450–1516), especially because the latter's many paintings are certainly determined by the grotesque[30] and defy easy interpretation.[31] However, Bosch specifically pursued a spiritual perspective, warning his spectators about the Apocalypse, the Seven Deadly Sins, and other fundamental human shortcomings that would be punished in the afterworld. Heinrich von dem Türlin demonstrates much more interest in the secret as such, expressed both in visual and narrative terms, and once those images have been witnessed, they also disappear again without leaving a trace.

Gawein is impressed, deeply moved, filled with pity, with many questions and concerns, but he does not engage with those phantasmagorias, passes by them, leaves them behind, as he is regularly instructed, and can thus protect himself effectively from whatever challenge might have waited for him in any of those three "Wunderketten." Alienation on the part of the protagonist and also the audience is constantly at work, and the more Gawein tries to probe the inner aspects of those secrets, the more he discovers that there is nothing to find, both in spatial and practical terms (actions, fights, defense, support, etc.).[32] In a way, the protagonist roams through a world of images, but those deny him concrete insights and refuse to release the key with which they could be unraveled or explained. We could thus argue that Heinrich von dem Türlin operates very deliberately with the notion of the "secret" and identifies it as a crucial epistemological phenomenon not available or accessible to most people here in this world. Gawein is privileged to witness those secrets, the greatest of which appears to be the Grail, but they all disappear again from view because they are beyond human comprehension and serve only as cues or markers of another world which the romance indicates subtly without allowing us to gain entrance. In short, *Diu Crône* demonstrates that human existence is determined both by the known and the unknown, and the many secrets passing by in front of Gawein's eyes and our minds are only there to provide us with a sense of the other dimension, but not to reveal it to us specifically.

It deserves to be mentioned also that Marie de France had already underscored the epistemological importance of obscurity in the prologue to her *lais* (ca. 1190). Referring to early sixth-century grammarian Priscian, the poet states: "It was the custom of the ancients, / . . . in the books that they once used to make / to speak quite obscurely / for those who were to come / and who would have to learn them" (9–14; "oscurement," 12). The literary discourse thus served her, and so also Heinrich von dem Türlin, to probe the deeper meaning of the literary words and to acknowledge them as essential secrets which not even the protagonist was allowed to understand.[33]

We can certainly agree with Johannes Keller that we should not overemphasize the Christian typology behind the images presented in the various "Wunderketten," but he tries himself very hard to associate those marvels with the Grail and previous literary elements discussed by his predecessors in France, Germany, and Italy.[34] It is true, at least on the surface, that Gawein displays in face of those strange scenarios a lack of decision-making power, but would we really have to subsume every aspect presented here under the Grail as the guiding power behind all episodes in this romance?[35] Gawein's inability to think through what the meaning of the "Wunderketten" might imply, his failing reflections and the silence following to appearance and disappearance of those marvels indicate that traditional epistemology is no longer working, while a new one, such as mystical vision, is not yet available to Heinrich. But the narrative discourse does not break down, after all, although Gawein performs only as an observer who cannot grasp what is happening in front of his eyes.[36]

The ultimate meaning seems to be not the Grail, not knighthood, not King Arthur's court, and not any of the traditional themes and topoi pertaining to chivalry, courtly honor and love, or the Christian faith, but the secret itself which gains here a certain degree of independence and operates virtually all by itself within an obscure world, just as Bosch was later to depict it in his apocalyptic paintings.

It is the secret itself that demands all our attention, that is, the human (in)ability to comprehend the world in its material and spiritual dimensions. The poet seems to be filled with considerable doubt about human rationality and comprehensibility and proposes to see the world in quite different terms because there are so many secrets that no one can fully fathom. Of course, Heinrich draws intensively from hellish iconography, apocalyptic images, and traditional concepts of the monstrous, but despite the certain degree of familiarity the framework provides, the world of *Diu Crône* is veiled because secrets have blocked our view. Maybe that's one of the reasons why the contemporary audience was apparently not so enthused about Heinrich's work, considering the fairly poor transmission of the text in surviving manuscripts.

NOTES

1. Heinrich von dem Türlin, *Die Krone (Verse 1–12281)*. Nach der Handschrift 2779 der Österreichischen Nationalbibliothek nach Vorarbeiten von Alfred Ebenbauer, Klaus Zatloukal und Horst P. Pütz, ed. Fritz Peter Knapp and Manuela Niesner. Altdeutsche Textbibliothek, 112 (Tübingen: Max Niemeyer, 2000); Heinrich von dem Türlin, *Die Krone* (Verse 12282–30042). Nach der Handschrift Cod. Pal. germ. 374 der Universitätsbibliothek Heidelberg nach Vorarbeiten von Fritz Peter Knapp und Klaus Zatloukal, ed. Alfred Ebenbauer and Florian Kragl. Altdeutsche Textbibliothek, 118 (Tübingen: Max Niemeyer, 2005). It is a very unfortunate situation that the various editors could not agree on their editorial principles due to the differences in the manuscripts. For an English translation, see Heinrich von dem Türlin, *The Crown: A Tale of Sir Gawein and King Arthur's Court*, trans. and with an intro. by J. W. Thomas (Lincoln, NE, and London: University of Nebraska Press, 1989). See also the original edition, *Diu Crône von Heinrich von dem Türlin*, ed. Gottlob Heinrich Friedrich Scholl. Bibliothek des Litterarischen Vereins in Stuttgart, XXVII. Reprint (1852; Amsterdam: Editions Rodopi, 1966).

2. For a helpful plot summary, see Karin R. Gürtler, "Heinrich von dem Türlin," *The New Arthurian Encyclopedia*, ed. Norris J. Lacy. Garland Reference Library of the Humanities, 931 (1991; New York and London: Garland, 1996), 227–28. However, she, like many other scholars, ultimately gives up engaging with all the adventures experienced by Gawein. Much better in detail and critical discussion proves to be Ernst S. Dick, "Heinrich von dem Türlin," *German Writers and Works of the High Middle Ages: 1170–1280*, ed. James Hardin and Will Hasty. Dictionary of Literary Biography, 138 (Detroit, MI, Washington, DC, and London: Gale Research, 1994), 44–49. See now also Gudrun Felder, *Kommentar zur "Crône" Heinrichs von dem Türlin* (Berlin and New York: Walter de Gruyter, 2006); Christine Zach, *Die Erzählmotive der Crône Heinrichs von dem Türlin und ihre altfranzösischen Quellen: ein kommentiertes Register*. Passauer Schriften zu Sprache und Literatur, 5 (Passau: Wiss.-Verl. Rothe, 1990); Annegret Wagner-Harken, *Märchenelemente und ihre Funktion in der Crône Heinrichs von dem Türlin: ein Beitrag zur Unterscheidung zwischen "klassischer" und "nachklassischer" Artusepik*. Deutsche Literatur von den Anfängen bis 1700, 21 (Bern, Berlin, et al.: Peter Lang, 1995); Justin Vollmann, *Das Ideal des irrenden Lesers: ein Wegweiser durch die "Krone" Heinrichs von dem Türlin*. Bibliotheca Germanica, 53 (Tübingen and Basel: Francke, 2008).

3. We rarely hear about winter as a specific season with its uncomfortable conditions in medieval literature; but see Albrecht Classen, "Winter as a Phenomenon in Medieval Literature: A Transgression of the Traditional Chronotopos?," *Mediaevistik* 24 (2011): 125–50. The poet does not draw from topical images but presents the cold and snow in realistic terms.

4. Christiane Schonert, *Figurenspiele: Identität und Rolen Keies in Heinrichs von dem Türlin "Crône."* Philologische Studien und Quellen, 217 (Berlin: Erich Schmidt Verlag, 2009).

5. Guillaume de Lorris and Jean de Meun, *The Romance of the Rose*, trans. into English verse by Harry W. Robbins. Ed., and with an intro. by Charles W. Dunn (New York: E. P. Dutton, 1962), ch. 99, vv. 21346–694, pp. 454–61.

6. Albrecht Classen, *Sexual Violence and Rape in the Middle Ages: A Critical Discourse in Premodern German and European Literature*. Fundamentals of Medieval and Early Modern Culture, 7 (Berlin and Boston: Walter de Gruyter, 2011), ch. 4, 83–112.

7. Elisabeth Schmid, "Text über Texte: Zur *Crône* des Heinrich von dem Türlin," eadem, *Poetik und Anthropologie: Gesammelte Aufsätze zum höfischen Roman*, ed. Dorothea Klein. Spolia Berolinensia, 41 (Hildesheim: Weidmann, 2021; orig. 1994), 203–27. She calls Heinrich's effort to appropriate Wolfram's *Parzival* into his own text an "aggressives Herabsetzen und ehrgeizige[] Aneignung" (207; aggressive put-down and ambitious appropriation).

8. Karin Cieslik, "Heinrich von dem Türlin: Die Krone," *Dichtungen des europäischen Mittelalters: Ein Führer durch die erzählende Literatur*, ed. Rolf Bräuer (Munich: C. H. Beck, 1990), 351–53.

9. Dick, "Heinrich von dem Türlin" (1994), 48. He also highlights, as other scholars such as Christoph Cormeau have done, the absence of the ultimate spiritualization of the courtly world; there is no spiritual crisis, and even the Grail simply disappears after Gawein has redeemed it: "The emphasis of the work is on the secular, and Gawein assumes the role of a secular savior" (48).

10. For a listing of all manuscripts, see https://handschriftencensus.de/werke/470 (last accessed on May 16, 2022).

11. Christine Zach, *Die Erzählmotive der* Crône *Heinrichs von dem Türllin und ihre altfranzösischen Quellen: Ein kommentiertes Register*. Passauer Schriften zu Sprache und Literatur, 5 (Passau: Wissenschaftsverlag Richard Rothe, 1990), 375–86.

12. Fritz Peter Knapp, *Chevalier errant und* fin'amor*: Das Ritterideal des 13. Jahrhunderts in Nordfrankreich und im deutschsprachigen Südosten. Studien zum Lancelot en prose, zum Moriz von Craûn, zur Krone Heinrichs von dem Türlin, zu Werken des Strickers und zum Frauendienst Ulrichs von Lichtenstein*. Schriften der Universität Passau: Reihe Geisteswissenschaften, 8 (Passau: Passavia-Universitätsverlag, 1986).

13. Fritz Peter Knapp, *Blüte der europäischen Literatur des Hochmittelalters*. Part 2: *Roman—Kleinepik—Lehrdichtung* (Stuttgart: S. Hirzel Verlag, 2019), 111–16.

14. Max Wehrli, *Geschichte der deutschen Literatur im Mittelalter: Von den Anfängen bis zum Ende des 16. Jahrhunderts*. 3rd ed. (1980; Stuttgart: Philipp Reclam jun., 1997), 479.

15. Wehrli, *Geschichte* (1997), 479–80: "Man könnte entschuldigend sagen, der Leser vollziehe in diesem Gewirr der inkommensurablen Ereignisse tatsächlich nichts anderes als eben die Existenz des Chevalier errant. Anstelle des Abenteuers, das zuerst und zuletzt ein Mittel der Selbstbegegnung war, tritt . . . die Fortuna (*Saelde*) und ihr Rad" (One could say in an exculpating manner that the reader re-enacts in this maze of incommensurable events in fact nothing else but the existence of the Chevalier errant. Instead of the adventure, which first and last was a medium of finding

oneself, . . . there is Fortuna (*Saelde*) and her wheel). *Diu Crône* thus appears to be, according to Wehrli, "Literatur über Literatur" (literature about literature).

16. Lewis Jilling, *Diu Crone of Heinrich von dem Türlein: The Attempted Emancipation of Secular Narrative*. Göppinger Arbeiten zur Germanistik, 258 (Göppingen: Kümmerle, 1980).

17. Thomas Gutwald, *Schwank und Artushof: Komik unter den Bedingungen höfischer Interaktion in der 'Crône' des Heinrich von dem Türlin*. Mikrokosmos, 55 (Frankfurt a. M., Berlin, et al.: Peter Lang, 2000).

18. Christoph Cormeau, *"Wigalois" und "Diu Crône": Zwei Kapitel zur Gattungsgeschichte des nachklassischen Artusromans*. Münchener Texte und Untersuchungen zur deutschen Literatur des Mittelalters, 57 (Munich: Artemis, 1977), 155–65; Mike Malm, "Heinrich von dem Türlin," *Deutsches Literatur-Lexikon: Das Mittelalter*, ed. Wolfgang Achnitz. Vol. 5: *Epik (Vers—Strophe—Prosa) und Kleinformen* (Berlin and Boston: Walter de Gruyter, 2013), 411–21. She offers an extensive updated bibliography. See also Christoph Cormeau, "Heinrich von dem Türlin," *Die deutsche Literatur des Mittelalters: Verfasserlexikon*, ed. Kurt Ruh. Sec. completely rev. ed. Vol. 3.1 (Berlin and New York: Walter de Gruyter, 1980), 894–99. J. W. Thomas's introduction to his English translation of *The Crown* (1989), xi–xxvii, presents in essence all we can say about Heinrich von dem Türlin; modern research since then has not yielded any significantly new insights.

19. For commentaries of those "Wunderketten," see Justin Vollmann, *Das Ideal des irrenden Lesers: Ein Wegweiser durch die 'Krone' Heinrichs von dem Türlin* (2008), 126–35.

20. Annegret Wagner-Harken, *Märchenelemente und ihre Funktion in der* Crône *Heinrichs von dem* Türlin (1995), 321–27. She attempts to correlate fairy-tale elements with the motives included in Heinrich's *Crône*.

21. Nicola Kaminski, *»Wâ ez sich êrste ane vienc, Daz ist ein teil unkunt«: Abgründiges Erzählen in der* Krone *Heinrichs von dem Türlin*. Beiträge zur älteren Literaturgeschichte (Heidelberg: Universitätsverlag Winter, 2005). Unfortunately, as much as she attempts to explore the narrative underground of this romance, as much does she create her own secret structures and discussions, which leave us at the end only with puzzlement.

22. Older research had still assumed that these sequences of infernal themes would support the claim that Heinrich lacked in structuring his work and pursuing a consistent thematic orientation; see, for instance, Bernd Kratz, "Rosengarten und Zwergenkönig in der Crone Heinrichs von dem Türlin," *Medieval Bohemia* 1 (1969): 21–29; here 25.

23. For a critical assessment of the relevant research, see Markus Wennerhold, *Späte mittelhochdeutsche Artusromane: 'Lanzelt,' 'Wigalois,' 'Daniel von dem Blühenden Tal,' 'Diu Crône.' Bilanz der Forschung 1960–2000*. Würzburger Beiträge zur deutschen Philologie, 27 (Würzburg: Königshausen & Neumann, 2005), 183–253; here 220–23.

24. Johannes Keller, *Diu Crône Heinrichs von dem Türlin: Wunderketten, Gral und Tod*. Deutsche Literatur von den Anfängen bis 1700, 25 (Bern, Berlin, et al.: Peter Lang, 1997), 413–29.

25. Keller, Diu Crône *Heinrichs von dem Türlin* (1997), 428: "Die Rückkehr an den Hof vollendet die 'Crône' und erübrigt damit jede Fortsetzung" (The return to the court is completed in the *Crown*, which makes any continuation unnecessary).

26. Albrecht Classen, *Tracing the Trails in the Medieval World: Epistemological Explorations, Orientation, and Mapping in Medieval Literature*. Routledge Studies in Medieval Literature and Culture (New York and London: Routledge, 2021). There, I engage with numerous parallel cases, but it had not occurred to me then that *Diu Crône* might also present valuable material to explore this topic further. But see now Fabian David Scheidel, "*Si muosen machen niwe slâ* ('Parzival,' 821,1): Zur Semantik von Spur und Weg im 'Parzival,' in der 'Crône' und dem 'Hohen Lied' Bruns von Schönebeck—mit einem Umweg zum Gral," *Aventiure: Ereignis und Erzählung*, ed. Michael Schwarzbach-Dobson and Franziska Wenzel, Beiheft zur ZfdPh, 21 (Berlin: Erich Schmidt, 2022), 127–151; here 139–45. He was not aware of my study, or of any non-German research literature, a typical feature, I am afraid, of the current academic situation in German universities.

27. It is worth mentioning here that the author includes a most important comment on a mother's grief over her dead child, which confirms, if ever so slightly, once again that our previous assumptions about the allegedly lacking emotional bonds between parents and children during the pre-modern era really have to be reassessed. See the contributions to *Childhood in the Middle Ages and the Renaissance: The Results of a Paradigm Shift in the History of Mentality*, ed. Albrecht Classen (Berlin and New York: Walter de Gruyter, 2005).

28. Konrad von Würzburg's *Partonopier und Meliur*, ed. Karl Bartsch. Mit einem Nachwort von Rainer Gruenter. Deutsche Neudrucke. Reihe: Texte des Mittelalters (1871; Berlin: Walter de Gruyter, 1970); online at https://archive.org/details/konradsvonwrzbu00bartgoog (last accessed on May 16, 2022). Cf. Rüdiger Brandt, Konrad von Würzburg. Wege der Forschung (Darmstadt: Wissenschaftliche Buchgesellschaft, 1987), 152–73; Hartmut Kokott, *Konrad von Würzburg: ein Autor zwischen Auftrag und Autonomie* (Stuttgart: S. Hirzel, 1989).

29. Johannes Keller, Diu Crône *Heinrichs von dem Türlin* (1997), 398: "Diese Struktur deutet an, daß alle Informationen das grundlegende Geheimnis nicht offenbaren können. Erwartet man im Zentrum der Rede die substantiellsten Aussagen, wird diese Erwartung durch die punktuelle Andeutung von 'gotes tougen' (v. 29544) ins Geheimnisvolle zurückgebogen" (This structure indicates that none of all that information can reveal the fundamental secret. If we might expect in the center of the speech the most substantial statements, that expectation is turned back into the secretive through the punctual indication of "God's secret" (v. 29544).

30. For an attempt to identify the grotesque in medieval verse narratives, see Reinhard Berron, *Elemente grotesken Erzählens in der europäischen Versnovellistik*. Kölner Germanistische Studien, Neue Folge, 13 (Vienna, Cologne, and Weimar: Böhlau Verlag, 2021). He mostly equates excessive human behavior (gluttony, lust, scatology, violence) with the grotesque, which leaves not much room for truly critical assessments of the grotesque as we discover it in Heinrich von dem Türlin's work. See my review forthcoming in *Mediaevistik* 35 (2023).

31. Charles de Tolnay, *Hieronymus Bosch* (1965; n.l.: Reynal & Company, in association with William Morrow & Company, 1966); R.-H. Marijnissen, K. Blockx, P. Gerach, H.-T. Piron, J.-H. Plokker, and V. H. Bauer, *Jhyronimus Bosch* (Geneva: Weber, 1972); Walter S. Gibson, *Hieronymus Bosch*. The World of Art Library: Artists (London: Thames and Hudson, 1973); Wilhelm Fraenger, *Hieronymus Bosch* (Dresden: VEB Verlag der Kunst, 1975); Wolfgang Wintermeier, *Hieronymus Bosch* (Hildesheim: Gerstenberg, 1983); Roger H. Marijnissen, *Hieronymus Bosch: das vollständige Werk*, trans. from the Dutch (Weinheim: Acta Humaniora, 1988); Hans Holländer, *Hieronymus Bosch: Weltbilder und Traumwerk*. 3rd updated and expanded ed. DuMont-Taschenbücher, 28 (Cologne: DuMont, 1988); Hans Belting, *Hieronymus Bosch: Garten der Lüste* (Munich: Prestel, 2002); Stefan Fischer, *Hieronymus Bosch: Malerei als Vision, Lehrbild und Kunstwerk*. Atlas—Bonner Beiträge zur Kunstgeschichte, Neue Folge, 6 (Cologne, Weimar, and Vienna: Böhlau, 2009); Reindert Falkenburg, *The Land of Unlikeness: Hieronymus Bosch, The Garden of Earthly Delights*. Studies in Netherlandish Art and Cultural History, 10 (Zwolle, Netherlands: W Books, 2011); Matthijs Ilsink, *Hieronymus Bosch, Painter and Draughtsman: Catalogue raisonné* (New Haven, CT: Yale University Press, 2016); Debra Higgs Strickland, *The Epiphany of Hieronymus Bosch: Imagining Antichrist and Others from the Middle Ages to the Reformation* (London: Harvey Miller Publishers, 2016); Joseph Leo Koerner, *Bosch & Bruegel: From Enemy Painting to Everyday Life* (Princeton, NJ, and Oxford: Princeton University Press, 2018); see also Albrecht Classen, "Imagination, Fantasy, Otherness, and Monstrosity in the Middle Ages and the Early Modern Age," *Imagination and Fantasy in the Middle Ages and Early Modern Times: Projections, Dreams, Monsters, and Illusions*, ed. Albrecht Classen. Fundamentals of Medieval and Early Modern Culture, 24 (Berlin and Boston: Walter de Gruyter, 2020), 1–229; here 168–71; 175–81.

32. See now Jordan Kirk, *Medieval Nonsense: Signifying Nothing in Fourteenth-Century England* (New York: Fordham University Press, 2021); see my review in *sehepunkt* 22.3 (2022): http://www.sehepunkte.de/2022/03/36498.html (last accessed on May 16, 2022).

33. Päivi Mehtonen, *Obscure Language, Unclear Literature: Theory and Practice from Quintilian to the Enlightenment*. Suomalaisen Tiedeakatemian toimituksia: Sarja Humaniora, 320. Trans. Robert MacGilleon (Helsinki: Acad. Scientiarum Fennica, 2003), 103–22; see also the contributions to *Illuminating Darkness: Approaches to Obscurity and Nothingness in Literature*, ed. Päivi Mehtonen. Suomalaisen Tiedeakatemian toimituksia: Humaniora, 348 (Helsinki: Acad. Scientiarum Fennica, 2007). With the exception of Pekka Kuusisto (Dante in comparison with Paul de Man's concepts), the contributions do not deal with pre-modern literature. Nevertheless, the theoretical ideas help us to gain a better understanding of the secretive nature of Marie's and Heinrich von dem Türlin's strategy to hide deliberately the deeper meaning of their texts and thus to challenge their audiences with literary secrets.

34. Keller, *Diu Crône Heinrichs von dem Türlin* (1997), 69–70.

35. Keller, *Diu Crône Heinrichs von dem Türlin* (1997), 72–74.

36. Keller, *Diu Crône Heinrichs von dem Türlin* (1997), 81, seems to indicate that he himself cannot make sense out of the "Wunderketten": "Man weiß nicht,

ob ritterliche Pflichterfüllung angesichts dieser irreal wirkenden Szenen überhaupt gefragt ist" (One does not know whether knightly fulfilment of obligations is even requested in face of these unreal seeming scenes). At the end of his monograph, Keller focuses increasingly on the Grail as the ultimate source of meaning, but even this remains rather elusive (428–29).

Chapter Six

Secrets and the Secret World in *Huon de Bordeaux* Foreign and Yet Not Alien

The Good King Auberon

It is not unusual that protagonists of courtly romance and heroic epics encounter magical beings, dwarfs, giants, or that they receive mysterious weapons and armor, that they reach enchanted castles, and have to fend hard to cope in worlds that belong rather to the sphere of fairy tales and mystery. As we have already observed in the previous chapters, secrets loom large in medieval literature and assume a big role determining the protagonist's lives.[1] Hagen in the Middle High German *Nibelungenlied* (ca. 1200), for instance, runs into a group of nixies in a body of water near the Danube River who provide him, after a short attempt to deceive him, with information about the future doom of their entire company in the land of the Huns.

There is no explanation for the existence of the nixies; we are not told why and how they know about the future events at the Hunnish court, but Hagen is curious about them and senses that they might hold the key to the secret of their survival. He steals their clothing and hides it and can thus force them to answer his question; nevertheless, after the first nixie has told him a lie, the second one then volunteers and reveals the truth, as far as she knows it. However, she does not advise him at all to return home, since that seems not to be an option for them; instead, she simply states the inevitable, to which Hagen can respond or not. In this sense, the nixies represent time as such since they can see into the future. Significantly, the nixies are swimming in a pond next to the mighty river, and rivers have always symbolized barriers in human life, whether we think of the Styx River or the mythologized Rhine River, the Ganges River, or the Volga.[2]

At first, Hagen is not prepared to believe them, but once he and his companions are in the middle of the river, he tests the validity of fairies' or nixies' prophecy. According to these mysterious beings, only the chaplain would survive among them all, whereas all of them would certainly suffer their death in the long run. So, he resolutely tosses the chaplain into the water although the poor man cannot swim. Near drowning, he desperately tries to climb back on board, but Hagen pushes him back, waiting to see whether the chaplain might sink or not.

Once he has witnessed that the man of the Church manages somehow to swim back to the shore, he realizes, indeed, that they all will die at the end of their journey to the land of the Huns. Consequently, accepting their destiny or doom, once the entire army has reached the other shore, Hagen destroys the ferry boat, allegedly to avoid that any of the knights might become victims of fear and cowardice. In reality, this is a symbolic action indicating that none of them will ever return home because death is awaiting them in Etzel's (Attila's) kingdom.[3]

Hagen's encounter with the nixies represents his own adventure with secret creatures (not magic!), and even here he has problems with female knowledge and female power, although this time he does not engage with the nixies in a hostile manner, apart from stealing their clothes.[4] Siegfried before him, this outlandish Netherlandish hero who had arrived at the Burgundian court in Worms like a usurper, had experienced much more than Hagen with respect to secret forces, and he almost seems to be intimately associated with the underworld. As Hagen reports himself, he had defeated the king of dwarfs, Alberich and had thus gained complete dominion over the underworld, ominously identified with the "Nibelungs," a mighty force always ready to come from a hidden realm in the mountains to Siegfried's assistance, such as when he fetches them at the end of the Burgundians' adventure in Iceland after Brünhild's defeat and when Gunther wants to force her to accept him as her future husband.

Most significantly, Siegfried's victory also gave him possession of Alberich's invisibility cloak, which he later uses particularly when he helps King Gunther to cheat the Icelandic Queen Brunhild and to defeat her in her own competition which serves to determine whether a suitor might be able to defeat her. No ordinary man would be capable of achieving these goals, but the protagonist, hidden under his mysterious cloak, has more strength than anyone else and can thus secretly lead Gunther's hand.

Further, Siegfried had killed a dragon and then had taken a bath in its blood, which gave him a completely impenetrable skin, except for a little spot on his shoulder blade where a leaf of a linden tree—a symbolic tree representing, since classical-Roman time, the pain and happiness of love—had protected his body from the blood. Nevertheless, none of his secret power that he had secured from the underworld can protect him against Hagen's intrigue, envy, and outright hatred,[5] and since Siegfried proves to be such a naive hero, he never understands the consequences of his own words and deeds among the members of the Burgundian court.[6] In fact, there are no indications in the entire poem that Siegfried himself was aware in any particular way about the meaning of that secret world of dwarfs, dragons, and mysterious people, the Nibelungs, never indicating any awareness about the implications for him through his close association with them. He only uses the paraphernalia taken from the "other side" for his own purposes, without realizing how much he insults and belittles everyone else by means of those extra, or super-human powers. His death at Hagen's hands is an almost natural outcome of his association with secret forces which the Burgundians do not know much about at all and obviously do not want to tolerate in their midst. Siegfried and his secrets are simply uncanny, and no one knows how to handle him in his physical superiority. As intriguing as secret powers might be at times, they simply disturb the ordinary people, heroic, or courtly society, at times to such an extent that murder is the only option for the one bold enough to pursue it to eliminate the superhero.

Other heroic epics normally do not incorporate such secret elements, whether we think of the *Chanson de Roland* (ca. 1150), the *Poema de Mío Cid* (ca. 1050), or any of the Middle High German poems dealing with the hero Dietrich (e.g., *Rabenschlacht, Dietrichs Flucht*, etc.). In *Beowulf* (ca. 700), however, the protagonist has to struggle first against Grendel, then against Grendel's mother, and finally against the dragon. Ultimately, he can no longer defeat the ominous threats and is killed himself, although his retainer Wyclaf helps him to kill the monster. Beowulf's physical capacity, his ability to dive deep into the water for many hours, and to fight against the monstrous mother using an ancient weapon he discovers deep down in the monster mother's cave, and later his heroic struggle against the dragon all closely associate him with another world, but once he has died, his successors have no longer any direct connection with the secret as such.[7]

Max Weber had coined the intriguing term of the "disenchantment of the world," referring to a phenomenon from the end of the eighteenth or early nineteenth century, a fascinating but problematic notion determined by the belief in the rise of modernity since then. The emergence of rationality as the dominant principle in all of human interactions would have closed off the door to a previous world determined by enchantment, or magic. But if such a disenchantment actually ever happened, then its early process set in already at the turn of the twelfth century, if we take the *Nibelungenlied* as a benchmark.[8] With the death of Siegfried, and with the subsequent disappearance of the Nibelungen gold which his widow Kriemhilt had fetched from the underworld for her own use to avenge her husband's death and which Hagen had subsequently appropriated and dumped into the Rhine River, the dimension of magic and secret seems to have come to an end, with the exception of the nixies who will later tell Hagen about their doom.

The thirteenth-century Old French *Huon de Bordeaux*—the full title reads: *Les Prouesses et faitz du noble Huon de Bordeaux*—a mixture of a *chanson de geste* and a courtly romance, allows us to examine this curious phenomenon further in greater detail because here the protagonist is critically supported by a most secretive individual who commands enormous powers, has unparalleled insight, and enjoys prophetic abilities without being characterized as evil, dangerous, or threatening, although he is at first deeply feared.

King Auberon, ruler of the fairies, or later known as Oberon, experienced a significant popularity in the later periods well into the late eighteenth century (William Shakespeare; Christoph Martin Wieland),[9] if not even until today,[10] but the post-medieval authors considerably changed his character and purpose. *Huon de Bordeaux* was first translated into English by John Bourchier, Lord Berners, in 1533, which is often said to have been the source of inspiration for William Shakespeare's *A Midsummer Night's Dream* with the appearance of the king of fairies, Oberon (1595–1596). But Shakespeare's play is otherwise far removed from the original Old French version transforming the medieval heroic or courtly framework into a spoof of confused love relationships brought about by magical charms.

In 1601, the London publisher Purfoot produced *The ancient history of Huon of Bordeaux*. In 1780, the German Enlightenment poet Christoph Martin Wieland (1733–1813) created his epic poem *Oberon*, based both on *Huon de Bordeaux* and on Shakespeare's *Midsummer's Night's Dream*, but it reached its final version only after seven rewrites in 1796, surprisingly maintaining many of the medieval narrative features and moving significantly beyond Shakespeare. *Oberon* in turn deeply impacted Friedrich Schiller's *Don Carlos*, Johann Wolfgang von Goethe's *Faust: The Second Part of the Tragedy*, and Amadeus Mozart's *The Magic Flute*, as well as the Portuguese Romantic poet Francisco Manoel de Nascimento with his *Contos*. Henry Purcell (*The Fairy Queen*, 1692) and Benjamin Britten (*A Midsummer Night's Dream*, premiered in 1960) based their libretti on Shakespeare's play, and thus also on the Old French version. In 1826, the German composer Carl Maria von Weber published his last opera, *Oberon*, directly based on Wieland's work, that is, once again on the Old French *chanson de geste*. The centrally shared motif is always the appearance of the king of fairies, Auberon, or Oberon, hence the world of secrets, incomprehensible to human beings, but certainly existing either to support or harm them.[11]

In the *Nibelungenlied*, the secretive domain from below (dwarfs) constitutes a threat to the world above (humans), undermining the traditional power structure there with the Burgundian kings at the top of the hierarchy. In *Huon de Bordeaux*, by contrast, the protagonist would certainly fail completely, either being killed by his opponents or taken prisoner for the rest of his life, if he did not gain access to the underworld. Certainly, Auberon withdraws from Huon for a while because he commits too many transgressions against him, but at the very end, when Huon's destiny seems to be finished, he returns and rescues him after all. Although the poet does not fully explain where this secret power originates from, he certainly positions it as a crucial force that helps Huon to overcome all the machinations of evil traitors at King Charlemagne's court. The narrator makes numerous attempts to explain the mysterious nature of Auberon, combining historical with mythical aspects, and he certainly confirms that this strange king is not a pagan, a powerful ancient god, or a magician. Instead, we are regularly informed that he fully embraces Christianity and believes, if not knows, that he will end up in heaven right next to God, once he will have died. But Auberon also emphasizes that he would die only when he himself would be ready for it. In short, this curious figure represents a fictional riddle of an extraordinary kind.

Before we turn to some of the details associated with secrets, let us first get a quick understanding of the text itself and its history. *Huon de Bordeaux* has survived in three manuscripts, which does not seem much compared to some real "bestsellers" from the Middle Ages. However, the creation of this mythical King Auberon had a huge impact on late medieval and early modern imagination, and this well into the late eighteenth, perhaps even the nineteenth century.[12] In fact, since the late 1890s, many new versions for young readers have appeared in France, meaning that this work continues to enjoy considerable popularity.[13]

The romance, if we might not want to call it a *chanson de geste*, essentially consists of two parts. In the first section, King Charlemagne calls the young prince Huon de Bordeaux to his court to serve as his vassal. But in the background, the courtier Amaury attempts a secret coup d'etat, first inciting Charlemagne's son Charlot to attack Huon and his brother Gerard. Charlot is strong enough to injure Gerard badly, but he is defeated and killed by Huon. The latter did not realize his opponent's identity and seeks refuge at the royal court, where the king promises him absolute and complete safety. However, when Amaury delivers the dead son and identifies Huon as the killer, Charlemagne explodes and turns into a tyrant who tries everything in his might to get Huon killed, irrespective of his own oath and the laws protecting the young man. Since Amaury accuses Huon of treason and the latter defends himself energetically, the issue represents a legal dilemma.

This then leads to the decision to have both men enter a duel by swords since God would help the innocent one triumph over the other. However, Charlemagne, contrary to all traditions and laws, suddenly imposes an additional rule, which guarantees, to the horror of everyone, that no justice can be achieved. Only if the defeated person were to confess publicly and audibly for everyone to hear his guilt, would the winner be free to go. Specifically, Huon would be exculpated and receive his inheritance of Bordeaux back from the king only under that condition. Despite vehement protests by Charlemagne's councilor, Duke Naimes, and Huon himself, not to speak of the other members of the royal council, the duel is conditioned in that way. After a long, painful, and bitter fight, Huon triumphs over his opponent, who indeed confesses his guilt, but only to Huon, so no one else hears it.

This infuriates the king so much that he would like to have Huon hanged at the gallows but can ultimately be convinced to replace this sentence with an alternative one according to which Huon has to travel to distant Muslim countries and achieve a number of virtually impossible tasks. Although everyone protests against this unfair treatment and the disregard of the duel, Huon accepts this command and departs, which then leads over to the second part of the romance. All this reveals strong structural parallels with the Middle High German goliard narrative, *Herzog Ernst* (ms. B, ca. 1220), despite the fact that the text is strongly determined by the protagonist's encounter with monsters.[14] Huon does not yet know how to handle the many challenges, but it is certain that they are almost insurmountable for an ordinary person. Early on, however, he encounters the King of the Fairies, Auberon, and this unique person becomes the protagonist's crucial helper.

The purpose of this chapter cannot be to investigate the various adventures which Huon has to go through, whether he is fighting against giants, or whether he is forced to pretend to be a Muslim to get out of a dangerous situation. I will also leave aside the curious phenomenon that this young man causes many of the problems himself because he regularly disregards commands, instructions, strict orders, and firm rules, which in turn means that he subsequently must go through a long period of suffering. I will also disregard many different topics characterizing his continuous struggle to regain his political power back home by means of facing enormous challenges in the Orient.[15] There is the theme of the Saracene princess who elopes with Huon and subsequently converts to Christianity, which was popular throughout medieval literature[16]; and, almost centrally, there is the topic of treason which permeates the entire work.[17] Huon discovers many of his countrymen in the east, some of whom had been sent into exile because they had killed an opponent in a tournament (3091–92). At closer analysis, *Huon de Bordeaux* emerges as a rather complex narrative, rich with many different themes and topics, motifs, and references to everyday courtly culture.

The narrator also includes numerous secrets that are never really solved, all of them pertaining to Auberon. This king is very little understood and deeply feared because people do not know anything about him. Huon learns of Auberon first through the hundred-year-old penitent Geriaume, brother of the provost Guiret whom Huon had tasked with governing his country during his absence. This is a very common feature in this narrative, with Huon regularly encountering Frenchmen somewhere in the Orient who are connected with him either through blood ties or through friendship/vassalage bonds. So, there is little surprise that Huon immediately trusts Geriaume, who has learned after thirty years abroad (3115) to speak Arabic (3107) and believes everything he is telling him about Auberon.

Geriaume informs him that this mysterious king is not more than three feet tall and a hunchback, yet displays the most attractive appearance (3154), features we are going to hear about many times throughout the rest of the narrative. Nevertheless, Auberon is to be feared because whoever might speak with him, would be forced to stay with him in his forest for the rest of his life (3157–60). In fact, Geriaume knows horror stories of this magical figure who can create all kinds of mirages to scare those who cross his forest, though he cannot harm anyone if one does not speak to him (3184).

For a long time, Huon believes all those claims, and he and his men are terribly scared when Auberon actually appears. The narrator then supplies us with a number of details about this mysterious person that deserve to be examined more closely. First, with his bow, Auberon can catch and kill any prey during a hunt (3223–24). A fairy had given Auberon an ivory horn with an extraordinary property, that is, whoever would hear its sounds would immediately be healed (3230–31)—despite the resonance with the horn Olifant in the *Chanson de Roland*, the secretive property of Auberon's horn is unsurpassed and inexplicable.

Another fairy had given to the horn the attribute that whoever possessed it would never be short of food (3235) and drink (3236). A third fairy had endowed the horn with the power that anyone who would hear its sound would begin to sing, irrespective of his own physical strength (3238–39). The fourth fairy had granted the property to the horn that Auberon would always hear its sound whenever its owner would blow into it, no matter where he would be situated (3243–47). Huon will later profit from all four gifts by the fairies to his own advantage, which then actually makes it possible for him to meet the life-threatening challenges in the Orient.

Auberon desperately tries to make the protagonist speak to him, affirming that he is a good Christian, but the company of men does not believe and flee from him. During the second encounter, the dwarf king assures Huon that he is neither an enemy nor the devil (3336), and he repeats again that he believes in the same God. This does not change Huon's mind, and filled with fear, they all run away one more time. Auberon gets so upset and angry about their refusal to speak to him that he is prepared to kill them, but some of his knights beg him to preserve the foreigners' lives. Shifting the narrative focus, we learn of Huon's exchange with Geriaume, whom he assures that he would certainly talk with the dwarf king the next time. The old penitent is deeply frightened and informs Huon that Auberon was born before Christ (3426), as if he could scare the young man enough to listen to his advice not to speak to the strange figure.

The next time Auberon appears, he shares more about himself, which underscores his mysterious, secretive nature even further. Auberon knows everything about Huon, which he quickly relates, and then he reveals that Huon would never achieve his goal without Auberon's help (3456). He ridicules the "old fool, Geriaume" (3468) and urges Huon to speak to him, which then actually happens, and this without any of the horrible consequences the penitent had warned him about. Instead, Auberon emphasizes that he holds strong affections for Huon and will provide him with all the help he will need to succeed with his plans. Then we learn more about the biography of Auberon whose parents were Julius Cesar (3492) and Morgan la Fée (3493), an intriguing combination of Roman historiography and medieval mythography.

At his birth, a number of fairies appeared and endowed him with a variety of gifts. While the first condemned him to the status of a hunchback, she then compensated that by ensuring that he would be regarded as the most beautiful man who had ever existed since Jesus (3508–09). A second fairy bestowed the gift upon him to "know the hearts and thoughts of man / . . . / As well as all his mortal sins" (3513–15). Auberon also enjoys the power to wish himself anywhere on the world by the speed of thought, and to get everything created he might imagine, whether a palace or any kind of food and drink, in seconds.

The list of Auberon's secret powers is not even exhausted yet. He also has the gift to control all animals and birds, making them tame immediately, coming to him upon his command. Most astoundingly, he also claims that he knows all the secrets of paradise and can hear the angels sing. He will never grow old (3559) and will die only when he himself might so desire (3560). If that were not enough to characterize him like a god, the narrator goes one step further and has Auberon claim that his "throne is ready next to God's" (3562), as if he were actually part of the divinity, a physical manifestation of God's creative power.

When the two men sit down together for dinner, Auberon is seated upon his throne, which itself is characterized by many secretive properties:

> It could be placed on a fire without burning;
> Anyone who sat upon it could rest assured
> That he could never be poisoned
> Or harmed by any venom,

For he could detect any poison as soon as it was brought to him (3615–19).

Curiously, neither Huon nor any of his comrades express particular surprise or astonishment about all those amazing skills, which make it possible for Auberon to control his own life; he is his own destiny and hence God-like, which no one even dares to question. But there is also no special amazement, and we are supposed simply to accept the numerous secrets surrounding this mythical figure. However, even though Auberon commands all those powers and abilities, he operates very much like any other ordinary person, repeatedly displaying his strong feelings for Huon, crying when he is worried about his tragic suffering, expressing anger when Huon has abused the horn and only tested its true power to call Auberon for help, and true wrath when he finally went too far with this magical instrument. In other words, despite being incredibly powerful according to the gifts bestowed upon him, Auberon operates in a very human-like manner, cries and laughs when the situation allows, interacts with his friend Huon in deeply emotional terms, and supports him like a father would treat his son. He himself affirms repeatedly: "I am a man like any other mortal / And I believe in the crucified Christ" (3338–39). Most definitely, Auberon is neither a religious person nor an evil force, that is, he cannot be associated with angels or devils. Nevertheless, he represents a major secret for everyone involved, which they simply acknowledge, but do not question at all. Auberon knows the past, the present, and the future, which often makes him rather sad because he can forsee Huon's subsequent sufferings, mostly brought about by himself out of his stubbornness to pay attention to his advice and to accept it as a guiding rod for his own life.

Auberon's entire *raison d'être*, at least in this romance/*chanson de geste*, seems to be to lend his helping hand to Huon, although that young man often does not obey him, contradicts him, and disregards even those instructions which Auberon had given him, warning that he would have to suffer badly if he were to disregard his teachings. There is no clear explanation for why he takes on such a strong liking of the protagonist, apart from the fact that the narrator needs his mysterious involvement to protect Huon; otherwise, the narrative would have come to an abrupt ending without any results; Huon would have been killed or rotted away in prison.

By associating Auberon with the world of fairies, the narrator has avoided any religious conflicts between him and the courtly world, especially because the king regularly identifies himself as a good Christian and appeals to the Christian God to assist them all to achieve a good outcome. In fact, this king of the fairies appears to be closely associated with Christ himself who had granted to him a mysterious goblet with which he can demonstrate his divine power. While the goblet is empty, as soon as Auberon has traced the circle of the rim three times and has made the sign of the cross, it is filled with white wine (3660–62).[18] Two properties characterize this goblet and the magic producing the liquid. First, the goblet would never empty, irrespective of the number of people drinking from it. Second, only those who are truly virtuous can drink from it; and when a non-virtuous person tries to enjoy the wine, it would be completely gone: "As soon as an evildoer touches it, / The goblet loses all of its powers, / Regaining them only when a virtuous man reclaims it" (3676–78). This is a common trope in medieval literature, the test of virtuousness, whether it is a vessel that spills on those who try to drink from it and are not truly worthy, or a bridge that only the virtuous can cross.[19] The fact itself that Auberon can recreate this miracle with the goblet indicates that he is blessed by God and that he is completely free of all sinfulness or vice. Similarly, Huon proves to be worthy of it, since he has already confessed all of his sins to the pope in Rome and has put aside all possible hatred he might feel toward any person (3687–89). When Auberon recognizes the protagonist's complete virtuosity, as demvonstrated by the filled goblet, he embraces him joyfully and hands over the goblet to him, and then also the magical ivory horn (3713), promising him that he would help him whenever it would be necessary. We might want to go so far as to identify Auberon as God's manifestation here on earth, or as Christ's tool because of the extraordinary power associated with that horn, allowing the king to come immediately to the rescue of the one who blows in it is derived from Jesus (3722).

Sadly, however, even though Auberon then admonishes the protagonist to observe carefully the limitations and conditions, Huon will transgress them without much concern for the consequences:

> I forbid you at the risk of having all your limbs cut off,
> to sound the horn without good reason.
> So help me God if you sound the horn
> Without being in dire need,
> You will find yourself in such a dreadful situation
> That every man alive will pity you. (3735–40)

Even though Huon earnestly promises to uphold the pledge, we know that he will break it right away, obviously because he cannot handle the secrets of Auberon's magical power. However, the term "magic" would be inappropriate because it is closely associated with the Christian faith, so when Auberon sends off Huon with his blessing: "Go with God, for I will not accompany you any farther" (3761). We are also later told about a noteworthy difference between magic and a secret power, or knowledge (5082). The protagonist has many doubts about the true nature and intentions of this curious fairy king, identifies some of the strange phenomena as "magic spell" (3792), and believes that he can do as it pleases him because they are, as he believes, a short time later out of danger (3794). Curiously, however, when the company encounters a delightful garden and a dinner table with plenty of food, they all accept it all happily as Auberon's gifts (3812), although Huon only refers to God who had graced him so marvelously (3821).

Then, having blown the horn, Auberon is forced to appear and to rescue Huon from mortal danger, which is not the case at all. The king gets furious, but he only warns him not to abuse the horn again, otherwise he would lose his friendship and would suffer badly from his transgression (3914–21). Of course, Huon, in his foolishness, will act contrary to this strict warning, as Auberon knows only too well, who then bursts out in tears because he knows of the dire consequences: "You will have even more / Hardships to bear, / Thanks to your foolishness" (3936–38). There is no clear sense of whether Huon really understands the true nature of the fairy king since he regularly disregards his commands and instructions. Auberon remains in the background of the narrative, but he is, to be sure, the strongest force and can overpower any enemy whom his young friend encounters. The audience is not really informed where this power originates from, and why this is not dangerous magic. As the giant Arrogant will later indicate, there is magic, but also "marvelous knowledge" (5082), hence a different epistemological dimension. But we are supposed to accept that Auberon does not embrace devilish forces and, instead, is directly related to Christ the Lord, although he never claims to be a religious person. Undoubtedly, we are left puzzling about this secret which is never fully revealed. It remains clear throughout the text that Auberon is a being beyond all time, even beyond all space limitations, can create miracles, can read people's minds, and knows both past and future. The narrator simply teases us and provokes confusion, amazement, and maybe even some fear because the king operates like God in person here on earth.

As much as Huon tends to question Auberon's trustworthiness, he finally accepts him as a reliable helper, especially when he himself is in dire need and resorts to the horn to call him in for his aid. It is clear to everyone that the horn and the goblet represent major secrets, as Geriaume expresses clearly when he warns Huon not to blow the horn and thus to reveal the secret when they are in the city of Tormont. Huon had left it behind in the house of the provost Hondré (4512). But the young man does not care about this problem, as he regularly disregards all advice, and simply resorts to the secret object with which he can call Auberon in for help: "I'll blow the horn, no matter what anyone says!" (4521).

Indeed, once again, the king of the fairies appears with his hundred thousand men and make it possible for Huon to overcome the Muslim enemies, and especially his own uncle Dudon who had converted to Islam and had turned into a bitter enemy of all Christians. The narrator calls him a "wicket traitor" (4561), and Huon cuts off his head with one strike of his sword. Then, however, Auberon has to leave him again, but not without appealing to Christ to succor Huon (4577), which underscores the king's deeply held Christian faith. He informs him about the mysterious tower Dunestre where a giant named Arrogant resides and warns him not to go there because it would mean his certain death. This tower was constructed by Julius Caesar, Auberon's father, whom the king gives full credit for having raised him well (4598), which reconnects this mysterious figure once again with human history, as imaginary as this reference certainly proves to be.

Arrogant had stolen that incomparable tower from Auberon, along with a miraculous hauberk which is as light as a loaf of white bread and yet makes its wearer perfectly protected from being wounded or from drowning, if he were to fall into water. Moreover, no fire could harm him (4617–24), which thus proves to be an appropriate armor for an inexplicable figure such as Auberon. The giant also explains that this hauberk can be worn only by a person who is completely free of any mortal sin and whose mother never had sexual intercourse with any man other than her husband (5091–96). Although Arrogant is an evil force, he operates under the same premises as Auberon, testing whether Huon might meet the highest ethical and moral standards in the world.

It might amount to a narrative inconsistency that Auberon introduces all those aspects and at the same time warns Huon ever to turn to that tower because he would certainly die there and could not count on his help in time of greatest need (4626–32). Of course, the very threat provokes the protagonist, and he disregards all warnings, which thus leads over to the next adventure. For our purposes, however, we gain more insights into the secrets behind Auberon's character, who is neither a magician nor a god, but simply a secret force which is never being completely explained, not even at the very end of the narrative. We can rest assured that Huon will never succumb to any danger because the narrator has included this secret guarantee, as much as Auberon regularly expresses his grave exasperation about the young hero's profound disrespect and disregard of his admonishments. Surprisingly, however, as Auberon also informs him, he will not come to Huon's rescue in his fight against the giant, which he confirms with a reference to the crucified Christ (4648–51).

When Huon and his men arrive at the tower, they discover marvels of yet another kind, this time automatons, that is, two metal figures constantly swinging maces which make it impossible for anything alive to enter the castle. But a lady, who is later identified as Huon's cousin, then opens a door which lets air enter inside, creating a huge suction that quickly stops the automata (4825).[20] All this leaves us as the audience completely baffled because there is, once again, no explanation. Without secrets, we might say, this romance would not move forward, and these automata constitute some of the typical medieval mechanical secrets.[21] In our case, they are most threatening, but female cunning quickly defeats them, which then makes it possible for the male hero to move forward and to confront the giant, whom he can kill with God's help.

A very similar strategy can be observed in the more or less contemporary Middle High German *Daniel von dem Blühenden Tal* by the Austrian or Bavarian poet The Stricker, where a mechanical or robotized giant challenges King Arthur and his Round Table and where its "brother," equally threatening in its automatic military power, guards the passage to King Matûr's kingdom.[22] Both were created by the Old Man from the Mountain, who later tries to avenge their destruction at the hand of Daniel, but then has to learn of all their wrongdoing, which settles the scores and appeases both sides.[23]

In the case of *Huon de Bordeaux*, the giant explains, parallel to Auberon, his mythical and also demonic origin: "The demon Beelzebub is my father, / And Lady Murgale, a sea-dwelling giant, / Bore me in her womb" (5140–42). All this remains similarly mysterious as with Auberon's family, but the latter turned into a good helper, whereas Arrogant proves to be his deadly opponent. Nevertheless, Huon more or less needs the former to overcome the latter, even though Auberon stays away in that situation which allows the protagonist to demonstrate his own heroic qualities. We also have to keep in mind that Arrogant explains that he was much stronger and powerful than Auberon: "All of his magic and marvelous knowledge / Could not harm me in the slightest" (5082–83).

The poet thus projects two separate worlds that interact with each other at times, but there are no epistemological bridges, especially because those secret forces never engage with the traditional courts of King Charlemagne (or King Arthur, in The Stricker's case). The concept of magic seems to apply superficially, but the notion of "secret" works better because neither Auberon nor Arrogant endeavors to create something miraculous; they both simply have the power to achieve whatever they want, and Huon learns about that only because he encroaches upon their territory and challenges their authority. This is the stuff of fantasy and imagination, of course,[24] and as such it helps us to understand more in-depth medieval mentality, which has transpired to the modern world through fairy tales, but then also countless science-fiction novels, computer games, graphic novels, videos, musical performances, and artwork. The human protagonist is fundamentally challenged by these secret forces that simply exist and interact with him either upon their own volition (Auberon) or in defense against him (Arrogant). The former voluntarily equips him with some of his magical objects for his protection, while Huon takes the mysterious golden ring from the giant once he has killed him

(5370–71). That ring protects the wearer from all harm at the court of Emir Gaudisse (5171–78), another secretive object, which finds an interesting parallel in the many different versions of *Floris and Blanchefleur* highly popular throughout the thirteenth century.[25] Floris's mother had given it to him to ensure that he would stay alive even under the worst conditions, but when he is discovered in bed with his beloved, and both are to be executed, they fight over who would die for the other, and thus the ring falls on the ground. But the lovers do not need the ring because their willingness to die for the other finally moves the Emir of Babylon's heart, and he entirely changes his mind, accepting the young people as true lovers who deserve his acceptance and recognition. The various poets make no effort to explain the origin of this mysterious ring and simply throw it in as a wonderful secret in the lives of the two lovers.[26]

In Huon de Bourdeaux, we know, at least that the giant had received it from the Emir Gaudisse as a token of his submission, whom Huon will kill later as well, then with Auberon's help, and offers it to the protagonist as a reward if he breaks off his aggressive approach, which fails, of course because Huon needs to accomplish his tasks without fail and without any deviations from Charlemagne's instructions. Ironically, however, Huon is distrustful of these secret objects, especially the hauberk which is supposed to keep him from drowning under any circumstances: "And I don't dare trust this hauberk, / Because if I went in, I'm afraid I'd drown" (5393–94). For him, thus, the secret world represented by Auberon, the giant, and others continues to baffle him, and if he could, he would simply put a stop to it because it is so inexplicable to him. Of course, he willingly accepts all magical help, so when Auberon's brother Malabron arrives to provide him with a ride across the sea, he simply embraces the idea, but not with full understanding or a grasp of the subsequent transition.

Even though Malabron, Auberon's liegeman, assures him of his own Christian faith and deep desire to support Huon, the latter is rather distrustful and worries that this strange person might deceive him (5473). However, since the transport would be possible only after Huon would have made the sign of the cross, he finally believes the stranger and jumps onto his back and can thus cross the ocean. This ambivalent attitude toward the secret objects, people, and maneuvers characterizes the entire epic poem, that is, the ambivalence regarding acceptance and rejection of the secret, all of which seems to result essentially from a fundamental lack of understanding. Magic is also incomprehensible, but it is normally associated with necromancy and a certain form of learning, whereas the secret dimension is altogether alien and baffling without being evil, either in moral or ethical terms.

Huon utilizes the mysterious powers and properties by default, but he is never completely assured that it will work out for himself, hence his appeal to

God to have "pity and watch over us!" (5483). Tellingly, however, the secret people also warn him never to transgress his ethical standards. In Malabron's words: "For the moment you tell a lie, / You will lose Auberon's friendship" (5507–08). Of course, already in the next situation, he lies blatantly to the bridge keeper, claiming to be a Muslim so that he can deceive him (5552), which causes yet another rift between him and the king of Fairies, who knows, of course, what Huon has said (5552–53). As much as Huon really needs Auberon, their relationship proves to be rather tenuous because the world of humans and the world of secrets do not easily merge, as we have already seen in the case of the *Nibelungenlied* (above).

Nevertheless, Huon then freely uses the golden ring and can thus convince all three other porters to open the gate for him and to let him pass. So, on the one hand, he does not hesitate to employ the magical objects, all of them representing secret powers, on the other, there is no explanation either for him or for us as to where this power really came from; so the golden ring effects all the tasks, but it remains a riddle by itself. Once he has entered the Emir's miraculous garden—there is even a spring/fountain of youth (5663–68)—and called for Auberon's help, he has to realize that the fairy king is no longer coming to his rescue because he himself had lied at the first bridge (laisse 55). As much as Huon had often expressed disrespect of Auberon and his secret powers, when those are no longer available to him, he is deeply stressed and worried because he has entered the most dangerous stage of his series of adventures, the court of the emir of Babylon. In fact, suddenly Huon is afraid that he might fail in his mission and thus would never be able to return to France (5739, or 5742).

Yet, he is wearing the mysterious hauberk which Arrogant had foolishly lent him, which guarantees him his life (5765). Moreover, he utilizes the golden ring which protects him from the attackers at Gaudisse's court after he has killed the princess's suitor. In other words, although he had viewed the secret world occupied by Auberon with considerable ambivalence, he fully embraces it when it is serving to his advantage. Moreover, he is also deeply afraid of lying once again when the emir asks him where he had received the golden ring from, finally being mindful of Auberon's warning (5908). Nevertheless, at the end of much fighting he loses his sword, is then knocked down, and taken prisoner, deprived of all of his magical objects, including the hauberk and the horn.

This then means long imprisonment of Huon, but help in the form of the emir's daughter Esclarmonde is not far away, and ultimately he is freed again, can kill the brother of the giant Arrogant, Agrapart, then call in Auberon with the help of the magical horn, who then overpowers the emir and kills him, pulls out four of his molars, and removes his white mustache, as commanded by Charlemagne as a condition for the protagonist to return to the court. Huon has resorted to the secret power again, and Auberon has forgiven him, although he still has to warn his young friend sternly not to commit yet another mistake (6974–75), which is, however, in vain, as the protagonist then transgresses once again.

But true to form, although Auberon had told him in most explicit terms not to have a sexual affair with the princess until he has married her (7005), Huon does just that, sleeps with Esclarmonde immediately after Auberon has disappeared, which then causes another series of miseries for the protagonist. And yet, Huon survives and can regain his previous status, return to France, where he faces the greatest threat yet, his brother Gerard's betrayal. Finally, demonstrating endless patience and virtually parental forgiveness, Auberon reappears at the court of King Charlemagne and can rescue Huon once again, which completes the narrative.

Auberon does not only save the protagonist's life; he also exposes Charlemagne's moral deficiency by means of the magical goblet which becomes empty as soon as the king touches it. Although he does not reveal the full truth, Auberon signals: "I happen to know a serious sin you committed / A very long time ago" (10561–62).[27] He does not go into details, but he can intimidate Charlemagne enough to save Huon from almost certain death, to bring the traitors, especially Huon's own brother Gerard, to justice by getting them hanged at the gallows, and to absolve the protagonist from all charges of wrongdoing or failures.

Charlemagne, and so the audience, becomes a witness of Auberon's enormous powers and he expresses deep fear that the king of the fairies might get them all killed (10684). Moreover, he equates him with God (10683) because he belongs to the world of secrets. Auberon rejects this false impression and emphasizes, once again: "I am not God. I am a man of flesh and blood" (10687). He retells part of his entire life story once again, outlining to the court what some of his secrets consist of, keeping others to himself (10713), and gives the highest praise to Huon for his "righteousness, faithfulness, and loyalty" (10717). Charlemagne extends his complete favor to the young prince, and peace is concluded (10735), which settles all political and military conflicts.

Yet, there is one final event, the transition of the secret force of Auberon to Huon whom he appoints as his heir of Monmur (10741–46), whereas the old Geriaume is to take over Bordeaux (10747–51) as a most loyal and trustworthy friend and vassal. Auberon himself then announces his departure from this world, something only he would be empowered to decide on: "I no longer wish to live in this world. / I must make my way to heaven, / For our Lord has called me there. / My seat by his side has been prepared" (10756–59). In a certain way, this mysterious king portrays himself as a new Christ, although he is specifically identified as the king of the fairies. He strictly forbids Huon to allow any conflict with Charlemagne to erupt in the future, and then he disappears, whereas Huon settles all remaining problems, especially with the king and the Church (abbey).

Undoubtedly, much of this romance/*chanson de geste* is predicated on literary fiction, but it mirrors in an intriguing fashion the extent to which the poet and his audience enjoy playing with secret forces, mysterious figures, magical objects, prophecies, and quasi-religious powers, combining ancient folkloric religion with Christianity, and naturalistic secrets with political and ecclesiastical issues. What we can learn from *Huon de Bordeaux* is the fact that medieval literature was often an outlet of archetypal concerns with secret dimensions which apparently never fully disappeared despite the best efforts by the Christian Church. This narrative does not fall into the category of fairy tales, but it is deeply infused with the same shared worldview according to which this material existence is intimately tied in with a different one manifesting itself as a secret.[28]

NOTES

1. Robert Bartlett, *The Natural and the Supernatural in the Middle Ages* (Cambridge: Cambridge University Press, 2008); Heinz Sieburg, "Magie und Wunder: Elemente und Funktionen des Übernatürlichen in der epischen mittelhochdeutschen Literatur um 1200," *Hexenwissen: Zum Transfer von Magie- und Zauberei-Imaginationen in interdisziplinärer Perspektive*, ed. id., Rita Voltmer, and Britta Weimann. Trierer Hexenprozesse, 9 (Trier: Spee, 2017), 181–93.

2. Albrecht Classen, "The Symbolic Meaning of Water in Medieval Literature: A Comparative Approach," *Mittellateinisches Jahrbuch* 46.2 (2011): 245–67; id., *Water in Medieval Literature: An Ecocritical Reading*. Ecocritical Theory and Practice (Lanham, MD, Boulder, CO, et al.: Lexington Books, 2018); Sudipta Sen, *Ganges: The Many Pasts of an Indian River* (New Haven, CT, and London: Yale University Press: 2019); Janet M. Harley, *The Volga: A History of Russia's Greatest River* (New Haven, CT, and London: Yale University Press, 2021). For the Rhine River, see Albrecht Classen, "Der Mythos vom Rhein: Geschichte, Kultur, Literatur und Ideologie. Die Rolle eines europäischen Flusses vom Mittelalter bis zur Gegenwart," *Mittelalter-Mythen*, vol. V. Ed. Ulrich Müller and Werner Wunderlich (St. Gall: UVK, 2008), 711–25.

3. *The* Nibelungenlied, *with the* Klage, trans. William Whobrey (Indianapolis and Cambridge: Hackett Publishing, 2019); Hermann Reichert, *Das* Nibelungenlied: *Text und Einführung, nach der St. Galler Handschrift*, ed. and commented. 2nd rev. and expanded ed. (Berlin and Boston: Walter de Gruyter, 2017). There is a legion of editions, translations, and research on this epic poem, which I cannot review here. But for a recent commentary, see Hermann Reichert, *Nibelungenlied-Lehrwerk: sprachlicher Kommentar, mittelhochdeutsche Grammatik, Wörterbuch: passend zum Text der St. Galler Fassung ("B")*. 2nd rev. ed. (Vienna: Praesens Verlag, 2019).

4. Ingeborg Robles, "Subversives weibliches Wissen im 'Nibelungenlied,'" *Zeitschrift für deutsche Philologie*, 124.3 (2005): 360–74.

5. Albrecht Classen, "Hate, Lies, and Violence: The Dark Side of Pre-Modern Literature: Why would we care? And yet, the key rests in the past to solve our issues today. With a Focus on the Stricker (Thirteenth Century)," *Journal of Humanities and Applied Social Sciences* 5.2 (2021): 281–94; online at: http://www.hillpublisher.com/UpFile/202112/20211231163859.pdf.

6. For a comprehensive discussion of the *Nibelungenlied* and its conclusion in an Armageddon, see Jan-Dirk Müller, *Spielregeln für den Untergang: die Welt des Nibelungenliedes* (Tübingen: Max Niemeyer, 1998); for a deconstructive critique of Siegfried, see Albrecht Classen, "The Downfall of a Hero: Siegfried's Self-Destruction and the End of Heroism in the *Nibelungenlied*," *German Studies Review* XXVI.2 (2003): 295–314.

7. *A Critical Companion to Beowulf*, ed. Andy Orchard (Woodbridge: D. S. Brewer, 2003); *Beowulf: An Edition with Relevant Shorter Texts. Including Archaeology and Beowulf*, ed. Leslie Webster (Oxford: Blackwell, 1998).

8. For the digital copy of Weber's essay, see https://www.molnut.uni-kiel.de/pdfs/neues/2017/Max_Weber.pdf (last accessed on Dec. 30, 2021); for critical studies, see Malcolm H. MacKinnon, "Max Weber's Disenchantment: Lineages of Kant and Channing," *Journal of Classical Sociology* 1.3 (2001): 329–51; for medieval and early modern approaches, see Michael Bailey, "The Disenchantment of Magic: Spells, Charms, and Superstition in Early European Witchcraft Literature," *The American Historical Review* 111.2 (April 2006): 383–404; *Marvels, Monsters, and Miracles: Studies in the Medieval and Early Modern Imaginations*, ed. Timothy S. Jones (Kalamazoo, MI: Medieval Institute Pub., Western Michigan University, 2002); Jibu Matthew George, *The Ontology of Gods: An Account of Enchantment, Disenchantment, and Re-Enchantment* (Cham, Germany: Springer International Publishing—Palgrave Macmillan, 2017); Jason Ananda Josephson, *The Myth of Disenchantment: Magic, Modernity, and the Birth of the Human Sciences* (Chicago and London: The University of Chicago Press, 2017); cf. now Allison P. Coudert, "Rethinking Max Weber's Theory of Disenchantment," *Magic and Magicians in the Middle Ages and the Early Modern Time: The Occult in Pre-Modern Sciences, Medicine, Literature, Religion, and Astrology*, ed. Albrecht Classen. Fundamentals of Medieval and Early Modern Culture, 20 (Berlin and Boston: Walter de Gruyter, 2017), 701–35.

9. David J. Buch, *Magic Flutes and Enchanted Forests: The Supernatural in Eighteenth-Century Musical Theater* (Chicago: University of Chicago Press, 2008). Wieland's *Oberon* stays surprisingly close to the Old French *Huon de Bordeaux*, although he replaces some of the names.

10. For a good list of modern uses of the figure of Oberon in popular culture and even sciences, which other scholarship has not yet covered, see https://en.wikipedia.org/wiki/Oberon (last accessed on Jan. 2, 2022). For Wieland's and Heinrich Heine's take on the myth, see Robert Steegers, "'Wie weiland Ritter Hüon von Bordeaux': Christoph Martin Wielands 'Oberon' und Heinrich Heines erzählende Versdichtungen," *Von Sommerträumen und Wintermärchen. Versepen im Vormärz*, ed. Bernd

Füllner and Karin Füllner. Vormärz-Studien, 12 (Bielefeld: Aisthesis-Verlag, 2007), 179–203.

11. Caroline Cazanave, "*Huon de Bordeaux* au Theâtre: Les Temps Modernes," *Études médiévales*, ed. Danielle Buschinger (Amiens: Presses du Centre d'études médiévales, Université de Picardie-Jules Verne, 1999), 71–102; for the sources used by Wieland, see Max Koch, *Das Quellenverhältniss von Wielands Oberon* (Marburg: Elwert, 1880); online at: https://archive.org/details/dasquellenverhl00wielgoog/page/n22/mode/2up?view=theater.

12. *Huon de Bordeaux: Chanson de geste du XIIIe siècle, publiéed'après le manuscrit Paris BNF fr. 22555*, ed. and trans. William W. Kibler and François Suard (Paris: Champion, 2003); *Huon of Bordeaux*, trans. Catherine Jones and William W. Kibler. Medieval & Renaissance Text Series (New York and Briston: Italica Press, 2021); *Le Huon de Bordeaux en prose du XVème siècle*, ed. William W. Kibler, Jean-Louise G. Picherit, and Thelma S. Fenster. 2 vols. (Geneva: Droz, 1980); cf. also *Huon de Bordeaux*, ed. Pierre Ruelle (Brussels: Presses Universitaires de Bruxelles, 1960); for subsequent versions, see Barbara Anne Brewka, "Esclarmonde, Clarisse et Florent, Yde et Olive I, Croissant, Yde et Olive II, Huon et les géants: Sequels to 'Huon de Bordeaux': An Edition," Ph.D. diss., Vanderbilt University, Nashville, TN, 1977.

13. For a good introduction, see Jones and Kibler, trans., *Huon of Bordeaux* (2021), ix–xxiii; cf. now also Albrecht Classen, "Huon de Bordeaux," *Literary Encyclopedia*, Dec. 30, 2021 (3302 words), online at: https://www.litencyc.com/php/sworks.php?rec=true&UID=40688. (last accessed on May 16, 2022).

14. *Herzog Ernst. Mittelhochdeutsch/Neuhochdeutsch: in der Fassung B mit den Fragmenten der Fassungen A, B und Kl nach der Leithandschrift*, ed. and trans. Mathias Herweg (Stuttgart: Philipp Reclam Jun., 2019).

15. See, for instance, Anne Berthelot, "L'Autre Monde féerique comme distortion de l'Orient dans *Maugis d'Aigremont, Huon de Bordeaux* t *Le Roman d'Auberon*," *L'Épopée Romane: actes du XV Congrès International Rencesvals, Poitiers, 21–27 août 2000*, ed. Gabriel Bianciotto. Civilisation médiévale, 13 (Poitiers: Centre d'Études Supérieures de Civilisation Médiévale, Université de Poitiers, 2002), 647–53; Caroline Cazane, "*Huon de Bordeaux* à la sauce enfantine," *Grands textes du moyen âge à l'usage des petits*, ed. Caroline Cazanave and Yvon Houssais (Besançon: Presses Universitaires de Franche-Comté, 2010), 123–62; Catherine M. Jones, "'Je ne soz queil homme j'oz ocis': Ignorance et innocence dans *Huon de Bordeaux* et *Garin le Lorrain*," *La faute dans l'épopée médiévale: ambiguité de jugement*, ed. Bernard Ribémont (Rennes: Presses Universitaires de Rennes, 2012), 123–36; Luke Sunderland, "Genre, Ideology and Utopia in *Huon de Bordeaux*," *Medium Ævum* 81 (2012): 289–302; Caroline Cazanave, "L'Espace maritime dans le *Huon en prose*," *Le Moyen Français* 83 (2018): 15–27; William Burgwinkle, "*Huon de Bordeaux*: The Cultural Dream as Palimpsest," *Shaping Identity in Medieval French Literature: The Other Within*, ed. Adrian P. Tudor and Kristin L. Burr (Gainesville, FL: University Press of Florida, 2019), 42–52.

16. Norman Daniel, *Heroes and Saracens: An Interpretation of the Chansons de Geste* (Edinburgh: University Press, 1984), 69–93; Sharon Kinoshita, "The Politics of Courtly Love: *La Prise d'Orange* and the Conversion of the Saracen Queen,"

Romanic Review 86 (1995): 265–88; Jaqueline de Weever, *Shela's Daughters: Whitening and Demonizing the Saracen Women in Medieval French Epic*. Garland Reference Library of the Humanities, 2077 (New York and London: Garland, 1998); Albrecht Classen, "Confrontation with the Foreign World of the East: Saracen Princesses in Medieval German Narratives," *Orbis Litterarum* 53 (1998): 277–95; Lynn Tarte Ramey, *Christian, Saracen, and Genre in Medieval French Literature* (New York and London: Routledge, 2001), 93–149.

17. See the contributions to *Treason: Medieval and Early Modern Adultery, Betrayal, and Shame*, ed. Larissa Tracy. Explorations in Medieval Culture, 10 (Leiden and Boston: Brill, 2019); Albrecht Classen, "Treason: Legal, Ethical, and Political Issues in the Middle Ages: With an Emphasis on Medieval Heroic Poetry," *Journal of Philosophy and Ethics* 1.4 (2019): 13–29; https://www.sryahwapublications.com/journal-of-philosophy-and-ethics/pdf/v1-i4/2.pdf (last accessed on May 16, 2022).

18. Jones and Kibler, trans. (2021), 111, note 29, annotate this passage because the magical gesture is unclear according to the manuscript.

19. Christine Kasper, *Von miesen Rittern und sündhaften Frauen und solchen, die besser waren: Tugend- und Keuschheitsproben in der mittelalterlichen Literatur*. Göppinger Arbeiten zur Germanistik, 547 (Göppingen: Kümmerle, 1995).

20. Jean Subrenat, "D'étrances machines étrangières dans le cycle de *Huon de Bordeaux*: Les automates, gardiens de Dunostre," *De l'étranger à l'étrange ou la conjointure de merveille: (en hommage à Marguerite Rossi et Paul Bancourt)*. Sénéfiance, 25 (Aix-en-Provence: Presses Universitaires de Provence, 1988), 463–80.

21. For this unique topic, automata in the Middle Ages, and similar mechanical objects or devices, see Lambertus Okken, *Das goldene Haus und die goldene Laube. Wie die Poesie ihren Herren das Paradies einrichtete*. Amsterdamer Publikation zur Sprache und Literatur, 72 (Amsterdam: Rodopi, 1987); E. R. Truitt, *Medieval Robots: Mechanism, Magic, Nature, and Art*. The Middle Ages Series (Philadelphia, PA: University of Pennsylvania Press, 2015).

22. Der Stricker, *Daniel von dem Blühenden Tal*, ed. Michael Resler. 3rd ed. Altdeutsche Textbibliothek, 92 (Berlin and Boston: Walter de Gruyter, 2015); Albrecht Classen, "The Role and Function of Women in the Stricker's *Daniel von dem Blühenden Tal*," *Die deutsche Frau als Dichterin und Protagonistin im Mittelalter*, ed. A. Classen. GAG 528 (Göppingen: Kümmerle, 1991), 87–103; rpt. *Classical and Medieval Literature Criticism*, ed. Jelena Krstović. CMCL 75 (Detroit, et al.: Thomson, 2005), 364–72; Markus Wennerhold, *Späte mittelhochdeutsche Artusromane: 'Lanzelet,' 'Wigalois,' 'Daniel von dem Blühenden Tal,' 'Diu Crône': Bilanz der Forschung 1960–2000* (Würzburg: Königshausen & Neumann, 2005).

23. Albrecht Classen, "Assassins, the Crusades, and the Old Man from the Mountains in Medieval Literature: With an Emphasis on The Stricker's *Daniel von dem Blühenden Tal*," *Marginal Figures in the Global Middle Ages and the Renaissance*, ed. Meg Lota Brown. Arizona Studies in the Middle Ages and the Renaissance, 47 (Turnhout: Brepols, 2021), 123–40.

24. See the contributions to *Imagination and Fantasy in the Middle Ages and Early Modern Times: Projections, Dreams, Monsters, and Illusions*, ed. Albrecht Classen.

Fundamentals of Medieval and Early Modern Culture, 24 (Berlin and Boston: Walter de Gruyter, 2020).

25. Christine Putzo, *Konrad Fleck: Flore und Blanscheflur: Text und Untersuchungen*. Münchener Texte und Untersuchungen zur deutschen Literatur des Mittelalters, 143 (Berlin and Boston: Walter de Gruyter, 2015).

26. For the Middle English version, see the text edited by Erik Kooper, *Floris and Blancheflour*, in *Sentimental and Humorous Romances*. Middle English Text Series (Kalamazoo, MI: Medieval Institute Publications, 2006), stanza 375, now online at https://d.lib.rochester.edu/teams/text/kooper-sentimental-and-humorous-romances-floris-and-blancheflour (last accessed on Jan. 2, 2022).

27. Suzanne Hafner, "Charlemagne's Unspeakable Sin," *Modern Language Studies* 32 (2002): 1–14; Jones and Kibler, trans., *Huon of Bordeaux* (see note 12), 311, note 54.

28. Anne Berthelot, "*Huon de Bordeaux* ou l'irruption de la féerie dans la geste," *L'Épopée romane au moyen âge et aux temps modernes: Actes du XIVe Congrés International de la Société Rencesvals*, ed. Salvatore Luongo. 2 vols. (Naples: Fridericiana Editrice Universitaria, 2001), 829–42.

Chapter Seven

Secrets of the Mystical World

Mysticism and the Absolute Other in Divine Terms

It is one thing to examine magic, magical objects, magicians, sorcerers, or state secrets, personal secrets, collective secrets, and the like in the Middle Ages. It is a very different thing to analyze religious secrets, the ultimate messages contained in religious texts, whether the Old and the New Testament, the Qur'an, the Torah, or the Bhagavad Gita, to name just some of the best-known Scriptures the world over. The religious experience itself, the *numinous*, as Rudolf Otto once called it,[1] constitutes the ultimate secret of them all, and so it is appropriate to conclude this study with a final chapter on mysticism as the most fundamental medium for the exploration of the divine secret.[2] More so than in all other cases discussed so far, the religious secret constitutes an essence or entity for which there are no appropriate words, and hence those who have sought to find human expressions for the divine or any spiritual experience have always struggled hard to come to terms with this task, often acknowledging that they were striving toward the impossibility of coining human words for the very apophatic dimension.[3]

What the mystics—here broadly defined, including all comparable figures in the various religions across the world—ultimately seek, or experience first-hand, constitutes the ultimate secret, which is not to be confused with magic, the miracle, the wonder, or the fabulous. The secret is tantamount to the holy, so this chapter in a way will supersede all previous ones, taking us far beyond the topics addressed in courtly romances, heroic epics, sagas, and related texts, diving into the sphere of mysticism.[4] As much as mystics have reported and recorded their experiences orally and in writing, the challenges of engaging with the secret of the divine have much resisted those efforts. Just as much as poets can only indicate through their verses a subtle hunch of their understanding of inner forces of life, so mystics have regularly struggled hard to formulate the essence of their out-of-world experiences. The late medieval German Dominican Meister Eckhart (ca. 1260–1328) might have reached some of the deepest insights when he developed the notion of "negative theology," to use a modern term, acknowledging that the divine secret was not truly accessible via human language.[5] Or we could also refer to one of his own sources, the ninth-century *Periphyseon: De divisione naturae* by John Scottus Eriugena, who already had conceived of the notion of the impossibility of grasping God in human terms.[6]

Although Rudolf Otto was not the first one at all to use this term, "the holy," and to analyze its meaning in a comparative and philosophical manner, he deserves credit for having developed it thoroughly and in-depth and having created a universal religious universal phenomenology on that basis. He refers to the Romantic philosopher Friedrich Schleiermacher, and then also to Martin Luther, Albrecht Ritschl, Immanuel Kant, and Jakob Friedrich Fries, as sources of his inspiration, but he himself might have been the most prominent author to address the idea of the "holy" so explicitly. It represents the complete "other" in all human epistemology and defies all rational endeavors to understand its working. It seems appropriate to begin with a brief reflection on his approach and notions before we engage with medieval mystical texts as mediums of the secret, perhaps the most mysterious of them all.[7]

As Otto states in the fourth chapter on the "Mysterium tremendum," that is, the one aspect of mysticism which is closely mirrored by the other:

> The feeling of it may at times come sweeping like a gentle tide pervading the mind with a tranquil mood of deepest worship. It may pass over into a more set and lasting attitude of the soul, continuing, as it were, thrillingly vibrant and resonant, until at last it dies away and the soul resumes its "profane," non-religious mood of everyday experience.... It has its crude, barbaric antecedents and early manifestations, and again it may be developed into something beautiful and pure and glorious. It may become the hushed, trembling, and speechless humility of the creature in the presence of—whom or what? In the presence of that which is a Mystery inexpressible and above all creatures. (12–13)

Otto himself reveals the difficulties he has to find the right word because the awe in face of the divine, for instance, finds no good expression. The "mystical awe" (17) might come close to describing the experience the individual might have in face of encountering the Godhead or another spiritual power. Pursuing the numinous further within the context of divine wrath, Otto observes:

> 'Wrath' here is the 'ideogram' of a unique emotional moment in religious experience, a moment whose singularly *daunting* and awe-inspiring character must

be gravely disturbing to those persons who will recognize nothing in the divine nature but goodness, gentleness, love, and a sort of confidential intimacy. (19)

But whether we talk about horror of the divine or about fascination with the divine, there is always the realization of "inapproachability" (19), that is, an intellectual divide that makes the communication between God and the individual ultimately impossible. God thus proves to be a secret which the rational mind cannot even aspire to comprehend or to incorporate within human thinking.

As to mysticism, Otto observes that "one of the chiefest and most general features of mysticism is just this *self-depreciation*, . . . the estimation of the self, of the personal 'I,' as something not perfectly or essentially real, or even as mere nullity, a self-depreciation" (21). Only when we recognize the very nature of mysticism, rejecting rationality as a means of comprehending God, would we be able to grasp this religious movement (22). Insofar as the divine is identified by its being non-rational, human communicative skills are of no use because the divine will thus stay outside of the rational world (23). Whether we talk about ghosts, god/God, or angels, we always face a secret "because it is a thing that 'doesn't really exist at all,' the 'wholly other,' something which has no place in our schema of reality but belongs to an absolutely different one, and which at the same time arouses an irrepressible interest in the mind" (29). The faithful person, or the mystic—in a more intensified sense—tries to reach out to the divine, or is met by the divine, but the essential realization is always that the other being or power "belongs to an absolutely different [scheme of reality], and which at the same time arouses an irrepressible interest in the mind" (29). Mysticism thus amounts to witnessing of the absolute and ultimate "other" in human life, the direct encounter with the greatest secret in all existence (29). I concluded my introduction to Thomas à Kempis, who also had pursued strong religious ideals, and both here and in the world of mysticism, secrets abound because the divine itself is a secret. The vernacular authors also dealt with this phenomenon, but they resorted more to metaphorical expressions of this mysterium.[8]

The experience of the "holy," or of the completely "other," evokes both terror and fascination, which justifies us to correlate it with the "secret," an equally irrational and incomprehensible phenomenon. Everything which Otto had to say about the "holy" with respect to "wrath," certainly also applies to the "fascination," as we observe regarding his comments on mysticism and other features. In his own words: "It is through this positive feeling-content that the concept of the 'transcendent' and 'supernatural' become forthwith designations for a unique, 'wholly other' reality and quality, something of whose special character we can *feel*, without being able to give it clear conceptual expression" (30). For mystics, the encounter with this secret being, the Godhead, constitutes "grace," and it is no surprise that for many of them, the new state of grace amounts to a form of sought-after privilege so that the individual can live within the spirit (33). However, as Otto also noted, and as we will discover in the subsequent analysis, all human attempts to express this "other," the secret of the divine encounter, basically fail because human language is not adequate for coming to terms with this mystical experience (34). Finally, comparing and contrasting the rational with the irrational, Otto confirms:

> the relation of the rational to the non-rational element in the idea of the holy or sacred is just such a one of 'schematization,' and the non-rational numinous fact, schematized by the rational concepts we have suggested above, yields us the complex category of 'holy' itself, richly charged and complete and in its fullest meaning. (45)

Whether we talk about the "holy" or the "sublime," the "mystery" or the "secret" (45–46), at the end we always encounter a hidden or locked door, and hence the mystical experience which remains so elusive for us in rational thought.[9]

Of course, what magicians produce, what berserks do, or what mysterious objects achieve also constitutes a complete irritation, confusion, a sense of helplessness, or of wonder on the part of outsiders. In either case, the individual is suddenly faced with a force that defies all traditional explanations and operates in a world all by itself, though it certainly exerts an impact on human existence both in a dangerous and in a fruitful manner. The secret, as we can accept it, thus represents an epistemological key to a foreign level to which we as human beings sometimes have access, and often not at all. Undoubtedly, religion as a universally shared experience is mostly predicated on this realization of the clear demarcation between, on the one hand, the material, earthly existence, and, on the other, a spiritual dimension that might grace us through a short-term visit, but which tends to abscond itself.

Little wonder that throughout times there have thus been many prophets, visionaries, religious leaders, but also charlatans, hypocrites, actors, liars, and hypnotists. Anyone who has ever claimed to belong to the former group, has regularly faced both severe criticism by the Church authorities, the state, and other power entities (courts), and profound admiration, respect, even veneration. The phenomenon of mysticism illustrates this most dramatically, as it bloomed first in the early and high Middle Ages, experienced its apogee in the late Middle Ages, and was then increasingly subjugated by the Church as a form of heresy. Nevertheless, until today, there are individuals both in the West and the East who claim to have been granted visions, revelations, stigmatization, and similar experiences. The secrets behind all that have not been solved and have not disappeared until today, when most individuals who claim to have witnessed those are conveniently moved to a mental asylum.

Many times we hear about individuals throughout the Middle Ages and beyond who experienced some visions, faced revelations, and personal contacts with a spiritual being. The entire movement of mysticism, carried both by men and women (if not a majority of women), represented a most amazing and until today little-understood phenomenon. This final chapter intends to probe a little into a variety of mystical texts in order to uncover yet another angle of secrets as epistemological challenges in medieval literature. Both here and in all previous chapters, the focus does not rest on the secret as such, that is, on a factual entity that we would have to embrace in our lives in spiritual or religious terms, but as a critically important dimension of the prevalent discourse.

Until today, mystical visions represent major religious claims that do not find easy, if any, answers as to their origin, meaning, value, and relevance. After all, religion as such, and mysticism in particular, defy rational explanations and require, instead, a phenomenological approach. Here I do not want to take the route as favored by some scholars with a psychological bend to equate mysticism with the individual's personal conflicts in childhood, or with personality disorder, or attacks of schizophrenia. Those attempts have been made, but they seem to be simply cheap shots against a vast corpus of mystical texts in which primarily women finally found a meaningful medium to express themselves.[10] As Peter Dinzelbacher now emphasizes, however we might evaluate mysticism as such, it represented a profound transformation of emotional history and the concept of the self since the twelfth century, at least for some individuals who were graced, as they perceived it, with being included into the highest secret of all human epistemology, the divine.[11]

Many scholars have, of course, already engaged intensively with the history of mysticism, and it would be unnecessary to revisit the many different contributions, whether we consider the gender angle, the linguistic and musical dimension, the spiritual level, the political position of the mystic within his/her community and at large, or the literary aspects pertinent to the narrative accounts provided by the mystics.[12] One of the most influential mystics, Hildegard of Bingen (1098–1179), was not only a most gifted visionary, but also a highly talented monastic administrator, running her own monastery near Bingen on the Rhine (west of Mainz), Rupertsberg, after she had left the monastery Disibodenberg quite some distance south of it in protest against the local abbot there who wanted to control her and use her as a *cause celèbre* to attract pilgrims to his own site.

She enjoys until today high respect for her musical, compositional skills, her pharmaceutical expertise, her medical knowledge about human sexuality, her linguistic competence (creating her own language for her fellow sisters), and her extraordinary ability to express her visions in letters, narratives, and poems.[13] In fact, Hildegard constitutes such a media presence until today that it would be unnecessary to go into specific details about her work and life. All we need to re-emphasize here is that she was graced with mystical visions since 1141, and that she worked on one of her most famous works, her *Scivias*, for more than ten years, drawing from the help of her scribe Volmar and her friend, the sister Richardis of Stade. Numerous other treatises and narratives followed, which established her reputation even further both in worldly and in religious terms. After 1158, with her monastery in steady conditions and well endowed, Hildegard went on several major preaching tours throughout Germany, reaching thousands of faithful who wanted to listen to this mystically endowed woman.

As Barbara J. Newman notes,

> The essentially prophetic character of Hildegard's spirituality explains the startling lack of interest in her own subjectivity. In spite of her unusual inner experiences, she recorded only as much as she had to reveal in order to authenticate her work. . . . Hildegard's prophetic self-awareness pervades all her writings except for her scientific works. . . . Because she saw herself as the voice of another, not as a speaker in her own right, she often seems disturbingly unaware of the human element in her writings. (17)

Instead of offering a detailed discussion of Hildegard's mystical visions, which would require a whole book-length investigation all by itself, much of which has already been done in a multiplicity of approaches, the purpose of this chapter is to give us a taste of the many secrets which Hildegard had to deal with, some of which were self-evident and obvious, whereas many others of her visions prove to be discursive and are only approximative regarding the secret behind the mystical vision. We could easily draw from countless other medieval and early modern mystics insofar as they all consistently refer to visions of a spiritual otherness, that is, secrets, but Hildegard serves us sufficiently to examine this phenomenon at greater length.[14]

The many manuscript illustrations accompanying her narrative in her *Scivias* are already most telling as to the impossibility to follow the mystic in her spiritual experience by means of a rational mind. The images present a variety of stunning scenes in which we are made privy to extraordinary scenes where the mystic's mind is opened up to light, streams, beams, and visions that are not of this earth and yet appear, at first sight, as relatively realistic. Of course, Hildegard operated with the artistic means available to her, and could not endeavor to create abstract paintings as in our modern world. As simple as the images might be on the surface, they relate in dramatic terms the impossibility for the human mind to follow rationally what happened in that very moment of Hildegard's vision.

When we turn to her narratives, we observe fairly similar strategies insofar as the author resorts to a wide range of well-known tropes and topoi in traditional religious, especially prophetic writing dating as far back as to the Old Testament. Self-negation and self-humiliation are some of the most effective strategies, such as when she emphasized about herself that she was nothing "but a tender and fragile rib imbued with a mystical breath" (149). Her visions are deeply determined by concepts of light, flashing in the dark, breaking open her mind: "The atmosphere suddenly rose up in a dark sphere of great magnitude, and that flame hovered over it and gave it one blow after another" (149). The dynamics of her visual observations speak volume of the intensity of her experience, while the author reveals at the same time a significant capability of expressing herself in poetic terms: "the blazing fire, by means of that flame which burned ardently with a gentle breath, offered to the human a white flower, which hung in that flame as dew hangs on the grass" (149). This is then coupled with an olfactory sensation, the smell, and an enormous tableau of astronomical images, all of which then serves to prepare the arrival of the "Supreme Will" (149). While observing the vision speechlessly, the mystic then hears the voice of the Godhead alerting her that she would not be able to perceive anything unless she would be granted the "miracle of faith" (149). Darkness is chased away by a human coming forth, and then a series of events take place which all support the realization of a mystical experience for which there are no words, only images. Yet, then she is addressed by the voice, praising her for her privilege of being "touched by My light, which kindles in you an inner fire like a burning sun; cry out and relate and write My mysteries that you see and hear in mystical vision" (150).

Undoubtedly, Hildegard relates some of the most stunning revelations that remain mysterious and cannot be fully deciphered because they are secrets of a divine nature. At the same time, she is encouraged to accept her role as a mouthpiece of the Godhead: "do not be timid, but say those things you understand in the Spirit as I speak them through you; so that those who should have shown My people righteousness, but who in their perversity refuse to speak openly of the justice they know" (150). Both here and in Otto's reflection, we observe the same intellectual dilemma, of being confronted by a divine or spiritual "other," being forced to address it or to come to terms with it in one way or the other, while not being able to speak about it because human language is not equipped for that purpose. Hildegard struggles hard with this very issue, seeking all kinds of terms to address God's properties: "He cannot be divided by any division or known as He is by any part of any of His creatures' knowledge" (150). Here we also come across two key terms: "incomprehensible" and "inextinguishable" (150). Paradoxes are the best she can come up with because this secret is ineffable: "He is that Fullness that no limit ever touched" (150).

Hildegard quickly switches from reporting about her mystical observations to a critical examination of what they all might mean and how they would apply to human existence in symbolic, material, and spiritual terms. However, she also laments that most people are far removed from this fundamental understanding and thus stay outside of the secret that she was privileged to witness: "O human, you are wholly in every creature, and you forget your Creator" (151). Yet, the mystic is blessed with having gained a new understanding of the divine, calling it the "Word" itself, the medium of communication amongst all living (151). More or less in common with the traditional teachings of the Catholic Church, Hildegard refers to God as "inextinguishable eternal life" (151), underscoring the impossibility to grasp the Godhead in human terms since we are all subject to time and the limitations of material existence.

When we then follow Hildegard's expounding of the religious meaning of her visions, she draws heavily from traditional Church teachings and treats her revelations as a basis for theological reflections, transforming thus the secrets she had been privileged to espy into a medium for didactic strategies to convert her social environment into devout Christians. However, even in this context, she conceives of a secret dimension to which only the blessed would have access, when she concludes: "But let the one who sees with watchful eyes and hears with attentive ears welcome with a kiss My mystical words, which proceed from Me Who am life" (157).

The spiritual dimension is incomprehensible to human beings, so Hildegard took it upon herself to serve as a translator for the ordinary people, presenting her visions and interpreting them at length, There is a consistent emphasis on light, brilliance, and fire, all of which interacted with each other and enveloped the human creature: "the glowing fire bathed the bright light; and the bright light and the glowing fire poured over the whole human figure, so that the three were one light in one power of potential" (161). At issue is both here and elsewhere the fundamental question of how to explain the mystery of the divine, and this beyond the biblical narrative, here drawing not on authoritative texts, but on visions that she experienced, which makes her entire theological endeavor to a very personal strategy, although even Hildegard cannot reveal much more than the images that had appeared to her. Naturally, she just makes her best attempts to translate those and connect them with biblical teachings, but it all remains a rather intimate situation, comparable to that of the prophets in the Old Testament. As much as she offers detailed interpretations, as much is the audience in the long run only receiving an approximate message concerning the meanings of those visions, and the secret remains as it was before: "This is the perception of God's mysteries, whereby it can be distinctly perceived and understood what is that Fullness, Whose origin was never seen, and in Which that lofty strength never fails that founded all the sources of strength" (161). After all, Hildegard is dealing intimately with the mysteries of the Christian faith and is given mystical images only that force her to figure out their meaning and to render those in terms manageable for ordinary people who might not have experienced visions.

The focus of this study is not directed toward the religious component as such, for which there are already countless other investigations. The specific issue addresses, by contrast, the very nature of the secret that Hildegard suddenly had to face when she experienced her visions. Obviously, she tried very hard to offer detailed interpretations of those images, and this over many pages. But in essence, as is always the case with mystical vision, even she failed because she could only marshal human terms for the apophatic experience and hence for the ultimate secret which rests far beyond any rational approach to the facts of this life. Each chapter begins thus with a description of her vision, which is then followed by the detailed analysis in practical terms.

As we can observe throughout her *Scivias*, Hildegard first describes her vision most visually and materially, and then picks out individual statements which she subsequently analyzes in theological and allegorical categories. The author operates as a teacher and uses her own revelations as a basis for her instructions, discussing the details, figures, colors, events, movements, and words uttered by the visionary characters. We could thus call Hildegard as a visionary who had been privy to the world of religious secrets and who was then inspired to relate her new understanding to the world of her audience. For instance, referring to the image of a woman, she explains that it "designates the Bride of My Son, who always hears her children by regeneration in the Spirit and in water, for the great crowd of His elect" (170).

Most remarkably, Hildegard never questions the validity of her visions and only strives to explain them as concretely as possible, so when she comments: "She expels unbelief and expands belief, by which it should be understood that in the mortal world each of the faithful is an example to his neighbor, and so they do great works of virtue in Heaven" (170).

Hildegard herself was clear enough that her visions represented not only images but secrets of the otherworld, the divine, such as in chapter eight of book three, in the third vision: "The human mind cannot fully understand the secrets of the Church" (172). As to be expected from an author/prophet/visionary such as this mighty woman, she claims the authority to understand her own visions, and thus proffers detailed discussions and explanations of her specific observations: "for, as you are now given to understand, all believers should join with their whole will in celebrating the virginity of that spotless Virgin in the Church" (172). That also means that she acknowledges the secret nature of her revelations and understands that she is dealing with most mysterious insights about the Godhead and the world beyond.

Hildegard, like many other mystics, makes many attempts to understand her physical world in spiritual terms by means of analogy, correlating, for instance, the light shining through balsam, the onyx, and the diamond with the light through which Christ was born, "unopposed by corruption" (174). Similarly, she identifies baptism as the armor and weapons which a young man would carry with him during a journey to defend himself against danger (175). Her entire world becomes decipherable by means of translating visionary elements into theological reasoning, such as in the case of chapter 20, "On the three wings and what they signify" (176). She goes so far as to refer also to the female body which is not to be circumcised "since the maternal tabernacle is hidden within her body and cannot be touched except as flesh embraces flesh" (177).

Both here and in some of her other works, such as her *Book of Secrets in Nature and Creatures* (*Liber Subtilitatum Diversarum Naturarum Creaturarum*), completed shortly before her death, Hildegard draws from her understanding of male and female sexuality and discusses it both medically and spiritually.[15] There would be many other theological issues of importance for her, but she approaches them all in a similar fashion, drawing some details from her vision and then translating them in religious terms. In a way, we could call her a translator of divine secrets which had been shared with her through the revelations. Another example would be the image of her vision in chapter four: "And there I saw the image of an immense round tower, all made of a single white stone, with three windows in its summit, from which shone so much brilliance that even the roof of the tower, which was constructed like a cone, showed very clearly in its light" (189). But Hildegard is not left alone in her struggle to come to terms with images like these, mysterious and secret in many respects. Instead, a voice from heaven speaks to her directly and offers a specific explanation and gives commands to her.

We also notice that she associates herself with the prophet Ezekiel in the Old Testament, claiming thus an ancient authority for herself. There is a universal secret, as she also was able to witness, and she promises here to reveal it to her audience by means of the divine grace granted to her: "But let the one who sees with watchful eyes and hears with attentive ears welcome with a kiss My mystical words, which proceed from Me Who am life" (197). As opaque as these words might sound, they are certainly the keys for the ultimate secret, and Hildegard thus claims to be the one privileged to interpret it for her secular audience. Moreover, she does not only render words but, above all, the pictures of the divine revelations. Both lightness and darkness compete against each other, and Hildegard is blessed by the divine voice to witness their presence, the movements of the colors, and the proportions of the objects in the images (201–02).

If not for the mystic's critical stance, coupled with a deep sense of wonder and amazement, and filled with profound faith, all those visions would simply pass by and lose their meaning. However, Hildegard serves both as the conveyer of the images and as the translator, emerging both as a visionary and a teacher, such as when she emphasizes, "This is to say that noble Virginity is surrounded and ardently embraced by a wonderful crowd of virgins" (205). Indirectly, the mystic confirms that she is dealing with secrets of the divine and understands that those cannot be easily understood by ordinary people.

Because she identifies herself as graced by spiritual enlightenment, or revelations, she regularly serves as translator of those secrets into the language of the common people. This does not, however, change any of the secret properties of those visions. Like a good philologist and theologian, she parses all those images and explains them to the smallest detail. She knows only too well that the visions might be theologically perplexing, but they are most powerful secrets she was graced with and could hence take the title of religious authority figure entitled to expound them to her listeners/readers.[16] Of course, we could also assume speculatively that these visions were nothing but expressions of her psychosis, the output of a certain type of neurosis, but this would not lead us far at all in analyzing the images themselves as powerful expressions of a secret world as perceived by her as an eyewitness: "And while I looked at these things, suddenly there appeared before my eyes as if in a mirror the symbols of the Nativity, Passion and burial, Resurrection and Ascension of our Savior, God's Only-Begotten" (237). This particular vision occurred to her during the celebration of the Eucharist, and disappeared once the priest had withdrawn from the altar: "the calm light from Heaven, which, as said, had shone round the whole altar, was drawn up again into the secret places of Heaven" (238).

As Hildegard emphasizes over and over again, her revelations were signs of her personal blessing because they refused to reveal themselves to other people and thus remained secrets. As such, those secrets revealed themselves only partially and then only to the mystic as a sign of grace. She, in turn, was then privileged to examine those images and offer her interpretation, which thus allows us to identify the visions as unique categories separate from those we have observed in the various contemporary secular romances and other narratives. After all, as we observe throughout, Hildegard perceived herself as uniquely called upon to divulge the meanings and thus to offer preliminary insights into the mysteries revealed to her: "let the one who has ears sharp to hear inner meanings ardently love My reflections and pant after My words, and inscribe them in his soul and conscience" (339). This becomes a trope that is repeated many times, as a signal signpost for Hildegard's personal approach to the divine secrets (e.g., 536).

It is also worth considering the probably most famous image projected or received by Hildegard as an expression of the inner core of the universe, the cosmic egg: "And in that fire there was a globe of sparkling flame so great that the whole instrument was illuminated by it, over which three little arches were arranged in such a way that by their fire they held up the globe lest it fall" (93). As she then interprets it, here we face a concrete and yet ineffable expression of the Creator: "faithfully shows Omnipotent God, incomprehensible in His majesty and inestimable in His mysteries and the hope of all the faithful" (94).[17] Similarly, turning to the placement of the sun and the three stars, we are told that within God the Father is His ineffable Only-Begotten, the sun of justice with the brilliance of burning charity, of such great glory that every creature is illumined by the brightness of His light" (94).[18] In the subsequent paragraphs, the author investigates further a variety of other cosmic phenomena and extols and interprets them all as reflections of the Godhead, thus theologizing the universe, as "scientific" as her visions appear to be at first sight. The audience is specifically instructed on how to perceive the stellar bodies and the explosions of light, but always in spiritual terms.[19]

Hildegard was certainly not a modern astronomer and scientist, but she regarded all the natural phenomena as expressions of the divine cosmos, a secret world all by itself that needed her interpretation to make it approximately comprehensible for the non-mystics. In other words, she specifically projected herself as the analyst, the mediator, the conveyor of the divine messages, or secrets, to humankind. The material existence both here on earth and in the universe beyond does not constitute the Godhead Itself, but a medium to make the latter manifest Itself, which would be possible only through the mystical vision, as Hildegard at least perceived it. She regarded herself hence both as a teacher and, above all, blessed individual empowered to explore the divine secrets and to translate them into human terms.

When we turn to her *Liber Vitae Meritorum*, or *The Book of the Rewards of Life* (ca. 1150–1160; three manuscripts),[20] we have yet another opportunity to identify her unique approach to the "truth" of all existence as revealed to her in her visions:

> This was the first year after that vision had shown me the *simplicity of the various natural creatures* with responses and warnings for greater and lesser people. It had also shown me the *symphony of the harmony of heavenly revelations, and an unknown language with letters* with certain other explanations.[21]

The Godhead instructed her to speak up and to reveal the secrets of the divine to the people, differentiating between the various types of knowledge, here identified as types of food (sweet and soft, solid and perfect, etc.): "Speak and write, therefore, now according to me and not according to yourself" (10). In this way, Hildegard revealed that she became God's mouthpiece and was entitled to reveal His secrets as far as she was capable to express them in her own terms. We do not need to follow the lengthy discourse which then follows, and it suffices to highlight only briefly some of the key aspects: words of worldly love (no. 1), heavenly love (no. 2), words of impudence (no. 3), discipline (no. 4), jesting (no. 5), etc. But we can conclude here with one final reference to how Hildegard perceived God as the one who controls all secrets:

> God, however, knows the number of all things. There are many, many secrets in God which he reveals to no one except partially and according to what pleases him and [what] he wishes. For he alone knows all things and holds all things together. And he preserves all things according to the plan of his grace. (No. 19, 19)

Altogether, Hildegard, and with her many other mystics and visionaries, recognized the Godhead as the source of all existence, most of which, however, would remain a secret, incomprehensible for ordinary people. In these spiritual terms, hence, secrets rule supreme.

From here we could dive into an ocean of other mystical texts, many of which prove to be highly poetic, musical, philosophical, and, of course, religious.

Mysticism was, after all, not only a pan-European phenomenon, not only a characteristic feature of the Middle Ages, but it found expression in other continents, in other religions, and in other historical periods, and might well be present even today despite the radically changed external circumstances.[22] One of the most moving and poetically skilled mystic addressing these religious experiences as expressions of the secret was the Beguine Mechthild of Magdeburg, who lived by herself for most of her life until she later joined the Cistercian convent of Helfta near Eisleben around 1272—the birthplace of the famous founder of the Protestant Reformation, Martin Luther (1483–1546).

Mechthild is best known today for her collection of mystical thoughts, poems, dialogues, and narratives compiled in her *Flowing Light of the Godhead*, which she composed with the help of her Dominican confessor, the priest Heinrich (Henry) of Halle. Helfta was the ideal location for Mechthild because she did not only receive the necessary care in her old age, but she was also highly respected there for her mystical visions, especially because two other members of the monastery, Mechthild of Hackeborn (ca. 1240–1298) and Gertrude the Great (1256–1302), also experienced profound mystical visions, which they recorded in Latin. Mechthild, by contrast, wrote in Middle Low German. The original text is lost today, but the first six books of the *Flowing Light* were translated into Latin by the Dominican friars of the Halle community around 1290, and in the middle of the fourteenth century, Heinrich (Henry) of Nördlingen rendered the text into Middle High German (Alemannic). The subsequent centuries witnessed a tremendous popularity of Mechthild's mystical reflections, although her name soon disappeared, which made the reception of the text even more acceptable for male audiences.[23]

Here is not the room to engage intensively with the *Flowing Light of the Godhead*, but a few observations about how Mechthild engaged with the phenomenon of the secret are certainly appropriate. Since she allows various voices to enter her discourse, it often remains uncertain who is really speaking, but the multiplicity of voices ultimately facilitates the profound engagement with the divine other. Right at the beginning, we hear a dialogue between the soul and the Godhead, the latter explaining why the book was created, "for I cannot restrain myself as to my gifts."[24] Even the book title originated from the Godhead, as we learn here, which underscores the extent to which Mechthild regarded herself merely just as God's mouthpiece and did not claim personal authorship, at least at first.

We become witnesses of the erotic exchange between the soul (the mystic) and Love (the divine), a medium probably quite familiar to Mechthild's contemporary audience through courtly love poetry.[25] The religious dimension, however, is never lost, and it proves to be quite remarkable the extent to which the author thereby opens many windows toward a secret world, without fully explaining what that all might mean. She complains that Lady Love has robbed her of her childhood, and has to learn that she gained instead "heavenly freedom" (40). Similarly, she laments that she lost all of her worldly joys, honor, and riches, and is then told that she gained in turn the Holy Spirit. Her physical weakness is substituted with "much sublime knowledge" (40), that is, knowledge of secrets, and at the end, the mystic realizes the full transformation of her inner self.

The mystical experience has a huge impact on the person and pushes her to her own physical limits, where the secrets actually begin: "God's true greeting, coming from the heavenly flood out of the spring of the flowing Trinity, has such force that it takes away all the body's strength and reveals the soul to herself" (40). However, the "first cause of the Three Persons" (41), that is, God Himself, remains hidden, although the soul is then granted the privilege of being taken "to a secret place" (41). The entire passages brims with references to the unique situation into which only the mystic is permitted to enter and where God then plays a game with her that is unknown to her own body, not known among the peasants, the knights, and not even by "his lovely mother, Mary" (41).

As the mystic then reveals, she was allowed to soar further "to a blissful place of which I neither will nor can speak. It is too difficult" (41), certainly a universal experience in many religions, if not all, a specific reference to the numinous by itself.[26] The soul realizes its complete transposition from the earthly existence to a divine dimension and even begins to forget its material origin. Tragically, however, which is characteristic of much of mystical experience, "when the game is at its best, one has to leave it" (41). The soul tries to resist the return, but she knows that there is no alternative. Even her pleading that she would not be able to praise God in an appropriate fashion when she would have returned to her body does not achieve the desired effect because the response is, again sort of secretive, "Your voice is string music to my ears. / Your words are spices for my mouth. / Your longings are the lavishness of my gift" (41).[27] Subsequently, a conflict between soul and body arises since the dwelling in the secret hiding place has transformed the former so much that she does not seem to fit into the latter any longer. The experience of and with the Godhead is of the most extreme kind, impossible to render in human terms, and Mechthild actually suggests that only the dissolution of the self into nothingness would create the necessary foundation to achieve the goal: "No one is able or is permitted to receive this greeting unless one has gone beyond oneself and has become nothing. In this greeting I want to die living" (42).

Many times, the mystical author includes dialogues between Love and the Soul, using almost violent images of capturing and wounding, of death and resurrection, of the conflict between body and soul, and then also employing highly erotic terms, so when the Soul informs Love: "Tell my Lover that his bed is made ready. / And that I am weak with longing for him" (43). In fact, only a short time later she formulates in concrete terms her ardent love for her Lord and thus combines the human-erotic with the spiritual secret of God.[28] Although she acknowledges openly that she can only approximate the essence of the divine through her mystical images, her entire *Flowing Light of the Godhead* represents a seemingly never-ending attempt to achieve a comprehension of this ultimate secret. In that process, she resorts to many different literary genres, images, topoi, tropes, and modes of speech, and we notice a fundamental strategy throughout to rely on the language of the courts, of the erotic, in order to come close to the mystery of her vision: "She remains silent, longing boundlessly for his praise. With great longing he reveals to her his divine heart. It resembles red gold burning in a great fire of coals. He places her into his glowing heart" (43). Examining closely her expressions of love for the Godhead, we recognize in Mechthild a potent poet who draws from nature images in order to formulate her deep feelings: "My desire, / My flowing fount, / My sun; / And I am your reflection" (44). In accordance with the main title of the book, she regularly resorts to images of flowing, desire, longing, and blissful feelings, but despite all of her efforts, the secret itself does not allow itself to be fully revealed, and it remains a mystery, whether the poet talks about God's curses, praises of God (45), battles for God (46), or the union with God (47).

The Flowing Light of the Godhead is filled with astoundingly poetic expressions and images, which serve to elevate the mystic from her material prison here on earth and to merge her with the Godhead in another dimension, so when she formulates: "I come to my beloved as the dew upon the flower" (47). Nevertheless, she ardently desires to gain knowledge of the Godhead (49), of the workings of the soul (49), and how the Redeemer became her bridegroom (50). The deeper we dive into Mechthild's poetic and religious outpouring, and the closer we get, so it seems, to a full understanding of the famous *unio mystica*, the more the very secret then slips out of our hands, as is commonly the case with some of the best poems ever written.

The mystic employs many elements of the traditional love discourse, but she also relies much on a strategy to systematize her thoughts and emotions, her visions and hopes. In that process, she appears to circulate around the secret, the Godhead, that is, her burning love, and adds ever more images or verbal exchanges to pinpoint this mystery. We seem to approximate it along with the poet, but only infinitesimally, and the more we hear the mystic engaged in dialogues with God, with Love, etc., the less the secret reveals itself and remains what it essentially is, incomprehensible and yet intimately part of human existence, the soul. However, it proves to be her own nature to follow the path of absolute love for the Godhead: "How, then, am I to resist my nature? / I must go from all things to God, / Who is my Father by nature, / My Brother by his humanity, / My Bridegroom by love, / And I his bride from all eternity" (61). In many ways, Mechthild engulfs herself deeply in an erotic discourse, relies on the traditional imagery, develops those further for her specific purpose, and yet, particularly because of the theme of love, denies the final access to the secret, which is nothing less but the Godhead Itself.

We could easily peruse *The Flowing Light of the Godhead* to find further confirmation. One of the most dramatic passages, however, where the experience of divine love for the mystic finds tentatively, if not paradoxically, most vivid expression, and where the notion of the secret comes most clearly to the surface, can be detected in the third book where we are informed about sixteen kinds of love (ch. 13). Many times, the statements there parallel rather standard religious perspectives combining erotic with spiritual love.[29] But then we also encounter rather mysterious comments, underscoring the incomprehensibility of passionate love: "Stormy love arising from great power—that is something no one can grasp" (120). She refers, of course, to her own passionate love for the Godhead, and insists that this represents a unique, deeply hidden secret. She herself has learned much about this love, but she also underscores that the Holy Spirit has withheld certain things from her (121). At least, she is to understand that even the best humility "without the fire of love ends in open hypocrisy" (121). But what is the connection between justice and God's humility (121)? Happiness cannot be achieved without adversity, and patience without turning one's heart to God would result "in secret guilt" (121). And ultimately, as the Holy Spirit insists, "Love that does not have humility as its mother and holy fear as its father is orphaned from all virtues" (121). All the virtues listed here are identified as contingent on additional values, such as peace which would require the support of the Holy Spirit would become "empty frenzy" (121). Or, poverty would need to be coupled with "constant cupidity," otherwise it would turn into "sinful prodigality" (121).

It also needs to be stressed that Mechthild, like many other mystics, combined the experience of pain and suffering with the illuminating force of love, and at the same time the Godhead tells her that He would follow her if she is walking in a humble fear and sorrow, and would approach her if she came toward him with "the blossoming yearning of flowing love" (122). At the same time, Mechthild also included theological issues and warned about heretics whom she blamed for having "sinned in secret" (123). We face, in other words, a plethora of efforts to come to terms with both big and large secrets, with personal experiences with the Godhead, and reports about religious deviants and hence enemies of the Church.

Altogether, however, as impressive and poetic Mechthild's account proves to be, it does not intend to be a teaching manual, or a guidebook toward the Godhead. Instead, and this proves to be the essential secret behind her countless meditations, ruminations, dialogues, and exchanges, she realizes that she is the object of God's love, but a love which is hidden behind pain, sickness, suffering, anguish, and torture. As she formulates it at the very end, "But the everyday work clothes are fasting, keeping vigils, scourging oneself, going to confession, sighing, weeping, praying, fearing sin, severely curbing the senses and the body in God for love of God" (335). The soul identifies its existence within the body as a prison and appeals to the body to hold fast to the hope that in the future when "everything that God has done with us / Will suit us just fine" (336).

Undoubtedly, Mechthild formulates deeply held Catholic concepts, many of which appear most difficult to comprehend, let alone talking about subscribing to them, which would be difficult for most modern readers. But we can conclude that both here and in Hildegard's works, not ignoring the vast number of other mystical narratives and poems (e.g., Hadewijch of Brabant, Richard Rolle, Julian of Norwich, Birgitta of Sweden, etc.), the mystical voice endeavors to transgress a fundamental epistemological barrier and to reach beyond its own physical limitations. Obviously, a secret world emerges at that very point, and the mystical poet can only resort to metaphors, erotic language, or biblical text in order to circumscribe that secret, without, maybe, breaking the code. The secret is there to challenge the mystic, or the faithful, and yet it also refuses, just as in the case of the Grail, to be revealed. Its very function appears to be the human struggle to come to terms with that which cannot be understood and yet certainly exists, either "the holy," in the way as Rudolf Otto had defined it, or as the ultimate Godhead, as the mystics tended to say.

We could easily gain further confirmation for these observations by examining additional examples from the vast corpus of mystical literature, whether by Heinrich Seuse (Henry Suso, 1295–1366)[30] or Julian of Norwich (1343–after 1416).[31] But all this might not be only a medieval phenomenon, as we could argue in light, for instance, of the famous German poet Rainer Maria Rilke (1875–1926), such as his *Sonnets to Orpheus* (1922).[32] It might be appropriate, even within our medieval context, to conclude with the first stanza in this collection:

> A tree was there! O pure and higher growing!
> O Orpheus sings! O tall tree in the ear!
> And all fell still. Yet even in the unknowing
> a new start grew, signal, and atmosphere.

After all, poetry is one of the critical keys for a door to another world, whether we call it "the holy" or "the Godhead," "love" or "epiphany." The human word, as flippantly as it tends to be used, proves to be a mystery, and the mystical authors, along with countless later poets, powerfully approached it and accepted it as a key for something which always looms large on the horizon of all epistemology, and yet always escapes from our critical grasp. This is, however, not a reflection or expression of escapism, a form of mystification of reality, but the realization by the mystics and others of a truth, whether divine or material, which simply tends to inaccessible for the human mind.

One of the most intriguing metaphors for the secret of the divinity and creation might be the hazelnut, as Julian of Norwich described it in her *Revelation of Love*. Wondering what this little object might be, she is suddenly told: "It is all that is made. . . . It lasteth and ever shall, for God loveth it. And so hath all thing being by the love of God" (139). Julian recognizes here the three major properties or forces in and by God, the fact that God made the earth, that He loves it, and that He will keep it forever. Without going into further details here, we can simply conclude with noting that Julian, just as Hildegard and Mechthild, recognized a secret for which there is no real key to gain understanding: "For this is the kinde yerning of the soule by the touching of the holy ghost, as by the understanding that I have in this shewing: 'God, of thy goodnes geve me thyselfe. For thou art inough to me, and I may aske nothing that is lesse that maybe full worshippe to thee'" (141).[33]

As to the Godhead, the mystic comments, also deeply insightfully, "For his goodnes comprehendeth all his creatures and all his blessed workes and overpasseth without end. For he is the endlesshead, and he hath made us only to himselfe and restored us by his precious passion, and ever kepeth us in his blessed love. And all this is of his goodnes" (141–42). The secret is there to be explored, and it allows the mystic to peer into it, maybe even to embrace it altogether, but the hazelnut itself remains an intellectual and spiritual riddle with no solution.[34] We recognize, in other words, a fundamental phenomenon of all spirituality which approximates human existence, or allows humans to come close, but ultimately refuses full illumination since it is beyond human capacity.[35]

To avoid the wrong impression that these phenomena were characteristic of women mystics only, we also could refer to the writings by Henry Suso, who was similarly inspired by mystical visions and put down in writing what he had witnessed, such as in his *Büchlein der Wahrheit* (Little Book of Truth) written between 1328 and 1334, and his *Das Büchlein der ewigen Weisheit* (The Little Book of Eternal Wisdom), written around 1328–1330.[36] Just one quote from his *The Life of the Servant* will suffice to underscore the elusive nature of the mystical secrets, that is, the visions and revelations. One day, having entered the church after lunch, suffering from various ailments, being completely alone,

> he saw and heard what all tongues cannot express. It was without form or definite manner of being, yet it contained within itself the joyous, delightful wealth of all forms and manners. His heart was full of desire, yet sated. His mind was cheerful and pleased. . . . It was a bursting forth of the delight of eternal life, present to his awareness, motionless, calm.[37] (66)

He describes an out-of-body experience and hence also the pain he suffered when his soul returned to the body: "When he had come to himself again, he felt in every respect like a person who has come from a different world" (66). Although the revelation lasted only temporarily, "his soul and mind were full of heavenly marvels within. Flashes from heaven came time and again deep within him and it seemed to him somehow that he was floating in the air" (66). Suso does not offer any explanations and does not fully know what had happened with him, but he confirms that he had entered the world of secrets and was thus transformed entirely: "The powers of his soul were filled with the sweet taste of heaven, just as when one pours fragrant balm from a container and the container keeps the pleasant aroma" (66–67).[38] Mysticism, as formulated by Suso, thus can be identified as the ultimate secret, a domain that we can hardly grasp or intellectualize. However, we might want to explain these phenomena, for the many different mystical authors there was only the realization that they had left this life, their bodily existence, and had witnessed another world, the secret.

NOTES

1. Rudolf Otto, *Das Heilige: Über das Irrationale in der Idee des Göttlichen und sein Verhältnis zum Rationalen* (Breslau: Trewendt & Granier, 1917); reprinted and translated many times thereafter; see now *Die Quellen der Philosophie und Phänomenologie der Religion: Überlegungen zu Rudolf Ottos "Das Heilige"* = *Sources of the Philosophy and Phenomenology of Religion*, ed. Dominika Jacy (Frankfurt a. M., Berlin, et al.: Peter Lang, 2010); *100 Jahre "Das Heilige": Beiträge zu Rudolf Ottos Grundlagenwerk*, ed. Wolfgang Gantke and Vladislav Serikov. Theion, 32 (Frankfurt a. M.: PL Academic Research, 2017).

2. Martin Honecker, "Spiritualität und Geheimnis," *Zeitschrift für Theologie und Kirche* 118.2 (2021): 184–215.

3. Alois M. Haas, "Die Verständlichkeit mystischer Erfahrung," *Deutsche Mystik im abendländischen Zusammenhang: Neu erschlossene Texte, neue methodische Ansätze, neue theoretische Konzepte. Kolloquium Kloster Fischingen 1998*, ed. Walter Haug and Wolfram Schneider-Lastin (Tübingen: Max Niemeyer, 2000), 9–29; Sebastian Neumeister, "Die Sprache als Weg in die Transzendenz," *Literarische und religiöse Kommunikation in Mittelalter und Früher Neuzeit*, ed. Peter Strohschneider (Berlin and New York: Walter de Gruyter, 2008), 930–52; Bruce Milem, *The Unspoken Word: Negative Theology in Meister Eckhart's German Sermons* (Washington, DC: The Catholic University of America Press, 2002).

4. Alois M. Haas, *Mystik als Aussage: Erfahrungs-, Denk- und Redeformen christlicher Mystik*. Suhrkamp-Taschenbuch Wissenschaft, 1196 (1996; Frankfurt a. M.: Verlag der Weltreligionen, 2007); see also the contributions to *The Wiley-Blackwell Companion to Christian Mysticism*, ed. Julia A. Lamm (Hoboken, NJ: J. Wiley, 2013). The phenomenon of mysticism has already been discussed from many different perspectives, both in print and online.

5. Joanna Maria Godlewicz-Adamiec and Paweł Piszczatowski, "Mystisches Geheimnis zwischen Sprachschöpfung und bildhafter Aussage," *Geheimnis und Verborgenes im Mittelalter: Funktion, Wirkung und Spannungsfelder von okkultem Wissen, verborgenen Räumen und magischen Gegenständen*, ed. Stephan Conermann, Harald Wolter-von dem Knesebeck, and Miriam Quiering. Das Mittelalter: Perspektiven mediävistischer Forschung, Beihefte, 15 (Berlin and Boston: Walter de Gruyter, 2021), 89–106.

6. Johannes Scotus Eriugena, *Periphyseon: De divisione naturae*, in Joannis Scoti, *Opera*, ed. Henricus Josephus Floss. Patrologiae Cursus Completus: Patrologia Latinae, 122 (Paris: J. P. Migne, 1865), cols. 439–1022; id., *Periphyseon (The Division*

of Nature), trans. I. P. Sheldon-Williams. Rev. ed. John J. O'Meara (Montreal and Washington, DC: Éditions Bellarmin/Dumbarton Oaks, 1987).

7. Here I draw from the English translation, Rudolf Otto, *The Idea of the Holy; An Inquiry into the Non-Rational Factor in the Idea of the Divine and Its Relation to the Rational*, trans. John W. Harvey. 2nd ed. (1950; London and New York: Oxford University Press, 1970). For an online version, see https://archive.org/details/in.ernet .dli.2015.22259 (last accessed on May 8, 2022).

8. Todd A. Gooch, *The Numinous and Modernity: An Interpretation of Rudolf Otto's Philosophy of Religion*. Beihefte zur Zeitschrift für die alttestamentliche Wissenschaft, 293 (Berlin and New York: Walter de Gruyter, 2000); Peter Schütz, *Mysterium tremendum: zum Verhältnis von Angst und Religion nach Rudolf Otto*. Beiträge zur historischen Theologie, 178 (Tübingen: Mohr Siebeck, 2016).

9. For a recent study on Otto, see Yoshitsugu Sawai, *Rudolf Otto and the Foundation of the History of Religions* (London: Bloomsbury Academic, 2022).

10. See, for instance, Ralph Frenken, "Childhood and Fantasies of Medieval Mystics," *The Journal of Psychohistory* 28 (2000): 150–72; online at:

http://www.primal-page.com/frenken.htm (last accessed on May 12, 2022); see also Becky R. Lee, "The Medieval Hysteric and the Psychedelic Psychologist: A Revaluation of the Mysticism of Margery Kempe in the Light of the Transpersonal Psychology of Stanislav Grof," *Studia Mystica* 23 (2002): 102–26; Jerome Kroll and Bernard S. Bachrach, *The Mystic Mind: The Psychology of Medieval Mystics and Ascetics* (New York and London: Routledge, 2005).

11. Peter Dinzelbacher, *Structures and Origins of the Twelfth-Century "Renaissance."* Monographien zur Geschichte des Mittelalters, 63 (Stuttgart: Anton Hiersemann, 2017), 172–79. See also his overview in *Christliche Mystik im Abendland: Ihre Geschichte von den Anfängen bis zum Ende des Mittelalters* (Paderborn and Munich: Ferdinand Schöningh, 1994), and his *Deutsche und niederländische Mystik des Mittelalters: Ein Studienbuch* (Berlin and Boston: Walter de Gruyter, 2012).

12. See, for example, Kurt Ruh, *Frauenmystik und Franziskanische Mystik der Frühzeit*. Geschichte der abendländischen Mystik, II (Munich: C. H. Beck, 1993); id., *Die Mystik des deutschen Predigerordens und ihre Grundlegung durch die Hochscholastik*. Geschichte der abendländischen Mystik III (Munich: C. H. Beck, 1996); Amy Hollywood, *The Soul as Virgin Wife: Mechthild of Magdeburg, Marguerite Porete, and Meister Eckhart*. Studies in Spirituality and Theology (Notre, Dame, IN, and London: University of Notre Dame Press, 1995); Bernard McGinn, *The Flowering of Mysticism: Men and Women in the New Mysticism (1200–1350)*. The Presence of God, 3 (New York: Crossroad, 1998); id., *The Growth of Mysticism*. The Presence of God, 2 (New York: Crossroad, 1999).

13. See the introduction to Hildegard of Bingen, *Scivias*, trans. Mother Columba Hart and Jane Bishop, intro. by Barbara J. Newman, preface by Caroline Walker Bynum (New York and Mahwah, NJ: Paulist Press, 1990). See also the contributions to *Hildegard von Bingen 1098–1179*, ed. Hans-Jürgen Kotzur (Mainz: Verlag Philipp von Zabern, 1998 *Hildegard von Bingen in ihrem historischen Umfeld: Internationaler wissenschaftlicher Kongreß zum 900jährigen Jubiläum, 13.–19. September 1998, Bingen am Rhein*, ed. Alfred Haverkamp (Mainz: Verlag Philipp von Zabern, 2000);

for an extensive bibliography, see *Hildegard von Bingen: Internationale Wissenschaftliche Bibliographie*, ed. Marc-Aeilko Aris, Michael Embach, et al. Quellen und Abhandlungen zur mittelrheinischen Kirchengeschichte, 84 (Mainz: Gesellschaft für mittelrheinische Kirchengeschichte, 1998); most recently, see *A Companion to Hildegard of Bingen*, ed. Beverly Mayne Kienzle, Debra L. Stroudt, and George Ferzoco. Brill's Companions to the Christian Tradition, 45 (Leiden and Boston: Brill, 2014); *The Cambridge Companion to Hildegard of Bingen*, ed. Jeniffer Bain (Cambridge: Cambridge University Press, 2021).

14. Änne Bäumer, *Wisse die Wege: Leben und Werk Hildegards von Bingen; eine Monographie zu ihrem 900. Geburtstag* (Frankfurt a. M., Bern, et al.: Peter Lang, 1998); Honey Meconi, *Hildegard of Bingen. Women Composers* (Urbana, Chicago; Springfield, IL: University of Illinois Press, 2018); Timothy K. Beal, *The Book of Revelation: A Biography* (Princeton, NJ: Princeton University Press, 2018); for a recent text anthology, see *Das große Hildegard von Bingen Lesebuch: Worte wie von Feuerzungen*, ed. Maura Zátonyi (Munich: Verlag Herder, 2022). The book markets are flooded with studies, editions, translations of Hildegard's works, many of which are more trade books than serious examinations. Hildegard is simply "in" both for young and old, for musicians and pharmacologists, for spiritualists and gender scholars.

15. This has been discussed, of course, already many times; see, most recently, *Medizin im Mittelalter: zwischen Erfahrungswissen, Magie und Religion: Hildegard von Bingen, missverstandene Ikone der Klostermedizin: die Pest, die überraschenden Folgen der Seuche: Sex in the City, Geschlechtsverkehr als Heilmittel*, ed. Carsten Könneker. Spektrum der Wissenschaft. Spezial. Archäologie, Geschichte, Kultur, 2019.2 (Heidelberg: Spektrum der Wissenschaft Verlagsgesellschaft, 2019); cf. also Winfried Wilhelmy, *Sexualität, Schwangerschaft und Geburt in den Schriften Hildegards von Bingen* (Mainz: Zabern, 1998); Stefanie Rinke, *Das "Genießen Gottes": Medialität und Geschlechtercodierungen bei Bernhard von Clairvaux und Hildegard von Bingen*. Berliner Kulturwissenschaft, 3 (Freiburg i. Br. and Berlin: Rombach, 2006). For a selection of relevant texts by this mystic, see Hildegard of Bingen, *On Natural Philosophy and Medicine: Selections from Cause et cure*. Library of Medieval Women (Cambridge and Rochester, NY: D. S. Brewer, 1999).

16. Margot Schmidt, "Hildegard von Bingen als Lehrerin des Glaubens: Speculum als Symbol des Transzendenten," *Hildegard von Bingen, 1179–1979: Festschrift zum 800. Todestag der Heiligen*, ed. Anton Ph. Brück. Quellen und Abhandlungen zur mittelrheinischen Kirchengeschichte, 3 (Mainz: Selbstverlag der Gesellschaft für Mittelrheinische Kirchengeschichte, 1979), 95–157.

17. Heinrich Schipperges, *Hildegard of Bingen: Healing and the Nature of the Cosmos*, trans. from German by John A. Broadwin (1995; Princeton: Wiener, 1997).

18. Renate Craine, *Hildegard: Prophet of the Cosmic Christ* (New York: Crossroad Publ., 1998); Kevin Duffy, SM, *Christian Solar Symbolism and Jesus the Sun of Justice* (London and New York: T & T Clark, 2022); see also the contributions to *Full of Your Glory: Liturgy, Cosmos, Creation: Papers from the 5th Yale ISM Liturgy Conference, June 18–21, 2018*, ed. Teresa Berger (Collegeville, MN: Liturgical Press Academic, 2019). Undoubtedly, here we encounter numerous studies that are deeply

religious (Catholic), which makes it difficult to discriminate between solid scholarship and open advocacy for the faith through the study of Hildegard's visions.

19. María José Ortúzar Escudero, *Die Sinne in den Schriften Hildegards von Bingen: Ein Beitrag zur Geschichte der Sinneswahrnehmung*. Monographien zur Geschichte des Mittelalters, 62 (Stuttgart: Anton Hiersemann, 2016).

20. Barbara Newman, "Hildegard of Bingen and the 'Birth of Purgatory,'" *Mystics Quarterly* 19 (1993): 90–97; Joanna Godlewicz-Adamiec, "Das Unsagbare sagen: Bilder der Natur und Naturmetapher im 'Liber Vitae Meritorum' der Hildegard von Bingen," *Studia germanica Gedanensia* 38 (2018): 11–25; Melanie Glier, "Aspekte der inhaltlich-strukturellen Beschaffenheit des 'Liber vitae meritorum' von Hildegard von Bingen," *Autour de Hildegarde de Bingen: Actes du Colloque du Centre d'Etudes Médiévales de l'université de Picardie-Jules Verne Saint-Riquier, 5–8 Décembre 1998*, ed. Kerstin Koch and Danielle Buschinger. Médiévales, 10 (Amiens: Presses du "Centre d'Etudes Médiévales" Université de Picardie—Jules Verne, 2000), 51–62.

21. Hildegard of Bingen, *The Book of the Rewards of Life (Liber Vitae Meritorum*, trans. Bruce W. Hozeski (New York and Oxford: Oxford University Press, 1994), 9.

22. Philip C. Almond, *Mystical Experience and Religious Doctrine: An Investigation of the Study of Mysticism in World Religions*. Rpt. (1982; Berlin and Boston: Walter de Gruyter, 1982). For a most useful lexicon, see *Wörterbuch der Mystik*, ed. Peter Dinzelbacher. Kröners Taschenausgabe, 456 (Stuttgart: Alfred Kröner Verlag, 1989); Louise Nelstrop, with Kevin Magill and Bradley B. Onishi, *Christian Mysticism: An Introduction to Contemporary Theoretical Approaches* (Farnham, Surrey: Ashgate, 2009); *Mysticism Without Bounds: Essays from the International Conference on Mysticism. Human Transcendence, Economic Life, Medical Materialism*, ed. Kurian Kachappilly (New Delhi: Christian World Imprints, 2015). The literature on this topic is truly legion, especially because individual forms of mysticism can be found in virtually all religions. For an excellent summary and critical discussion, see now Jerome Gellman, "Mysticism," *Stanford Encyclopedia of Philosophy*, first published Nov 11, 2004; substantive revision Jul. 31, 2018, online at https://plato.stanford.edu/entries/mysticism/ (last accessed on May 12, 2022).

23. Sara S. Poor, *Mechthild of Magdeburg and Her Book: Gender and the Making of Textual Authority*. The Middle Ages Series (Philadelphia, PA: University of Pennsylvania Press, 2004), esp. ch. 5, 173–203.

24. Mechthild of Magdeburg, *The Flowing Light of the Godhead*, trans. and intro. by Frank Tobin (New York and Mahwah, NJ: Paulist Press, 1998), 39. For the historical-critical edition, see Mechthild von Magdeburg, *Das fließende Licht der Gottheit*, ed. Gisela Vollmann-Profe. Bibliothek des Mittelalters, 19, Bibliothek deutscher Klassiker, 181 (Frankfurt a. M.: Deutsche Klassiker Verlag, 2003); Mechthild von Magdeburg, *'Lux divinitatis'—'Das liecht der gotheit.' Der lateinischfrühneuhochdeutsche Überlieferungszweig des 'Fließenden Lichts der Gottheit.' Synoptische Ausgabe*, ed. Balázs J. Nemes and Elke Senne, under the guidance of Ernst Hellgardt (Berlin and Boston: Walter de Gruyter, 2019).

25. Albrecht Classen, "The Dialectics of Mystical Love in the Middle Ages: Violence/Pain and Divine Love in the Mystical Visions of Mechthild of Magdeburg and Marguerite Porète," *Studies in Spirituality* 20 (2010): 143–60; id., "Mystical

Literature for the Modern Reader – Responses to a Dilemma and Pragmatic Suggestions: With a Focus on Mechthild of Magdeburg," *Studies in Spirituality* 28 (2018): 145–67.

26. Hildegard Gosebrink, *Das Geheimnis schauen: Grundkurs christliche Mystik* (Munich: Kösel, 2007). For parallels in early modern mystical literature, see Jacob Vance, *Secrets: Humanism, Mysticism, and Evangelism in Erasmus of Rotterdam, Bishop Guillaume Briçonnet, and Marguerite de Navarre*. Brill's Studies in Intellectual History, 231 (Leiden and Boston: Brill, 2014). See now the contributions to *Darstellung und Geheimnis in Mittelalter und Früher Neuzeit*, ed. Jutta Eming und Volkhard Wels. Episteme in Bewegung, 21 (Wiesbaden: Harrassowitz Verlag, 2021).

27. As to music as the ultimate aesthetic and spiritual secret, at least in medieval literature, see Albrecht Classen, "Music as a Universal Bond and Bridge Between the Physical and the Divine: Transcultural and Medieval Perspectives," *Rupkatha Journal on Interdisciplinary Studies in Humanities* 13.3 (2021): 1–30; online at: https://rupkatha.com/V13/n3/v13n301.pdf; or: DOI: 10.21659/rupkatha.v13n3.01.

28. Albrecht Classen, "The Dialectics of Mystical Love in the Middle Ages: Violence/Pain and Divine Love in the Mystical Visions of Mechthild of Magdeburg and Marguerite Porète," *Studies in Spirituality* 20 (2010): 143–60. See also Elizabeth A. Andersen, *The Voices of Mechthild of Magdeburg* (Oxford, Bern, et al.: Peter Lang, 2000).

29. Wouter J. Hanegraaff and Jeffrey J. Kripal, *Hidden Intercourse: Eros and Sexuality in the History of Western Esotericism*. Aries Book Series, 7 (Leiden and Boston: Brill, 2008).

30. Henry Suso, *The Exemplar, with Two German Sermons*, trans., ed., and intro. by Frank Tobin (New York and Mahwah, NJ: Paulist Press, 1989).

31. *The Writings of Julian of Norwich: A Vision Showed to a Devout Woman and A Revelation of Love*, ed. Nicholas Watson and Jacqueline Jenkins (University Park, PA: The Pennsylvania State University Press, 2006). For critical comments on English mystics, see now *The Cambridge Companion to Medieval English Mysticism* (Cambridge: Cambridge University Press, 2011).

32. Rainer Maria Rilke, *The Sonnets to Orpheus*, trans. from the original German by Leslie Norris and Alan Keele. Studies in German Literature, Linguistics, and Culture, 42 (Columbia, SC: Camden House, 1989); see also Rilke, *The Duino Elegies*, trans. by Leslie Norris and Alan Keele. Studies in German Literature, Linguistics, and Culture, 42 (Columbia, SC: Camden House, 1993).

33. Jeanette S. Zissell, "Universal Salvation in the Earthly City: *De Civitate Dei* and the Significance of the Hazelnut in Julian of Norwich's *Showings*," *Urban Space in the Middle Ages and Early Modern Times*, ed. Albrecht Classen. Fundamentals of Medieval and Early Modern Culture, 4 (Berlin and New York: Walter de Gruyter, 2009), 331–51.

34. Wolfgang Riehle, *The Secret Within: Hermits, Recluses, and Spiritual Outsiders in Medieval England*, trans. from the German by Charity Scott-Stokes (2011; Ithaca, NY: Cornell University Press, 2014). See also Hans G. Kippenberg and Guy G. Stroumsa, *Secrecy and Concealment: Studies in the History of Mediterranean and*

Near Eastern Religions. Studies in the History of Religions, 65 (Leiden and New York: E. J. Brill, 1995).

35. See, for instance, Moshe Idel, *Absorbing Perfections: Kabbalah and Interpretation* (New Haven, NJ: Yale University Press, 2002); Vita Daphna Arbel, *Beholders of Divine Secrets: Mysticism and Myth in Hekhalot and Merkavah Literature* (Albany, NY: State University of New York Press, 2003); Kocku von Stuckrad, *Locations of Knowledge in Medieval and Early Modern Europe: Esoteric Discourse and Western Identities*. Brill's Studies in Intellectual History, 186 (Leiden and Boston: Brill, 2010).

36. Kurt Ruh, *Die Mystik des deutschen Predigerordens* (1996), 417–75. See also the contributions to *Die deutschen Dominikaner und Dominikanerinnen im Mittelalter*, ed. Elias H. Füllenbach, Sabine von Heusinger, Walter Senner, and Klaus-Bernward Springer. Quellen und Forschungen zur Geschichte des Dominikanerordens, Neue Folge, 21 (Berlin and Boston: Walter de Gruyter, 2016); cf. also Silvia Bara Bancel, *Teología mística alemana: estudio comparativo del 'Libro de la Verdad' de Enrique Suso con el Maestro Eckhart*. Beiträge zur Geschichte der Philosophie und Theologie des Mittelalters, Neue Folge, 78 (Münster: Aschendorff Verlag, 2015).

37. For the critical edition, see Heinrich Seuse, *Die deutschen Schriften des Seligen Heinrich Seuse aus dem Predigerorden*, ed. Heinrich Denifle (1880; Norderstedt: Hansebooks GmbH, 2018); *Des Mystiker Heinrich Seuse O. Pr. Deutsche Schriften*, eingeleitet, übertragen und erläutert von Nikolaus Heller (Regensburg: Verlagsanstalt vorm. G. J. Manz, 1926).

38. Markus Enders, *Das Gottesverständnis der deutschen Mystik (Meister Eckhart, Johannes Tauler, Heinrich Seuse) und die Frage nach seiner Orthodoxie*. Heinrich-Seuse-Jahrbuch, 4 (Berlin and Münster: Lit, 2011).

Epilogue
Have We Now Found the Secret? Or Are There No Secrets?

This study has endeavored to isolate and analyze the phenomenon of the "secret" as it emerges in a number of medieval literary texts from across Europe, both fictional and mystical—which might be an artificial distinction. The "secret" as an epistemological term serves well to address many different aspects in the literary discourse because it encapsulates a range of unusual and often astonishing experiences where the individual finds him/herself within a situation that is not being explained and cannot be fully understood. Here I was not concerned with "magic" or "religion" in the narrow sense of the word, and I have also not examined secret strategies within the political sphere when rulers negotiate, for instance, privately with their confidants or councilors. On the other hand, I have also occasionally considered the role of secrets in ordinary life, such as when marriage partners keep secrets from each other for a variety of reasons (Heinrich Kaufringer), but this only in the longer introduction to this study.

Instead, the focus has rested on critical moments when the protagonist faces mysterious forces, figures, objects, or words and cannot deal with them rationally, yet often happily engages with them and/or profits from their abilities and powers for his/her own purposes. Hagen in the *Nibelungenlied* or Reymund in the *Melusine* have to cope with fairy-like figures, either water nixies or a hybrid woman who transforms into a being that is half human and half snake. Those beings often can prophesy the future, or they impose conditions on their human companions that amount to taboos, which are then regularly transgressed, leading to catastrophic outcomes for husband and wife.

Many times, authors of courtly romances and other texts present inexplicable forces or beings that are of supernatural power and yet are not the same as God. Here I am not concerned with dark or evil forces, such as the devil,

evil spirits, ghosts, revenants, and the like. Rather, at issue are phenomena that evade ordinary understanding and yet seem actually to exist in concrete terms. Often, the poets seem to make rather naïve assumptions or pretend to operate on a simplistic level, as if there were really berserks, dragons, dwarfs, mysterious objects, such as rings or crowns, etc. The secrets exert uncanny influence, as many poets confirm, without questioning really what those secrets might essentially be. Maybe, we might say, medieval poets simply enjoyed playing with secrets as convenient instruments of narration to address critical issues and to promote their fictional plots. However, at closer analysis, we have regularly recognized the degree to which secrets emerge as actual entities that exist within the ordinary context and exert huge influence, yet without ever fully revealing their identities or properties. Many times, they are simply mysterious, at other times they are awesome and impressive, but they always refuse to let the human individuals look behind the screen and understand in practical terms what those secrets might really be. Such secrets are not deceptive forces or masks, hence illusions as is the case in the famous American musical fantasy film "The Wizard of Oz" (1939). Both in Wolfram von Eschenbach's *Parzival* and in the anonymous *Huon de Bordeaux*, the protagonist encounters either the Grail or the magical sorcerer Auberon, and it is his obligation to reach a goal, to assume a role, to meet expectations, or also to rely on that mysterious figure as the ultimate helper in order to rectify this world and cleanse it from evil.

Secrets separate people from each other and divide them into those who are initiates and those who are not, such as in Gottfried von Straßburg's *Tristan* and in some of the *lais* by Marie de France. Secrets point the way toward the inside, the hidden, and the mysterium behind life itself. When we examine the examples of secrets in a variety of medieval texts, we discover the extent to which the phenomenon of the inexplicable and stupefying mattered deeply. But the poets did not simply play with an aspect of fantasy; instead, they regularly explored new dimensions of the inexplicable features of life itself but cast in literary terms, or in mystical images (Mechthild of Magdeburg, Heinrich Seuse, Bridgit of Sweden, or Richard Rolle).

As I have indicated in the introduction, there are many secrets in our contemporary lives as well, as much as modern science and medicine have progressed tremendously, pushing the limit of the unknown further and further away from the boundaries of what an ordinary person or a non-specialist can understand. However, the push itself indicates that we just cannot tell what lies beyond the limits of human intelligence, whether in the nanosphere down here on earth or in the cosmic worlds beyond our solar system. This book does not intend to suggest or imply anything regarding any better or worse comprehension of human existence in the Middle Ages. Nevertheless, it is very clear that ultimate questions concerning God, life, death, or love continue to be unanswered, and will probably never be answered because they are the building blocks of all existence all by itself, and so we could identify them as the most profound secrets.

Literature serves many purposes, and one of them certainly addresses the issue of how to make sense of our lives, studied through a narrative lens. Romantic poets had a clear impression of the relevance of medieval poetry and imitated, translated, or edited many texts from that time. Hence, we can witness here the emergence of the theme of the secret during that period as well (E. T. A. Hoffmann). There are, of course, many modern writers and poets who are engaged with the secret as well and conceive of it in a myriad of fashions.

The same applies to the pre-modern world where we discover a strong awareness of otherness within the physical dimension, whether this pertains to the Grail, to magical figures, objects, or mystical visions. Many times, of course, there is magic involved, but more often than not, the narrators deliberately present curious cases of berserks, secret objects, prophets, nixies, hybrid creatures, fairies, sorcerers, and other beings, all so powerful beyond human comprehension and significantly not associated with magic as such.

In order to confirm the ubiquity of this phenomenon, the individual chapters of this volume address a wide range of different medieval fictional texts, both from medieval Germany and France, from Anglo-Norman England, Wales, and Iceland, which clearly distinguishes it from all recent attempts to tackle the same issue. I could have easily expanded the selection to include also examples from Castile, Portugal, the Netherlands, Denmark, etc. To round off my investigations, however, I finally turn to mystical literature in Latin, Middle Low German, Middle English, etc. After all, mystical phenomena represent the greatest secrets and have challenged both medieval and modern readers as the ultimate realization of the Godhead within the human context.

Of course, mysticism represents a very different aspect than, for instance, the treatment and appearance of the Grail, of magical ships, berserks, otherworld monsters, and other phenomena. However, drawing from and employing the category of the secret offers the significant opportunity to reflect on the deeper meaning of literature and of human life both in the medieval and modern context. While most readers have regularly looked for simple education, the true relevance of fictional, philosophical, and religious texts rests in their efforts to engage with epistemology. The narrative itself suggests possibilities, which are actually infinite, such as perceiving life through a fictional or imaginary lens and hence of learning about alternatives beyond our basic rationality and sense of logic. Many a medieval poet and visionary author demonstrated a considerable willingness to listen to voices from another reality, or level of existence, although they commonly leave the audience with an uncanny sense of incomprehensibility.

But would it really be so surprising to read about secrets, such as magical charms, riddles, prophetic comments, and remarks about the Grail, if not the Godhead, when even we, in the post-modern world, have to admit regularly that we might have a hunch about some gadgets, powers, or phenomena in our lives but ultimately do not understand them? This book hence suggests an interpretive approach to literature at large and medieval literature in particular informed by a sensitivity toward the ineffable and apophatic. As the various voices from the pre-modern world signal to us, despite a certain sense of reality that determines our existence, in essence, we know very little and can only imagine alternatives as they fleetingly enter our lives and alert us about the existence of different dimensions.

All authors of utopian narratives from throughout time have embraced this concept, and now we can simply step a little further back into the Middle Ages where we discover to our surprise, perhaps, a rather similar willingness and sensitivity to acknowledge the existence of many different forces, beings, and objects from other worlds that somehow interact with us here and there and yet then disappear again, such as Melusine in the various pan-European romances and novels. Maybe facetiously, I would like to conclude with the claim that "secrets are with us!" Both secular and religious poets in the pre-modern world were deeply aware about that phenomenon and continue to invite us to examine this epistemological conundrum. Dante's *Divina Commedia* (completed ca. 1320), illustrates this powerfully, although the pilgrim Dante is allowed to gain some insights into Inferno, Purgatorio, and even Paradiso; his path takes him from death to love, and hence to eternal life in and with God, certainly the ultimate secret, at least in his opinion.

Bibliography

To be systematic and comprehensive, this bibliography includes all primary and secondary material in one list. I use a strictly alphabetical system, even when a book title begins with the concrete article "the," which then places it in the "T"-range. A few times I have included cross-references to connect primary material throughout although there are differences between the English and the German versions.

100 Jahre "Das Heilige": Beiträge zu Rudolf Ottos Grundlagenwerk, ed. Wolfgang Gantke and Vladislav Serikov. Theion, 32 (Frankfurt a. M.: PL Academic Research, 2017).
A Companion to Hildegard of Bingen, ed. Beverly Mayne Kienzle, Debra L. Stroudt, and George Ferzoco. Brill's Companions to the Christian Tradition, 45 (Leiden and Boston: Brill, 2014).
A Companion to Marie de France, ed. Logan E. Whalen. Brill's Companions to the Christian Tradition, 27 (Leiden and Boston: Brill, 2011).
A Companion to Old Norse-Icelandic Literature and Culture, ed. Rory McTurk. Blackwell Companions to Literature and Culture, 31 (Malden, MA, Oxford, and Carlton, Victoria, Australia: Blackwell, 2007).
A Companion to the Gawain-Poet, ed. Derek Brewer and Jonathan Gibson. Arthurian Studies, 38 (Woodbridge, Suffolk; Rochester, NY: D. S. Brewer, 1997).
A Companion to Wolfram's Parzival, ed. Will Hasty. Studies in German Literature, Linguistics, and Culture (Columbia, SC: Camden House, 1999).
A Critical Companion to Beowulf, ed. Andy Orchard (Woodbridge: D. S. Brewer, 2003); *Beowulf: An Edition with Relevant Shorter Texts. Including Archaeology and Beowulf*, ed. Leslie Webster (Oxford: Blackwell, 1998).
Abecedarium: erzählte Dinge im Mittelalter, ed. Peter Glasner, Sebastian Winkelsträter, and Birgit Zacke (Berlin: Schwabe Verlag, 2019).
Ackermann, Christiane, *Im Spannungsfeld von Ich und Körper: Subjektivität im 'Parzival' Wolframs von Eschenbach und im 'Frauendienst' Ulrichs von Liechtenstein*. Ordo, 12 (Cologne, Weimar, and Vienna: Böhlau, 2009).

Alice Brittan, *The Art of Astonishment: Reflections on Gifts and Grace* (London: Bloomsbury Publishing, 2022).
Allen, Richard F., *Fire and Iron: Critical Approaches to Njáls saga* ([Pittsburgh, PA]: University of Pittsburgh Press, 1971).
Almond, Philip C., *Mystical Experience and Religious Doctrine: An Investigation of the Study of Mysticism in World Religions*. Rpt. (1982; Berlin and Boston: Walter de Gruyter, 1982).
Althoff, Gerd, *Spielregeln der Politik im Mittelalter: Kommunikation in Frieden und Fehde* (Darmstadt: Wissenschaftliche Buchgesellschaft, 1997).
Amour et merveille: Les Lais de Marie de France. Collection Unichamp, 46 (Paris: Champion, 1995).
Andersen, Elizabeth A., *The Voices of Mechthild of Magdeburg* (Oxford, Bern, et al.: Peter Lang, 2000).
Andersson, Ida, Julia Persson, and Petri Kajonius, "Even the Stars Think that I am Superior: Personality, Intelligence and Belief in Astrology," *Personality and Individual Differences* Nov. 2011, online at: https://www.sciencedirect.com/science/article/pii/S0191886921007686.
Arbel, Vita Daphna, *Beholders of Divine Secrets:Mysticism and Myth in Hekhalot and Merkavah Literature* (Albany, NY: State University of New York Press, 2003). Stuckra,
Archibald, Elizabeth, "Questioning Arthurian Ideals,"*The Cambridge Companion to the Arthurian Legend*, ed. eadem and Ad Putter (Cambridge: Cambridge University Press, 2009), 139–53.
Asmark, Ulla, "Magikyndige kvinder i islændingesagaerne—terminologi, værdiladning og kausalitet," *Arkiv för Nordisk Filologi/Archives for Scandinavian Philology* 121 (2006): 113–20.
Assmann, Aleida and Jan Assmann, "Das Geheimnis und die Archäologie der literarischen Kommunikation: Einführende Bemerkungen," *Schleier und Schwelle: Archäologie der literarischen Kommunikation V*. Vol. 1: *Geheimnis und Öffentlichkeit*, ed. Aleida und Jan Assman (Munich: Wilhelm Fink, 1997), 7–16.
Aucassin and Nicolette: A Facing-Page Edition and Translation by Robert S. Sturges (East Lansing, MI: Michigan State University Press 2015).
Aucassin et Nicolette, ed. critique. 2nd rev. and corrected ed. by Jean Dufournet (Paris: GF-Flammarion, 1984). See also *Aucassin et Nicolette*, trans. and photo-ill. by Katharine Margot Toohey (2017), online at: https://quemarpress.weebly.com/uploads/8/6/1/4/86149566/aucassin_and_nicolette_-_translation_by_k.m._toohey.pdf.
Axen, Christine, "Kissing in the Middle Ages," *Medievalists.net*, online at: https://www.medievalists.net/2022/02/kissing-middle-ages/
Bailey, Michael, "The Disenchantment of Magic: Spells, Charms, and Superstition in Early European Witchcraft Literature," *The American Historical Review* 111.2 (April 2006): 383–404.
Bambeck, Manfred, *Wiesel und Werwolf: typologische Streifzüge durch das romanische Mittelalter und die Renaissance*. Landeskundliche Vierteljahrsblätter, 36.1 (Stuttgart: Steiner, 1990).

Bancel, Silvia Bara, *Teología mística alemana: estudio comparativo del 'Libro de la Verdad' de Enrique Suso con el Maestro Eckhart*. Beiträge zur Geschichte der Philosophie und Theologie des Mittelalters, Neue Folge, 78 (Münster: Aschendorff Verlag, 2015).
Banisalamah, Ahmed Muhammed Faleh, "Gender, Reason, and Androgyny in the Role of Righteousness in Marie de France's 'Bisclavret,'" *Interactions: Ege Journal of British and American Studies/Ege İngiliz ve Amerikan İncelemeleri Dergisi* 26.1–2 (2017): 55–63.
Barragán Nieto, José Pablo, *El "De Secretis Mulierum" atribuido a Alberto Magno: estudio, edición crítica y traducción*. Textes et études du Moyen-Age, 63 (Porto: Fédération Internationale des Instituts d'Études Médiévales; Turnhout: Brepols, 2012).
Bartlett, Robert, *The Natural and the Supernatural in the Middle Ages* (Cambridge: Cambridge University Press, 2008).
Baumberg, Jeremy J., *The Secret Life of Science: How It Really Works and Why It Matters* (Princeton, NJ: Princeton University Press, 2018).
Bäumer, Änne, *Wisse die Wege: Leben und Werk Hildegards von Bingen; eine Monographie zu ihrem 900. Geburtstag* (Frankfurt a. M., Bern, et al.: Peter Lang, 1998).
Beal, Timothy K., *The Book of Revelation: A Biography* (Princeton, NJ: Princeton University Press, 2018).
Bechmann, Roland, *Trees and Man: The Forest in the Middle Ages*, trans. Katharyn Dunham (1984; New York: Paragon House, 1990).
Behmenburg, Lena, "Die Semantisierung des Raumes: Öffentlichkeit und Geheimnis," eadem, *Philomela: Metamorphosen Eines Mythos in der deutschen und französischen Literatur des Mittelalters* (Berlin and Berlin: Walter de Gruyter, 2009), 244–58.
Behmenburg, Lena, *Philomela: Metamorphosen eines Mythos in der deutschen und französischen Literatur des Mittelalters*. Trends in Medieval Pilology, 15 (Berlin and New York: Walter de Gruyter, 2009), 244–58.
Bekker, Hugo, *Gottfried von Strassburg's Tristan: Journey Through the Realm of Eros*. Studies in German Literature, Linguistics, and Culture (Columbia, SC: Camden House, 1987).
Belting, Hans, *Hieronymus Bosch: Garten der Lüste* (Munich: Prestel, 2002).
Benati, Chiara, "*À la guerre comme à la guerre* but with caution: Protection Charms and Blessings in the Germanic Tradition," *Revista Brathair* 17.1 (2017): 155–91.
Bennett, Jane, *Vibrant Matter: A Political Ecology of Things* (Durham, NC: Duke University Press, 2010).
Benz, Maximilian, "Verrätseltes Erzählen vom Mysterium: Wer nimmt was auf Munsalvæsche wahr?," *Darstellung und Geheimnis in Mittelalter und Früher Neuzeit*, ed. Jutta Eming and Volkhard Wels. Episteme in Bewegung, 21 (Wiesbaden: Harrassowitz, 2021), 125–40.
Beowulf. The Beowulf *Manuscript: Complete Texts and* The Fight at Finnsburg, ed. and trans. by R. D. Fulk. Dumbarton Oaks Medieval Library, 3 (Cambridge, MA, and London: Harvard University Press, 2010).

Berron, Reinhard, *Elemente grotesken Erzählens in der europäischen Versnovellistik.* Kölner Germanistische Studien, Neue Folge, 13 (Vienna, Cologne, and Weimar: Böhlau Verlag, 2021).

Berthelot, Anne, "Huon de Bordeaux ou l'irruption de la féerie dans la geste," *L'Épopée romane au moyen âge et aux temps modernes: Actes du XIVe Congrés International de la Société Rencesvals*, ed. Salvatore Luongo. 2 vols. (Naples: Fridericiana Editrice Universitaria, 2001), 829–42.

Berthelot, Anne, "L'Autre Monde féerique comme distortion de l'Orient dans *Maugis d'Aigremont, Huon de Bordeaux* t *Le Roman d'Auberon*," *L'Épopée Romane: actes du XV Congrès International Rencesvals, Poitiers, 21–27 août 2000*, ed. Gabriel Bianciotto. Civilisation médiévale, 13 (Poitiers: Centre d'Études Supérieures de Civilisation Médiévale, Université de Poitiers, 2002), 647–53.

Bestiari tardoantichi e medievali: i testi fondamentali della zoologia sacra cristiana, ed. Francesco Zambon with Roberta Capelli, Silvia Cocco, Claudia Cremonini, Manuela Sanson, and Massimo Villa. Classici della letteratura europea (Florence: Bompiani, 2018).

Bibring, Tovi, "'Quant il le pout partir de sei!' Les départs amoureux dans les Lais de Marie de France," *Atant m'en vois: Figures du départ au Moyen Âge*, ed. Nelly Labère and Luca Pierdominici. Piccola biblioteca di studi medievali e rinascimentali, 4 (Fano: Aras edizioni, 2019), 333–62.

Bierce, Vincent, *Le sentiment religieux dans La Comédie humaine: foi, ironie et ironisation* (Paris: Classiques Garnier, 2019).

Bildhauer, Bettina, *Medieval Things: Agency, Materiality, and Narratives of Objects in Medieval German Literature and Beyond.* Interventions: New Studies in Medieval Culture (Columbus, OH: The Ohio State University Press, 2020).

Biographies des troubadours: textes provençaux des XIIIe et XIVe siècles, ed. Jean Boutière, Alexander Hermann Schutz, and Irénée Marcel Cluzel. Bibliothèque Méridionale, First Series, 27 (Paris: Didier, 1950).

Black, Nancy B., *Medieval Narratives of Accused Queens* (Gainesville, Tallahassee, Tampa, et al.: University Press of Florida, 2003).

Bladen Ogle, Marbury, "Some Theories of Irish Literary Influence and the Lay of *Yonec*," *Romanic Review* 10 (1919): 123–48.

Blamires, Alcuin, *The Case for Women in Medieval Culture* (Oxford: Clarendon Press, 1997).

Bloch, Howard R., "Silence and Roles: *The Roman de Silence* and the Art of the Trouvère." *Yale French Studies* 70 (1986): 81–90.

Bloch, R. Howard, *The Anonymous Marie de France* (Chicago and London: The University of Chicago Press, 2003).

Blud, Victoria, "Wolves' Heads and Wolves' Tales: Women and Exile in *Bisclavret* and *Wulf and Eadwacer*," *Exemplaria: A Journal of Theory in Medieval and Renaissance Studies* 26.4 (2014): 328–46.

Böhme, Gernot, "Zeitphilosophie in Michael Endes '"Momo,"'" *Philosophie im Spiegel der Literatur*, ed. Gerhard Gamm. Zeitschrift für Ästhetik und allgemeine Kunstwissenschaft. Sonderheft, 9 (Hamburg: Meiner, 2007), 79–89.

Boucher, Philip P., *Cannibal Encounters. Europeans and Island Caribs, 1492–1763.* Johns Hopkins Studies in Atlantic History and Culture (Baltimore, MD, and London: Johns Hopkins University Press, 1992).
Bourns, Timothy, "Becoming-Animal in the Icelandic Sagas," *Neophilologus* 105.4 (2021): 633–53.
Boutang, Pierre, *Ontologie du secret* (Paris: Presses Universitaires de France, 1973).
Boyd, Matthieu, "The Ring, the Sword, the Fancy Dress, and the Posthumous Child: Background to the Element of Heroic Biography in Marie de France's Yonec," *Romance Quarterly* 55.3 (2008): 205–30.
Bozkaya, Inci, "Illuminiertes Schweigen. Zur Überlieferung des »Roman de Silence« im Codex WLC/LM/6," *Der Ritter, der ein Mädchen war: Studien zum Roman de Silence von Heldris de Cornouailles*, ed. Inci Bozkaya, Britta Bußmann, and Katharina Philipowski. Aventiuren, 13 (Göttingen: V&R unipress, 2020), 75–114.
Brandt, Rüdiger, "... his stupris incumbere non pertimescit publice. Heimlichkeit zum Schutz sozialer Konformität im Mittelalter," *Schleier und Schwelle: Archäologie der literarischen Kommunikation V.* Vol. 1: *Geheimnis und Öffentlichkeit*, ed. Aleida und Jan Assman (Munich: Wilhelm Fink, 1997), 71–88.
Brandt, Rüdiger, *Enklaven—Exklaven. Zur literarischen Darstellung von Öffentlichkeit und Nichtöffentlichkeit im Mittelalter. Interpretationen, Motiv- und Terminologiestudien.* Forschungen zur Geschichte der älteren deutschen Literatur, 15 (Munich: Wilhelm Fink, 1993).
Brandt, Rüdiger, Konrad von Würzburg. Wege der Forschung (Darmstadt: Wissenschaftliche Buchgesellschaft, 1987).
Braunfels, S., "Wiesel," *Lexikon der christlichen Ikonographie*, ed. Engelbert Kirschbaum SJ, Vol. 4: *Allgemeine Ikonographie* (Rome, Freiburg i. Br., Basel, and Vienna: Herder, 1972), 528.
Breeze, Andrew, *The Origins of the Four Branches of the Mabinogi* (Leominster, Herefordshire: Gracewing, 2009).
Brenner, Andreas, "Mystiker und Wahnsinnige, eine Beängstigung der Philosophie: Die Ausgrenzung a-rationaler Erkenntnisformen als Methode," *Religion und Gesundheit: Der heilkundliche Diskurs im 16. Jahrhundert*, ed. Albrecht Classen. Theophrastus Paracelsus Studies, 3 (Berlin and Boston: Walter de Gruyter, 2011), 381–96.
Brewka, Barbara Anne, "Esclarmonde, Clarisse et Florent, Yde et Olive I, Croissant, Yde et Olive II, Huon et les géants: Sequels to 'Huon de Bordeaux': An Edition," PhD diss., Vanderbilt University, Nashville, TN, 1977.
Brook, Leslie, "Guigemar and the White Hind," *Medium Ævum* 56 (1987): 94–101.
Brunner, Horst, "*Von Munsalvaesche wart gesant / der den der swane brahte*: Überlegungen zur Gestaltung des Schlusses von Wolframs Parzival," *Germanisch-Romanische Monatsschrift* 41.4 (1991): 369–84.
Buch, David J., *Magic Flutes and Enchanted Forests: The Supernatural in Eighteenth-Century Musical Theater* (Chicago: University of Chicago Press, 2008).
Buhr, Christian, "*dar nâch underkusten sich diu bilde mê danne tûsent stunt*. Automaten und Sprechpuppen in der deutschen und französischen Literatur

des hohen Mittelalters," *Technik und Science-Fiction in Mittelalter und Früher Neuzeit*, ed. Brigitte Burrichter and Dorothea Klein. Würzburger Ringvorlesungen, 17 (Würzburg: Königshausen & Neumann, 2018), 87–108.

Bumke, Joachim, *Die Blutstropfen im Schnee: Über Wahrnehmung und Erkenntnis im 'Parzival' Wolframs von Eschenbach*. Hermaea. Germanistische Forschungen, Neue Folge, 94 (Tübingen: Max Niemeyer, 2001).

Bumke, Joachim, *Wolfram von Eschenbach*. 8th completely rev. ed. (Stuttgart and Weimar: Metzler, 2004).

Burgess, Glyn S., *The Lais of Marie de France: Text and* Context (Athens, GA: The University of Georgia Press, 1987).

Burgwinkle, William, "*Huon de Bordeaux*: The Cultural Dream as Palimpsest," *Shaping Identity in Medieval French Literature: The Other Within*, ed. Adrian P. Tudor and Kristin L. Burr (Gainesville, FL: University Press of Florida, 2019), 42–52.

Burkhardt, Julia, *Von Bienen lernen. Das* Bonum universale de apibus *des Thomas von Cantimpré als Gemeinschaftsentwurf: Analyse, Edition, Übersetzung, Kommentar*. 2 vols. Klöster als Innovationslabore, 7 (Regensburg: Schnell & Steiner, 2020).

Bußmann, Britta, *Wiedererzählen, weitererzählen und beschreiben: der "Jüngere Titurel" als ekphrastischer Roman*. Studien zur historischen Poetik, 6 (Heidelberg: Universitätsverlag Winter, 2011).

Campbell, Emma, "Political Animals: Human/Animal Life in *Bisclavret* and *Yonec*," *Exemplaria: A Journal of Theory in Medieval and Renaissance Studies* 25.2 (2013): 95–109.

Campbell, Emma, "Translating Gender in Thirteenth-Century French Cross-Dressing Narratives: *La Vie de Sainte Euphrosine* and *Le Roman de Silence*," *The Journal of Medieval and Early Modern Studies* 49.2 (2019): 233–64.

Campbell, Laura Chuhan, *The Medieval Merlin Tradition in France and Italy: Prophecy, Paradox, and Translatio*. Gallica, 42 (Cambridge: D. S. Brewer, 2017).

Carey, John, *Magic, Metallurgy and Imagination in Medieval Ireland* (2019).

Carré, Yannick, *Le baiser sur la bouche au moyen âge: rites, symboles, mentalités, à travers les textes et les images, XIe–XVe siècles* (Paris: Le Léopard d'Or, 1992).

Cazanave, Caroline, "*Huon de Bordeaux* au Theâtre: Les Temps Modernes," *Études médiévales*, ed. Danielle Buschinger (Amiens: Presses du Centre d'études médiévales, Université de Picardie-Jules Verne, 1999), 71–102.

Cazanave, Caroline, "L'Espace maritime dans le *Huon en prose*," *Le Moyen Français* 83 (2018): 15–27.

Cazane, Caroline, "*Huon de Bordeaux* à la sauce enfantine," *Grands textes du moyen âge à l'usage des petits*, ed. Caroline Cazanave and Yvon Houssais (Besançon: Presses Universitaires de Franche-Comté, 2010), 123–62.

Chaganti, Seeta, "The Space of Epistemology in Marie de France's 'Yonec,'" *Romance Studies* 28.2 (2010): 71–83.

Chari, Raj and Isabel Rozas, *Viruses, Vaccines, and Antivirals: Why Politics Matters* (Berlin and Boston: Walter de Gruyter, 2022).

Childhood in the Middle Ages and the Renaissance: The Results of a Paradigm Shift in the History of Mentality, ed. Albrecht Classen (Berlin and New York: Walter de Gruyter, 2005).
Christus in natura: Quellen, Hermeneutik und Rezeption des 'Physiologus,' ed. Zbyněk Kindschi Garský and Rainer Hirsch-Luipold. Studies of the Bible and Its Reception, 11 (Berlin and Boston: Walter de Gruyter, 2019).
Cieslik, Karin, "Heinrich von dem Türlin: Die Krone," *Dichtungen des europäischen Mittelalters: Ein Führer durch die erzählende Literatur*, ed. Rolf Bräuer (Munich: C. H. Beck, 1990), 351–53.
Classen, Albrecht, "Angst vor dem Tod: Jämmerliche Männerfiguren in der deutschen Literatur des Spätmittelalters (von *Mauritius von Craûn* zu Heinrich Kaufringer und *Till Eulenspiegel*)," *Jenseits: Eine mittelalterliche und mediävistische Imagination: Interdisziplinäre Ansätze zur Analyse des Unerklärlichen*, ed. Christa Agnes Tuczay. Beihefte zur Mediävistik, 21 (Frankfurt a. M.: Peter Lang, 2016), 213–31.
Classen, Albrecht, "Assassins, the Crusades, and the Old Man from the Mountains in Medieval Literature: With an Emphasis on The Stricker's *Daniel von dem Blühenden Tal*," *Marginal Figures in the Global Middle Ages and the Renaissance*, ed. Meg Lota Brown. Arizona Studies in the Middle Ages and the Renaissance, 47 (Turnhout: Brepols, 2021), 123–40.
Classen, Albrecht, "Aucassin et Nicolette," *Encyclopedia of Medieval Literature*, ed. Jay Ruud (New York: Facts on File, 2005), 44–46.
Classen, Albrecht, *Charlemagne in Medieval German and Dutch Literature*. Bristol Studies in Medieval Culture (Cambridge: D. S. Brewer, 2021).
Classen, Albrecht, "Communication in the Middle Ages," *Handbook of Medieval Studies: Terms—Methods—Trends*, ed. Albrecht Classen (Berlin and New York: Walter de Gruyter, 2010), vol. 1, 330–43.
Classen, Albrecht, "Complex Relations Between Jews and Christians in Late Medieval German and Other Literature," *Jews in Medieval Christendom: "Slay them Not,"* ed. Kristine T. Utterback and Merrall Llewelyn Price. Études sur le judaïsme médiéval, 60 (Leiden and Boston: Brill, 2013), 313–38.
Classen, Albrecht, "Confrontation with the Foreign World of the East: Saracen Princesses in Medieval German Narratives," *Orbis Litterarum* 53 (1998): 277–95.
Classen, Albrecht, "Contracting Love Versus Courtly Love: Jans Enikel's 'Friedrich von Auchenfurt,' the Anonymous *Mauritius von Craûn*, and Dietrich von der Gletze's 'Der Borte,'" *Neohelicon* 46.1 (2019): 159–81.
Classen, Albrecht, "Das Paradox der widersprüchlichen Urteil[s]sprechung und Weltwahrnehmung: göttliches vs. menschliches Recht in Heinrich Kaufringers 'Die unschuldige Mörderin'—mit paneuropäischen Ausblicken und einer neuen Quellenspur ('La femme du roi de Portugal')," *Neuphilologische Mitteilungen* CXX.II (2019): 7– 28.
Classen, Albrecht, "Der Gürtel als Objekt und Symbol in der Literatur des Mittelalters. Marie de France, *Nibelungenlied, Sir Gawain and the Green Knight* und Dietrich von der Glezze," *Mediaevistik* 21 (2008, appeared in 2010): 11–37.

Classen, Albrecht, "Der Mythos vom Rhein: Geschichte, Kultur, Literatur und Ideologie. Die Rolle eines europäischen Flusses vom Mittelalter bis zur Gegenwart," *Mittelalter-Mythen*, vol. V. Ed. Ulrich Müller and Werner Wunderlich (St. Gall: UVK, 2008), 711–25.

Classen, Albrecht, "Der Text der nie enden will. Poetologische Überlegungen zu fragmentarischen Strukturen in mittelalterlichen und modernen Texten," *Zeitschrift für Literaturwissenschaft und Linguistik*, vol. 99: *Anfang und Ende*, ed. Wolfgang Haubrichs (1995), 83–113.

Classen, Albrecht, "*Der Wunderer*. Hybridität, Erzähllogik und narrative Fragmentierung in der Literatur des deutschen Spätmittelalters," *Wirkendes Wort* 66.3 (2016): 371–84.

Classen, Albrecht, "Die Suche nach der Utopie in der Gralswelt. Albrechts (von Scharfenberg) *Der jüngere Titurel*," *Parzival. Reescritura y Transformación*, ed. Berta Raposo Fernández (Valencia: Universitat de València, 2000), 133–56.

Classen, Albrecht, "Disguises, Gender-Bending, and Clothing Symbolism in Dietrich von der Gletze's *Der Borte*," *Seminar* XLV.2 (2009): 95–110.

Classen, Albrecht, "Dreams and Visions, in a Historical Perspective," *The Living Pulpit* Oct. 17, 2020; http://www.pulpit.org/2020/10/dreams-and-visions-a-historical-perspective/.

Classen, Albrecht, "Female Agency and Power in Gottfried von Strassburg's *Tristan*: The Irish Queen Isolde: New Perspectives," *Tristania* XXIII (2005): 39–60.

Classen, Albrecht, *Freedom, Imprisonment, and Slavery in the Pre-Modern World: Cultural-Historical, Social-Literary, and Theoretical Reflections*. Fundamentals of Medieval and Early Modern Culture, 25 (Berlin and Boston: Walter de Gruyter, 2021).

Classen, Albrecht, "Globalism before Globalism: The Alexander Legend in Medieval Literature (Priest Lambrecht's Account as a Pathway to Early Global Perspectives)," *Esboços: histories in global contexts Florianópolis* 28/49 (Aug./Sept. 2021): 813–33, set./dez. 2021.ISSN 2175–7976 DOI https://doi.org/10.5007/2175-7976.2021.e79311).

Classen, Albrecht, "Guildeluëc in Marie de France's 'Eliduc' as the Avatar of Heloise? The Destiny of Two Twelfth-Century Women," *Quaestiones Medii Aevii Novae* (Poland) 20 (2015): 395–412.

Classen, Albrecht, "Hate, Lies, and Violence: The Dark Side of Pre-Modern Literature: Why would we care? And yet, the key rests in the past to solve our issues today. With a Focus on The Stricker (Thirteenth Century)," *Journal of Humanities and Applied Social Sciences* 5.2 (2021): 281–94; online at: http://www.hillpublisher.com/UpFile/202112/20211231163859.pdf.

Classen, Albrecht, "Hermann Hesses *Glasperlenspiel* (1943) und James Hiltons *Lost Horizon* (1933). Die Intertextualität zweier utopischer Entwürfe," *Studia Neophilologica* 72 (2000): 190–202.

Classen, Albrecht, "Hunde als Freunde und Begleiter in der deutschen Literatur vom Mittelalter bis zur Gegenwart: Reaktion auf den 'Animal Turn' aus motivgeschichtlicher Sicht," *Etudes Germaniques* 73.4 (2018): 441–66.

Classen, Albrecht, "Huon de Bordeaux," *Literary Encyclopedia*, Dec. 30, 2021 (3302 words), online at: https://www.litencyc.com/php/sworks.php?rec=true&UID =40688.
Classen, Albrecht, "Imagination, Fantasy, Otherness, and Monstrosity in the Middle Ages and the Early Modern Age," *Imagination and Fantasy in the Middle Ages and Early Modern Times: Projections, Dreams, Monsters, and Illusions*, ed. Albrecht Classen. Fundamentals of Medieval and Early Modern Culture, 24 (Berlin and Boston: Walter de Gruyter, 2020), 1–229.
Classen, Albrecht, "Introduction: The Authority of the Written Word, the Sacred Object, and the Spoken Word: A Highly Contested Discourse in the Middle Ages, With a Focus on the Poet Wolfram von Eschenbach and the Mystic Hildegard von Bingen," *Authorities in the Middle Ages: Influence, Legitimacy, and Power in Medieval Society*, ed. Sini Kangas, Mia Korpiola, and Tuija Aionen. Fundamentals of Medieval and Early Modern Culture, 12 (Berlin and Boston: Walter de Gruyter, 2013), 1–24.
Classen, Albrecht, "Jewish-Christian Relations in Medieval Literature," Peter Meister, ed., *German Literature Between Faiths: Jew and Christian at Odds and in Harmony*. Studies in German Jewish History, 6 (Oxford, Bern, Berlin, et al.: Peter Lang, 2004), 53–65.
Classen, Albrecht, "Madness in the Middle Ages—An Epistemological Catalyst? Literary, Religious, and Theological Perspectives in Caesarius of Heisterbach's *Dialogus Miraculorum*," *Hermeneutics of Textual Madness: Re-Readings*, ed. M. J. Muratore. 2 vols. Biblioteca della Ricerca: Mentalità e scrittura, 38 (Fasano, Italy: Schena Editore, 2016), vol. I, 339–68.
Classen, Albrecht, "Marie de France," *The Literary Encyclopedia*, ed. Robert Clark, online at: (http://www.litencyc.com/php/speople.php?rec=true&UID=5494; Sept. 2003).
Classen, Albrecht, "Multilingualism and Multiculturalism in the Pre-Modern Age: Medieval Welsh and Icelandic Literature in a Literature Survey Course. Interdisciplinary Approaches on a Pan-European Level," *Leuvense Bijdragen* 102 (2018–2020): 357–82.
Classen, Albrecht, "Music as a Universal Bond and Bridge Between the Physical and the Divine: Transcultural and Medieval Perspectives," *Rupkatha Journal on Interdisciplinary Studies in Humanities* 13.3 (2021): 1–30; online at: https://rupkatha.com/V13/n3/v13n301.pdf; or: DOI: 10.21659/rupkatha.v13n3.01.
Classen, Albrecht, "Mystical Literature for the Modern Reader—Responses to a Dilemma and Pragmatic Suggestions: With a Focus on Mechthild of Magdeburg," *Studies in Spirituality* 28 (2018): 145–67.
Classen, Albrecht, "Noch einmal zu Wolframs 'spekulativer' Kyôt-Quelle im Licht jüdischer Kultur und Philosophie des zwölften Jahrhunderts," *Studi Medievali* XLVI (2005): 281–308.
Classen, Albrecht, "Outsiders, Challengers, and Rebels in Medieval Courtly Literature: The Problem with the Courts in Courtly Romances," *Arthuriana* 26.3 (2016): 67–90.

Classen, Albrecht, "Rabbi Nissim and His Influence on Medieval German Literature: Rudolf von Ems's Der guote Gêrhart and Heinrich Kaufringer's 'Der Einsiedler und der Engel': Jewish Wisdom Teachings in the Middle High and Early Modern German Context," *Aschkenas* 108.4 (2017): 349– 69.

Classen, Albrecht, *Freedom, Imprisonment, and Slavery in the Pre-Modern World: Cultural-Historical, Social-Literary, and Theoretical Reflections*. Fundamentals of Medieval and Early Modern Culture, 25 (Berlin and Boston: Walter de Gruyter, 2021).

Classen, Albrecht, "Reading, Writing, and Learning in Wolfram von Eschenbach's *Parzival*," *A Companion to Wolfram's Parzival*, ed. Will Hasty. Studies in German Literature, Linguistics, and Culture (Columbia, SC: Camden House, 1999), 189–202.

Classen, Albrecht, "Reflections on Key Issues in Human Life: Gottfried von Strassburg's Tristan, Dante's Divina Commedia, Boccaccio's Decameron, Michael Ende's Momo, and Fatih Akın's Soul Kitchen Manifesto in Support of the Humanities—What Truly Matters in the End?," *Humanities Open Access* Nov. 16, 2020, online at: https://www.mdpi.com/2076-0787/9/4/121.

Classen, Albrecht, *Sexual Violence and Rape in the Middle Ages: A Critical Discourse in Premodern German and European Literature*. Fundamentals of Medieval and Early Modern Culture, 7 (Berlin and Boston: Walter de Gruyter, 2011).

Classen, Albrecht, "Smart Marie de France Knew the Ways of this World—Medieval Advice Literature (Fables) and Social Criticism in Its Relevance for Us Today," *International Journal of History and Cultural Studies* 5.4 (2019), online at: https://www.arcjournals.org/pdfs/ijhcs/v5-i4/4.pdf.

Classen, Albrecht, "Soundscapes in Medieval German Literature," to appear in *A Companion to Sound Studies in German-Speaking Cultures*, ed. Rolf J. Goebel (Rochester, NY: Camden House, forthcoming).

Classen, Albrecht, "Symbolic Significance of the Sword in the Hero's Hand: *Beowulf*, The *Nibelungenlied*, *El Poema de Mio Cid*, the *Volsunga Saga*, and the *Njál's Saga*. Thing Theory from a Medieval Perspective," *Amsterdamer Beiträge zur älteren Germanistik* 80 (2020): 346–70.

Classen, Albrecht, "The Agency of Female Characters in Late Medieval German Verse Narratives: "Aristotle and Phyllis," Dietrich von der Gletze's "Der Borte," "Beringer," and Ruprecht von Würzburg's "Die zwei Kaufleute," *Totius mundi philohistor: Studia Georgio Strzelczyk octuagenario oblata*, ed. Małgorzata Delimata-Proch, Adam Krawiec, Jakub Kujawiński (Poznań: UAM/Adami Mickiewicz University Press, 2021), 227–42.

Classen, Albrecht, "The Agency of Wives in High Medieval German Courtly Romances and Late Medieval Verse Narratives: From Hartmann von Aue to Heinrich Kaufringer," *Quidditas* 39 (2018): 25–53.

Classen, Albrecht, "The Amazing East and the Curious Reader: Twelfth-Century World Exploration through a Writer's Mind: Lamprecht's *Alexander*," *Orbis Litterarum* 55.5 (2000): 317–39.

Classen, Albrecht, "The Book of Kells—The Wonders of Early Medieval Christian Manuscript Art Within a Pagan World," *Mediaevistik* 32 (2019; appeared in 2020): 55–69.

Classen, Albrecht, "The Dialectics of Mystical Love in the Middle Ages: Violence/ Pain and Divine Love in the Mystical Visions of Mechthild of Magdeburg and Marguerite Porète," *Studies in Spirituality* 20 (2010): 143–60.

Classen, Albrecht, "The Dialectics of Mystical Love in the Middle Ages: Violence/ Pain and Divine Love in the Mystical Visions of Mechthild of Magdeburg and Marguerite Porète," *Studies in Spirituality* 20 (2010): 143–60.

Classen, Albrecht, "The Downfall of a Hero: Siegfried's Self-Destruction and the End of Heroism in the *Nibelungenlied*," *German Studies Review* XXVI.2 (2003): 295–314.

Classen, Albrecht, "The Fairy Tales by the Brothers Grimm and Their Medieval Background," *German Quarterly* 94.2 (2021): 165–75.

Classen, Albrecht, "The Kiss in Medieval Literature: Erotic Communication, with an Emphasis on *Roman de Silence*: Erotic Communication, with an Emphasis on *Roman de Silence*," *Journal of Humanities, Arts and Social Science* 6.2 (2022): 227–32; online at: chrome-extension://efaidnbmnnnibpcajpcglclefindmkaj/https: //www.hillpublisher.com/UpFile/202206/20220609154525.pdf; DOI: 10.26855/ jhass.2022.06.009.

Classen, Albrecht, "The Role and Function of Women in the Stricker's *Daniel von dem Blühenden Tal*," *Die deutsche Frau als Dichterin und Protagonistin im Mittelalter*, ed. A. Classen. GAG 528 (Göppingen: Kümmerle, 1991), 87–103; rpt. *Classical and Medieval Literature Criticism*, ed. Jelena Krstović. CMCL 75 (Detroit, et al.: Thomson, 2005), 364–72.

Classen, Albrecht, "The Symbolic Meaning of Water in Medieval Literature: A Comparative Approach," *Mittellateinisches Jahrbuch* 46.2 (2011): 245–67.

Classen, Albrecht, "Thomas a Kempis," in *Literary Encyclopedia* (2005), http://www .litencyc.com/php/speople.php?rec=true&UID=2.

Classen, Albrecht, "Transpositions of Dreams to Reality in Middle High German Narratives," *Shifts and Transpositions in Medieval Narratives. A Festschrift for Dr. Elspeth Kennedy*, ed. Karen Pratt (Woodbridge, Suffolk: D. S. Brewer, 1994), 109–120.

Classen, Albrecht, "Treason: Legal, Ethical, and Political Issues in the Middle Ages: With an Emphasis on Medieval Heroic Poetry," *Journal of Philosophy and Ethics* 1.4 (2019): 13–29; https://www.sryahwapublications.com/journal-of-philosophy -and-ethics/pdf/v1-i4/2.pdf.

Classen, Albrecht, "Winter as a Phenomenon in Medieval Literature: A Transgression of the Traditional Chronotopos?," *Mediaevistik* 24 (2011): 125–50.

Classen, Albrecht, "Wolfram von Eschenbach," *Arthurian Writers: A Biographical Encyclopedia*, ed. Laura Cooner Lambdin and Robert Thomas Lambdin (Westport, CT, and London: Greenwood Press, 2008), 70–80.

Classen, Albrecht, "Wolfram von Eschenbach," *Medieval Folklore. An Encyclopedia of Myths, Legends, Tales, Beliefs, and Customs*, ed. John Lindow, John McNamara, and Carl Lindahl (Santa Barbara et al.: ABC-CLIO, 2000), 1062–63.

Classen, Albrecht, "Wolfram von Eschenbach," *Oxford Bibliographies*, online (an extensive commented bibliography on this poet) at: http://www.oxfordbibliographies .com/view/document/obo-9780195396584/obo-9780195396584-0163.xml?rskey =JnnNSa&result=1&q=Wolfram#firstMatch.

Classen, Albrecht, *The Forest in Medieval German Literature: Ecocritical Readings from a Historical Perspective*. Ecocritical Theory and Practice (Lanham, Boulder, et al.: Lexington Books, 2015).

Classen, Albrecht, *Tracing the Trails in the Medieval World: Epistemological Explorations, Orientation, and Mapping in Medieval Literature*. Routledge Studies in Medieval Literature and Culture (New York and London: Routledge, 2021).

Classen, Albrecht, *Utopie und Logos. Vier Studien zu Wolframs von Eschenbach Titurel. Beiträge zur älteren Literaturgeschichte* (Heidelberg: Carl Winter Universitätsverlag, 1990).

Classen, Albrecht, *Verzweiflung und Hoffnung. Die Suche nach der kommunikativen Gemeinschaft in der deutschen Literatur des Mittelalters*. Beihefte zur Mediaevistik, 1 (Frankfurt a. M., Berlin, et al.: Peter Lang, 2002).

Classen, Albrecht, *Water in Medieval Literature: An Ecocritical Reading*. Ecocritical Theory and Practice (Lanham, MD, Boulder, CO, et al.: Lexington Books, 2018).

Cline, Austin, "Why Does Religion Exist?" *Learn Religions*, Sep. 4, 2021, learnreligions.com/why-does-religion-exist-250557.

Communication, Translation, and Community in the Middle Ages and Early Modern Period: New Cultural-Historical and Literary Perspectives, ed. Albrecht Classen. Fundamentals of Medieval and Early Modern Culture, 26 (Berlin and Boston: Walther de Gruyter, forthcoming).

Cordez, Philippe, *Treasure, Memory, Nature: Church Objects in the Middle Ages* (2015, in German; 2016, in French; London and Turnhout: Harvey Miller Publishers, 2020).

Cormeau, Christoph, "Heinrich von dem Türlin," *Die deutsche Literatur des Mittelalters: Verfasserlexikon*, ed. Kurt Ruh. Sec. completely rev. ed. Vol. 3.1 (Berlin and New York: Walter de Gruyter, 1980), 894–99.

Cormeau, Christoph, *"Wigalois" und "Diu Crône": Zwei Kapitel zur Gattungsgeschichte des nachklassischen Artusromans*. Münchener Texte und Untersuchungen zur deutschen Literatur des Mittelalters, 57 (Munich: Artemis, 1977).

Coudert, Allison P., "Rethinking Max Weber's Theory of Disenchantment," *Magic and Magicians in the Middle Ages and the Early Modern Time: The Occult in Pre-Modern Sciences, Medicine, Literature, Religion, and Astrology*, ed. Albrecht Classen. Fundamentals of Medieval and Early Modern Culture, 20 (Berlin and Boston: Walter de Gruyter, 2017), 701–35.

Cox, Jennifer K., "Symbiotic Werewolves and Cybernetic Anchoresses: Premodern Posthumans in Medieval Literature," *Quidditas: Online Peer-reviewed Journal of the Rocky Mountain Medieval and Renaissance Association* 36 (2015): 84–105.

Coxon, Sebastian, English translation of *Deutsche Versnovellistik des 13. bis 15. Jahrhunderts*, ed. Klaus Ridder and Hans-Joachim Ziegeler (Berlin: Schwabe Verlag, 2020), vol. 5.

Craine, Renate, *Hildegard: Prophet of the Cosmic Christ* (New York: Crossroad Publ., 1998). Duffy, Kevin, SM, *Christian Solar Symbolism and Jesus the Sun of Justice* (London and New York: T & T Clark, 2022).
Cross, Tom Peete, "The Celtic Origin of the Lay of Yonec," *Studies in Philology* 11 (1913): 26–60.
Damon, S. Foster, "Marie de France: Psychologist of Courtly Love," *PMLA* 44 (1929): 96–96.
Daniel, Norman, *Heroes and Saracens: An Interpretation of the* Chansons de Geste (Edinburgh: University Press, 1984), 69–93.
Dante Alighieri, *Paradiso*. The Italian text with an English verse translation, intro., and commentary by Allen Mandelbaum (Berkeley, CA: University of California Press, 1982).
Dante Alighieri, *The Divine Comedy*. Vol. I: *Inferno*, trans. with an intro., notes, and commentary by Mark Musa (1971; London: Penguin, 1984).
Darstellung und Geheimnis in Mittelalter und Früher Neuzeit, ed. Jutta Eming and Volkhard Wels. Episteme in Bewegung, 21 (Wiesbaden: Harrassowitz, 2021).
Das Alexanderlied des Pfaffen Lamprecht (Strassburger Alexander. Text, Nacherzählung, Worterklärungen by Irene Ruttmann (Darmstadt: Wissenschaftliche Buchgesellschaft, 1974).
Das Öffentliche und Private in der Vormoderne, ed. Gert Melville and Peter von Moos. Norm und Struktur, 10 (Cologne, Weimar, and Vienna: Böhlau, 1998).
Davidson, H. R. Ellis, "Hostile Magic in the Icelandic Sagas," *The Witch Figure: Folklore Essays by a Group of Scholars in England Honouring the 75th Birthday of Katharine M. Briggs*, ed. Venetia Newall (London: Routledge & K. Paul; 1973), 20–41.
Davidson, H. R. Ellis, "Shape-Changing in the Old Norse Sagas," *Animals in Folklore*, ed. Joshua R. Porter and William M. S. Russell (Cambridge and Totowa, NJ: D. S. Brewer; Rowman & Littlefield for Folklore Soc; Rowman & Littlefield for Folklore Soc.; Rowman & Littlefield Publishers, 1978), 126–42.
Dawson, Anna, *Studying the Lord of the Rings*. Studying Films Ser. (Oxford: Auteur Publishing, 2021).
Dawson, Lesel, *Lovesickness and Gender in Early Modern English Literature* (Oxford: Oxford University Press, 2008).
De Frédéric II à Rodolphe II: Astrologie, divination et magie dans les cours (XIIIe–XVIIe siècle), ed. Jean-Patrice Boudet, Martine Ostorero, and Agostino Paravicini Bagliani. Micrologus Library, 85 (Florence: SISMEL—Edizioni del Galluzzo, 2017).
de Weever, Jaqueline, *Shela's Daughters: Whitening and Demonizing the Saracen Women in Medieval French Epic*. Garland Reference Library of the Humanities, 2077 (New York and London: Garland, 1998).
Der "Jüngere Titurel" zwischen Didaxe und Verwilderung: neue Beiträge zu einem schwierigen Werk, ed. Martin Baisch, Johannes Keller, Florian Kragl, and Matthias Meyer (Göttingen: V&R unipress, 2010).
Der Stricker, *Daniel von dem Blühenden Tal*, ed. Michael Resler. 3rd ed. Altdeutsche Textbibliothek, 92 (Berlin and Boston: Walter de Gruyter, 2015).

Dick, Ernst S., "Heinrich von dem Türlin," *German Writers and Works of the High Middle Ages: 1170–1280*, ed. James Hardin and Will Hasty. Dictionary of Literary Biography, 138 (Detroit, MI, Washington, DC, and London: Gale Research, 1994), 44–49.

Die deutschen Dominikaner und Dominikanerinnen im Mittelalter, ed. Elias H. Füllenbach, Sabine von Heusinger, Walter Senner, and Klaus-Bernward Springer. Quellen und Forschungen zur Geschichte des Dominikanerordens, Neue Folge, 21 (Berlin and Boston: Walter de Gruyter, 2016).

Die Quellen der Philosophie und Phänomenologie der Religion: Überlegungen zu Rudolf Ottos "Das Heilige" = Sources of the Philosophy and Phenomenology of Religion, ed. Dominika Jacy (Frankfurt a. M., Berlin, et al.: Peter Lang, 2010).

"Die Tücke des Objekts": vom Umgang mit Dingen, ed. Katharina Ferus and Dietmar Rübel. Schriftenreihe der Isa-Lohmann-Siems-Stiftung, 2 (Berlin: Reimer, 2009).

Dingkulturen: Objekte in Literatur, Kunst und Gesellschaft der Vormoderne, ed. Anna Mühlherr, Heike Sahm, Monika Schausten, and Bruno Quast, together with Ulrich Hoffmann. Literatur | Theorie | Geschichte, 9 (Berlin and Boston: Walter de Gruyter, 2018).

Dinzelbacher, Peter, *Christliche Mystik im Abendland: ihre Geschichte von den Anfängen bis zum Ende des Mittelalters* (Paderborn and Munich: Ferdinand Schöningh, 1994).

Dinzelbacher, Peter, *Deutsche und niederländische Mystik des Mittelalters: Ein Studienbuch* (Berlin and Boston: Walter de Gruyter, 2012).

Dinzelbacher, Peter, *Structures and Origins of the Twelfth-Century "Renaissance."* Monographien zur Geschichte des Mittelalters, 63 (Stuttgart: Anton Hiersemann, 2017).

Dohrn-van Rossum, Gerhard, *History of the Hour: Clocks and Modern Temporal Orders*, trans. Thomas Dunlap (1992; Chicago and London: The University of Chicago Press, 1996).

Draesner, Ulrike, *Wege durch erzählte Welten: intertextuelle Verweise als Mittel der Bedeutungskonstitution in Wolframs Parzival*. Mikrokosmos, 36 (Frankfurt a. M., Bern, et al.: Peter Lang, 1993).

DuBois, Thomas A., "Magic and Witchcraft Historicized, Localized, and Ethnicized: A Response to Stephen Mitchell's *Witchcraft and Magic in the Nordic Middle Ages*," *Magic, Ritual, and Witchcraft* 8.1 (2013): 82–89.

Dubuis, Roger, "La notion de *druerie* dans les Lais de Marie de France," *Le Moyen Âge Revue d'Histoire et de Philologie* 98 (1992): 391–413.

Eamon, William, *Science and the Secrets of Nature: Books of Secrets in Medieval and Early Modern Culture* (1994; Princeton, NJ: Princeton University Press, 2021).

Eckhart, see Meister Eckhart

Eddings, Sarah, "Infertility and the Marvel-Less in Marie de France's *Deus Amanz*," *Romance Notes* 57.1 (2017): 157–65.

Egil, the Viking Poet: New Approaches to 'Egil's Saga,' ed. Laurence de Looze, Jón Karl Helgason, Russell Poole, and Torfi H. Tulinius. Toronto Old Norse and Icelandic Series, 9 (Toronto, Buffalo, and London: University of Toronto Press, 2015).

Egil's Saga, trans. Bernard Scudder, ed. with an intro. and notes by Svanhildur Óskarsdóttir (London: Penguin, 1997).
Egills saga, ed. Bjarni Einarsson (London: Viking Society for Northern Research, 2003; available now online at http://www.vsnrweb-publications.org.uk/Egla/Egils_saga.pdf).
Egills saga: Með formála, viðaukum, skýringum og skrám, ed. Bergljót Kristjánsdóttir and Svanhildur Óskarsdóttir. Sígildar sögur, 2 (Reykjavík: Mál og menning, 1994).
Elena, Santiago F. and Ricard Solé, *Viruses as Complex Adaptive Systems* (Princeton, NJ: Princeton University Press, 2019).
Eming, Jutta, " Evokation und Episteme: Zu Wissensmodi des Wunderbaren im Späthöfischen Roman," *Darstellung und Geheimnis in Mittelalter und Früher Neuzeit*, ed. Jutta Eming and Volkhard Wels. Episteme in Bewegung, 21 (Wiesbaden: Harrassowitz, 2021), 25–47.
Encyclopedia of Medieval Literature, ed. Jay Ruud (New York: Facts on File, 2006).
Encyclopedia of Medieval Pilgrimage, ed. Larissa J. Taylor, Leigh Ann Craig, et al. (Leiden and Boston: Brill, 2010).
Enders, Markus, *Das Gottesverständnis der deutschen Mystik (Meister Eckhart, Johannes Tauler, Heinrich Seuse) und die Frage nach seiner Orthodoxie*. Heinrich-Seuse-Jahrbuch, 4 (Berlin and Münster: Lit, 2011).
Eriugena, Johannes Scotus, *Periphyseon: De divisione naturae*, in Joannis Scoti, *Opera*, ed. Henricus Josephus Floss. Patrologiae Cursus Completus: Patrologia Latinae, 122 (Paris: J. P. Migne, 1865).
Eriugena, John the Scot, *Periphyseon (The Division of Nature)*, trans. I. P. Sheldon-Williams. Rev. ed. John J. O'Meara (Montreal and Washington, DC: Éditions Bellarmin/Dumbarton Oaks, 1987).
Erotic Tales of Medieval Germany, selected and trans. by Albrecht Classen. Sec. ed., rev. and expanded. Medieval and Renaissance Texts and Studies, 328 (2007; Tempe, AZ: Arizona Center for Medieval and Renaissance Studies, 2009).
Exploring the Fantastic: Genre, Ideology, and Popular Culture, ed. Ina Batzke, Eric C. Erbacher, and Linda Hess (Bielefeld: transcript, 2018).
Falkenburg, Reindert, *The Land of Unlikeness: Hieronymus Bosch, The Garden of Earthly Delights*. Studies in Netherlandish Art and Cultural History, 10 (Zwolle, Netherlands: W Books, 2011).
Felder, Gudrun, *Kommentar zur "Crône" Heinrichs von dem Türlin* (Berlin and New York: Walter de Gruyter, 2006).
Fenske, Claudia, *Muggles, Monsters and Magicians: A Literary Analysis of the Harry Potter Series*. Kulturelle Identitäten, 2 (Frankfurt a. M. et al.: Peter Lang, 2008).
Findon, Joanne, "Supernatural Lovers, Liminal Women, and the Female Journey," *Florilegium: The Journal of the Canadian Society of Medievalists/La revue de la Société canadienne des médiévistes* 30 (2013): 27–52.
Fischer, Stefan, *Hieronymus Bosch: Malerei als Vision, Lehrbild und Kunstwerk*. Atlas—Bonner Beiträge zur Kunstgeschichte, Neue Folge, 6 (Cologne, Weimar, and Vienna: Böhlau, 2009).
Floris and Blancheflour, in *Sentimental and Humorous Romances: Floris and Blancheflour, Sir Degrevant, The Squire of Low Degree, The Tournament of*

Tottenham, and The Feast of Tottenham, ed. Erik Kooper. Middle English Text Series (Kalamazoo, MI: Medieval Institute Publications, 2006).

Flynn, Christopher P., "Fontenoy and the Justification of Battle-Seeking Strategy in the Ninth Century," to appear in *Mediaevistik* 35 (2023).

Forster, Regula, *Das Geheimnis der Geheimnisse: die arabischen und deutschen Fassungen des pseudo-aristotelischen Sirr al-asrar / Secretum Secretorum*. Wissensliteratur im Mittelalter, 43 (Wiesbaden: Reichert, 2006).

Fraenger, Wilhelm, *Hieronymus Bosch* (Dresden: VEB Verlag der Kunst, 1975); Wolfgang Wintermeier, *Hieronymus Bosch* (Hildesheim: Gerstenberg, 1983).

Frenken, Ralph, "Childhood and Fantasies of Medieval Mystics," The Journal of Psychohistory 28 (2000): 150–72; online at: http://www.primal-page.com/frenken.htm.

Frog, M., "Rituelle Autoritäten und narrativer Diskurs: Vormoderne finno-karelische Sagenüberlieferungen als analoges Modell für die Annäherung an mittelalterliche Quellen," *Magie und Literatur: erzählkulturelle Funktionalisierung magischer Praktiken in Mittelalter und Früher Neuzeit*, ed. Andreas Hammer, Wilhelm Heizmann, and Norbert Kössinger. Philologische Studien und Quellen, 280 (Berlin: Erich Schmidt Verlag, 2022), 153–207.

Full of Your Glory: Liturgy, Cosmos, Creation: Papers from the 5th Yale ISM Liturgy Conference, June 18–21, 2018, ed. Teresa Berger (Collegeville, MN: Liturgical Press Academic, 2019).

Galván Alvarez, Enrique, "Aspectos místicos y religiosos del amor cortés en *Guigemar*, de María de Francia," *Nerter* 11 (Fall 2007): 97–105.

Geertz, Clifford, "Religion as a Cultural System," id., *The Interpretation of Cultures: Selected Essays* (London: Fontana Press, 1993), 87–125.

Gellman, Jerome, "Mysticism," *Stanford Encyclopedia of Philosophy*, first published Nov 11, 2004; substantive revision Jul 31, 2018, online at: https://plato.stanford.edu/entries/mysticism/.

Gelzer, Heinrich, "Der Silenceroman von Heldris de Cornualle," *Zeitschrift für romanische Philologie* 47 (1927): 87–99; Frederick Augustus Grant, "Origins and Peregrinations of the Laval-Middleton Manuscript," *Nottingham Medieval Studies* 3 (1959): 3–18.

George, Jibu Matthew, *The Ontology of Gods: An Account of Enchantment, Disenchantment, and Re-Enchantment* (Cham, Germany: Springer International Publishing—Palgrave Macmillan, 2017).

Gęsicka, Anna, "Sacrum et profanum dans Yonec de Marie de France (XIIe siècle)," *Quêtes Littéraires* 3 (2013): 9–15.

Gibbs, Marion E., "Parzival," *The Literary Encyclopedia*. First published 09 January 2004 [https://www.litencyc.com/php/sworks.php?rec=true&UID=13213.

Gibson, Walter S., *Hieronymus Bosch*. The World of Art Library: Artists (London: Thames and Hudson, 1973).

Gilbert, Dorothy, "The Beast in You: On Teaching Bisclavret," *Le Cygne: Journal of the International Marie de France Society* 7.2 (2020): 53–68.

Gilmore, Gloria Thomas, "*Le Roman de Silence*: Allegory in Ruin or Womb of Irony?," *Arthuriana* 7.2 (1997): 111–23.

Glier, Melanie, "Aspekte der inhaltlich-strukturellen Beschaffenheit des 'Liber vitae meritorum' von Hildegard von Bingen," *Autour de Hildegarde de Bingen: Actes du Colloque du Centre d'Etudes Médiévales de l'université de Picardie-Jules Verne Saint-Riquier, 5–8 Décembre 1998*, ed. Kerstin Koch and Danielle Buschinger. Médiévales, 10 (Amiens: Presses du "Centre d'Etudes Médiévales" Université de Picardie—Jules Verne, 2000), 51–62.
Glosecki, Stephen O., "Wolf and Werewolf," *Medieval Folklore: An Encyclopedia of Myths, Legends, Tales, Beliefs, and Customs*, ed. Carl Lindahl, John McNamara, and John Lindow (Santa Barbara, CA, Denver, CO, and Oxford: ABC-CLIO, 2000), vol. 2, 1057–61.
Göck, Roland, *Die letzten Rätsel dieser Welt: unerklärliche Phänomene, letzte Geheimnisse, Jenseits des Begreifens, Mythen und Mysterien, Grenzen des Wissens* (Augsburg: Weltbild Verlag, 1994).
Godlewics-Adamiec, Joanna and Pawel Piszczatowsky, "Mystisches Geheimnis zwischen Sprachschöpfung und bildhafter Aussage, " *Geheimnis und Verborgenes im Mittelalter: Funktion, Wirkung und Spannungsfelder von okkultem Wissen, verborgenen Räumen und magischen Gegenständen*, ed. Stephan Conermann, Harald Wolter-von dem Knesebeck, and Miriam Quiering. Das Mittelalter: Perspektiven mediävistischer Forschung. Beihefte, 15 (Berlin and Boston: Walter de Gruyter, 2021), 89–106.
Godlewicz-Adamiec, Joanna Maria and Paweł Pisczatowski, "Mystisches Geheimnis zwischen Sprachschöpfung und bildhafter Aussage," *Geheimnis und Verborgenes im Mittelalter: Funktion, Wirkung und Spannungsfelder von okkultem Wissen, verborgenen Räumen und magischen Gegenständen*, ed. Stephan Conermann, Harald Wolter-von dem Knesebeck, and Miriam Quiering. Das Mittelalter: Perspektiven mediävistischer Forschung, 15 (Berlin and Boston: Walter de Gruyter, 2021), 89–106.
Godlewicz-Adamiec, Joanna, "Das Unsagbare sagen: Bilder der Natur und Naturmetapher im 'Liber Vitae Meritorum' der Hildegard von Bingen," *Studia germanica Gedanensia* 38 (2018): 11–25.
Goebel, Rolf J., "Auditory Resonance: A Transdisciplinary Concept?," *Humanities* 11.6 (2022): https://doi.org/10.3390/h11010006.
Gooch, Todd A., *The Numinous and Modernity: An Interpretation of Rudolf Otto's Philosophy of Religion*. Beihefte zur Zeitschrift für die alttestamentliche Wissenschaft, 293 (Berlin and New York: Walter de Gruyter, 2000).
Goodich, Michael E., *Miracles and Wonders: The Development of the Concept of Miracle, 1150–1350*. Church, Faith and Culture in the Medieval West (Aldershot: Ashgate, 2007).
Gosebrink, Hildegard, *Das Geheimnis schauen: Grundkurs christliche Mystik* (Munich: Kösel, 2007).
Gottfried von Strassburg, *Tristan and Isolde, with Ulrich von Türheim's* Continuation, ed. and trans., with an intro. by William T. Whobrey (Indianapolis, IN, and Cambridge: Hackert, 2020).

Gottfried von Strassburg, *Tristan*, newly edited on the basis of the edition by Friedrich Ranke, trans. into New High German, with a commentary and an epilogue by Rüdiger Krohn (Stuttgart: Philipp Reclam jun., 1980).
Greco, Pietro, *Trotula: la prima donna medico d'Europa*. Profilo di donna, 7 (Rome: L'asino d'oro edizioni, 2020).
Green, Monica H., *Women's Healthcare in the Medieval West: Texts and Contexts*. Collected Studies Series, 680 (Aldershot: Ashgate, 2000).
Grubmüller, Klaus, *Die Ordnung, der Weitz und das Chaos: Eine Geschichte der europäischen Novellistik im Mittelalter: Fabliau—Märe—Novelle* (Tübingen: Max Niemeyer, 2006).
Grünkorn, Gertrud, *Die Fiktionalität des höfischen Romans um 1200*. Philologische Studien und Quellen, 129 (Berlin: Erich Schmidt, 1994).
Guillaume de Lorris and Jean de Meun, *The Romance of the Rose*, trans. into English verse by Harry W. Robbins. Ed., and with an intro. by Charles W. Dunn (New York: E. P. Dutton, 1962).
Guillaume de Palerne: An English Trans. of the 12th Century French Verse Romance, trans. and ed. Leslie A. Sconduto (Jefferson, NC, and London: McFarland, 2004).
Guntram Haag, *Traum und Traumdeutung in mittelhochdeutscher Literatur: theoretische Grundlagen und Fallstudien* (Stuttgart: S. Hirzel, 2003).
Gurevitch, Danielle, "The Weasel, the Rose and Life after Death: Representations of Medieval Physiology in Marie de France's *Eliduc*," *Restoring the Mystery of the Rainbow: Literature's Refraction of Science*, ed. Valeria Tinkler-Villani and C. C. Barfoot (Amsterdam: Brill/Rodopi, 2011), 209–23.
Gürtler, Karin R., "Heinrich von dem Türlin," *The New Arthurian Encyclopedia*, ed. Norris J. Lacy. Garland Reference Library of the Humanities, 931 (1991; New York and London: Garland, 1996), 227–28.
Gutwald, Thomas, *Schwank und Artushof: Komik unter den Bedingungen höfischer Interaktion in der 'Crône' des Heinrich von dem Türlin*. Mikrokosmos, 55 (Frankfurt a. M., Berlin, et al.: Peter Lang, 2000).
Haage, Bernhard Dietrich, "Liebe als Krankheit in der medizinischen Fachliteratur der Antike und des Mittelalters," *Würzburger medizinhistorische Mitteilungen* 5 (1987): 173–208.
Haas, Alois M., *Mystik als Aussage: Erfahrungs-, Denk- und Redeformen christlicher Mystik*. Suhrkamp-Taschenbuch Wissenschaft, 1196 (1996; Frankfurt a. M.: Verlag der Weltreligionen, 2007).
Haas, Alois M., "Die Verständlichkeit mystischer Erfahrung," *Deutsche Mystik im abendländischen Zusammenhang: Neu erschlossene Texte, neue methodische Ansätze, neue theoretische Konzepte. Kolloquium Kloster Fischingen 1998*, ed. Walter Haug and Wolfram Schneider-Lastin (Tübingen: Max Niemeyer, 2000), 9–29.
Haeseli, Christa M., *Magische Performativität. Althochdeutsche Zaubersprüche in ihrem Überlieferungskontext*. Philologie der Kultur, 4 (Würzburg: Königshausen & Neumann. 2011).
Hafner, Suzanne, "Charlemagne's Unspeakable Sin," *Modern Language Studies* 32 (2002): 1–14.

Hahn, Alois, "Geheimnis," *Vom Menschen. Handbuch Historische Anthropologie*, ed. Christian Wulf. Beltz-Handbuch (Weinheim and Basel: Beltz, 1997), 1105–18.
Hahn, Alois, "Geheimnis," *Vom Menschen: Handbuch Historische* Anthropologie, ed. Christoph Wulf (Weinheim and Basel: Beltz Verlag, 1997), 1105–18.
Hall Martin, June, *Love's Fools: Aucassin, Troilus, Calisto and the Parody of the Courtly Lover*. Colleción Tamesis, A, 21 (London: Tamesis Books, 1972).
Hall McCash, June, "The Curse of the White Hind and the Cure of the Weasel: Animal Magic in the *Lais* of Marie de France," *Literary Aspects of Courtly Culture: Selected Papers from the Seventh Triennial Congress of the International Courtly Literature Society; University of Massachusetts, Amherst, USA, 27 July–1 August 1992*, ed. Donald Maddox, Sara Sturm-Maddox (Cambridge: D. S. Brewer, 1994), 199–209.
Hall McCash, June, "The Mulier Mediatrix in the Deus Amanz of Marie de France," *Courtly Arts and the Art of Courtliness*, ed. Keith Busby and Christopher Kleinhenz (Cambridge: D. S. Brewer, 2006), 455–65.
Hammond, Wayne G. and Christina Scull, *The Lord of the Rings: A Reader's Companion* (London: HarperCollins, 2014).
Hanegraaff, Wouter J. and Jeffrey J. Kripal, *Hidden Intercourse: Eros and Sexuality in the History of Western Esotericism*. Aries Book Series, 7 (Leiden and Boston: Brill, 2008).
Harley, Janet M., *The Volga: A History of Russia's Greatest River* (New Haven, CT, and London: Yale University Press, 2021).
Hartmann, Heiko, *Einführung in das Werk Wolframs von Eschenbach*. Einführungen Germanistik (Darmstadt: Wissenschaftliche Buchgesellschaft, 2015).
Hasker, William, *God, Time, and Knowledge* (Ithaca, NY: Cornell University Press, 1998).
Hassig, Debra, *Medieval Bestiaries: Text, Image, Ideology* (Cambridge: Cambridge University Press, 1995).
Hasty, Will, *The Medieval Risk-Reward Society: Courts, Adventure, and Love in the European Middle Ages* (Columbus, OH: The Ohio State University Press, 2016).
Haug, Walter, "Erzählen vom Tod her: Sprachkrise, gebrochene Handlung und zerfallende Welt in Wolframs 'Titurel,'" id., *Strukturen als Schlüssel zur Welt: kleine Schriften zur Erzählliteratur des Mittelalters*. Kleine Schriften, 1 (1980; Tübingen: Max Niemeyer, 1989), 541–53.
Haug, Walter, "Erzählen vom Tod her: Sprachkrise, gebrochene Handlung und zerfallende Welt in Wolframs 'Titurel,'" *Wolfram-Studien* VI, ed. Werner Schröder (Berlin: Erich Schmidt Verlag, 1980): 8–24.
Haug, Walter, "Lesen oder Lieben? Erzählen in der Erzählung: vom 'Erec' bis zum 'Titurel,'" *Beiträge zur Geschichte der deutschen Sprache und Literatur* 166 (1994): 302–22.
Haug, Walter, "Vom Tristan zu Wolframs *Titurel* oder die Geburt des Romans aus dem Scheitern am Absoluten," *Deutsche Vierteljahrsschrift für Literaturwissenschaft und Geistesgeschichte* 82.2 (2008): 193–204.
Hebert, Jill M., *Morgan le Fay, Shapeshifter*. Arthurian and Courtly Cultures (New York: Palgrave Macmillan, 2013).

Heck, Christian and Rémy Cordonnier, *The Grand Medieval Bestiary: Animals in Illuminated Manuscripts* (New York: Abbeville Press, 2012).
Heinrich von dem Türlin, *Die Krone (Verse 1–12281)*. Nach der Handschrift 2779 der Österreichischen Nationalbibliothek nach Vorarbeiten von Alfred Ebenbauer, Klaus Zatloukal und Horst P. Pütz, ed. Fritz Peter Knapp and Manuela Niesner. Altdeutsche Textbibliothek, 112 (Tübingen: Max Niemeyer, 2000).
Heinrich von dem Türlin, *Die Krone* (Verse 12282–30042). Nach der Handschrift Cod. Pal. germ. 374 der Universitätsbibliothek Heidelberg nach Vorarbeiten von Fritz Peter Knapp und Klaus Zatloukal, ed. Alfred Ebenbauer and Florian Kragl. Altdeutsche Textbibliothek, 118 (Tübingen: Max Niemeyer, 2005).
Heinrich von dem Türlin, *Diu Crône von Heinrich von dem Türlin*, ed. Gottlob Heinrich Friedrich Scholl. Bibliothek des Litterarischen Vereins in Stuttgart, XXVII. Reprint (1852; Amsterdam: Editions Rodopi, 1966).
Heinrich von dem Türlin, *The Crown: A Tale of Sir Gawein and King Arthur's Court*, trans and with an intro. by J. W. Thomas (Lincoln, NE, and London: University of Nebraska Press, 1989).
Heinzle, Joachim, *Wolfram von Eschenbach: Dichter der ritterlichen Welt: Leben, Werke, Nachruhm* (Basel: Schwabe Verlag, 2019).
Heldris de Cornuälle. *Le Romanc de Silence*, trans. Regina Psaki. Garland Library of Medieval Literature, Series B, 63 (New York and London: Garland Press, 1991).
Heldris of Cornwall, *Silence: A Thirteenth-Century French Romance*, newly ed. and trans., with intro. and notes by Sarah Roche-Mahdi (East Lansing, MI: Colleagues Press, 1992).
Hemming, Jessica, "Reflections on Rhiannon and the Horse Episodes in *Pwyll*," *Western Folklore* 57.1 (1998): 19–40.
Heng, Geraldine, "Cannibalism, The First Crusade and the Genesis of Medieval Romance," *differences: A Journal of Feminist Cultural Studies* 10.1 (1998): 98–174.
Hermeneutics of Textual Madness: Re-Readings, ed. M. J. Muratore. 2 vols. Biblioteca della Ricerca: Mentalità e scrittura, 38 (Fasano, Italy: Schena Editore, 2016).
Herrschaft, Ideologie und Geschichtskonzeption in Alexanderdichtungen des Mittelalters, ed. Ulrich Mölk. Veröffentlichungen aus dem Göttinger Sonderforschungsbereich 529 "Internationalität nationaler Literaturen," 2 (Göttingen: Wallstein Verlag, 2002).
Hertz, Wilhelm and Rudolf Leubuscher, *Der Werwolf/Werwölfe und Tierverwandlungen im Mittelalter: Zwei ungekürzte Quellenwerke in einem Band* (1862; Norderstedt: Books on Demand, 2018).
Herzog Ernst: Mittelhochdeutsch/Neuhochdeutsch, in der Fassung B mit den Fragmenten der Fassungen A, B und Kl nach der Leithandschrift, ed, trans., and commentary by Mathias Herweg (Stuttgart: Philipp Reclam jun., 2019).
Hess, Erika E., *Literary Hybrids: Cross-Dressing, Shapeshifting, and Indeterminacy in Medieval and Modern French Narrative*. Studies in Medieval History and Culture, 21 (New York: Routledge, 2004).

Higgs Strickland, Debra, *The Epiphany of Hieronymus Bosch: Imagining Antichrist and Others from the Middle Ages to the Reformation* (London: Harvey Miller Publishers, 2016).
Hildegard of Bingen, *On Natural Philosophy and Medicine: Selections from* Cause et cure. Library of Medieval Women (Cambridge and Rochester, NY: D. S. Brewer, 1999).
Hildegard of Bingen, *Scivias*, trans. Mother Columba Hart and Jane Bishop, intro. by Barbara J. Newman, preface by Caroline Walker Bynum (New York and Mahwah, NJ: Paulist Press, 1990).
Hildegard of Bingen, *The Book of the Rewards of Life (Liber Vitae Meritorum*, trans. Bruce W. Hozeski (New York and Oxford: Oxford University Press, 1994).
Hildegard von Bingen 1098–1179, ed. Hans-Jürgen Kotzur (Mainz: Verlag Philipp von Zabern, 1998 *Hildegard von Bingen in ihrem historischen Umfeld: Internationaler wissenschaftlicher Kongreß zum 900jährigen Jubiläum, 13.–19. September 1998, Bingen am Rhein*, ed. Alfred Haverkamp (Mainz: Verlag Philipp von Zabern, 2000).
Hildegard von Bingen: *Das große Hildegard von Bingen Lesebuch: Worte wie von Feuerzungen*, ed. Maura Zátonyi (Munich: Verlag Herder, 2022).
Hildegard von Bingen: Internationale Wissenschaftliche Bibliographie, ed. Marc-Aeilko Aris, Michael Embach, et al. Quellen und Abhandlungen zur mittelrheinischen Kirchengeschichte, 84 (Mainz: Gesellschaft für mittelrheinische Kirchengeschichte, 1998).
Hodgson, Eleanor, "Rewriting the Werewolf: Transformations of Bisclavret in Guillaume de Palerne," *French Studies Bulletin: A Quarterly Supplement* 37 (138) (2016): 9–13.
Holländer, Hans, *Hieronymus Bosch: Weltbilder und Traumwerk*. 3rd updated and expanded ed. DuMont-Taschenbücher, 28 (Cologne: DuMont, 1988).
Hollywood, Amy, *The Soul as Virgin Wife: Mechthild of Magdeburg, Marguerite Porete, and Meister Eckhart*. Studies in Spirituality and Theology (Notre, Dame, IN, and London: University of Notre Dame Press, 1995).
Holzmann, Verena, *"Ich beswer dich wurm vnd wyrmin . . . " Formen und Typen altdeutscher Zaubersprüche und Segen*. Wiener Arbeiten zur germanischen Altertumskunde und Philologie, 36 (Bern, Berlin, et al: Peter Lang, 2001).
Honecker, Martin, "Spiritualität und Geheimnis," *Zeitschrift für Theologie und Kirche* 118.2 (2021): 184–215.
Honegger, Thomas, *Introducing the Medieval Dragon* (Cardiff: University of Wales Press, 2019).
Horn, András, *Das Schöpferische in der Literatur: Theorien der dichterischen Phantasie* (Würzburg: Königshausen & Neumann, 2000).
Hornaday, Aline G., "Visitors from Another Space: The Medieval Revenant as Foreigner," *Meeting the Foreign in the Middle Ages*, ed. Albrecht Classen (New York and London: Routledge, 2002).
Hotchkiss, Valerie R., *Clothes Make the Man: Female Cross Dressing in Medieval Europe*. Garland Reference Library of the Humanities. New Middle Ages, 1 (New York: Routledge, 2012).

Huber, Christoph, *Gottfried von Straßburg: Tristan*. Klassiker-Lektüren, 3. 3rd, newly rev. and expanded ed. (2000; Berlin: Erich Schmidt Verlag, 2013).
Huemer, Werner, *Warum wir durch den Tod nicht sterben: die großen Geheimnisse am Ende des Lebens* (Leipzig and Frankfurt a. M.: Deutsche Nationalbibliothek, 2021).
Huon de Bordeaux, ed. Pierre Ruelle (Brussels: Presses Universitaires de Bruxelles, 1960).
Huon de Bordeaux: Chanson de geste du XIIIe siècle, publiéed'après le manuscrit Paris BNF fr. 22555, ed. and trans. William W. Kibler and François Suard (Paris: Champion, 2003).
Huon of Bordeaux, trans. Catherine Jones and William W. Kibler. Medieval & Renaissance Text Series (New York and Briston: Italica Press, 2021).
Huon of Bordeaux: First Modern English Translation by Catherine M. Jones and William W. Kibler. Medieval & Renaissance Text Series (New York and Bristol: Italica Press, 2021).
Huon: Le Huon de Bordeaux en prose du XVème siècle, ed. William W. Kibler, Jean-Louise G. Picherit, and Thelma S. Fenster. 2 vols. (Geneva: Droz, 1980).
Hutton, Ronald, "Stephen Mitchell's *Witchcraft and Magic in the Nordic Middle Ages*: An Assessment and Appreciation," *Magic, Ritual, and Witchcraft* 8.1 (2013): 75–81.
Ich—Ulrich von Liechtenstein: Literatur und Politik im Mittelalter. Akten der Akademie Friesach "Stadt und Kultur im Mittelalter" 1996, ed Franz Viktor Spechtler and Barbara Maier (Klagenfurt: Wieser, 1999).
Idel, Moshe, *Absorbing Perfections: Kabbalah and Interpretation* (New Haven, NJ: Yale University Press, 2002).
Ifor Williams, *The Beginnings of Welsh Poetry* (Cardiff: University of Wales Press, 1990).
Illingworth, R. N., "Celtic Tradition and the *Lai of Yonec*," *Études Celtiques* 9 (1961): 501–20.
Illuminating Darkness: Approaches to Obscurity and Nothingness in Literature, ed. Päivi Mehtonen. Suomalaisen Tiedeakatemian toimituksia: Humaniora, 348 (Helsinki: Acad. Scientiarum Fennica, 2007).
Ilsink, Matthijs, *Hieronymus Bosch, Painter and Draughtsman: Catalogue raisonné* (New Haven, CT: Yale University Press, 2016).
Imagination and Fantasy in the Middle Ages and Early Modern Times: Projections, Dreams, Monsters, and Illusions, ed. Albrecht Classen. Fundamentals of Medieval and Early Modern Culture, 24 (Berlin and Boston: Walter de Gruyter, 2020).
Jilling, Lewis, *Diu Crone of Heinrich von dem Türlein: The Attempted Emancipation of Secular Narrative*. Göppinger Arbeiten zur Germanistik, 258 (Göppingen: Kümmerle, 1980).
Jones, Catherine M., "'Je ne soz queil homme j'oz ocis': Ignorance et innocence dans *Huon de Bordeaux* et *Garin le Lorrain*," *La faute dans l'épopée médiévale: ambiguïté de jugement*, ed. Bernard Ribémont (Rennes: Presses Universitaires de Rennes, 2012), 123–36.

Josephson, Jason Ananda, *The Myth of Disenchantment: Magic, Modernity, and the Birth of the Human Sciences* (Chicago and London: The University of Chicago Press, 2017).
Jouffroy, Théodore, *Cours d'esthetique: suivi de la thèse du mème auteur sur le semtiment du beau et de deux fragments inédits* (Paris: Hachette, 1843).
Journey, Florence Ramond, "Secret Identities: (Un)Masking Gender in *Le Roman de Silence* by Heldris de Cornouaille and *L'enfant de sable* by Tahar Ben Jelloun," *Dalhousie French Studies* 55 (2001): 3–10.
Julian of Norwich: *The Writings of Julian of Norwich: A Vision Showed to a Devout Woman and A Revelation of Love*, ed. Nicholas Watson and Jacqueline Jenkins (University Park, PA: The Pennsylvania State University Press, 2006).
Kaminski, Nicola, *»Wâ ez sich êrste ane vienc, Daz ist ein teil unkunt«: Abgründiges Erzählen in der* Krone *Heinrichs von dem Türlin*. Beiträge zur älteren Literaturgeschichte (Heidelberg: Universitätsverlag Winter, 2005).
Kampfhammer, Hans-Peter, "Das Geheimnis mystischer Zustände: Klinische und neurobiologische Aspekte," *Das Geheimnis: Psychologische, psychopathologische und künstlerische Ausdrucksformen im Spektrum zwischen Verheimlichen und Geheimnisvollem*, ed. Daniel Sollberger, Jobst Böning, Erik Boehlke, and Gerhard Schindler. Schriftenreihe der Deutschsprachigen Gesellschaft für Kunst und Psychopathologie des Ausdrucks e.V., 35 (Berlin: Frank & Timme, 2016), 103–32.
Karnes, Michelle, *Medieval Marvels and Fictions in the Latin West and Islamic World* (Chicago and London: University of Chicago Press, 2022).
Kasper, Christine, *Von miesen Rittern und sündhaften Frauen und solchen, die besser waren: Tugend- und Keuschheitsproben in der mittelalterlichen Literatur*. Göppinger Arbeiten zur Germanistik, 547 (Göppingen: Kümmerle, 1995).
Kaufringer, Heinrich, English translation: Albrecht Classen. *Love, Life, and Lust in Heinrich Kaufringer's Verse Narratives*. 2nd rev. ed. Medieval and Renaissance Texts and Studies, 467. MRTS Texts for Teaching, 9 (2014; Tempe, AZ: Arizona Center for Medieval and Renaissance Studies, 2019).
Kaufringer, Heinrich, *Werke*, ed. Paul Sappler (Tübingen: Max Niemeyer, 1972)
Kauth, Jean-Marie, "Barred Windows and Uncaged Birds: The Enclosure of Woman in Chrétien de Troyes and Marie de France," *Medieval Feminist Forum* 46.2 (2010): 34–67.
Keller, Hildegard Elisabeth, *My Secret is Mine: Studies on Religion and Eros in the German Middle Ages*. Studies in Spirituality, 4 (Leuven: Peeters, 2000).
Keller, Johannes, *Diu Crône Heinrichs von dem Türlin: Wunderketten, Gral und Tod*. Deutsche Literatur von den Anfängen bis 1700, 25 (Bern, Berlin, et al.: Peter Lang, 1997).
Kibler, William W., "Merlin," *The New Arthurian Encyclopedia*, ed. Norris J. Lacy. Garland Reference Library of the Humanities, 931 (New York and London: Garland, 1996), 319–21.
Kinoshita, Sharon and Peggy McCracken, *Marie de France: A Critical Companion*. Gallica, 24 (Cambridge: D. S. Brewer, 2012).
Kinoshita, Sharon, "The Politics of Courtly Love: *La Prise d'Orange* and the Conversion of the Saracen Queen," *Romanic Review* 86 (1995): 265–88.

Kinoshita, Sharon, "Two for the Price of One: Courtly Love and Serial Polygamy in the *Lais* of Marie de France," *Arthuriana* 8.2 (1998): 23–55.
Kirchhoff, Anne and Matthias, commentary to no. 43: *Deutsche Versnovellistik des 13. bis 15. Jahrhunderts*, ed. Klaus Ridder and Hans-Joachim Ziegeler. Vol. 2 (Berlin: Schwabe Verlag, 2020), 103–26.
Kirk, Jordan, *Medieval Nonsense: Signifying Nothing in Fourteenth-Century England* (New York: Fordham University Press, 2021).
Kissle, Alexander and Carsten S. Leimbach, *Alles über Patrick Süskinds "Das Parfüm"* (Munich: Heyne, 2006).
Klingner, Jacob, "Der Sündenfall als Glücksfall?: Zur Deutung des Gürtels in Dietrichs von der Glezze 'Borte,'" *Liebesgaben: kommunikative, performative und poetologische Dimensionen in der Literatur des Mittelalters und der Frühen Neuzeit*, ed. Margreth. Egidi, Ludger Lieb, Mireille Schnyder, and Moritz Wedell. Philologische Studien und Quellen, 240 (Berlin: Erich Schmidt Verlag, 2012), 163–79.
Knapp, Fritz Peter, "Der Gral zwischen Märchen und Legende," id., *Historie und Fiktion in der mittelalterlichen Gattungspoetik: Sieben Studien und ein Nachwort* (Heidelberg: Universitätsverlag C. Winter, 1997; orig. 1996), 133–51.
Knapp, Fritz Peter, *Blüte der europäischen Literatur des Hochmittelalters*. Part 2: *Roman—Kleinepik—Lehrdichtung* (Stuttgart: S. Hirzel Verlag, 2019).
Knapp, Fritz Peter, *Chevalier errant und* fin'amor*: Das Ritterideal des 13. Jahrhunderts in Nordfrankreich und im deutschsprachigen Südosten. Studien zum Lancelot en prose, zum Moriz von Craûn, zur Krone Heinrichs von dem Türlin, zu Werken des Strickers und zum Frauendienst Ulrichs von Lichtenstein*. Schriften der Universität Passau: Reihe Geisteswissenschaften, 8 (Passau: Passavia-Universitätsverlag, 1986).
Knapton, Antoinette, *Mythe et psychologie chez Marie de France*. North Carolina Studies in the Romance Languages and Literatures, 142 (Chapel Hill, NC: University of North Carolina Department of Romance Languages, 1975), 69.
Knight, Stephen, *Merlin: Knowledge and Power through the Ages* (Ithaca, NY, and London: Cornell University Press, 2016).
Koch, Max, *Das Quellenverhältniss von Wielands Oberon* (Marburg: Elwert, 1880).
Koerner, Joseph Leo, *Bosch & Bruegel: From Enemy Painting to Everyday Life* (Princeton, NJ, and Oxford: Princeton University Press, 2018).
Kokott, Hartmut, *Konrad von Würzburg: ein Autor zwischen Auftrag und Autonomie* (Stuttgart: S. Hirzel, 1989).
Kolb, Herbert, *Munsalvaesche: Studien zum Kyotproblem* (Munich: Eidos-Verlag, 1963).
Konrad von Würzburg, *Goldene Schmiede*, ed. Edward Schröder. 2nd ed. (Göttingen: Vandenhoeck & Ruprecht, 1969).
Konrad von Würzburg's *Partonopier und Meliur*, ed. Karl Bartsch. Mit einem Nachwort von Rainer Gruenter. Deutsche Neudrucke. Reihe: Texte des Mittelalters (1871; Berlin: Walter de Gruyter, 1970).
Korngiebel, Diane, "Mabinogion, The," *Encyclopedia of Medieval Literature*, ed. Jay Ruud (New York: Facts on File, 2006), 416–17.

Korotayev, Andrey, *World Religions and Social Evolution of the Old World Oikumene Civilizations: A Cross-cultural Perspective* (Lewiston, NY: Edwin Mellen Press, 2004).
Körper—Kultur—Kommunikation: = Corps—Culture—Communication, ed. Alexander Schwarz, Catalina Schiltknecht and Barbara Wahlen. Tausch, 18 (Bern: Peter Lang, 2014).
Kratz, Bernd, "Rosengarten und Zwergenkönig in der Crone Heinrichs von dem Türlin," *Medieval Bohemia* 1 (1969): 21–29.
Kroll, Jerome and Bernard S. Bachrach, *The Mystic Mind: The Psychology of Medieval Mystics and Ascetics* (New York and London: Routledge, 2005).
Krueger, Roberta L., "Questions of Gender in Old French Courtly Romance," *The Cambridge Companion to Medieval Romance Cambridge*, ed. Roberta L. Krueger. Cambridge and New York: Cambridge University Press, 2000, 132–49.
Kruger, Steven F., *Dreaming in the Middle Ages* (Cambridge: Cambridge University Press, 1992).
Kruse, Britta-Juliane, *Verborgene Heilkünste: Geschichte der Frauenmedizin im Spätmittelalter*. Quellen und Forschungen zur Literatur- und Kulturgeschichte, 239 (Berlin and New York: Walter de Gruyter, 1996).
Kühne, Anja, *Vom Affekt zum Gefühl: Konvergenzen von Theorie und Literatur im Mittelalter am Beispiel von Konrads von Würzburg "Partonopier und Meliur."* Göppinger Arbeiten zur Germanistik, 713 (Göppingen: Kümmerle, 2004).
Kulturelle Inszenierungen von Transgender und Crossdressing: grenz(en)überschreitende Lektüren vom Mythos bis zur Gegenwart, ed. Anne-Berenike Rothstein. GenderCodes - Transkriptionen zwischen Wissen und Geschlecht, 20 (Bielefeld: transcript, 2021).
Kunert, Günter, "Der verschlossene Raum," id., *Die geheime Bibliothek* (Berlin and Weimar: Aufbau Verlag, 1973), 9–10.
Kvideland, Reimund, "Schiff," *Enzyklopädie des Märchens*, ed. Rolf Wilhelm Brednich. Vol. 11.3 (Berlin and New York: Walter de Gruyter, 2004), 1416–21.
La matière arthurienne tardive en Europe: 1270–1530, ed. Christine Ferlampin-Acher (Rennes: Presses universitaires de Rennes, 2020).
Labbie, Erin F., "The Specular Image of the Gender-Neutral Name: Naming Silence in *Le Roman de Silence*," *Arthuriana* 7.2 (1997): 63–77.
Lamprecht, *Alexanderroman. Mittelhochdeutsch/Neuhochdeutsch*, ed. Elisabeth Lienert (Stuttgart: Philipp Reclam jun., 2007).
Lamprecht, see also *Das Alexanderlied*
Larrington, Carolyne, *King Arthur's Enchantresses: Morgan and Her Sisters in Arthurian Tradition* (London: I. B. Tauris, 2006),
Laxdæla Saga, trans. with an intro. by Magnus Magnusson and Hermann Pálsson (London: Penguin, 1969).
Le Roman de Silence: A Thirteenth-Century Arthurian Verse-Romance by Heldris de Cornuälle, ed. Lewis Thorpe (Cambridge: W. Heffer and Sons, 1972).
Lee, Ashley, "The Hind Episode in Marie de France's *Guigemar* and Medieval Vernacular Poetics," *Neophilologus* 93.2 (2009): 191–200.

Lee, Becky R., "The Medieval Hysteric and the Psychedelic Psychologist: A Revaluation of the Mysticism of Margery Kempe in the Light of the Transpersonal Psychology of Stanislav Grof," *Studia Mystica* 23 (2002): 102–26.

Lemay, Helen Rodnite, *Women's Secrets: A Translation of Pseudo-Albertus Magnus's De secretis mulierum with Commentaries*. SUNY Series in Medieval Studies (Albany, NY: SUNY Press, 1992).

Lembke, Astrid, *Inschriftlichkeit: Materialität, Präsenz und Poetik des Geschriebenen im höfischen Roman*. Deutsche Literatur, 37 (Berlin and Boston: Walter de Gruyter, 2020).

Lerchner, Karin, *Lectulus Floridus: Zur Bedeutung des Bettes in Literatur und Handschriftenillustrationen des Mittelalters* (Cologne, Weimar, and Vienna: Böhlau Verlag, 1993).

Leventhal, Cassidy, "Finding Avalon: The Place and Meaning of the Otherworld in Marie de France's *Lanval*," *Neophilologus* 98.2 (2014): 193–204.

Lexikon der Geisteswissenschaften: Sachbegriffe—Disziplinen—Personen, ed. Helmut Reinaler and Peter J. Brenner (Vienna, Cologne, and Weimar: Böhlau Verlag, 2011).

Das Lexikon des Mittelalters, ed. Bruno Mariacher. Vol. IV (Munich and Zürich: Artemis, 1989), 1172–73.

Liebe als Krankheit, ed. Theo Stemmler. Kolloquium der Forschungsstelle für Europäische Lyrik des Mittelalters, 3 (Tübingen: Narr, 1990).

Liendo, Elizabeth, "The Wound that Bleeds: Violence and Feminization in the *Lais* of Marie de France," *Neophilologus* 104 (2020): 19–32.

Lönnroth, Lars, *Njáls saga: A Critical Introduction* (Berkeley, CA: University of California Press, 1976).

Losch, Andreas, *What is Life?: On Earth and Beyond* (Cambridge: Cambridge University Press, 2017).

Mabinogi: *The Mabinogi: Legend and Landscape of Wales*, trans. J. K. Bollard (Llandysul: Gomer, 2006).

Mac Cana, Proinsias, *Celtic Mythology* (London: Hamlyn, 1970).

Mac Cana, Proinsias, *The Mabinogi*. Writers of Wales (Cardiff: University of Wales, 1992).

Macdonald, Aileen Ann, *The Figure of Merlin in Thirteenth Century French Romance*. Studies in Medieval Literature, 3 (Lewiston, Lampeter, and Queenston: Edwin Mellen Press, 1990).

MacKinnon, Malcolm H., "Max Weber's Disenchantment: Lineages of Kant and Channing," *Journal of Classical Sociology* 1.3 (2001): 329–51.

Magic and Magicians in the Middle Ages and the Early Modern Time: The Occult in Pre-Modern Sciences, Medicine, Literature, Religion, and Astrology, ed. Albrecht Classen. Fundamentals of Medieval and Early Modern Culture, 20 (Berlin and Boston: Walter de Gruyter, 2017).

Mai und Beaflor. Herausgegeben, übersetzt, kommentiert und mit einer Einleitung von Albrecht Classen. Beihefte zur Mediaevistik, 6 (Frankfurt a. M.: Peter Lang, 2006).

Malm, Mike, "Heinrich von dem Türlin," *Deutsches Literatur-Lexikon: Das Mittelalter*, ed. Wolfgang Achnitz. Vol. 5: *Epik (Vers—Strophe—Prosa) und Kleinformen* (Berlin and Boston: Walter de Gruyter, 2013), 411–21.

Mandach, André de, *Auf den Spuren des Heiligen Gral: die gemeinsame Vorlage im pyrenäischen Geheimcode von Chrétien de Troyes und Wolfram von Eschenbach*. Göppinger Arbeiten zur Germanistik, 596 (Göppingen: Kümmerle, 1995).

Manzalaoui, Mahmoud, "The Pseudo-Aristotelian Kitab Sirr al-asrar: Facts and Problems," *Oriens* 23–24 (1974): 146–257.

Maraschi, Andrea, "Taboo or Magic Practice? Cannibalism as Identity Marker for Giants and Human Heroes in Medieval Iceland," *Parergon: Journal of the Australian and New Zealand Association for Medieval and Early Modern Studies* 37.1 (2020): 1–25.

Mären als Grenzphänomen, ed. Silvan Wagner. Bayreuther Beiträge zur Literaturwissenschaft, 37 (Berlin: Peter Lang, 2018).

Marie de France, *Fables*, ed. and trans. Harriet Spiegel. Medieval Academy Reprints for Teaching (Toronto, Buffalo, and London: University of Toronto Press, 1994).

Marie de France, *The Lais by Marie de France: Text and Translation*, ed. and trans. Claire M. Waters (Peterborough, Ont.: broadview editions, 2018).

Marijnissen, R.-H., K. Blockx, P. Gerach, H.-T. Piron, J.-H. Plokker, and V. H. Bauer, *Jhyronimus Bosch* (Geneva: Weber, 1972).

Marijnissen, Roger H., *Hieronymus Bosch: das vollständige Werk*, trans. from the Dutch (Weinheim: Acta Humaniora, 1988).

Marvels, Monsters, and Miracles: Studies in the Medieval and Early Modern Imaginations, ed. Timothy S. Jones (Kalamazoo, MI: Medieval Institute Pub., Western Michigan University, 2002).

Marxhausen, Thomas, "Geheimnis," *Historisch-kritisches Wörterbuch des Marxismus*, vol. 5 (Hamburg: Argument-Verlag, 2001), cols. 48–53.

Masterson, Patrick, *In Reasonable Hope: Philosophical Reflections on Ultimate Meaning* (Washington, DC: The Catholic University of America Press, 2021).

Matthews, Caitlín, *Mabon and the Mysteries of Britain: An Exploration of the Mabinogion* (London and New York: Arkana, 1987).

McCaughan, Michael, "Symbolism of Ships and the Sea: From Ship of the Church to Gospel Trawler," *Folk Life* 40.1 (2001): 54–61.

Mcculloch, Florence, *Medieval Latin and French Bestiaries*. North Carolina Studies in the Romance Languages and Literatures (Chapel Hill, NC: University of North Carolina at Chapel Hill Department of Romance Studies, 2017).

McGinn, Bernard, *The Flowering of Mysticism: Men and Women in the New Mysticism (1200–1350)*. The Presence of God, 3 (New York: Crossroad, 1998).

McGinn, Bernard, *The Growth of Mysticism*. The Presence of God, 2 (New York: Crossroad, 1999).

McLemore, Emily, "Queer Bodies, Sexual Possibility, and Violent Misogyny in Bisclavret," *Le Cygne: Journal of the International Marie de France Society* 7.1 (2020): 9–31.

McMunn, Meredith T. and Willene B. Clark, *Beasts and Birds of the Middle Ages: The Bestiary and Its Legacy*. The Middle Ages Series (1989; Philadelphia, PA: University of Pennsylvania Press, 2016).
Mecham, Jane L., "Cooperative Piety Among Monastic and Secular Women in Late Medieval Germany," *Church History and Religious Culture* 88 (2008): 581–611.
Mechthild of Magdeburg, *The Flowing Light of the Godhead*, trans. and intro. by Frank Tobin (New York and Mahwah, NJ: Paulist Press, 1998).
Mechthild von Magdeburg, *'Lux divinitatis'—'Das liecht der gotheit.' Der lateinisch-frühneuhochdeutsche Überlieferungszweig des 'Fließenden Lichts der Gottheit.' Synoptische Ausgabe*, ed. Balázs J. Nemes and Elke Senne, under the guidance of Ernst Hellgardt (Berlin and Boston: Walter de Gruyter, 2019).
Mechthild von Magdeburg, *Das fließende Licht der Gottheit*, ed. Gisela Vollmann-Profe. Bibliothek des Mittelalters, 19, Bibliothek deutscher Klassiker, 181 (Frankfurt a. M.: Deutsche Klassiker Verlag, 2003).
Meconi, Honey, *Hildegard of Bingen. Women Composers* (Urbana, Chicago; Springfield, IL: University of Illinois Press, 2018).
Medizin im Mittelalter: zwischen Erfahrungswissen, Magie und Religion: Hildegard von Bingen, missverstandene Ikone der Klostermedizin: die Pest, die überraschenden Folgen der Seuche: Sex in the City, Geschlechtsverkehr als Heilmittel, ed. Carsten Könneker. Spektrum der Wissenschaft. Spezial. Archäologie, Geschichte, Kultur, 2019.2 (Heidelberg: Spektrum der Wissenschaft Verlagsgesellschaft, 2019).
Mehtonen, Päivi, *Obscure Language, Unclear Literature: Theory and Practice from Quintilian to the Enlightenment*. Suomalaisen Tiedeakatemian toimituksia: Sarja Humaniora, 320. Trans. Robert MacGilleon (Helsinki: Acad. Scientiarum Fennica, 2003).
Meister Eckhart, *Deutsche Predigten und Traktate*, ed. and trans. Josef Quint (Munich: Carl Hanser Verlag, 1955).
Meister, Peter, *The Healing Female in the German Courtly Romance*. Göppinger Arbeiten zur Germanistik, 523 (Göppingen: Kümmerle, 1990).
Merkelbach, Rebecca, *Monsters in Society: Alterity, Transgression, and the Use of the Past in Medieval Iceland*. The Northern Medieval World (Berlin and Boston: Walter de Gruyter, 2019).
Merlin in der europäischen Literatur des Mittelalters, ed. Silvia Brugger-Hackett. Helfant-Studien, 8 (Stuttgart: Helfant, 1991).
Merzetti, Monia, *I volti della moglie di Putifarre nella letteratura francese (sec. XII–XX)* (Pisa: Edizioni ETS, 2010).
Meyer, Evelyn, "Wolfram von Eschenbach's *Parzival*: A Complex Reshaping and Expansion of a Source," *A Companion to World Literature*, ed. Ken Seigneurie. Vol. 2: *601 CE to 1450 CE*, ed. Christine Chism. Blackwell Companions to Literature and Culture (Hoboken, NJ, and Chichester, West Sussex, 2020), 967–77.
Michaela Willers, *Heinrich Kaufringer als Märenautor: das Oeuvre des cgm 270* (Berlin: Logos-Verlag, 2002).
Mikota, Jana, "Zeitdiebe in unterschiedlichen Jahrzehnten: narratologische Untersuchungen zu Zeit—Raum—Figur in ausgewählten Beispielen," *Kinder- und Jugendliteratur und Narratologie*, ed. Carsten Gansel and Hermann Korte.

Deutschsprachige Gegenwartsliteratur und Medien, 2 (Göttingen: V & R Unipress, 2009), 67–79.
Milem, Bruce, *The Unspoken Word: Negative Theology in Meister Eckhart's German Sermons* (Washington, DC: The Catholic University of America Press, 2002).
Milin, Gaël, *Les chiens de Dieu:* Matthew Beresford, *The White Devil: The Werewolf in European Culture* (London: Reaktion Books, 2013)*la représentation du loup-garou en Occident, XIe–XXe siècles* (Brest: Centre de recherche bretonne et celtique, Université de Bretagne occidentale, 1993).
Mirakel im Mittelalter: Konzeptionen, Erscheinungsformen, Deutungen, ed. Martin Heinzelmann, Klaus Herbers und Dieter R. Bauer. Beiträge zur Hagiographie, 3 (Stuttgart: Steiner, 2002).
Mitchell, Stephen A., *Magic, Ritual and Witchcraft in the Nordic Middle Ages*. The Middle Ages Series (Philadelphia, PA: University of Pennsylvania Press, 2011).
Mitchell, Stephen, "Magic as Acquired Art and the Ethnographic Value of the Sagas," *Old Norse Myths, Literature and Society*, ed. Margaret Clunies Ross (Odense: University Press of Southern Denmark, 2003), 132–52.
Moebius, Stephan, *Simmel lesen: moderne, dekonstruktive und postmoderne Lektüren der Soziologie von Georg Simmel* (Stuttgart: Ibidem-Verlag, 2002).
Mondschein, Ken and Denis Casey, "Time and Timekeeping," *Handbook of Medieval Culture: Fundamental Aspects and Conditions of the European Middle Ages*, ed. Albrecht Classen (Berlin and Boston: Walter de Gruyter, 2015), vol. 3, 1657–79.
Mondschein, Ken, *On Time: A History of Western Timekeeping* (Baltimore, MD: Johns Hopkins University Press, 2020).
Montésinos, Christian, *Les étranges symboles des cathédrales, basiliques et églises de la France médiévale*. Les lieux de la tradition (Paris: Éditions Dervy, 2018).
Morgan, Hollie L. S., *Beds and Chambers in Late Medieval England* (Woodbridge, Suffolk: Boydell & Brewer, 2017).
Mühlenfeld, Stephanie, *Konzepte der "exotischen" Tierwelt im Mittelalter* (Göttingen: V&R unipress, 2019).
Mühlhausen, Ludwig, ed., *Die vier Zweige des Mabinogi (Pedeir Ceinc y Mabinogi)*. 2nd rev. and expanded ed. Buchreihe der Zeitschrift für celtische Philologie, 7 (1925; Tübingen: Max Niemeyer, 1988).
Müller, Jan-Dirk, *Spielregeln für den Untergang: die Welt des Nibelungenliedes* (Tübingen: Max Niemeyer, 1998).
Murray, Alan V., "Tourney, Joust, Foreis and Round Table: Tournament Forms in the Frauendienst of Ulrich von Liechtenstein," *Pleasure and Leisure in the Middle Ages and Early Modern Age: Cultural-Historical Perspectives on Toys, Games, and Entertainment*, ed. Albrecht Classen (Berlin and Boston: Walter de Gruyter, 2019), 365–94.
Mysticism Without Bounds: Essays from the International Conference on Mysticism. Human Transcendence, Economic Life, Medical Materialism, ed. Kurian Kachappilly (New Delhi: Christian World Imprints, 2015).
Myth, Magic, and Memory in Early Scandinavian Narrative Culture: Studies in Honour of Stephen A. Mitchell, ed. Jörg Glauser, Pernille Hermann, Stefan Brink,

Joseph Harris, and Sarah Künzler. Acta Scandinavica, 11 (Turnhout: Brepols, 2021).
Nellmann, Eberhard, "Wolfram und Kyot als 'vindære wilder mære," *Zeitschrift für deutsches Altertum und deutsche Literatur* 117 (1988): 31–67.
Nellmann, Eberhard, *Wolframs Erzähltechnik: Untersuchungen zur Funktion des Erzählers* (Wiesbaden: Steiner, 1973).
Nelstrop, Louise, with Kevin Magill and Bradley B. Onishi, *Christian Mysticism: An Introduction to Contemporary Theoretical Approaches* (Farnham, Surrey: Ashgate, 2009).
Neukirchen, Thomas, *Die ganze aventiure und ihre lere: der "Jüngere Titurel" Albrechts als Kritik und Vervollkommnung des "Parzival" Wolframs von Eschenbach*. Beihefte zum Euphorion, 52 (Heidelberg: Universitätsverlag Winter, 2006).
Neumeister, Sebastian, "Die Sprache als Weg in die Transzendenz," *Literarische und religiöse Kommunikation in Mittelalter und Früher Neuzeit*, ed. Peter Strohschneider (Berlin and New York: Walter de Gruyter, 2008), 930–52.
New Studies in the Manuscript Tradition of Njál's Saga: The historia mutila of Njála, ed. Svanhildur Óskarsdóttir and Emily Lethbridge. The Northern Medieval World: On the Margins of Europe (Basel, Berlin, and Boston: Walter de Gruyter, 2018).
Newman, Barbara, "Hildegard of Bingen and the 'Birth of Purgatory,'" *Mystics Quarterly* 19 (1993): 90–97.
Newman, Barbara, *Medieval Crossover: Reading the Secular Against the Sacred* (University of Notre Dame Press, 2013).
Nibelungenlied: The Nibelungenlied *with* The Klage, ed. and trans., with an intro. by William Whobrey (Indianapolis, IN, and Cambridge: Hackett Publishing, 2018).
Nicolas, Catherine, "'Sun parastre ad le chief tolu': Vengeance, jugement et amour dans le lai d'*Yonec*," *Babel: Littératures Plurielles* 42 (2020): 115–32.
Nikolaus Henkel, Studien zum Physiologus im Mittelalter. Hermaea: Neue Folge, 38 (Tübingen: Max Niemeyer, 1976).
Njál's Saga, trans. from the Old Icelandic with intro. and notes by Carl F. Bayerschmidt and Lee M. Hollander (New York: New York University Press, 1955).
Njal's Saga, trans. with intro. and notes by Robert Cook. World of the Sagas (London: Penguin, 1997).
Norako, Leila K., "Morgan le Fay," *The Camelot Project*, online at: https://d.lib.rochester.edu/camelot/theme/morgan.
Nugent, Christopher G., "Reading Riannon: The Problematics of Motherhood in *Pwyll Pendeuic Dyuet*," *Domestic Violence in Medieval Texts*, ed. Eve Salisbury, Georgiana Donavin, and Merrall Llewelyn (Gainesville, Tallahassee, et al., FL: University Press of Florida; 2002), 180–202.
Nyrop, Krystoffer, *The Kiss and Its History*, trans. William Frederick Harvey (1901; Detroit, MI: Singing Tree Press, 1968).
O'Gorman, Richard, "Grail," *The New Arthurian Encyclopedia*, ed. Norris J. Lacy. Updated Paperback Ed. (1991; New York and London: Garland Publishing, 1996), 212–13.

Oberleitner, Alexander, *Michael Endes Philosophie im Spiegel von "Momo" und "Die unendliche Geschichte"* (Hamburg: Meiner, 2020).
Magical Realism and Literature, ed. Warnes, Christopher and Kim Anderson Sasser (Cambridge: Cambridge University Press, 2020).
Obermaier, Sabine, "Frauenlob und der 'Geblümte Stil,'" *Handbuch Frauenlob*, ed. Claudia Lauer and Uta Störmer-Caysa, together with Anna Sara Lahr. Beiträge zur älteren Literaturgeschichte (Heidelberg: Universitätsverlag Winter, 2018), 147–79.
Object Fantasies: Experience and Creation, ed. Philippe Cordez, Romana Kaske, Julia Saviello, and Susanne Thürigen. Object Studies in Art History, 1 (Berlin and Boston: Walter de Gruyter, 2018).
Ogden, Daniel, *The Werewolf in the Ancient World* (Oxford: Oxford University Press, 2020).
Okken, Lambertus, *Das goldene Haus und die goldene Laube: Wie die Poesi ihren Herren das Paradies einrichtete*. Amsterdamer Publikationen zur Sprache und Literatur, 72 (Amsterdam: Rodopi, 1987).
On the Margin of the Visible: Sociology, the Esoteric, and the Occult, ed. Edward A Tiryakian (New York: Wiley, 1974), 53–69.
Orlemanski, Julie, *Symptomatic Subjects: Bodies, Medicine, and Causation in the Literature of Late Medieval England*. Alembics: Penn Studies in Literature and Science (Philadelphia, PA: University of Pennsylvania Press, 2019).
Orton, Peter, "Pagan Myth and Religion," *A Companion to Old Norse-Icelandic Literature and Culture*, ed. Rory McTurk. Blackwell Companions to Literature and Culture, 31 (Malden, MA, Oxford, and Carlton, Victoria, Australia: Blackwell, 2007), 302–19.
Ortúzar Escudero, María José, *Die Sinne in den Schriften Hildegards von Bingen: Ein Beitrag zur Geschichte der Sinneswahrnehmung*. Monographien zur Geschichte des Mittelalters, 62 (Stuttgart: Anton Hiersemann, 2016).
Otto, Rudolf, *Das Heilige: Über das Irrationale in der Idee des Göttlichen und sein Verhältnis zum Rationalen* (Breslau: Trewendt & Granier, 1917).
Otto, Rudolf, *The Idea of the Holy; An Inquiry into the Non-Rational Factor in the Idea of the Divine and Its Relation to the Rational*, trans. John W. Harvey. 2nd ed. (1950; London and New York: Oxford University Press, 1970).
Page, Sophie, *Astrology in Medieval Manuscripts* (Toronto and Buffalo: University of Toronto Press, 2002).
Pals, Daniel L., *Eight Theories of Religion* (Oxford: Oxford University Press, 2006).
Parry, Thomas, *A History of Welsh Literature* (Oxford: Clarendon Press, 1955).
Partonopeus in Europe: An Old French Romance and Its Adaptations, ed, and with an intro. by Catherine Hanley, Mario Longtin, and Penny Eley. *Mediaevalia* 25.2, Special Issue (Binghamton, NY: The Center for Medieval and Renaissance Studies, 2004).
Paz, James, *Nonhuman Voices in Anglo-Saxon Literature and Material Culture* (Manchester: Manchester University Press, 2017).
Pensom, Roger, *Aucassin et Nicolete: The Poetry of Gender and Growing Up in the French Middle Ages* (Bern, Berlin, et al.: Peter Lang, 1999).

Perret, Michèle, "Travesties et transsexuelles: Yde, Silence, Grisandola, Blanchandine," *Romance Notes* 25.3 (1985): 328–40.
Petkov, Kiril, *The Kiss of Peace: Ritual, Self, and Society in the High and Late Medieval West.* Cultures, Beliefs and Traditions, 17 (Leiden and Boston: Brill, 2003).
Petrarch, Francesco, *The Secret, with Related Documents*, ed. with an intro. by Carol E. Quillen. The Bedford Series in History and Culture (Boston: Bedford/St. Martin's, 2003).
Petrarch and Boccaccio: The Unity of Knowledge in the Pre-Modern World, ed. Igor Candido. Mimesis, 61 (Berlin and Boston: Walter de Gruyter, 2018).
Petrarch: *Petrarch's Secret: or The Soul's Conflict with Passion. Three Dialogues Between Himself and S. Augustine*, trans. from the Latin by William H. Draper (Westport, CT: Hyperion Press, 1911).
Pfeiffer, Jens, "Verirrungen im Dickicht der Wörter: die Wälder der Ritter und der Wald Dantes," *Das Mittelalter: Der Wald im Mittelalter* (2008): 136–51.
Physiologus, trans. Michael J. Curley (Chicago and London: University of Chicago Press, 1979).
Picard, Hans Rudolf, "Ei wie gut, daß niemand weiß, daß ich Rumpelstilzchen heiß'!: Das Geheimnis und seine Entdeckung im Märchen," *Archäologie der literarischen Kommunikation. Geheimnis und Öffentlichkeit*, ed. Aleida und Jan Assman (Munich: Wilhelm Fink, 1997), vol. 3: *Geheimnis und Neugierde* (1999), 253–59.
Pickens, Rupert T., "Grail and Grail Romances," *Medieval France: An Encyclopedia*, ed. William W. Kibler and Grover A. Zinn (New York and London: Garland Publishing, 1995), 409–10.
Pigg, Daniel F., "Who is Grendel in *Beowulf?* Ambiguity, Allegory, and Meaning," *Imagination and Fantasy in the Middle Ages and Early Modern Times: Projections, Dreams, Monsters, and Illusions*, ed. Albrecht Classen. Fundamentals of Medieval and Early Modern Culture, 24 (Berlin and Boston: Walter de Gruyter, 2020), 303–19.
Pilch, Herbert, "Mabinogion," *Lexikon des Mittelalters*, vol. VI (Munich and Zürich: Artemis & Winkler Verlag, 1993), 54.
Pilgrimage in the Middle Ages: A Reader, ed. Brett Edward Whalen. Readings in Medieval Civilizations and Cultures, XVI (Toronto: University of Toronto Press, 2011).
Pilgrimage to Jerusalem and the Holy Land, 1187–1291, ed. Denys Pringle. Crusade Texts in Translation (Farnham, Surrey, and Burlington, VT: Ashgate, 2012).
Pongratz-Leisten, Beate and Karen Sonik, *The Materiality of Divine Agency*. Studies in Ancient Near Eastern Records (SANER), 8 (Berlin and Boston: Walter de Gruyter, 2015).
Poor, Sara S., *Mechthild of Magdeburg and Her Book: Gender and the Making of Textual Authority*. The Middle Ages Series (Philadelphia, PA: University of Pennsylvania Press, 2004).
Przybilski, Martin, *sippe und geslehte: Verwandtschaft als Deutungsmuster im "Willehalm" Wolframs von Eschenbach*. Imagines medii aevi, 4 (Wiesbaden: Reichert, 2000).

Putzo, Christine, *Konrad Fleck: Flore und Blanscheflur: Text und Untersuchungen*. Münchener Texte und Untersuchungen zur deutschen Literatur des Mittelalters, 143 (Berlin and Boston: Walter de Gruyter, 2015).
Quenstedt, Falk, *Mirabiles Wissen: Deutschsprachige Reiseerzählungen um 1200 im transkulturellen Kontext arabischer Literatur:* Straßburger Alexander, Herzog Ernst, Reise-*Fassung des* Brandan. Episteme in Bewegung, 22 (Wiesbaden: Harrassowitz Verlag, 2021).
Rabanus Maurus, *Poenitentium Liber ad Otgarium*, in *Patrologia Latinae*, ed. J. P. Migne (Paris: Migne, 1852), 112: 1398–424.
Rahner, K., "Geheimnis," *Lexikon für Theologie und Kirche*. 2nd completely rev. ed. by Josef Höfer and Karl Rahner. Vol. 4 (Freiburg i. Br.: Herder, 1960), 593–97.
Ramey, Lynn Tarte, *Christian, Saracen, and Genre in Medieval French Literature* (New York and London: Routledge,2001), 93–149.
Ramm, Ben, *A Discourse for the Holy Grail in Old French Romance* (Cambridge: D. S. Brewer, 2012).
Rampau, Laetitia, "Der Sprung nach Avalon: Ritter, Ross und Raum bei Marie de France und Chrétien de Troyes," *Raumerfahrung—Raumerfindung. Erzählte Welten des Mittelalters zwischen Orient und Okzident*, ed. eadem and Peter Ihring (Berlin: Akademie Verlag, 2005), 119–48.
Rampau, Laetitia, "Die *aventure* der *escriture*: Zu einem poetologischen Strukturprinzip der *Lais* von Marie de France," *Das Wunderbare in der arthurischen Literatur*, ed. Friedrich Wolfzettel (Tübingen: Max Niemeyer, 2003), 249–80.
Raskolnikov, Masha, "Without Magic or Miracle: The Romance of Silence and the Prehistory of Genderqueerness," *Trans Historical: Gender Plurality before the Modern*, ed. Greta LaFleur, Masha Raskolnikov, Anna Kłosowska (Ithaca, NY, and London: Cornell University Press, 2021), 178–206.
Rauhut, Nils Ch., *Ultimate Questions: Thinking about Philosophy*. 4th edition. Penguin Academies (New York, Munich, et al.: Pearson Longman, 2021).
Reading the Natural World in the Middle Ages and Renaissance: Perceptions of the Environment and Ecology, ed. Thomas Willard. Arizona Studies in the Middle Ages and Renaissance, 46 (Turnhout: Brepols, 2020).
Rebschloe, Timo, *Der Drache in der mittelalterlichen Literatur Europas*. Beiträge zur älteren Literaturgeschichte (Heidelberg: Universitätsverlag Winter, 2014).
Reed, Thomas L. Jr., "Marie de France's *Guigemar* as Art of Interpretation (and Ambiguity)," *Speaking Images: Essays in Honor of V. A. Kolve*, ed. Robert F. Yeager and Charlotte C. Morse (Asheville, NC: Pegasus Books, 2001), 1–26.
Rees, E. A., *The Mabinogi Decoded* (Birmingham: University of Birmingham, 2012).
Reichert, Hermann, *Das* Nibelungenlied*: Text und Einführung, nach der St. Galler Handschrift*, ed. and commented. 2nd rev. and expanded ed. (Berlin and Boston: Walter de Gruyter, 2017).
Reichert, Hermann, *Nibelungenlied-Lehrwerk: sprachlicher Kommentar, mittelhochdeutsche Grammatik, Wörterbuch: passend zum Text der St. Galler Fassung ("B")*. 2nd rev. ed. (Vienna: Praesens Verlag, 2019).
Ribaj, Brikena, "Economics of Virtue in Dietrich von der Glezze 'der borte': A Wife Errant and a Husband Caught," *Neohelicon* 93.4 (2009): 647–57.

Ribard, Jacques, "Le Lai d'Yonec est-il une allégorie chrétienne? *The Legend of Arthur in the Middle Ages: Studies Presented to A. H. Diverres by Colleagues, Pupils, and Friends*, ed. P. B. Grouot, R. A. Lodge, C. E. Pickford, and E. K. C. Varty (Cambridge: D. S. Brewer, 1983), 160–69.

Riddles, Knights and Cross Dressing Saints: Essays on Medieval English Language and Literature, ed. Thomas Honegger. Collection Variations, 5 (Bern, Berlin, et al.: Peter Lang, 2004).

Riehle, Wolfgang, *The Secret Within: Hermits, Recluses, and Spiritual Outsiders in Medieval England*, trans. from the German by Charity Scott-Stokes (2011; Ithaca, NY: Cornell University Press, 2014).

Rilke, Rainer Maria, *The Duino Elegies*, trans. by Leslie Norris and Alan Keele. Studies in German Literature, Linguistics, and Culture, 42 (Columbia, SC: Camden House, 1993).

Rilke, Rainer Maria, *The Sonnets to Orpheus*, trans. from the original German by Leslie Norris and Alan Keele. Studies in German Literature, Linguistics, and Culture, 42 (Columbia, SC: Camden House, 1989).

Rippl, Coralie, *Erzählen als Argumentationsspiel: Heinrich Kaufringers Fallkonstruktionen zwischen Rhetorik, Recht und literarischer Stofftradition*. Bibliotheca Germanica, 61 (Tübingen: Francke, 2014).

Robles, Ingeborg, "Subversives weibliches Wissen im 'Nibelungenlied,'" *Zeitschrift für deutsche Philologie*, 124.3 (2005): 360–74.

Roman de Silence, see *Le Roman de Silence*

Rosenstein, Roy S., "*Mabinogion*," *The Oxford Dictionary of the Middle Ages*, ed. Robert E. Bjork, vol. 3 (Oxford: Oxford University Press, 2010), 1062.

Rößlin, Eucharius, *Der swangern Frauwen vnd Hebammen Rosegarten* (1513; Wutöschingen: Antiqua-Verlag, 1994).

Rösslin, Eucharius, *When Midwifery Became the Male Physician's Province: The Sixteenth Century Handbook "The rose garden for pregnant women and midwives newly Englished.*" Trans. from the German and with an intro. by Wendy Arons (Jefferson, NC, and London: Macfarland, 1994).

Ruh, Kurt, *Die Mystik des deutschen Predigerordens und ihre Grundlegung durch die Hochscholastik*. Geschichte der abendländischen Mystik III (Munich: C. H. Beck, 1996).

Ruh, Kurt, *Frauenmystik und Franziskanische Mystik der Frühzeit*. Geschichte der abendländischen Mystik, II (Munich: C. H. Beck, 1993).

Rühtemann, Julia, *Die Geburt der Dichtung im Herzen: Untersuchungen zu Autorschaft, Personifikation und Geschlecht im Minnesang, im "Parzival," in "Der Welt Lohn" und im "Roman de Silence."* Philologische Studien und Quellen, 283 (Berlin: Erich Schmidt Verlag, 2022), 313–39.

Rüthemann, Julia, "Silence als narratives Prinzip und poetologische Figuration. Oder: haben wir es mit einem weiblichen Merlin zu tun?," *Der Ritter, der ein Mädchen war: Studien zum* Roman de Silence *von Heldris de Cornouailles*, ed. Inci Bozkaya, Britta Bußmann, and Katharina Philipowski. Aventiuren, 13 (Göttingen: V&R unipress, 2020) (2020), 233–66.

Sacred and Profane in Chaucer and Late Medieval Literature: Essays in Honour of John V. Fleming, ed. Robert Epstein (Toronto: University of Toronto Press, 2010).
Sager, Alexander, *Minne von maeren: On Wolfram's Titurel*. Transatlantische Studien zu Mittelalter und Früher Neuzeit, 2 (Göttingen: Vandenhoeck & Ruprecht, 2006).
Saltzman, Benjamin A., *Bonds of Secrecy: Law, Spirituality, and the Literature of Concealment in Early Medieval England*. The Middle Ages Series (Philadelphia, PA: University of Pennsylvania Press, 2019).
Samson, Vincent, *Die Berserker: Die Tierkrieger des Nordens von der Vendelbis zur Wikingerzeit*. Ergänzungsbände zum Reallexikon der Germanischen Altertumskunde, 121 (Berlin and Boston: Walter de Gruyter, 2020).
Sangster, Minnie B., trans. Walter A. Blue, "A Study of the Legend and the Location of 'Les Deux Amanz' from the Middle Ages to Modern Times," *Le Cygne: Journal of the International Marie de France Society* 4 (1998): 11–27.
Sargent-Baur, Barbara, *Aucassin et Nicolete: A Critical Bibliography*. Research Bibliography & Checklists, 35 (London: Grant & Cutier, 1981).
Schausten, Monika, *Erzählwelten der Tristangeschichte im hohen Mittelalter: Untersuchungen zu den deutschsprachigen Tristanfassungen des 12. und 13. Jahrhunderts*. Forschungen zur Geschichte der älteren deutschen Literatur, 24 (Munich: Wilhelm Fink, 1999).
Scheidel, Fabian David, "*Si muosen machen niwe slâ* ('Parzival,' 821,1): Zur Semantik von Spur und Weg im 'Parzival,' in der 'Crône' und dem 'Hohen Lied' Bruns von Schönebeck—mit einem Umweg zum Gral," *Aventiure: Ereignis und Erzählung*, ed. Michael Schwarzbach-Dobson and Franziska Wenzel, Beiheft zur ZfdPh, 21 (Berlin: Erich Schmidt, 2022), 127–151.
Schipperges, Heinrich, *Hildegard of Bingen: Healing and the Nature of the Cosmos*, trans. from German by John A. Broadwin (1995; Princeton: Wiener, 1997).
Schleier und Schwelle: Archäologie der literarischen Kommunikation V. Vol. 1: Geheimnis und Öffentlichkeit, ed. Aleida und Jan Assman (Munich: Wilhelm Fink, 1997).
Schmid, Elisabeth, "Text über Texte: Zur *Crône* des Heinrich von dem Türlin," eadem, *Poetik und Anthropologie: Gesammelte Aufsätze zum höfischen Roman*, ed. Dorothea Klein. Spolia Berolinensia, 41 (Hildesheim: Weidmann, 2021; orig. 1994), 203–27.
Schmid, Elisabeth, *Familiengeschichten und Heilsmythologie: die Verwandtschaftsstrukturen in den französischen und deutschen Gralromanen des 12. und 13. Jahrhunderts*. Beihefte zur Zeitschrift für romanische Philologie, 211 (Tübingen: Max Niemeyer, 1986).
Schmidt, Margot, "Hildegard von Bingen als Lehrerin des Glaubens: Speculum als Symbol des Transzendenten," *Hildegard von Bingen, 1179–1979: Festschrift zum 800. Todestag der Heiligen*, ed. Anton Ph. Brück. Quellen und Abhandlungen zur mittelrheinischen Kirchengeschichte, 3 (Mainz: Selbstverlag der Gesellschaft für Mittelrheinische Kirchengeschichte, 1979), 95–157.
Schmidt-Cadalbert, Christian, "Der wilde Wald: Zur Darstellung und Funktion eines Raumes in der mittelhochdeutschen Literatur," *Gotes und der werlde hulde:*

Literatur in Mittelalter und Neuzeit. Festschrift für Heinz Rupp zum 70. Geburtstag, ed. Rüdiger Schnell (Bern and Stuttgart: Francke Verlag, 1989), 24–47.

Schmitt, Jean-Claude, *Ghosts in the Middle Ages: The Living and the Dead in Medieval Society*, trans. Teresa Lavender Fagan (1994; Chicago: University of Chicago Press, 1998).

Schmitz-Esser, Romedio, *Der Leichnam im Mittelalter: Einbalsamierung, Verbrennung und die kulturelle Konstruktion des toten Körpers*, translated by Albrecht Classen and Carolin Radtke as *The Corpse in the Middle Ages: Embalming, Cremation, and the Cultural Construction of the Dead Body* (orig. 2014) (Turnhout: Harvey Miller Publishers, Brepols, 2020).

Schnyder, Mireille, "Der Wald in der höfischen Literatur: Raum des Mythos und des Erzählens," *Das Mittelalter: Der Wald im Mittelalter* 13.2 (2008): 1220–35.

Scholz Williams, Gerhild, "Konstruierte Männlichkeit: Genealogie, Geschlecht und ein Briefwechsel in Heldris von Cornwalls 'Roman de Silence,'" *Gespräche—Boten—Briefe: Körpergedächtnis und Schriftgedächtnis im Mittelalter*, ed. Horst Wenzel. Philologische Studien und Quellen, 143 (Berlin: Erich Schmidt Verlag, 1997), 193–211.

Schonert, Christiane, *Figurenspiele: Identität und Rolen Keies in Heinrichs von dem Türlin "Crône."* Philologische Studien und Quellen, 217 (Berlin: Erich Schmidt Verlag, 2009).

Schreiner, Klaus, "'Er küsse mich mit dem Kuß seines Mundes' (Osculetur me oscuto oris sui, Cant 1,1). Metaphorik, kommunikative und herrschaftliche Funktionen einer symbolischen Handlung," *Höfische Repräsentation: Das Zeremoniell und die Zeichen*, ed. Hedda Ragotzky and Horst Wenzel (Tübingen: Max Niemeyer, 1990), 89–132.

Schrödinger, Erwin, *What is Life?: The Physical Aspect of the Living Cell: with Mind and Matter: & Autobiographical Sketches* (Cambridge: Cambridge University Press, 1992).

Schuler-Lang, Larissa, *Wildes Erzählen—Erzählen vom Wilden: "Parzival," "Busant" und "Wolfdietrich D."* Literatur—Theorie—Geschichte, 7 (Berlin and Boston: Walter de Gruyter, 2014).

Schulz, Armin, *Erzähltheorie in mediävistischer Perspektive*. Studienausgabe. 2nd rev. ed., ed. Manuel Braun, Alexandra Dunkel, and Jan-Dirk Müller (Berlin and Boston: Walter de Gruyter, 2015).

Schütz, Peter, *Mysterium tremendum: zum Verhältnis von Angst und Religion nach Rudolf Otto*. Beiträge zur historischen Theologie, 178 (Tübingen: Mohr Siebeck, 2016).

Science and the Secrets of Nature: Books of Secrets in Medieval and Early Modern Culture, ed. William Eamon (Princeton, NJ: Princeton University Press, 1994).

Sconduto, Leslie A., *Metamorphoses of the Werewolf: A Literary Study from Antiquity Through the Renaissance* (Jefferson, NC, and London: McFarland, 2008).

Scull, Andrew, *Madness in Civilization: A Cultural History of Insanity from the Bible to Freud, from the Madhouse to Modern Medicine* (Princeton, NJ, and Oxford: Princeton University Press, 2015).

Secrecy and Concealment: Studies in the History of Mediterranean and Near Eastern Religions, ed. Hans G. Kippenberg and Guy G. Stroumsa. Numen. Studies in the History of Religions (Leiden and New York: E. J. Brill, 1995).
Secrets and Discovery in the Middle Ages: Proceedings of the 5th European Congress of the Fédération Internationale des Instituts d'Études Médiévales (Porto, 25th to 29th June 2013), ed. José Meirinhos, Celia López Alcalde, and João Rebalde. Textes et études du Moyen Âge, 90 (Barcelona and Rome, 2017).
Secular Sacred: 11th–16th Century Works from the Boston Public Library and the Museum of Fine Arts, ed. Nancy Netzer (Chicago: University of Chicago Press, 2006).
Selmayr, Pia, *Der Lauf der Dinge: Wechselverhältnisse zwischen Raum, Ding und Figur bei der narrativen Konstitution von Anderwelten im "Wigalois" und im "Lanzelet."* Mikrokosmos, 82 (Frankfurt a. M., Bern, et al.: Peter Lang, 2017).
Sen, Sudipta, *Ganges: The Many Pasts of an Indian River* (New Haven, CT, and London: Yale University Press: 2019).
Seuse, *Des Mystiker Heinrich Seuse O. Pr. Deutsche Schriften*, eingeleitet, übertragen und erläutert von Nikolaus Heller (Regensburg: Verlagsanstalt vorm. G. J. Manz, 1926).
Seuse, Heinrich, *Die deutschen Schriften des Seligen Heinrich Seuse aus dem Predigerorden*, ed. Heinrich Denifle (1880; Norderstedt: Hansebooks GmbH, 2018).
Shearer Duncan, Thomas, "The Weasel in Religion, Myth and Superstititon," *Washington University Studies* 12 (1924–1925): 33–66.
Sherman Loomis, Roger, *The Grail: From Celtic Myth to Christian Symbol* (1963; Princeton, NJ: Princeton University Press, 1992; 2018).
Sieber, Andrea, "Paradoxe Geschlechterkonstruktionen bei Ulrich von Liechtenstein," *Ulrich von Liechtenstein: Leben—Zeit—Werk—Forschung*, ed. Sandra Linden and Christopher Young (Berlin and New York: Walter de Gruyter, 2010), 261–304.
Sieburg, Heinz, "Magie und Wunder: Elemente und Funktionen des Übernatürlichen in der epischen mittelhochdeutschen Literatur um 1200," *Hexenwissen: Zum Transfer von Magie- und Zauberei-Imaginationen in interdisziplinärer Perspektive*, ed. id., Rita Voltmer, and Britta Weimann. Trierer Hexenprozesse, 9 (Trier: Spee, 2017), 181–93.
Sievers, Burkard, *Geheimnis und Geheimhaltung in sozialen Systemen*. Studien zur Sozialwissenschaft, 23 (Wiesbaden: VS Verlag für Sozialwissenschaften, 1974).
Sign, Sentence, Discourse: The Ambiguity of Silence, ed. Peter Allen, Jennifer Wasserman, and Lois Roney (New York: Syracuse University Press, 1998).
Signori, Gabriele, "Wanderer zwischen den 'Welten': Besucher, Briefe, Vermächtnisse und Geschenke als Kommunikationsmedien im Austausch zwischen Kloster und Welt," *Krone und Schleier: Kunst aus mittelalterlichen Frauenklöstern, Ruhrlandmuseum, die frühen Klöster und Stifte 500–1200. Kunst- und Ausstellungshalle der Bundesrepublik Deutschland, die Zeit der Orden 1200–1500*, ed. Jutta Frings and Jan Gerchow (Munich: Hirmer, 2005), 130–41.
Simmel, Georg, *Essays on Art and Aesthetics*, ed. and with an intro. by Austin Harrington (Chicago and London: The University of Chicago Press, 2020).

Simmel, Georg, *Soziologie: Untersuchungen über die Formen der Vergesellschaftung*. Gesamtausgabe, vol. II. Suhrkamp-Taschenbuch Wissenschaft, 811 (1908; Berlin: Suhrkamp, 1992).
Simmel-Handbuch: Begriffe, Hauptwerke, Aktualität, ed. Hans-Peter Müller and Tilman Reitz (Berlin: Suhrkamp, 2018).
Simmel-Handbuch: Leben—Werk—Wirkung, ed. Jörn Bohr, Gerald Hartung, Heike Koenig, and Tim-Florian Steinbach (Stuttgart: J. B. Metzler, 2021).
Sir Gawain and the Green Knight: A Dual-Language Version, ed. and trans. by William Vantuono. Garland Reference Library of the Humanities, 1265 (New York and London: Garland, 1993).
Sobecki, Sebastian I., "A Source for the Magical Ship in the *Partonopeu de Blois* and Marie de France's *Guigemar*," *Notes and Queries* 48.3 (2001): 220–22.
Stauffer, Marianne, *Der Wald: Zur Darstellung und Deutung der Natur im Mittelalter*. Studiorum Romanicorum Collectio Turicensis, X (Bern: Francke Verlag, 1959).
Stede, Marga, *Schreiben in der Krise: Die Texte des Heinrich Kaufringer*. Literatur—Imagination—Realität (Trier: Wissenschaftlicher Verlag, 1993).
Steegers, Robert, "'Wie weiland Ritter Hüon von Bordeaux': Christoph Martin Wielands 'Oberon' und Heinrich Heines erzählende Versdichtungen," *Von Sommerträumen und Wintermärchen. Versepen im Vormärz*, ed. Bernd Füllner and Karin Füllner. Vormärz-Studien, 12 (Bielefeld: Aisthesis-Verlag, 2007), 179–203.
Stevens, John, *Medieval Romance: Themes and Approaches*. The Norton Library (London: 1973).
Stevenson, William Henry, *Report on the Manuscripts of Lord Middleton, preserved at Wollaton Hall, Nottinghamshire*, ed. W. H. Stevenson. Historical Manuscripts Commission (London: Stationery Office, 1911).
Stolz, Michael, "Kyot und Kundrie: Expertenwissen in Wolframs 'Parzival,'" *Wissen, maßgeschneidert: Experten und Expertenkulturen im Europa der Vormoderne*, ed. Björn Reich, Frank Rexroth, and Matthias Roickh. Historische Zeitschrift, Beiheft, N.F., 57 (Munich: Oldenbourg, 2012), 83–113.
Stricker, see Der Stricker
Strzelczyk, Jerzy, *Święci Władcy Europy*. Biblioteka Długosza, 3 (Częstochowa: Wydawnictwo Naukowe Uniwersytetu Humanistyczno-Przyrodniczego, 2020).
Stuckrad, Kocku von, *Locations of Knowledge in Medieval and Early Modern Europe: Esoteric Discourse and Western Identities*. Brill's Studies in Intellectual History, 186 (Leiden and Boston: Brill, 2010).
Stypczynski, Brent A., *The Modern Literary Werewolf: A Critical Study of the Mutable Motif* (Jefferson, NC, and London: McFarland, 2013).
Subrenat, Jean, "D'étrances machines étrangières dans le cycle de *Huon de Bordeaux*: Les automates, gardiens de Dunostre," *De l'étranger à l'étrange ou la conjointure de merveille: (en hommage à Marguerite Rossi et Paul Bancourt)*. Sénéfiance, 25 (Aix-en-Provence: Presses Universitaires de Provence, 1988), 463–80.
Sunderland, Luke, "Genre, Ideology and Utopia in *Huon de Bordeaux*," *Medium Ævum* 81 (2012): 289–302.
Suso, Henry, *The Exemplar, with Two German Sermons*, trans., ed., and intro. by Frank Tobin (New York and Mahwah, NJ: Paulist Press, 1989).

Suso, see Seuse
Sutter, Rolf E., *Mit saelde ich gerbet han den gral: genealogische Strukturanalyse zu Wolframs von Eschenbach Parzival*. Göppinger Arbeiten zur Germanistik, 705 (Göppingen: Kümmerle, 2003).
Sziráky, Anna, *Éros Lógos Musiké: Gottfrieds 'Tristan' oder eine utopische renovatio der Dichtersprache und der Welt aus dem Geiste der Minne und Musik?*. Wiener Arbeiten zur germanischen Altertumskunde und Philologie, 38 (Bern, Berlin, et al.: Peter Lang, 2003).
Tanner, Heather, "Lords, Wives and Vassals in the *Roman de Silence*," *Journal of Women's History* 24.1 (2012): 138–59.
Tax, Petrus W., "Zur Interpretation des 'Gürtels' Dietrichs von der Glezze," *Zeitschrift für deutsche Philologie* 124.1 (2005): 47–62.
Terrell, Katherine, "Competing Gender Ideologies and the Limitations of Language in Le Roman de Silence," *Romance Quarterly* 55.1 (2008): 35–48.
Terrell, Katherine, "Competing Gender Ideologies and the Limitations of Language in *Le Roman de Silence*." *Romance Quarterly* 55.1 (2008): 35–48.
The Astrological Autobiography of a Medieval Philosopher: Henry Bate's Nativitas (1280–81), ed. and intro. by Carlos Steel, Steven Vanden Broecke, and David Juste and Shlomo Sela. Ancient and Medieval Philosophy, XVII (Leuven: Leuven University Press, 2018).
The Book and the Magic of Reading in the Middle Ages, ed. Albrecht Classen. Garland Reference Library of the Humanities, 2118 (New York and London: Garland Publishing, 1999).
The Cambridge Companion to Fantasy Literature, ed. Edward James and Farah Mendlesohn (Cambridge: Cambridge University Press, 2012).
The Cambridge Companion to Hildegard of Bingen, ed. Jeniffer Bain (Cambridge: Cambridge University Press, 2021).
The Cambridge Companion to Medieval English Mysticism (Cambridge: Cambridge University Press, 2011).
The Cambridge Companion to Miracles, ed. Graham H. Twelftree. Cambridge Companions to Religion (Cambridge: Cambridge University Press, 2011).
The Cambridge History of Magic and Witchcraft in the West: From Antiquity to the Present, ed. David J. Collins (Cambridge: Cambridge University Press, 2015).
The Cambridge History of Welsh Literature, ed. Geraint Evans and Helen Fulton (Cambridge: Cambridge University Press, 2019).
The Celtic Heroic Age: Literary Sources for Ancient Celtic Europe and Early Ireland and Wales, ed. John T. Koch and John Carey (New York: David Brown, 2003).
The Four Branches of the Mabinogi, ed. and trans. by Matthieu Boyd (Peterborough, Ont.: Broadview Press, 2017).
The Ghost Story from the Middle Ages to the Twentieth Century: A Ghostly Genre, ed. Helen Conrad-O'Briain and Julie Anne Stevens (Dublin: Four Courts Press, 2010).
The Grail, the Quest and the World of Arthur, ed. Norris J. Lacy. Arthurian Studies, 72 (Cambridge: D. S. Brewer, 2008).
The Imitation of Christ: Being the Autograph Manuscript of Thomas à Kempis, De Imitatione Christi, ed. Charles Ruelens (London: Elliot Stock, 1885).

The Legend of Charlemagne: Envisioning Empire in the Middle Ages, ed. Jace Stuckey. Explorations in Medieval Culture, 15 (Leiden and Boston: Brill, 2022).
The Mabinogi and Other Medieval Welsh Tales, ed. and trans. Patrick K. Ford (Berkeley, CA: University of California Press, 2019).
The Mabinogi, ed. Proinsias Mac Cana. 2nd ed. (1977; Cardiff: University of Wales Press, 1992).
The Mabinogion, trans. Sioned Davie. Oxford World's Classics (Oxford: Oxford University Press, 2007).
The Marvels of the World: An Anthology of Nature Writing Before 1700, Rebecca Bushnell. Penn Studies in Landscape Architecture (Philadelphia, PA: University of Pennsylvania Press, 2021).
The Oxford Dictionary of the Middle Ages, ed. Robert E. Bjork. 4 vols. (Oxford: Oxford University Press, 2010).
The Palgrave Handbook of Magical Realism in the Twenty-First Century, ed. Richard Perez and Victoria A. Chevalier (Cham, Switzerland: Palgrave MacMillan, 2020).
The Routledge History of Medieval Magic, ed. Sophie Page and Catherine Rider. The Routledge Histories (London and New York: Routledge, 2019).
The Rusted Hauberk: Feudal Ideals of Order and Their Decline, ed. Liam O. Purdon and Cindy L. Vitto (Gainesville, Tallahassee, et al.: University Press of Florida, 1994).
The Sacred and the Secular in Medieval Healing: Sites, Objects, and Texts, ed. Barbara S. Bowers and Linda Migl Keyser. AVISTA Studies in the History of Medieval Technology, Science and Art, 10 (London: Routledge, 2016).
The Sociology of Georg Simmel, trans., ed., and with an intro. by Kurt H. Wolff (Glencoe, IL: The Free Press, 1950).
The Trotula: An English Translation of the Medieval Compendium of Women's Medicine, ed. and trans. by Monica H. Green. The Middle Ages Series (2001; Philadelphia, PA: University of Pennsylvania Press, 2002).
The Wiley-Blackwell Companion to Christian Mysticism, ed. Julia A. Lamm (Hoboken, NJ: J. Wiley, 2013).
Thomas von Kempen, *Von der Nachfolge Christi: Die Weisheit des mittelalterlichen Klosters*. Übersetzt und herausgegeben von Bernhard Lang (Stuttgart: Philipp Reclam jun., 2022).
Thorpe, Lewis, "*Le Roman de Silence*," *Nottingham Mediaeval Studies* 5 (1961): 33–74; 6 (1962): 18–69; 7 (1963): 34–52; 8 (1964): 35–61; 10 (1966): 25–69; 11 (1967): 19–56.
Tiemann, Manfred, *Josef und die Frau Potifars im populärkulturellen Kontext: transkulturelle Verflechtungen in Theologie, bildender Kunst, Literatur, Musik und Film* (Wiesbaden: Springer, 2020).
Todorov, Tzvetan, *The Fantastic* (1970: Ithaca, NY: Cornell University Press, 1975).
Tolnay, Charles de, *Hieronymus Bosch* (1965; n.l.: Reynal & Company, in association with William Morrow & Company, 1966).
Tolstoy, Nikolai, *The Oldest British Prose Literature: The Compilation of the Four Branches of the Mabinogi* (Lewiston, NY, Lampeter, Wales, Queenston, Victoria: Edwin Mellen Press, 2009).

Tomaryn Bruckner, Matilda, "Speaking Through Animals in Marie de France's *Lais* and *Fables*," *A Companion to Marie de France*, ed. Logan E. Whalen. Brill's Companions to the Christian Tradition, 27 (Leiden and Boston: Brill, 2011), 157–85.
Tomasek, Tomas, *Gottfried von Straßburg* (Stuttgart: Philipp Reclam jun., 2007).
Trajectoires européennes du "Secretum secretorum" du Pseudo-Aristote (XIIIe–XVIe siècle), ed. Catherine Gaullier-Bougassas, Margaret Bridges, and Jean-Yves Tilliette. Alexander Redivivus, 6 (Turnhout: Brepols, 2015).
Treason: Medieval and Early Modern Adultery, Betrayal, and Shame, ed. Larissa Tracy. Explorations in Medieval Culture, 10 (Leiden and Boston: Brill, 2019).
Truitt, E. R., *Medieval Robots: Mechanism, Magic, Nature, and Art*. The Middle Ages Series (Philadelphia, PA: University of Pennsylvania Press, 2015).
Tücke des Objekts, see *"Die Tücke des Objekts"*
Ulrich von Liechtenstein, *Frauendienst*, trans. Franz Viktor Spechtler. Göppinger Arbeiten zur Germanistik, 485 (Göppingen: Kümmerle, 1987).
Ulrich von Liechtenstein, *The Service of Ladies*, trans. J. W. Thomas (Woodbridge: Boydell & Brewer, 2004).
Ulrich von Liechtenstein: Leben—Zeit—Werk—Forschung, ed. Sandra Linden and Christopher Young (Berlin and New York: Walter de Gruyter, 2010).
Urscheler, Andreas, *Kommunikation in Wolframs "Parzival": Eine Untersuchung zu Form und Funktion der Dialoge*. Deutsche Literatur von den Anfängen bis 1700, 38 (Bern, Berlin, et al.: Peter Lang, 2002).
van Nahl, Jan Alexander, "Digital Norse," *The Routledge Research Companion to the Medieval Icelandic Sagas*, ed. Ármann Jakobsson and Sverrir Jakobsson (London: Routledge, 2017), 344–53.
Vance, Jacob, *Secrets: Humanism, Mysticism, and Evangelism in Erasmus of Rotterdam, Bishop Guillaume Briçonnet, and Marguerite de Navarre*. Brill's Studies in Intellectual History, 231 (Leiden and Boston: Brill, 2014).
Vietta, Silvio, *Literatur und Rationalität: Funktionen der Literatur in der europäischen Kulturgeschichte* (Munich: Wilhelm Fink, 2014).
Vollmann, Justin, *Das Ideal des irrenden Lesers: ein Wegweiser durch die "Krone" Heinrichs von dem Türlin*. Bibliotheca Germanica, 53 (Tübingen and Basel: Francke, 2008).
Wack, Mary Frances, *Lovesickness in the Middle Ages: The* Viaticum *and Its Commentaries*. Middle Ages Series (Philadelphia, PA: University of Pennsylvania Press, 1990).
Wagner-Harken, Annegret, *Märchenelemente und ihre Funktion in der Crône Heinrichs von dem Türlin: ein Beitrag zur Unterscheidung zwischen "klassischer" und "nachklassischer" Artusepik*. Deutsche Literatur von den Anfängen bis 1700, 21 (Bern, Berlin, et al.: Peter Lang, 1995).
Ward, Benedicta, *Miracles and the Medieval Mind: Theory, Record and Event 1000–1215* (London: Scolar Press, 1982).
Wehrle, Jan, "Dreams and Dream Theory," *Handbook of Medieval Culture: Fundamental Aspects and Conditions of the European Middle Ages*, ed. Albrecht Classen (Berlin and Boston: Walter de Gruyter, 2015), vol. 1, 329–46.

Wehrle, Jan, *Das Übernatürliche erzählen: die erzählerische Darstellung übernatürlicher Phänomene in sechs Isländersagas* (Munich: utzverlag, 2021).
Wehrli, Max, *Geschichte der deutschen Literatur im Mittelalter: Von den Anfängen bis zum Ende des 16. Jahrhunderts.* 3rd ed. (1980; Stuttgart: Philipp Reclam jun., 1997).
Welch, John, *An Interior Life: Rummaging Through the Christian Tradition* (Mahwah, NJ: Paulist Press, 2022).
Wennerhold, Markus, *Späte mittelhochdeutsche Artusromane: 'Lanzelt,' 'Wigalois,' 'Daniel von dem Blühenden Tal,' 'Diu Crône.' Bilanz der Forschung 1960–2000.* Würzburger Beiträge zur deutschen Philologie, 27 (Würzburg: Königshausen & Neumann, 2005).
Wenzel, Horst, "Boten und Briefe: Zum Verhältnis körperlicher und nicht-körperlicher Nachrichtenträger," *Gespräche—Boten—Briefe: Körpergedächtnis und Schriftgedächtnis im Mittelalter*, ed. id. together with Peter Göhler et al. Philologische Studien und Quellen, 143 (Berlin: Erich Schmidt Verlag, 1997), 86–105.
Wenzel, Horst, "Das höfische Geheimnis: Herrschaft, Liebe, Texte," *Archäologie der literarischen Kommunikation V*. Vol. 1: *Geheimnis und Öffentlichkeit*, ed. Aleida und Jan Assman (Munich: Wilhelm Fink, 1997), 53–69.
Wenzel, Horst, "Öffentlichkeit und Heimlichkeit in Gottfrieds, Tristan,'" *Zeitschrift für deutsche Philologie* 107 (1988): 335–61.
Wesselski, Albert, *Märchen des Mittelalters* (Berlin: H. Stubenrauch, 1925).
Westerbarkey, Joachim, *Das Geheimnis: Zur funktionalen Ambivalenz von Kommunikationsstrukturen* (Wiesbaden: VS Verlag für Sozialwissenschaften, 1991).
Whalen, Logan, "A Matter of Life or Death: Fecundity and Sterility in Marie de France's *Guigemar*," Shaping Courtliness in Medieval France, ed. Daniel E. O'Sullivan and Laurie Shepard (Woodbridge: D. S. Brewer, 2013), 139–149.
Wierenga, Edward R., *The Nature of God: An Inquiry into Divine Attributes* (Ithaca, NY: Cornell University Press, 2003).
Wilhelmy, Winfried, *Sexualität, Schwangerschaft und Geburt in den Schriften Hildegards von Bingen* (Mainz: Zabern, 1998); Stefanie Rinke, *Das "Genießen Gottes": Medialität und Geschlechtercodierungen bei Bernhard von Clairvaux und Hildegard von Bingen.* Berliner Kulturwissenschaft, 3 (Freiburg i. Br. and Berlin: Rombach, 2006).
Williams, Mark, "Magic and Marvel," *The Cambridge History of Welsh Literature*, ed. Geraint Evans and Helen Fulton (Cambridge: Cambridge University Press, 2019), 52–72.
Williams, Steven J., "The Early Circulation of the Pseudo-Aristotelian 'Secret of Secrets' in the West," *Micrologus* 2 (1994): 127–44.
Williams, Steven J., *The Secret of Secrets: The Scholarly Career of a Pseudo-Aristotelian Text in the Latin Middle Ages* (Ann Arbor, MI: University of Michigan Press, 2003).
Wolf, Ernst, *Beschwörungen und Segen. Angewandte Psychotherapie im Mittelalter* (Cologne, Weimar and Vienna: Böhlau, 2011).

Wolfram von Eschenbach, *Die Lieder Wolframs von Eschenbach*, ed., trans., and commentary by Joachim Heinzle (Stuttgart: S. Hirzel Verlag, 2021).
Wolfram von Eschenbach, *Parzival*. Studienausgabe. Mittelhochdeutscher Text nach der sechsten Ausgabe von Karl Lachmann. Übersetzung von Peter Knecht. Einführung zum Text von Bernd Schirok (Berlin and New York: Walter de Gruyter, 1998).
Wolfram von Eschenbach, *Titurel*, ed. Helmut Brackert and Stephan Fuchs-Jolie. With a [German] trans., commentary, and materials (Berlin and New York: Walter de Gruyter, 2002). Wolfram von Eschenbach, *Parzival* and *Titurel*, trans. and notes by Cyril Edwards. Oxford World's Classics (Oxford: Oxford University Press, 2004/2006).
Woman Defamed and Woman Defended: An Anthology of Medieval Texts, ed. Alcuin Blamires with Karen Pratt and C. W. Marx (Oxford: Clarendon Press, 1992).
Wörterbuch der Mystik, ed. Peter Dinzelbacher. Kröners Taschenausgabe, 456 (Stuttgart: Alfred Kröner Verlag, 1989).
Wouters, Dinah, "Revisiting Potiphar's Wife: A European Perspective on a Character in Early Modern Drama," *Medievalia et Humanistica* New Series, 47 (2022): 81–106.
Xia, Haoyu Irene, "La Symbolique des oiseaux de proie dans trois lais des douzième et treizième siècles," *The French Review: Journal of the American Association of Teachers of French* 89.4 (2016): 93–105.
Yohannan, John D., *Joseph and Potiphar's Wife in World Literature: An Anthology of the Story of the Chaste Youth and the Lustful Stepmother* (New York: New Directions, 1968).
Yoon, Ju Ok, "Lettre, Love, and Magic in Marie de France's *Les Deus Amanz*," *The Journal of English Language and Literature* 58.3 (2012): 427–46.
Yoshitsugu Sawai, *Rudolf Otto and the Foundation of the History of Religions* (London: Bloomsbury Academic, 2022).
Young, Charles R., *The Royal Forest of Medieval England* (Leicester: Leicester University Press, 1979).
Yun, Bee, *Wege zu Machiavelli: Die Rückkehr des Politischen im Spätmittelalter.* Beihefte zum Archiv für Kulturgeschichte, 91 (Vienna, Cologne, and Weimar: Böhlau, 2021).
Zach, Christine, *Die Erzählmotive der* Crône *Heinrichs von dem Türllin und ihre altfranzösischen Quellen: Ein kommentiertes Register.* Passauer Schriften zu Sprache und Literatur, 5 (Passau: Wissenschaftsverlag Richard Rothe, 1990).
Zach, Christine, *Die Erzählmotive der Crône Heinrichs von dem Türlin und ihre altfranzösischen Quellen: ein kommentiertes Register.* Passauer Schriften zu Sprache und Literatur, 5 (Passau: Wiss.-Verl. Rothe, 1990).
Ziolkowski, Theodore, *The Mirror of Justice: Literary Reflections of Legal Crises* (Princeton, NJ: Princeton University Press, 1997).
Zissell, Jeanette S., "Universal Salvation in the Earthly City: *De Civitate Dei* and the Significance of the Hazelnut in Julian of Norwich's *Showings*," *Urban Space in*

the Middle Ages and Early Modern Times, ed. Albrecht Classen. Fundamentals of Medieval and Early Modern Culture, 4 (Berlin and New York: Walter de Gruyter, 2009), 331–51.

Index

Aelfric, 8
Aesop, 69
Albert I, Count of Görtz and Tyrol, 167
Albertus Magnus, 12
Albrecht (von Scharfenberg), 116
Andechs-Meran, House of, 166
Apollinaris, St., 153
Aquinas, Thomas, 26
Arthur and Gorlagon, 67
Aucassin et Nicolette, 140
Augustine, St., 8, 12, 26, 33, 34

Bacon, Roger, 11
Beowulf, 86, 189
Bernard of Clairvaux, 8
Bonaventure, 8
Book of Fermoy, 74
Book of the Dun Cow. See *Lebhor eta h-Uidre*
Bourchier, John, Lord Berners, 190
Bridgit of Sweden, 236
Britten, Benjamin, 190
Buch der Sieben weisen Meister, 7

Caesarius of Heisterbach, 4
Chanson de Roland, 16, 189, 193
Charlemagne, 2, 191–92, 199, 201–2
Chrétien de Troyes, 59, 98, 118, 166
The Compert Mongain, 74

Coudrette, 27
cross-dressing, 143–44
Culhwch and Olwen, 93

Dante Alighieri, 37–38, 238
"Dark," 3
Der Stricker, 16, 30, 56, 199
Dietrich von der Glezze, 138–40
Dietrichs Flucht, 189
Dingtheorie, 10
Dinnshenchus, 74
Durkheim, Emile, 2

Egil's Saga, 86–87
Einstein, Albert, 6
Eliade, Mircea, 2
Ende, Michael, 27, 98
Eriugena, John Scottus, 210
Eugenia, St., 153
Euphrosyne, St., 153
Evans-Pritcha, E. E., 2

First Continuation, 119
Fleck, Konrad, 56
Flegetanis, 125–26
Flóamanna saga, 62
Floris and Blanchefleur, 200
Fortunatus, 27
Francisco Manoel de Nascimento, 190

Frazer, James, 2
Freud, Sigmund, 2
Fries, Jakob Friedrich, 210
Fuetrer, Ulrich, 167

Gautier li Leus, 142
Geertz, Clifford, 2
Gerbert de Montreuil, 119
Gereint and Enid, 94
Gertrude the Great, 221
Goethe, Johann Wolfgang von, 190
Gottfried von Strassburg, 13–16, 17
Graelent, 166
Guillaume de Palerne, 67–68
Guthrie, Stewart Elliot, 2

Hans von Bühel, 8
Hartmann von Aue, 167
Heinrich (Henry) of Halle, 221
Heinrich von dem Türlin, 20, 136, 163–80
Heldris de Cornuälle, 135–54
Hélinand of Froidmont, 118
Herzog Ernst, 18, 35, 192
Hildegard of Bingen, 13, 213–21
Hilton, James, 30
Hugh of St. Victor, 116
Huon de Bourdeaux, 16–17, 145, 187–203

Ille et Galeron, 142

Jacob, St., 62
Jacques de Vitry, 8
Jean d'Arras, 27
Joseph and Potiphar's wife, 147–48
Joseph of Arimathia, 119
Julian of Norwich, 225–27

Kant, Immanuel, 210
Kaufringer, Heinrich, 22–26, 235
Konrad von Würzburg, 59, 70, 98, 177
Kunert, Günter, 32
Kyot, 125–26

L'Estoire Merlin, 143, 145
La chanson d'Aspremont, 142
La Vengeance Raguidel, 142, 166
Lady of the Fountain. See *Owain*
Lamprecht, Priest, 19–20
Lancelot en prose, 56
Lanval, 166
Latini, Bruno, 70
Laxdaela Saga, 86, 90–91
Le Bel Inconnue, 166
Le Chevalier à L'Épée, 166
Le roman d'Alixandre, 142
Le roman de Troie, 142
Lebhor eta h-Uidre, 74
Li dis Raoul de Hosdaing, 142
Llyfr Coch Hergest. See *Red Book of Hergest*
Llyfr Gwyn Rhydderch. See *White Book of Rhydderch*
Longinus, 119
Luther, Martin, 12, 210

Mabinogi/Mabinogion, 19, 85–104, 169
Mai und Beaflor, 145
Manessier, 119
Marie de France, 18–19, 55–77, 92, 117, 147, 179–80, 236
Marina, St., 153
Márquez, Gabriel García, 27
Marx, Karl, 2
Maurilius, St., 62
Maurus, Rabanus, 24–25
Mechthild of Hackeborn, 221
Mechthild of Magdeburg, 221–25, 236
Meister Eckhart, 33, 70, 210
Melion, 67
Merlin, 9, 143–46, 152–53
"Merseburger Zaubersprüche," 17
Morgan le Fée, 9, 21, 194
Mozart, Wolfgang Amadeus, 30, 190

Nibelungenlied, 19, 88–89, 187, 189–90, 201, 235
Njál's Saga, 86–87
Notker Balbulus, 33

Ockham, William, 26
One Thousand and One Nights, 9
Oswald of Northumbria, King, 2
Otto, Rudolf, 209, 210, 215, 226
Owain, 93

Paien de Maisières, 166
Pañatantra, 8
Partonopeus de Blois, 59, 98
Pelagia, St., 153
Peredur, 94, 119
Perlesvaus, 119
Petrarch, Francesco, 12
Physiologus, 69–71
Poema de Mío Cid, 189
Première Continuation du Conte du Graal, 166
Prose Lancelot, 119
Purcell, Henry, 190

Queste del Saint Graal, 119

Rabenschlacht, 189
Red Book of Hergest, 93
Rilke, Rainer Maria, 226
Ritschl, Albrecht, 210
Robert de Boron, 119
Rolle, Richard, 236
Roman d'Alexandre, 118
Rösslin, Eucharius, 13
Rowling, J. K., 3, 27
Rudolf von Ems, 167

Schiller, Friedrich, 190
Schleiermacher, Friedrich, 210
Second Continuation, 119
Septem sapientes, 7
Seuse, Heinrich, 226, 236

Shakespeare, William, 16, 190
Simmel, Georg, 28–30
Sir Gawain and the Green Knight, 20–22, 95
Skiðblaðnir, 62
Straparola, Giovanni Francesco, 6, 8
Sueskind, Patrick, 27
Suso. *See* Seuse, Heinrich

Theodora, St., 153
Thing Theory. *See Ding* Theory
Thomas à Kempis, 36–37
Thomas de/of Cantimpré, 34, 116
Thomas of Brittany, 56
Thüring von Ringoltingen, 27
Tischlein-deck-dich, 122
Tolkien, J. R. R., 3
Tristan de Nanteuil, 145
Trotula, 58
Tylor, E. B., 2

Ulrich von Liechtenstein, 141–42

Vidal, Peire, 66
Vitus, St., 62

weasel, 71–72
Weber, Carl Maria von, 190
Weber, Max, 27, 189
White Book of Rhydderch, 93
Wieland, Christoph Martin, 190
William of Conches, 116
William the Conqueror, 93
Wirnt von Gravenberg, 167
"The Wizard of Oz," 236
Wolfram von Eschenbach, 18, 30, 113–29, 165, 167, 172, 173, 236

About the Author

Dr. Albrecht Classen is University Distinguished Professor of German Studies at the University of Arizona, Tucson. He has currently published 118 scholarly books on German and European medieval and early modern literature, most recently *Freedom, Imprisonment, and Slavery in the Pre-Modern Time* (2021), *Tracing the Trails in Medieval Literature* (Routledge, 2021), and *Wisdom from the European Middle Ages* (2022). In his other recent books, he explored the history of toleration and tolerance (2018 and 2020), prostitution in medieval literature (2019), the topics of the forest and of water in medieval literature (2015 and 2018), magic and magicians (2017), and the Paradigm Shift in the late Middle Ages (2019). He is the editor of the journals *Mediaevistik* and *Humanities Open Access*, and serves on many different boards of international journals dedicated to the Humanities. In 2004, he received the *Bundesverdienstkreuz am Band* (Order of Merit) from the German government. In 2012, he was awarded the Carnegie Foundation for the Advancement of Teaching Arizona Professor of the Year Award. In 2017, he was given the rank of Grand Knight Commander of the Most Noble Order of the Three Lions (GKCL) for his contributions to teaching and researching German language, literature, and culture. He is also the author of nine volumes of his own poetry, of four volumes with his essays and satires, and of one book for young readers dedicated to the Middle Ages. In 2021 he won the Tulliola Renato Filippelli World Award for his prose narratives, and also received the Chatfield Outstanding Tenured Researcher Award from the College of Humanities at the University of Arizona.

He served for close to three decades as the President of the Arizona Chapter of the American Association of Teachers of German (AATG); he was the Vice President/President/Past President of the Rocky Mountain Modern Language Association for four times, and he served twice on the Executive Board of the national AATG. Since 2021, he is Member of the Executive Board of the Arizona Humanities. He has received numerous research and teaching awards, especially the Five Star Faculty Award (2009), and several awards for his service as Director of Undergraduate Studies (2014 and 2015).

www.ingramcontent.com/pod-product-compliance
Lightning Source LLC
Chambersburg PA
CBHW020111010526
44115CB00008B/786